HARRY C. TREXLER
LIBRARY

PARENTS FUND
1988 - 1989

COLLEGE

The Political Logic of Economic Reform in China

California Series on Social Choice and Political Economy

EDITED BY BRIAN BARRY (1981 TO 1991), ROBERT H. BATES,
JAMES S. COLEMAN (FROM 1992), AND SAMUEL L. POPKIN

The Political Logic of Economic Reform in China

SUSAN L. SHIRK

University of California Press

BERKELEY   LOS ANGELES   OXFORD

University of California Press
Berkeley and Los Angeles, California

University of California Press, Ltd.
Oxford, England

©1993 by
The Regents of the University of California

Library of Congress Cataloging-in-Publication Data

Shirk, Susan L.
The political logic of economic reform in China / Susan L. Shirk.
    p. cm.—(California series on social choice and political
    economy; 24)
  Includes bibliographical references and index.
  ISBN 0-520-07706-7 (alk. paper).—ISBN 0-520-07707-5 (pbk. :
  alk. paper)
  1. China—Economic policy—1976– 2. China—Politics and
government—1976– I. Title. II. Series.
HC427.92.S55 1993
338.951—dc20   92-12030
                                                              CIP

Printed in the United States of America
9 8 7 6 5 4 3 2 1

To Sam, Lucy, and David Popkin

Contents

Acknowledgments

I am deeply grateful to the many individuals and organizations in China who helped me carry out the field research for this book. My research in China was generously supported by the Rockefeller Foundation International Relations Fellowship, the National Academy of Sciences Committee on Scholarly Communication with the People's Republic of China, and the University of California–San Diego.

My colleagues at UC–San Diego provided a stimulating, supportive environment in which to work out my ideas about communist political institutions. Most valuable were my almost daily discussions with Philip Roeder, who was writing his own book on Soviet political institutions; my teaching partnership with Mathew McCubbins, who was eager to reach beyond the United States to figure out how institutions work in other countries; and the patient help I received from Barry Naughton in understanding the Chinese economy. Other colleagues, especially Gary Cox, Francis Rosenbluth, T. J. Cheng, and Peter Gourevitch, cheerfully engaged me in many hours of conversation about the ideas in the book.

On other campuses, Christine Wong and James Tong shared information and ideas about the Chinese fiscal system. When I presented parts of the book at the University of California–Los Angeles, MIT, and Harvard, the tough questions helped me clarify my arguments. Robert Bates, Andrew Nathan, Michel Oksenberg, Lee Sands, Dorothy Solinger, and Andrew Walder read the entire manuscript and offered very valuable suggestions.

Zhao Suisheng, Michael Tierney, and Christopher Nevitt, graduate students at UC–San Diego, helped by acute questioning of arguments and tracking down sources. Joan Brunn did a fine job of manuscript preparation. Sheila Levine, Amy Klatzkin, and Dan Gunter at the University of California Press were a pleasure to work with during the publication process. Finally, I wish to thank Beverley Walton, Jaqueline Wheeler, Mary Tschosik, and, most of all, Jeanette Popkin, who took excellent care of my children while I was working on this book.

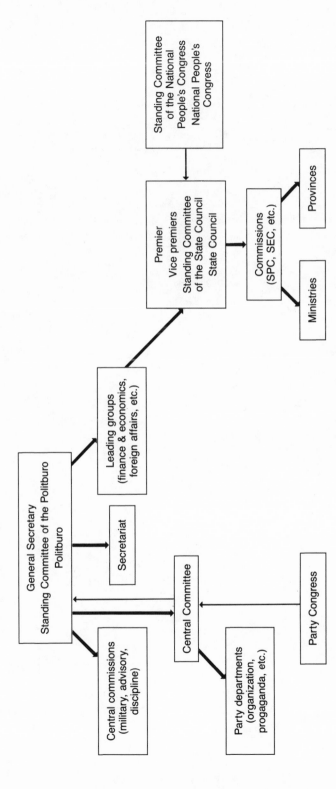

COMMUNIST PARTY

GOVERNMENT

Formal Authority Relations Among Central Communist Party and Government Institutions in the People's Republic of China

NOTE: This chart includes only the institutions discussed in this book. Thin lines indicate weaker authority.

1

INTRODUCTION

1 The Political Logic of Economic Reform

In the fall of 1991 I visited China and Russia. Urban economic conditions in the two countries presented a striking contrast. The streets of Chinese cities were bustling with commercial activity. Shoppers thronged private and collective shops displaying the latest Hong Kong fashions manufactured in China. Couples debated whether to spend their savings on microwave ovens or tape recorders. Doting parents purchased Japanese electronic keyboards for their children. Market counters displayed an abundance of vegetables, fruit, meat, and seafood. People said that nowadays there was more fresh produce available in winter than there used to be in summer. Black-market currency traders no longer prowled the streets because the Chinese *renminbi* had been gradually devalued almost to the market rate. Urbanites still went to work on bicycles or crowded buses; they still lived in tiny, dilapidated apartments; the newspapers still complained about the low efficiency of state-owned factories. But it was obvious that starting from a relatively low base, Chinese urban living standards had improved markedly during the past decade.

Conditions in Russian cities were much bleaker. Compared with China, the number of private or collective businesses was infinitesimal and their supply of consumer goods meager. People stood in line for hours, and when they finally made it inside the shops, they found little to buy. The shelves of state stores were even barer. Basic foods were in short supply, especially in Moscow. Sugar and cheese were impossible to find and eggs almost as scarce, even in private markets. Uncertainty about the political and economic future had driven the expected value of the ruble to almost zero. People waited in long lines outside hard-currency shops, the only steady supply of food and consumer goods. Some vegetable sellers in private markets demanded that their customers pay in U.S. dollars. Many mothers had quit their jobs because their ruble salaries were worthless and they had to forage for food. Russian émigrés arrived in the West with serious health and nutrition problems. Soviet living standards had started from a higher base than that of the Chinese, and Russian citizens still drove private cars and lived in more modern apartments than did their counterparts in China; nevertheless, the lack of food and everyday consumer goods meant that basic subsistence was now in doubt.

What paths brought China and the Soviet Union to such different economic outcomes? Both countries introduced economic reforms during the 1980s, but their reform strategies were completely different. Deng Xiaoping, the Chinese Communist Party (CCP) leader, attempted to carry out economic reforms without political reforms. By contrast, Mikhail Gorbachev, the Soviet Communist Party leader, decided that the only way to accomplish economic reforms was to introduce political reforms first.

By the end of the 1980s the Chinese strategy of economic reform without political reform appeared to have worked, at least in overall economic terms. The economy was growing, and people were living better. Real per capita gross national product increased 7.2 percent annually from 1978 to 1990 (McMillan and Naughton 1991, 3). The economy grew out of the plan so that more than half of all economic activity was governed by the market (Naughton forthcoming). Private, collective, and foreign joint venture enterprises produced more than half of national income. Despite these changes, progress toward a market economy was not smooth. At several times during the decade the reform drive appeared to have been derailed by economic problems and political conflicts. Economic overheating threatened to stall reforms and necessitate a return to central economic controls in 1981 and again in 1987–89. Over the course of the 1980s popular protests became more frequent (student demonstrations occurred in 1986, 1987, and 1989), and the conservative leaders in the party strengthened their hand. In 1989 Deng Xiaoping ordered the army to put down mass demonstrations in Beijing and more than eighty other cities. The violent repression, televised worldwide on CNN, tainted the CCP's international image as well as its domestic political legitimacy. After the Tiananmen crackdown, the CCP was split between a conservative leadership and a Central Committee that supported the reforms. With the party divided, the government bureaucracy was immobilized and economic policy was stuck. Despite the lack of new reform intiatives, the marketization of the Chinese economy expanded on its own momentum, and mass living standards continued to improve. Over the decade Chinese groups had acquired vested interests in the economic reforms, and no one suggested turning back to the command economy.

The Soviet strategy of political reform before economic reform produced political chaos and disintegration and a decline in living standards and growth rates.[1] Gorbachev dismantled the Communist Party's control over the government and the society and shifted authority to government institutions, including democratically elected legislatures. Despite radical political reforms, government officials continued to obstruct economic reform initiatives. After an abortive coup in August 1991 by conservative party and military leaders, the Communist Party was outlawed and the Soviet Union dissolved. The old centrally planned economy collapsed without a new economic system to take its place.

The overall economic success of the Chinese economic reform experience is surprising because we usually think of communist political institutions as rigid and hostile to innovation. We expect communist party and government officials to defend their vested interests in the command economy by blocking market reforms. Gorbachev's effort to change the political rules of the game before transforming the economic system accords with our views of communism better than Deng's strategy of economic reform without political reform does. Why, then, did China successfully achieve economic reform while the Soviet Union failed? How were the Chinese leaders able to introduce market reforms through communist political institutions?

In *The Political Logic of Economic Reform in China* I try to answer these questions by analyzing the political process of economic reform in China since 1979. The transformation of a Soviet-type centrally planned economy into a system of market socialism is an extremely complex and difficult task.[2] Most of the previous attempts

1. The United Nations estimated that Soviet economic output would decline by 15 percent in 1991 ("U.N. Calls" 1991).
2. Throughout this book I use the term *market reform* to describe the Chinese economic reforms. The Chinese version of market reform involved introducing the profit motive, competition, and managerial autonomy into a socialist state- and collectively owned economy, not substituting private

6 / Introduction

at economic reform—specifically, those in the Soviet Union in 1957 and 1965, Poland in 1956, Yugoslavia in 1952 and 1965, Hungary in 1968, Romania in 1967, and Czechoslovakia in 1968—failed, leading to no structural changes in the economy. Only in Yugoslavia did the decentralization of economic control proceed continuously to create a socialist economy with genuine markets.

We are right to believe that the limitations to economic reform in communist countries such as China exist more in the realm of politics than in the realm of economics. It is indeed extraordinarily difficult to introduce a market through a communist party-state bureaucracy. Yet communist political systems also have elements of flexibility and authority that offer opportunities for policy innovation. This book demonstrates that in some forms of communism, economic transformation can be achieved without changing the political rules of the game. Although communist political institutions are not in themselves insurmountable obstacles to economic reform, they do shape the economic reform policies that emerge from them.

The pattern of economic reform in China should be seen not merely as the trial-and-error attempts of Chinese leaders to find a formula that works or as the reflection of debates among economists over policy design. The real challenge of economic reforms was the political one. Every Chinese economist I've ever met believes that the path of reform reflects a political logic. As the Chinese economists put it, Deng Xiaoping and his reformist lieutenants, Zhao Ziyang and Hu Yaobang, pushed against the stone wall of the Chinese bureaucracy. Where they found loose stones, they pushed through; when stones would not move, they did not waste energy pushing. I try to make sense of Chinese economic reform policies by analyzing the construction of the "stone wall," that is, the institutional characteristics of the Chinese political system.

---

ownership for public ownership. It also involved combining market exchange among economic units with government planning, not substituting the market for planning. In other words, the Chinese market reform was intended to improve the economic performance of socialism, not to replace it with capitalism. Until 1992, the Chinese themselves always used the term *socialist commodity economy* (*shehuizhuyi de shangpin jingji*) because it was politically more palatable than the term *market economy* (*shichang jingji*). As the well-known reformist economist Chen Yizi argued, a commodity economy *is* a market economy, but no one in China was ready to say it (Chen Yizi 1990, 69–70).

An Institutional Approach to Explaining Economic Policies

This book explores the distinctive features of communist political institutions in order to discover the opportunities and limits for economic reform in all communist regimes. My starting point is the unusual idea that we can study policy-making in communist countries much as we would in noncommunist countries: by looking at the patterns of competition among politicians who operate in an institutionalized political setting. Scholars who study policy-making in democracies look at the way electoral, legislative, and executive powers and procedures create political incentives for politicians and set the ground rules for collective decision-making. Different sets of institutional arrangements generate distinctive political incentives and decision-making rules and thereby lead to predictable policy outcomes. Some scholars, most notably Robert Bates (1981; 1983) and Barry Ames (1987), have used a similar institutional analysis to understand economic policy-making in nondemocratic, authoritarian, less developed countries. I apply this kind of institutional analysis to the study of economic policy-making in communist countries.

Scholars of communist systems usually ignore the institutional framework of policy-making. They assume that institutional rules and lines of authority are irrelevant and that all decisions are made by one or a few individuals at the top of the nation's communist party.[3] And, depending on each scholar's perspective, they see communist leaders as choosing policies to solve the real problems confronting the country, to pursue their moral-ideological vision of the good society, or to defeat their rivals in factional power struggles.

My view is that policy-making in China has become a pluralistic process involving hundreds of officials from various Communist Party and government departments. And I believe that, although the informal power of a small number of Communist Party leaders such as Deng Xiaoping still influences the policy-making process, the formal and tacit rules of Chinese politics also shape policy out-

3. The most outstanding exceptions to this generalization are Jerry Hough's writings on "institutional pluralism" in the Soviet Union (especially 1969 and 1977), Philip Roeder's book (forthcoming) on the transformation of political institutions in the Soviet Union, and research on Chinese bureaucratic politics by Kenneth Lieberthal and Michel Oksenberg (especially their book, 1988) and by David Lampton (1987a).

comes. The authority to choose top party leaders granted by the CCP constitution to the Central Committee and the party's legal authority to appoint government officials set the context in which Chinese officials compete with one another to advance their careers and make economic policies.

Communist authoritarian regimes begin as revolutionary movements led by charismatic leaders. After Liberation these leaders continue to be the focus of loyalties, and personalistic authority dominates. As revolutionary regimes consolidate themselves and shift their attention from revolutionary transformation to economic modernization, their ruling parties begin to assert their collective authority, and political practices become regularized and institutionalized.

In China, Mao Zedong attempted to sustain his revolutionary charisma and stem the trend of institutionalization (disparagingly called "revisionism" by Mao) by launching mass campaigns such as the Great Leap Forward (1957–58) and the Cultural Revolution (1966–69). Thanks to Mao, China's evolution from personalistic rule to institutionalized authority was retarded.

China in the 1980s was far behind the Soviet Union in giving institutions and not personalities the authority to make decisions. The Central Committee of the Communist Party of the Soviet Union (CPSU) established once and for all its authority to choose party leaders in 1957 when it overruled the Politburo's firing of the party first secretary, Nikita Khrushchev; after defending Khrushchev in 1957, the Central Committee removed him from power in 1964 (Hough 1991, 95; Roeder forthcoming). Although the Chinese Central Committee has the same formal powers on paper (in the CCP constitution), its actual authority has not yet been definitively established. Whenever a party leader is selected, the Central Committee must share its role with other party elites, some of whom are retired elders who do not even hold official posts. The locus of authority is ambiguous because it is actually moving from an informal group of revolutionary elders to the collective institutions of the Communist Party; the pattern should be familiar to European historians who study political transitions from rule by royal courts to rule by parliaments.

Deng Xiaoping, who took over as China's preeminent leader in 1977, publicly declared his commitment to accelerating the long-delayed process of political institutionalization in China. In a landmark 1980 speech, "On the Reform of the System of Party and State

Leadership" (Deng Xiaoping 1980), Deng laid out a political reform agenda which, although falling far short of democratization, proposed a system governed by rules, clear lines of authority, and collective decision-making institutions to replace the overconcentration of power and patriarchal rule that had characterized China under Mao.

Not all the Maoist feudal, patriarchal ways criticized by Deng Xiaoping were actually eliminated, and the authority of institutions was not yet firmly established during the first decade of economic reform; nevertheless, Chinese officials themselves acted as if they believed that institutional rules now mattered more than they had before. In the history of economic reform policy decisions, communist politicians were obviously concerned as much with winning the support of the groups well represented in the CCP Central Committee, especially local officials, as with winning the approval of the retired elderly leaders who no longer had formal institutional positions.

Yet most observers of Chinese politics, not only foreign observers but also Chinese ones close to the action in Beijing, still view policymaking as a game played by only a few leading personalities. Because institutions such as the Central Committee almost never overrule the proposals of top leaders, the authority of such institutions is invisible to most observers.[4] Of course, Washington insiders have the same blindness to the role of institutions that Beijing insiders do; their stories about policy-making concentrate on the idiosyncrasies of the current president, the Speaker of the House, and key congressional leaders instead of the institutional relationships between the executive and legislative branches of

4.   Hough (1991, 94) points out that the same blindness to institutions has characterized the views of foreign scholars and Soviet intellectuals on Soviet politics: "We have become extraordinarily insensitive to institutions in the Soviet Union. The Soviet unwritten constitution put decision-making power in the party Central Committee and Politburo. . . . The political stability under Leonid Brezhnev left little reason for scholars to think about the institutional mechanisms through which power was acquired or maintained during his long reign. And the Soviet intellectuals on whom we have come to rely have understood nothing about intraparty mechanisms. They have talked about the resistance of 'bureaucrats' or 'the Party apparatus' to Gorbachev and about his need to create democratic institutions to circumvent them, but they have had no detailed sense of how the bureaucracy and Party apparatus are organized and how they interrelate. One thing is absolutely certain: Gorbachev understood the mechanisms of power in the Soviet system extremely well, and he set out to gain control of them in a very determined and even ruthless way."

government, the committee structure within the legislature, or the different electoral incentives facing presidents and legislative representatives.

Although I do not deny the continuing influence of leadership personalities in Chinese politics, I propose to place Chinese economic reform policy-making in a broader institutional context and to make explicit the rules of the political game in China. Part 2 (chapters 3–8) of this book maps the basic contours of the Chinese institutional landscape:

Authority relations. Who are the leaders with ultimate responsibility over policy, and who carries out policy? In the Chinese case, the Communist Party has supreme authority but delegates the job of making and implementing economic policy to the government.

Leadership incentives. To whom are leaders accountable and how are they chosen? In China, Communist Party leaders are chosen by an elite "selectorate" consisting of the members of the Central Committee, the revolutionary elders, and top military leaders— fewer than five hundred people in all. Party, government, and military officials in the selectorate are appointed by top CCP leaders but also have the authority to choose top CCP leaders, creating a relationship of "reciprocal accountability."

Bargaining arena. What is the institutional setting of collective choice? In China, economic policies generally are made in the government bureaucracy, with virtually no role for the legislature or judiciary.

Enfranchised participants.[5] Which groups are represented in policy deliberations? (Another way to phrase this question is, Who gets to sit around the bargaining table?) In China, economic decisions are made by ministries organized by function (e.g., education) and sector (e.g., machinery), and by province.

Decision rules. What are the rules of collective choice? Chinese economic policy-making operates according to delegation by consensus. If lower-level bureaucrats agree, the policy is automatically ratified by the upper level. If some lower-level bureaucrats refuse to agree, effectively vetoing the policy, it is referred to the upper level for resolution or tabled indefinitely.

These five features of Chinese communist institutions shaped the behavior of the officials who made economic reform policies from

5. Whereas I use the term *enfranchised participants* to describe groups who participate in policy-making, Roeder (forthcoming) uses the term in a more limited way to describe groups in the selectorate.

1979 to 1989. Analysis of these institutional features provides a framework for understanding the political logic of the reform drive and the sequencing, form, and content of reform policies.

The Political Strategy of Economic Reform: Why Gorbachev Decided to Change the Political Rules of the Game, and Why Deng Xiaoping Decided to Keep Them

Political institutions are not static. Economic reforms in communist states often are accompanied by some reform of the political system. Changes in institutional rules can modify the context in which bargaining over economic reform policies occurs. Thus, political reforms can be important elements of the political strategy of economic reform conducted by political elites.

The practical challenge of reforming a communist economy is how to manage politically the major redistributions of funds and power involved in the transition from central planning to market competition. Reformist leaders need simultaneously (1) to mobilize groups who will benefit from economic reforms into an effective coalition of support for the reforms and (2) to win over or render ineffective the groups who will lose as a result of the reforms. Otherwise, reform policies will be blocked by the groups most threatened by them.

The classical form in which this issue confronts reformist leaders in communist states is how to create an effective political counterweight to the center, the central communist party and government bureaucracies. The center has a strong vested interest in perpetuating central planning because it has the most to lose from reforms; moreover, it dominates the policy-making process in communist states.

China clearly differs from the Soviet Union in institutional strategies designed to tackle this issue. In the Soviet Union, Gorbachev decided that the only way to create a counterweight was to open up the political arena to mass participation and political competition. Changing the political rules of the game was a high-risk gamble—one that eventually led to the dismantling of Communist Party rule—but he believed he had no other choice. As he said in 1987, "Restructuring will only spin its wheels unless the main actor—the people—is included in it in a thoroughgoing way. . . . In order to make restructuring irreversible and to prevent a repetition of what happened in the past, everything must be placed under the control—once again—of the people. There is only one way to accomplish these tasks—through the broad democratization of Soviet society" (Gorbachev 1987, 7).[6]

Although Deng Xiaoping never publicly articulated his political strategy of economic reform, his actions show a very different calculation. He opted to retain the traditional communist bureaucratic polity with only minor modifications. He apparently believed that he could use local officials as an effective counterweight to the center without changing the political rules of the game. As a consequence, the Chinese processed economic reforms through the old decision-making channels.

Why did Deng and his political allies decide to stick with the authoritarian, bureaucratic system? Obviously, the political status quo was less risky than was a process of political change that might go out of control and subvert communism. From the perspective of Deng Xiaoping and his elderly colleagues in the founding generation of the CCP, what they feared most was what actually occurred in 1991 in the Soviet Union, namely, the overthrow of communist party rule.[7]

Another reason that Deng's strategy of reform differed from Gorbachev's was that China and the Soviet Union, although structurally very similar, differed in one important respect: in China, political and economic authority was more decentralized and less institutionalized than it had been in the Soviet Union. Mao Zedong's previous deliberate efforts at decentralization had left the Chinese center a less formidable threat to economic reform than its counterpart was in the Soviet Union.

6. Gorbachev's decision to risk mobilizing groups outside the bureaucracy in support of economic reform was based on a negative assessment of previous Soviet attempts at economic reform without political reform. The prominent Soviet sociologist Tatyana Zaslavskaya explained the lack of success of previous efforts to reform economic relations by the lack of "a strategy that would simultaneously stimulate the activity of groups interested in changing present relations and block the actions of groups capable of obstructing this change" (1984, 98).

7. The difference in the strategies of the Chinese and Soviet leaders may derive from their different generational perspectives. Deng's cohort of leaders are first-generation founders of the communist revolution in China, whereas Gorbachev belonged to the fourth generation of communist leaders in the Soviet Union (Hough 1980). Hong Yung Lee (1991) argues that the political evolution of the People's Republic of China was shaped by the peasant origins and the low educational standard of the founder generation, which remained in power for more than forty years.

The Stalinist model of a centrally planned economy was transferred to China from the Soviet Union less than forty years ago and was less deeply rooted in China than in the land of its origin. Forty years is a brief stretch of time from the perspective of twenty-five hundred years of Chinese history. Moreover, during the brief period when the Soviet-style system reigned in China, central control over economic life was never as extensive or effective as it was in the USSR itself. Especially after Mao Zedong purposefully shifted economic power down to provinces and cities during the Great Leap Forward and the Cultural Revolution, local governments played a much stronger economic role than did their counterparts in the Soviet Union. Chinese central planning was also more primitive and less inclusive than Soviet central planning had been; even during periods with a relatively high degree of centralization, the Chinese central bureaucracy (planning commission and ministries) controlled the production and allocation of fewer than 600 products, whereas the Soviets had central control over as many as 5,500 products (the Chinese categories were coarser so the numbers are not strictly comparable; Wong 1985). Under China's version of the command economy, a substantial share of economic activity went on outside the national plan, and much of it was administered at the provincial level.

China also had the "benefit" of the Cultural Revolution, which weakened central institutions and created a constituency for economic reforms. The normal operations of central party and government bodies were severely disrupted during the period following the Cultural Revolution (1966–76), with thousands of officials transferred to lower-level jobs or sent to the countryside for reeducation. As a result, central party and state bureaucracies were less daunting opponents to economic reform than they were in the Soviet Union and other communist states where their reign had been uninterrupted. In fact, central bureaucracies were active proponents of some reforms that they believed would rationalize and preserve their limited domain.

During the Cultural Revolution decade, social life became highly politicized and unpredictable. Thousands of intellectuals, professionals, and officials were pilloried in public meetings, fired from their jobs, and imprisoned. Ordinary citizens had to worry about being criticized by their coworkers and neighbors. Political campaigns disrupted the economy so that living standards stagnated and China fell increasingly behind its East Asian neighbors. The Cultural Revolution had a genuinely traumatic effect on Chinese urban society, compared by some Chinese to the social trauma of fascism in Europe. Having experienced the irrationalities of the communist system in such an extreme form, Chinese leaders and citizens alike were ready to consider changing the system.

The comparison between China and the Soviet Union illuminates the logic of the Chinese political strategy of economic reform. In China, the central party-state bureaucracies were a less formidable obstacle to market reforms, and previous waves of administrative decentralization had created the possibility that provincial politicians could become the reformist counterweight to the more conservative center. Although these provincial politicians were appointed by the central party organization, they were expected not only to enforce central directives but also to articulate local interests. With the support of provincial politicians, Deng Xiaoping was able to push his reform program through the bureaucratic decision-making process and avoid the risks of changing the political rules of the game.

The Path of Chinese Economic Reforms

The ramifications of Deng Xiaoping's crucial decision to retain the traditional communist polity were momentous. Economic reform policies were processed through the same bureaucratic authoritarian institutions that had existed in China since the 1950s. Yet even without changing the political process, the Chinese were able to make considerable progress toward a competitive socialist market economy. Contests for leadership succession—during 1978–80 between Deng Xiaoping and Hua Guofeng, during 1980–87 between Hu Yaobang and Zhao Ziyang, and during 1987–89 between Zhao Ziyang and Li Peng—motivated contenders to propose innovative solutions to China's problems. Various early moves—for instance, to decollectivize agriculture, expand foreign trade and investment, encourage private and collective business, decentralize fiscal revenues to local governments, and allow state factories to keep a share of their own profits—changed the economic and career incentives of bureaucrats and managers to give them a real interest in promoting reform. The dynamic growth of the nonstate sector during the long period of transition taught state industry bureaucrats and managers the advantages of getting free of the plan.[8] Over the course of the decade the momentum of the reform drive was sustained despite periodic retrenchments caused by economic difficulties.

Certainly the persistence of the old communist political institutions made the task of winning approval for reform policies difficult. The Chinese government bureaucracy, where most economic policies are made, always made decisions by consensus and not by majority rule.[9] Consensus decision-making institutions tend to be conservative because radical departures from the status quo are blocked by vetoes from groups who stand to lose. In a hierarchical bureaucracy, moreover, subordinates are less willing to compromise to achieve consensus when they perceive their leaders to be divided. Intense political competition at the top makes it harder to obtain consensus below.

The trajectory of Chinese industrial reforms over the decade in question was shaped by consensus decision-making. Instead of sweeping out central planning in one bold stroke, elements of market competition were introduced gradually and tacked onto central planning, prolonging the period of transition from planned to market economy. A radical agricultural decollectivization, which did not threaten the industrial ministries or the Ministry of Finance, was introduced ahead of industrial reform, which would diminish the control and resources of these powerful central ministries. Because local (provincial and municipal) officials were a large bloc in the CCP Central Committee and a critical ingredient for achieving a policy consensus, funds and authority were decentralized more to local governments than to the enterprises themselves. A dual-track price system combining floating market prices with administratively set plan prices was implemented to avoid tackling the radical redistribution among raw material and manufacturing sectors implied by a comprehensive price liberalization. Instead of attacking the perquisites and powers of the central bureaucracies head-on, Deng Xiaoping decided to encircle the bureaucracies by

8. In China, the nonstate sector is defined as all business not owned by the government, including both collectively and privately owned businesses.
9. The collective bodies of the CCP, including the Party Congress, the Central Committee, the Politburo, and the Standing Committee of the Politburo, appear to make decisions by majority rule and not by consensus. But the government bureaucratic meetings where most economic policies are hammered out make decisions by consensus.

creating new forms of business exempt from normal state rules, such as private and collective firms and Special Economic Zones designed to attract foreign investment. The dynamic growth of this nonstate sector put competitive pressure on state-owned firms and the government bureaucrats responsible for them; soon state managers and bureaucrats were demanding the same market freedoms for their state-owned firms.

In the context of leadership competition and consensus decision-making, proposals for industrial reform that would have applied the same economic rules to all enterprises or all localities drew bureaucratic opposition and either were defeated or barely passed after being modified by compromises and side payments. Such proposals, which can be called "standardization reforms" (the most obvious examples were tax reform and price reform), drew bureaucratic opposition because they were inherently redistributive, threatening the economic benefits of industries and regions favored under the centrally planned economy.

But surprisingly, some reform initiatives were easily approved by communist bureaucrats. Reform proposals that applied different rules to each enterprise and locality were widely popular and sailed through the bureaucracy. These proposals, which I call "particularistic contracting," gave party and government officials at every level opportunities to earn political support from subordinates in exchange for granting them generous contract terms. Particularistic contracting was politically successful in the context of Chinese political institutions because it mimicked the familiar pattern by which production and supply quotas were bargained out and political support networks built under traditional central planning. Moreover, particularistic contracting reforms were embraced because they were not redistributive; enterprises and localities could preserve their vested interests while carrying out reforms.

Out of China's authoritarian, bureaucratic policy came a reform package that was surprisingly successful in political terms. "Chinese-style economic reform"—consisting of particularistic contracting, a dual-track system combining market and plan, decentralization to local governments, agricultural decollectivization, stimulation of the nonstate sector, and special zones for foreign investment—was a winning formula given the rules of Chinese politics. To put this conclusion in the terms of institutional analysis, Chinese-style economic reform was a policy equilibrium in the context of Chinese political institutions. Every time politicians or economic advisors tried to deviate from this formula—for example, by introducing universalistic price and tax reforms or by recentralizing the fiscal system—they failed. The momentum of the reform drive was sustained by continuing to introduce policies based on this formula. Communist institutions proved their flexibility as the bureaucratic support for economic reforms snowballed over the decade. The simplistic notion that communist bureaucracies are so wedded to central planning that they block any attempts to change was proven false.

A reform package that is politically logical is not necessarily economically logical. The cumulative economic effect of China's economic reform policies was mixed. The positive result was that the economy grew rapidly and living standards improved. From 1980 to 1990 the average annual increase (adjusted for inflation) in GNP was 9.0 percent and in industrial output value was 12.6 percent (Li Peng 1991a, 9). Along with the growth came a rise in personal income. Urban per capita income rose from 500.4 yuan in 1981 to 1,387.81 yuan in 1989; adjusted for inflation, these figures translate into an average annual increase of 4.5 percent. Rural per capita income rose from 133.57 yuan in 1978 to 601.51 yuan in 1989; adjusted for inflation, these figures translate into an average annual increase of 9.2 percent.[10]

But the bad news was that industry grew and incomes increased with only modest improvement in the efficiency of state-owned factories.[11] The reform policies produced not intensive growth (increased efficiency in already existing factories) but extensive growth (rapid expansion of industrial capacity), albeit extensive growth un-

10.   The urban per capita income data are based on household survey data not available before 1981. Because there was a big jump in urban wages between 1978 and 1981, my figure understates the rate by which urban income increased over the total 1978–89 period. The urban income statistics are taken from the *Statistical Yearbook* (*Zhongguo tongji nianjian*) 1987 (691), and *Statistical Yearbook* 1990 (296). The rural income statistics based on household survey data are from the *Statistical Yearbook* 1991 (312). The urban income figures are adjusted for inflation by using the urban consumer price index in the *Statistical Yearbook* 1990 (250); and the rural income figures are adjusted for inflation by using the price index of consumer goods sold in the rural areas in the *Statistical Yearbook* 1990 (250).

11.   For Chinese data on industrial labor productivity, capital output ratio, fixed assets output ratio, consumption output ratio, and changes in fixed costs, see Zhu Mingchun 1990. Although the Chinese sources see no improvement in industrial efficiency during the decade of reform, Western economists find modest improvement (Kuan Chen et al. 1988; Jefferson et al. forthcoming).

der reform conditions. At the end of the 1980s the number of state factories operating in the red was conservatively estimated at one-third. Because the government continued to be responsible for bailing out losing firms, industrial waste and inefficiency translated into persistent budget deficits. Rapid extensive growth produced supply and energy shortages and inflation rates of more than 20 percent. For several years after 1985, inflation cut into the income gains Chinese citizens had enjoyed during the first half of the reform decade. Finally, the dual-track system, although a politically attractive approach to reform, stimulated corruption as officials exploited their role as gatekeepers to the lucrative market sector.

During the second half of the 1980s the economic problems provoked by overly rapid growth boomeranged, returning in the form of political opposition. Large numbers of CCP and government bureaucrats at the middle and lower levels of the system had become converted to the cause of economic reform, but conspicuous economic problems, particularly inflation and corruption, created doubts both at the top of the CCP and at the bottom, among ordinary citizens. Conflicts over economic reform strategy polarized the party elite into reformists (led by Premier Zhao Ziyang and CCP General Secretary Hu Yaobang) and conservatives (led by Chen Yun and other party elders). Inflation and corruption provided ammunition for the conservative elites to strengthen their position and defeat the reformists in CCP power struggles. As for ordinary citizens, inflation and corruption drove many of them into the streets in spring 1989.

Research Methodology

This book is based primarily on interviews I conducted in Chinese with Chinese economic officials. I made research visits to China from 1980 to 1991. My most valuable material was acquired in a period of intensive interviewing from August to December 1984 in Beijing and Shanghai.

Because I wanted to learn how economic reform policies were made and implemented, I interviewed economic officials who had participated in this process at the national level in Beijing and the municipal level in Shanghai. In 1984 I conducted fifty-four interviews, each two to three hours long, with forty-two different officials in China. I also participated in group discussions with national economic officials as a member of visiting delegations and had many brief discussions with officials at banquets and receptions. I was fortunate to be able to obtain interviews with officials from three industrial ministries and all the major comprehensive economic agencies of the central government, including the State Planning Commission, State Economic Commission, State Bureau of Material Supply, State Price Bureau, Ministry of Finance, Commission on Economic System Reform, Institute on Economic System Reform, Economic Research Center of the State Council, Policy Research Office of the Communist Party Secretariat, China International Trust and Investment Corporation, and Special Economic Zone Office. In Shanghai I had interviews with Mayor Wang Daohan and with officials from the Finance Bureau, Economic Commission, Planning Commission, Economic Reform Leading Small Group, Foreign Economic Relations and Trade Commission, International Trust and Investment Corporation, Material Supply Bureau, Number One Electrical Machinery Bureau, and Light Industrial Bureau.

Persuading these officials to talk frankly with me about the controversies and conflicts surrounding reform policies was a personal challenge. At first the officials were wary of revealing too much and presented only the official *People's Daily* version of events. I cracked this reserve by introducing several leading questions that told the interviewees that I already knew at least part of the real story. After that, all officials gave detailed, specific accounts reporting the different viewpoints of various organizations and individuals. They obviously spoke from the perspective of their particular organizations. I always compared the accounts of officials from different bureaucracies on the same issues and events.

In addition to these interviews, I gathered material during visits to the Special Economic Zones in Xiamen, Fujian Province (1982), and in Shenzhen, Guangdong Province (1984). I was also able to gain information on the evolution of reform policies in interviews with Chinese economic officials who visited the United States during the 1980s.

To learn about the implementation of economic reforms at the enterprise level, I conducted interviews with managers and workers at two large factories in Chongqing, Sichuan Province, during a month of research in 1980. I prepared for this factory research during four months in 1980 in Hong Kong interviewing émigrés who had formerly been employees in PRC factories. During 1984 I also interviewed the managers of three factories in Beijing.

My interviews with Chinese officials and factory managers were supplemented by extensive documentary research, especially articles from economics newspapers and journals I gathered in China and in U.S. libraries.

Finally, during the period 1980–84 I conducted interviews with foreigners who had done business with the Chinese under the new open policy. Their case histories of business dealings gave me a different and very valuable perspective on how the Chinese government bureaucracy implemented the new foreign trade and investment policies.

Social science field research by foreigners is a relatively new and controversial practice in China. The Chinese who agreed to be interviewed were taking a political risk. If the foreign scholar's writings offend higher Chinese officials or if the political line shifts, the interviewee could be tainted. It is therefore particularly important that the anonymity and confidentiality that protect interviewees in standard international social science practice be extended to Chinese interviewees. To guarantee an extra layer of protection I will not identify my interviewees even by institutional affiliation and will attribute information gathered from interviews reported in the book only by the designation "author's interviews." Specific documentary sources will be cited in references.

The Plan of the Book

What happens when you introduce a market through a communist bureaucracy? I try to answer this question by analyzing the course of Chinese industrial reform policies from 1979 to 1989. Of course, I cannot tell the whole story of China's economic reforms. Instead, I focus on the reforms in industrial management and finance and do not deal with the reforms in agriculture or in foreign trade and investment. Within industry, I do not cover changes in labor policies, nor do I deal with private and collective enterprises, only state-owned ones. Although the parts of the Chinese economy not discussed in this book are undeniably important, a large share of national output value and financial revenues is generated by the state-owned industrial enterprises that are my focus.

Chinese political institutions shaped industrial reform policies by establishing the incentives of political actors and the rules by which they made decisions. I do not claim that institutional incentives and rules can provide a complete explanation of every specific policy choice; the economic situation facing decisionmakers and their individual personalities and preferences certainly affected their choices as well. But I do hope to show that the overall path of

Chinese economic reform over the past decade can be best understood by focusing on the political institutions in which reform policies were made.

Chapter 2 provides background information on the prereform Chinese economic system. The chapter compares the Chinese version of the command economy with the Soviet one and identifies several reasons why the Chinese version performed more poorly. In the context of this comparison I suggest that the decision of Deng Xiaoping and other reformist party leaders to introduce market reforms was explicable more in political terms than in economic ones. The chapter concludes with a brief description of other parts of the economic reform package and their contributions to industrial reform.

Part 2 of the book includes six chapters. Five of them lay out the core characteristics of Chinese political institutions: chapter 3 on the authority relations between the CCP and the government; chapter 4 on party leadership incentives; chapter 5 on the government bargaining arena; chapter 6 on who is enfranchised in this arena; and chapter 7 on delegation by consensus decision-making in this arena. In chapter 8 I present an overview of industrial reform policy outcomes and relate them to the institutional context in which they were made. A comparison of the rocky course of industrial reform with the comparatively smooth progress of agricultural reform illustrates the consequences of institutional arrangements for policy outcomes.

Part 3 tells the story of Chinese industrial reforms. Chapter 9 focuses on one of the earliest and most significant moves in Deng Xiaoping's approach to economic reform, namely, fiscal decentralization to local governments. By "playing to the provinces" Deng hoped to give local officials an incentive to improve enterprise performance and to join his political coalition for reform. The strategy was politically successful, but its economic effects were mixed.

Chapters 10, 11, 12, and 13 present a chronological account of industrial reforms from 1979 to 1989. The evolution of policies governing the finance and management of enterprises vividly illustrates the institutional dynamics of reform policy-making. Chapter 10 describes the political success of enterprise profit retention experiments from 1978 to 1981. Chapter 11 reveals the close link between elite competition and economic policy-making in the decision to replace enterprise profit retention with a system based on tax payment in 1982–83. Chapter 12 focuses on the bureaucratic bargaining over the tax reform policy in 1983–84. And chapter 13 shows how, in the context of elite competition, the political logic of particularistic contracting overcame the economic logic of tax reform and price reform from 1985 to 1988.

Chapter 14 concludes the book by reconsidering the opportunities and limitations for economic reform built into communist political institutions and returning to the comparison between the Chinese and Soviet reform experiences introduced at the beginning of the book. The Chinese case raises important questions about the relationship between economic and political reform in communist states and suggests that the political preconditions for dynamic transformation from plan to market are institutional flexibility and authority.

2 The Prereform Chinese Economy and the Decision to Initiate Market Reforms

Scholars work backward to show how the seeds of revolution were laid long before the actual event. China's economic reform has been described by its leaders as a kind of revolution, and like other revolutions, once it happened, people believed it had been ordained by history.[1] At the end of Mao Zedong's reign, serious economic problems and a political legitimacy crisis threatened the Communist Party; the only way for the party to survive was to improve living standards by means of market reforms.

In reality, there was nothing inevitable about the decision of China's leaders to launch an economic reform drive in late 1978. The Chinese version of the command economy that operated under Mao's rule had produced accomplishments as well as problems. Moreover, China's economic problems were nothing new; they were apparent to many Chinese economists in the 1970s and even in the 1960s. And it was by no means obvious that market reforms were the only solution to these problems.

By the time of Mao's death in 1976, members of China's political elite did agree that restoring the CCP's prestige required improving economic performance and raising living standards. The traumatic experience of the Cultural Revolution had eroded popular trust in the moral and political virtue of the CCP. The party's leaders decided to shift the base of party legitimacy from virtue to competence, and to do that they had to demonstrate that they could deliver the goods. The self-doubt of the Chinese elite, brought back from their first trips abroad to more advanced countries during the 1970s, also motivated them to strong action on the economic front.

Despite an elite consensus on the political necessity of economic progress, there was no agreement on the means to achieve it. Econ-

1.   On the differences between great reform and revolution, see Oksenberg and Dickson 1991.

omists at universities and research institutes proposed intellectually attractive ideas about profit incentives and market competition. Market reforms, although politically threatening to the groups with vested interests in the command economy, might be the best economic solution to China's inefficiency and backwardness. But some members of the elite and some economists favored strengthening and improving the system of Soviet-style central planning that had first been introduced in China during the First Five-Year Plan (1953–57).

With many economic ideas in the wind and many policy solutions available to him, Deng Xiaoping chose to advocate market-type reforms, that is, profit incentives, market competition, and reduced scope for planning. His choice was shaped by his own political incentives, specifically his ambition to replace Hua Guofeng as Mao's successor, as well as by his desire to ameliorate China's economic condition.

The Performance of China's Command Economy

In the 1950s the Chinese established a Soviet-type centrally planned economy. This kind of economic system, often called a "command economy," included the following features:

State ownership of industrial enterprises.

Organization of agriculture into large-scale collective and state farms.

Centralized bureaucratic management of the economy with government planners setting output and supply quotas, prices, and wages.

Capital investment provided as free government grants; no land rents or land-use fees.

An extensive growth strategy designed to achieve high rates of growth and establish a heavy industrial base.

State revenues based almost entirely on industrial profits. To increase the profitability of industrial production, planners set the prices of agricultural commodities and raw materials low, and manufactured goods high. The result was a system of rich industry, poor agriculture.

Disparagement of the service sector and prohibitions on private business.

A closed economy with foreign trade plans treated as addenda to domestic plans; foreign trade held to low levels and aimed at the goal of import substitution; no foreign investment; a central foreign trade monopoly; nonconvertible currency; and the prevalence of barter trade.[2]

The Soviet-style system turned the Chinese economy into a gigantic corporation that we might call "China, Incorporated," managed by the government planners in Beijing and overseen by the Politburo, which was the equivalent of a board of directors. The planners determined all prices and wages and assigned output quotas to economic enterprises in terms of physical quantities. Managers of enterprises were evaluated and promoted according to their success in meeting output quotas. An enterprise had almost no responsibility to market its own products or procure its own inputs.[3] Allocations of labor, material supplies, and capital investment were centrally determined. All products were purchased and marketed by state monopolies. All foreign trade was conducted through the central ministry of foreign trade.

The strong point of command economies is supposed to be their ability to mobilize resources for rapid economic development. Bureaucratic controls on consumption (by means of rationing in cities and administrative allocation of grain in rural collective farms) enable planners to accumulate a high proportion of national output for reinvestment. In China this proportion was approximately 30 percent from the 1950s on, roughly the same as Soviet rates. Theoretically, the planners who allocate investment funds base their decisions on their assessment of the long-term needs of society as a whole, not on the narrow interests of individual sectors, regions, or enterprises. Unlike a market, the command economy can concentrate resources on priority or bottleneck sectors that are retarding overall economic progress.[4]

2. This list of features is drawn in part from Brown and Neuberger 1968 and Ward 1980.
3. In the Chinese version of the command economy, the central plan never provided 100 percent of inputs to state factories, and managers always were responsible for procuring some of their own materials.
4. In both the Soviet Union and China communist leaders used their centralized control of resources in the service of egalitarian redistribution among geographic regions. After 1949 the CCP gave priority to the industrial development of inland China, the poor, backward part of the country where the communists were based during the Civil War. In the first thirty years of communist rule the government invested approximately 40 percent of capital construction funds in industrial construction in the interior. The central government siphoned off the fiscal surpluses of provinces with large

In actuality, the decisions of central planners are as skewed toward short-term considerations as are those of market capitalists. Because their thinking is dominated by a desire to achieve high growth rates and an ideological preference for heavy industries such as steel, communist planners channel the lion's share of investment into industry instead of agriculture and, within industry, to heavy industry instead of light. In China, iron and steel and machine building, the backbone heavy industries, were given priority, consuming more than one-third of total investment in industrial capital construction (*Statistical Yearbook* 1990, 168). During the period 1949–78 the value of heavy industrial output multiplied 90.6 times, while agriculture and light industry rose only 2.4 times and 19.8 times, respectively (Dong Furen 1982).[5]

Meanwhile, energy and transportation infrastructure, essential for long-term progress but not reflected in annual growth rates, tends to be neglected in communist economies. One study comparing socialist and capitalist countries (not including China) found that contrary to expectations, capitalist countries had invested a *higher* share of capital and labor into infrastructure (transport, communications, housing, health, education, and culture) and therefore had a greater stock of infrastructure than socialist countries had (Ehrlich and Szilagyi 1980). Chinese planners made the same shortsighted choices, and as a result the Chinese economy was severely

---

industrial cities, mostly on the coast, and allocated those funds to deficit-ridden inland provinces (Maruyama 1981; Lardy 1979). The more populous, industrialized, and cosmopolitan coastal provinces were held back by redistributive fiscal policies; coastal provinces grew at a slower rate than did the inland provinces (Field 1986). The redistributive thrust of national economic policies was intensified during the Cultural Revolution, when Mao Zedong prepared for the threat of war with the United States or the Soviet Union by promoting regional economic autarky and accelerating industrial construction in the inland "Third Front" (Naughton 1988a; 1989). Resources flowed to the regions that were the most defensible or the most needy, not to regions that could make the most efficient use of resources. The economic waste created by regional redistribution was massive because the efficiency gap between inland and coastal China is so wide. The fourteen coastal cities that were granted special freedoms to attract foreign investment in 1984 realize output value per 100 yuan of original fixed assets 73.5 percent higher than the average level of the whole country, and the figure for Shanghai is more than double that of the country (Liu Rongcang 1987).
5. Although industrial growth certainly outpaced agricultural growth, these figures exaggerate the disparity between the two because Chinese planners always kept the prices of agricultural commodities low and of industrial goods high.

constrained by shortages of energy and transport. Because of energy shortages, industries lay idle two or three days a week. Finished products often failed to reach customers because of shortages of rail and roadway freight, the consequence of downgrading transport to the status of "nonproductive investment." Rail traffic increased ten times between 1948 and 1975, yet route length only doubled and overall track (because of double tracking) expanded only about three times (Clarke 1981).

The Soviet-style command of resources enabled China to achieve high rates of industrial growth, estimated to be approximately 10 percent per year from 1949 to 1980.[6] Yet the price of these high growth rates was steep. Because the economic system operated inefficiently, more and more capital and labor had to be pumped into industry to sustain high growth. During the period 1951–80 the average annual increase in total investment in industrial fixed assets (11.7 percent) exceeded the average annual growth rate of industrial and agricultural output value (8.6 percent); in advanced industrial countries, including the Soviet Union, the rate of production growth exceeded the growth rate of investment (Liu Rongcang 1987). From 1957 to 1978 the gross output value per every 100 yuan in industrial fixed assets fell by 25.4 percent (Ma Hong 1982). The economist Robert Dernberger estimates that total factor productivity (calculated as the gross value of output produced for every unit of capital and labor) declined between the early 1950s and 1979 at an annual rate of 2.75 percent (Dernberger 1981). In other words, the Chinese command economy produced "self-consuming growth" (Hirszowicz 1980), with industrial growth eating up an ever larger share of industrial output.[7]

What made statistics about declining factor productivity politically relevant to the post-Mao leadership was the fact that the costs of industrial growth were felt directly by consumers. During the thirty years when the Chinese were building 400,000 industrial en-

6. Barry Naughton (1989a) compares the two peak years of 1953 and 1978 and estimates that over that period the average annual growth of net material product, a version of national income, was 6 percent.
7. Economists who study socialist systems have noted that socialist states benefit from a "composition effect": because they can suppress consumption and services to preserve high rates of investment and concentrate resources in manufacturing, which is the sector with the highest productivity, they are able to compensate for lower rates of factor productivity growth (compared with capitalist systems) within individual sectors (Pryor 1985; Bergson 1978).

terprises with total assets of more than 500 billion U.S. dollars, people's living standards remained basically stagnant. Between 1952 and 1980, the gross output value of industry and agriculture increased by 810 percent and national income grew by 420 percent, but average individual income increased by only 100 percent (Ma Hong 1982). The planners diverted resources from mass consumption to feed industrial growth. Because of meager agricultural investment and lack of production incentives, grain output grew only 55 percent between 1953 and 1978; this pace of development, although quite respectable by comparative historical standards, failed to keep up with population growth, which was 64 percent over the same period (*Statistical Yearbook* 1990, 89, 363). The average amount of grain available to be consumed by each person was smaller in 1976–77 than in 1956–57 (Xue Muqiao 1981). Because planners neglected light industry, department stores had few consumer goods to offer customers, and whatever they had was of poor quality and limited variety. Urban housing was inadequate and run-down because government investment policies ignored nonproductive construction and state-set rents were too low to accumulate funds for housing construction, renovation, or maintenance.

During the first thirty years after 1949, the CCP and the government planners successfully achieved their goal of rapid industrialization, but the price of this accomplishment was continued low living standards. Western observers, swayed by Mao Zedong's rhetoric of rural populism, praised the Chinese model of development for promoting the livelihood of the masses much better than the Soviet model did. In reality, both China and the Soviet Union gave priority to industrial growth over mass living standards.

The crucial link in understanding how an industrial economy growing at 10 percent a year could fail to improve people's livelihood was the persistent low efficiency of Chinese factories and of the planning system as a whole. Some of the sources of inefficiency were common to all Soviet-style economies: the problem of poor information flowing from managers to planners, first noted by Frederick Hayek in 1935 (Hayek 1935); the impracticability of planning a huge, complex, interdependent economy, even with the best computers and planners (Nove 1983); the impossibility of making good investment decisions without rational prices; the lack of managerial incentives to undertake technological innovations (Ward 1967); the presence of monopolistic firms that faced no domestic or foreign competition; and the absence of managerial incentives to meet customer demand by improving the quality or variety of products. Efficiency was reduced both by the rigidity of central plans and by the illicit mechanisms (e.g., distorting information to resist excessive demands from planners, using networks of personal relations to get things done, stockpiling materials and labor to insure against uncertainties in the supply system) that managers devised to cope with the plans (Brus 1973; Ward 1967).

The Distinctive Features of China's Command Economy: Comparisons with the Soviet Union

The Chinese and Soviet economic systems were not identical. Compared with that of the USSR, the Chinese command economy was cruder, more decentralized, and more dominated by noneconomic, ideological considerations. The differences between the Chinese and Soviet economic systems had important consequences for their future patterns of reform.

LARGE NUMBER OF SMALL-SCALE FIRMS AND DECENTRALIZATION OF PLANNING AUTHORITY FROM CENTER TO LOCALITIES

The Chinese central plan managed a smaller share of economic activity and managed it less effectively than the Soviet plan did. Beginning in 1951, soon after the communist takeover, the Chinese system became a multitiered, regionally based system in which much of the responsibility for planning and coordination devolved to local governments. Large, key enterprises were under the central plan, receiving supply allocations from central government agencies and handing over their output to unified allocation by the central government. Less important enterprises were left to planning and management at the provincial, prefectural, and county levels. According to two prominent Chinese economists, "strict centralized management of the economy by directives, as under the pure Soviet model, has never existed in China. The 'decentralizing movement' which took place in 1958 and has been renewed from time to time ever since has eroded central planning and its power to control" (Wu Jinglian and Zhao Renwei 1987, 310).

The economic explanation usually given for this devolution of planning authority to local levels is the unusually large number of firms and the predominance of small firms in China. (There is also a political explanation for the tendency of Beijing leaders to grant power and resources to local officials; see chapter 9.) As of 1978

China had a total of 348,000 industrial firms, 344,000 of which were small (*Statistical Yearbook* 1984, 193).[8] Soviet industry was much more concentrated: the Soviet Union had only 40,000 factories in 1979, and firms with more than one thousand employees accounted for 74 percent of Soviet industrial output, compared with 41.8 percent in China.[9]

It was impossible for the technically unsophisticated Chinese planners to incorporate so many small firms into a central plan. As a result, the plan covered only part of China's economic activity (50–55 percent of gross value industrial output as of 1977–78), and local government planners allocated substantial portions of materials that normally were under central government control in Soviet-type economies. As of 1980 only 3 percent of Chinese state-owned factories were directly administered by central government ministries; the rest belonged to local governments, received their plan quotas mainly from local governments, and remitted their profits to local governments.[10]

8. Chinese industrial firms are categorized as small, medium, or large according to sector-specific productive capacities rather than by the number of workers. However, as a rule large and medium-sized firms have more than one thousand employees, and small firms have fewer than one thousand employees. Christine Wong (1987) states that as of 1984 only 0.6 percent of Chinese firms had more than 243 workers. Many of China's small firms (and some of its larger ones) are not state firms owned and run by different parts of the government but collective firms owned and operated by their employees. The Soviet Union never had any significant number of collective firms.
9. The Soviet figures are from Andrew Ferris, *The Soviet Enterprise* (London: Croom Helm, 1984), 9, cited in Naughton 1988, 2. The figure on the share of industrial output produced by large enterprises is also from Naughton 1988, 2. Although the Chinese figure is from 1987, Naughton has told me (personal communication) that in the late 1970s it was roughly the same—that is, between 40 and 50 percent.
10. The information in this paragraph comes from Wong 1986a and Wong 1987. Wong explains that China has a four-tier hierarchy of industrial firms. At the top are approximately 2,500 large enterprises controlled by the central government and its ministries; these enterprises produce 30–40 percent of industrial output. In the second tier are enterprises run by provinces and cities, including 30,000–40,000 state enterprises and 125,000 collective enterprises. In the third tier are prefectural and county enterprises, perhaps 40,000–50,000 in number and mostly small-scale. At the bottom are rural collective enterprises run by townships and villages (formerly called communes and brigades); 227,700 township enterprises were listed in national industrial statistics in 1984. The central plan governed all of the output of first-tier firms, perhaps one-half to two-thirds of the production

ADMINISTRATIVE ALLOCATION OF LABOR,
LIFETIME EMPLOYMENT, AND "UNITISM"

In one regard, the hand of the Chinese planners reached further than that of the Soviet planners, but it was all thumbs and no fingers (in the vivid phrase of Charles E. Lindblom [1977]). Beginning in the early 1960s, the Chinese government exercised strict control over industrial labor, setting enterprise labor quotas and assigning workers to enterprises. With the exception of the World War II period, the Soviet Union always had an industrial labor market; China had administrative allocation of labor and restriction of labor mobility instead. Soviet firms competed for labor, which was scarce, by ignoring central wage restrictions and raising pay levels. Chinese firms had no choice about which workers to hire and what to pay them even though the labor supply was plentiful. By assigning people to jobs and forbidding people to change jobs, the Chinese created an "iron rice bowl" employment system, with lifetime employment in one work unit.

Lifetime employment and restrictions on rural-urban migration in turn led to the emergence of "unitism," a system in which work units became total communities with full responsibility for the housing, welfare, retirement, and schooling of employees and their families and complete control over their lives (Walder 1986; Henderson and Cohen 1984). "Unitism" and the lack of a labor market undoubtedly diluted labor incentives and reduced efficiency in Chinese firms. According to one World Bank study, even after enterprise reforms were introduced, the dominant objective function of Chinese factories continued to be not the maximization of profit but the maximization of the welfare of employees' families (Byrd and Tidrick 1987).[11]

---

in provincial and city enterprises, and one-fourth of production in county and prefectural enterprises.

11. Why unitism was created in China in the early 1960s remains something of a mystery because it was economically irrational in the context of China's abundant supply of labor. In fact, it would have been more economically logical for Soviet industry, facing a labor shortage, to extend generous welfare and security privileges to its permanent workers than it was for Chinese industry, with its plentiful supply of labor. Most scholars explain the creation of permanent employment and unitism after the Great Leap Forward as a measure to prevent uncontrolled migration of peasants to cities (for example, see Walder 1986). But why were Chinese leaders so

LACK OF MATERIAL INCENTIVES

Maoism compounded the problem of crude planning and inadequate enterprise incentives in China. Unlike Soviet leaders who pragmatically introduced profit incentives for both managers and workers—firms were permitted to retain a small share of their profits, managers were rewarded with bonuses, and workers were motivated by "piecework" bonuses[12]—Mao Zedong was suspicious of individual material incentives. The idea of allowing firms to seek profits was anathema to him and his followers; only during years of exceptional liberalism when Mao's position was weak—for example, in 1961—could the word *profit* even be whispered in China (Xiao Min and Shao Fei 1961). Work bonuses were considered just as bad. Soviet-style piecework bonuses were abandoned in China during the Great Leap Forward and never restored. During most periods Chinese managers passed out (infrequent) raises according to seniority; they motivated workers with moral incentives and labor emulation.[13] During the rare periods when it was politically acceptable to pay bonuses, the bonuses turned into across-the-board wage supplements because they were distributed by democratic evaluations within work groups. Chinese managers never received the generous bonuses enjoyed by their Soviet counterparts. Compared with the Soviet system, the Chinese provided far weaker incentives for managers and workers. The income of managers and workers was not linked to the performance of the enterprise. Ideological purity was pursued to the detriment of industrial efficiency.

POORLY EDUCATED MANAGERS

Another liability of the Chinese system, compared to the Soviet Union, was the poor quality of its administrative and managerial

---

afraid of rural-urban migration? How did the urban industrial working class in the 1960s manage to obtain such a privileged position for itself?

12. David Granick (1987, 113) states that incentive pay in Soviet factories is sharply differentiated among employees, with employees of trades and skill levels that are in short supply receiving disproportionately higher shares of the pot. Thus, within a Soviet enterprise relative earnings are determined primarily by market forces rather than central authorities.

13. Andrew Walder (1986) stresses that labor models and activists received material benefits in the form of preferential housing assignment, access to consumer goods, loans, and the like. He also notes that one reason the Chinese abandoned piecework bonuses was that their managerial personnel lacked the technical skills to implement them.

manpower. As a result of Stalin's purges, the Soviet Union upgraded its economic administration in the 1930s, replacing its revolutionary veterans with better-trained technocrats. In China such a transformation failed to occur until the reform era. Mao Zedong and the Long March revolutionaries who dominated the CCP for thirty years always favored political loyalists over the professionally competent when appointing people to economic posts (H. Y. Lee 1991). In 1966 one study of Chinese factories found that managers averaged nine to eleven years of education (junior high graduation to some senior high education; Richman 1969, 145). In contrast, by that time most Soviet managers were college educated.

PARTY INTERFERENCE IN ENTERPRISE MANAGEMENT

To make matters worse, the CCP meddled in planning and managerial decisions more than the Soviet party ever did. Party leaders frequently imposed excessively ambitious plan targets on the government State Planning Commission. At the firm level, Chinese party secretaries took over leadership from managers, whereas managerial rule prevailed in the Soviet Union. Mao's insistence on placing politics in command interfered with economic performance at both ends of the industrial hierarchy.[14]

The Decision to Launch Reforms in 1978

The cumulative effect of crude planning, weak enterprise incentives, and political distortions caused Chinese industry to operate less efficiently than Soviet industry did.[15] What does this compar-

14. What Benjamin Ward (1967, 158) had to say about the Great Leap Forward could be generalized to the CCP's leadership of the national economy over the entire period after Liberation: "[They attempted] to apply the techniques of the Jesuits to the environment of the Navy. That is, the Chinese had a relatively favorable environment in terms of the attitudes and commitments of party members and others to the ideals and ideology of the leadership, but they did not appreciate the technical aspects of planning and controlling an economy which possesses a significant industrial sector. The requirements of coordinative activity were grossly underestimated, with reliance apparently placed on the ability of the party cadres to make wise decisions. Perhaps the cadres had the commitment to do so, but they lacked the appropriate information."
15. Although there are no published systematic comparisons of industrial efficiency in prereform China and the Soviet Union, forthcoming work by Barry Naughton will show that Chinese industry operated less efficiently than did Soviet industry, at least insofar as the efficiency of investment is concerned.

ative perspective on the performance of the Chinese command economy tell us about the Chinese decision to launch market reforms?

The comparison tells us that there was nothing inevitable about the Chinese market reforms (Dernberger 1986). Economic performance and living standards could have been substantially improved by simply upgrading the technical capacity of Chinese planning; letting managers instead of party secretaries run factories; evaluating managers on the basis of long-term performance, including profits; introducing a labor market and piecework bonuses; shifting investment to more efficient regions; and raising agricultural prices or increasing agricultural investment. The rapid growth under the reform conditions of the past decade shows that China, unlike the Soviet Union, had not reached the limits of extensive growth. China as of 1978 was still a predominantly agricultural country with massive reserves of labor. With a more technically sound system of planning and work incentives, the Chinese economy could have continued to grow with substantial improvements in industrial efficiency. (What is less clear is that a new, improved version of the command economy could have reoriented Chinese industry away from heavy industry toward consumer goods; the experiences of the Soviet Union and China suggest that without introducing market demand, planners find it impossible to accomplish that shift.)

In fact, many Chinese officials and even some economists believed that the road to prosperity was to restore and improve the command economy after the disruptions of the Cultural Revolution. They yearned to return to the supposed golden age of Chinese planning in the 1950s before the Great Leap Forward. But others, including Deng Xiaoping, held more fundamental doubts about the efficacy of central planning. After all, as early as 1956–57 Chinese leaders as diverse as Mao Zedong and Liu Shaoqi had criticized Soviet-style planning for being stereotyped and inflexible (MacFarquhar 1974).[16] The version of the command economy China was left with after the Great Leap Forward and the Cultural Revolution may have been less effective than the Soviet version, but by 1978 some Chinese believed nevertheless that the answer lay in market competition, not in central planning.

The Chinese leaders also may have believed the Chinese economy to be in even worse shape than it actually was. A greatly im-

16.   The most vocal critic of both rigid Soviet-style central planning and Mao's campaign-style alternatives to it was Chen Yun.

proved system for compiling economic statistics revealed declining factor productivity and made other deficiencies of the system more obvious than they had been in the past (Field 1986). When in the mid-1970s Chinese officials began to venture outside China to visit foreign countries, many of them for the first time, they were shocked and demoralized by what they saw. They had anticipated the technological and economic gap between China and the industrialized nations of the West, but they were surprised and humiliated to see that China lagged far behind even Japan and the newly industrialized countries of East Asia.

The immediate economic context of the CCP decision of late 1978 to undertake reforms was that Chinese leaders were searching for a solution to serious economic problems produced by Hua Guofeng, the man who had succeeded Mao Zedong as CCP leader after Mao's death in 1976. During his brief reign (1976–78) Hua tried to prove himself a worthy successor to Mao by draping himself in the mantle of Maoist tradition.[17] His approach to economic development was orthodox Maoism with an up-to-date, international twist. He promoted high-speed industrial growth (with a concentration on heavy industry) by a combination of Maoist campaign-style mass mobilization and foreign investment to develop China's oil reserves. Hua's "Great Leap Outward" (*yang yue jin*) collapsed in 1978, when estimates of the oil reserves were revised downward; commitments to import plants and expand heavy industry could not be sustained (Huan Gudan 1979). In the last part of 1978 the annual plan, which had been based on overly optimistic projections of oil production, essentially collapsed (Naughton 1989). Having made the decision to open the door to technology imports, the Chinese leaders suddenly realized that they had almost nothing other than oil to export for hard currency (Dong Furen 1982). A sense of economic crisis pervaded meetings of party leaders (author's interviews).

The CCP leadership faced real economic problems in 1978, but the choice of solutions was dictated by a political calculus. China was in the midst of a leadership succession struggle. Deng Xiaoping took advantage of the economic crisis to discredit Hua Guofeng and weaken the heavy industry czars who dominated the central economic bureaucracy (and who came to be known as the "Petroleum

17. Hua and his supporters were nicknamed the "whatever faction" (*fanshi pai*) because they took the position that whatever Mao said was right.

Faction" because many of them came from the Ministry of Petroleum and pushed an oil-based modernization strategy; Lieberthal and Oksenberg 1988). Reform policies became Deng's platform in his competition against Hua for post-Mao leadership.

Policy solutions designed to restore and improve planning rather than replace it with market competition received serious consideration during 1978 and 1979 (Fang Weizhong 1979; Guo Daimo and Yang Zhaoming 1979) and continued to attract substantial bureaucratic support throughout the reform decade (Xu Yi 1983). Prestigious revolutionary veterans such as Chen Yun and Yao Yilin advocated a "bird-cage" economic system in which the bird (economic activity) would be given more freedom and more rational economic signals but never allowed to escape from the cage (the planned economy).

Although Deng Xiaoping allied with the conservative reformers of Chen Yun's ilk in his campaign to defeat Hua Guofeng, he identified himself with a more radical version of reform aimed at creating a real socialist market economy. He promoted market reforms not only because he clearly believed they were the best solution to improving economic performance and raising living standards but also because they offered political advantages. Market reforms involving enterprise autonomy and competition presented a more dramatic political challenge to Hua Guofeng than merely a return to planning à la the First Five-Year Plan (1953–57). Market reforms also allowed Deng to make an end run around the central planners and industrial bureaucrats who supported Hua's policies or Chen Yun's conservative version of reform by appealing to other influential groups, namely, local officials, the military, and intellectuals.[18]

Market reforms also created political resources for Deng Xiaoping to employ in his succession contest with Hua Guofeng. Deng Xiaoping, challenging the incumbent Hua Guofeng for the position

18. Many of Deng Xiaoping's speeches in 1977–78 were directed toward intellectuals and argued that China had paid too high an economic price for the neglect and political oppression of science and education under Mao (and, by implication, Hua Guofeng). The call for an economy that operated according to objective economic laws (Hu Qiaomu 1978) was at the same time a call for professional autonomy for every field of intellectual endeavor (Tsou Tang 1983). As for the military, Carol Lee Hamrin (1984, 496–99) notes that during 1977–78 Deng stressed the seriousness of the Soviet threat and the need to obtain Western technology by tilting toward the United States to create a sense of crisis demanding radical solutions, build support for himself within the PLA, and discredit Hua Guofeng. See chapter 9 for a discussion of Deng's appeals to local officials.

as preeminent leader, sought to build up his network of supporters. He already could claim many allies among the older generation of party officials whom he helped rehabilitate after their humiliation during the Cultural Revolution, but he needed to augment this base. By selectively handing out to various bureaucracies and localities potentially profitable experiments with agricultural, industrial, and foreign trade reforms, Deng was able to build a coalition of support for himself as well as for the reforms. In exchange for receiving special economic treatment, local and ministry officials pledged political loyalty to Deng and his platform of economic reform.

In other words, the question of why the Chinese embarked on a set of ambitious market reforms during the decade after 1978 cannot be answered simply by pointing to the poor performance of China's prior economic system or to the post–Cultural Revolution crisis of confidence at elite and mass levels. The proximate cause of the 1978 initiatives was the succession contest between Deng Xiaoping and Hua Guofeng. Deng acted as political entrepreneur, using innovations in economic policy to discredit Hua Guofeng and attract support among groups in the CCP Central Committee and Politburo.

Thus, from its very origins Chinese economic reform bore the mark of political competition among ambitious politicians. The economic reform of the 1980s coincided with a period of leadership succession. Because of Deng Xiaoping's advanced age, just as soon as Deng succeeded in wresting the number one position from Hua Guofeng, the contest to succeed Deng began. The context of succession competition helps us understand why the Chinese version of industrial reform consistently followed the pattern of particularistic contracting instead of universalistic rules: different levels of the industrial hierarchy contracted to share power and resources on an ad hoc basis rather than according to universally applied rules for business competition. Politicians at every level of the system—from Deng Xiaoping and his lieutenants Hu Yaobang and Zhao Ziyang, who were competing to succeed him, to the local party secretary at the bottom—garnered the gratitude and political support of subordinates by selectively giving them special economic treatment. The particularistic formula of early reform experiments (see chapter 10) and subsequent reform policies had a compelling political logic that Deng Xiaoping and other aspiring leaders could exploit in their pursuit of power.

The Post-1978 Chinese Economic Reforms:
A Brief Description

Beginning with the Third Plenum of the Eleventh Communist Party Central Committee in December 1978, Deng Xiaoping and his allies initiated a series of policies designed to reform the structure of the Chinese economy. These reforms were far-reaching, extending to agriculture and foreign trade as well as industry. Although I concentrate on the reforms in state-run industrial enterprises from 1979 to 1989, a brief overview of the reforms in agriculture, private and collective industry and commerce, work incentives, and foreign trade and investment is called for because reforms in these other areas generated economic and political momentum for the changes in state industry.

DECOLLECTIVIZING AGRICULTURE

The 1978 Central Committee Third Plenum that launched the economic reform drive proposed only modest organizational changes in collective agriculture (an increase in the autonomy of production teams and greater freedom for peasants to sell their private plot output in rural free markets), and the Fourth Plenum in 1979 actually prohibited agricultural decollectivization to the household level. Yet at that time decollectivization was already happening on a large scale in Anhui Province. The provincial party secretary, Wan Li, was allowing teams to divide and lease the land to households who were responsible for providing a certain amount of product to the teams. During 1978–81 the household responsibility system, enthusiastically embraced by peasants, spread throughout rural China. In 1981 the central government acknowledged reality and officially endorsed the new system, and by 1983 nearly all farm households in China had implemented it.

The household responsibility system transferred decision-making power from collective production units (communes, brigades, and teams) to the family. Each family was assigned a plot of collective land and was responsible for every stage of cultivation on that land. Farmers signed contracts with the production team, promising to provide a certain amount of crops or services, and retained or sold the rest on their own. Farm households were allowed to invest their profits in farm machinery, trucks, or industrial equipment and to engage in private marketing and manufacturing. Land contracts were for fifteen years and were renewable and transferable by inheritance or lease.[19] Although the land continued to be owned collectively, farmers had the right to use the land as if it were their own. In effect, Chinese farmers became sharecroppers or tenants with the collectives as their landlords.[20]

The reorganization of agricultural production was supported by an increase in the purchase prices for major farm products. From 1978 to 1982 the procurement prices for the mandatory quotas of grain, cotton, and edible oil were raised by 26, 20, and 24 percent respectively, while above-quota state procurement prices were raised by 45, 56, and 43 percent (Perry and Wong 1985, 10). The price rises and the increase in state purchases of above-quota commodities put more money in farmers' pockets, but they also increased the burden of government subsidies. Keeping city food prices low while encouraging more farm output cost the central government 32 billion yuan (4.6 percent of GNP) in 1984, when the grain harvest was the largest in history (*Statistical Yearbook* 1989, X118).

To ease its financial burden, the government introduced a second set of structural reforms of agriculture in 1985 ("Nineteen Eighty-Five Document" 1985). Government mandatory purchases of grain, cotton, and edible oil, a fundamental feature of Soviet-type centrally planned economies, were replaced by long-term sales contracts between farmers and the government. This change increased the share of basic agricultural commodities sold on the market. At the same time, the city prices of fruit and vegetables, fish, meat, and eggs were freed from government controls so they could respond to market demand. Inflationary pressures later forced a reinstitution of price controls in most cities and a return to mandatory government sales for grain.

The decollectivization of agricultural production and gradual marketization of food distribution were accompanied by a surge of private and collective industry and commerce in the countryside. Farmers could reinvest their agricultural profits into family busi-

---

19. Leases were lengthened to fifteen years in 1984. A 1987 proposal to extend leases to fifty years was never promulgated. Land used for growing some specialized crops can be leased for thirty years. The actual length of leasing contracts is subject to local variation (Thomas P. Bernstein, personal communication).

20. For good discussions of the rural reforms and their political and economic consequences, see Lardy 1983; J. Lin 1988; McMillan, Whalley, and Zhu Lijing 1989; Nee 1989; Nee and Su Sijin 1990; Oi 1988; Oi 1989; Oi 1990; Parish 1985; Zweig, Hartford, Feinerman, and Deng Jianxu 1987.

nesses or pool them for group ventures. Collectively owned township (commune) and village (brigade) enterprises were leased to individuals or groups. Beginning in 1983 farmers were allowed to engage in private transport and marketing of commodities, even to distant provinces ("Chinese Communist Party Document" 1983). Individuals could escape the drudgery of agricultural work by transferring their contracts, leasing their land, moving to a small town, and getting a job in a local factory. By the end of 1988, of a rural labor force of 401 million, 86 million or 21 percent were engaged full-time in nonagricultural pursuits (*Statistical Yearbook* 1989, 161). The diversification of the rural economy reduced the share of agricultural output in the countryside's total output value from 68.9 percent in 1980 to 45.4 percent in 1990 (Li Peng 1991a, 9).

The post-1978 agricultural reforms, which were the most radical, far-reaching structural changes in the entire reform package, were a clear success (although after the grain harvest peaked in 1984, there were questions about the long-term sustainability of their impressive results). From 1978 to 1988 the net value of agricultural production rose from 98.6 billion yuan to 381.8 billion yuan; adjusted for inflation, this was an average annual increase of almost 7 percent, more than twice the average (1.9 percent) of the previous twenty-six years (*Statistical Yearbook* 1989, 29–30). Even with farmers concentrating more on the production of cash crops and nonagricultural activities than on grain production after 1984, grain output increased from 305 million tons in 1978 to 407 million tons in 1984 before leveling off.[21]

The increases in output were due to dramatic improvements in the productivity of agricultural labor and land. The decollectivization reforms—namely, managerial autonomy, market competition, financial risk, and rational prices—had created effective incentives for farm households to make their operations more efficient.[22] Still lacking were capital and labor markets and secure property rights to the land to encourage long-term private investment.

21. Grain production was 402 million tons in 1987, 394 million in 1988, and 407 million in 1989 (*Statistical Yearbook* 1990, 363).
22. There was considerable local variation in how thoroughly the agricultural economic environment was transformed. For example, in many villages, village leaders continued to interfere in farmers' decisions over cropping patterns, leasing arrangements, and the allocation of capital and labor (Rozelle forthcoming). In addition, prices, although more rational, were still constrained by state purchase prices.

The diversification and improved performance of the rural economy translated into better living standards for rural dwellers. Per capita rural income rose more than 9 percent per year over the decade. A substantial number of farm families who diversified into industry and trade became rich—the so-called 10,000 yuan households. With the increases in farm output and family income both rural and urban consumption standards improved.

The agricultural responsibility system was not part of a grand design by Deng Xiaoping; rather, it emerged spontaneously from Chinese villages. Once the system was a fait accompli, there was minimal bureaucratic opposition in Beijing to supporting and expanding it, especially compared to the industrial reforms (see chapter 8). None of the most powerful bureaucratic actors—the State Planning Commission, the Ministry of Finance, and the industrial ministries—was at all threatened by agricultural decollectivization.

Having agricultural reform precede industrial reform proved to be a great boon to the Chinese reform drive. The early success of the agricultural reforms generated tremendous momentum for industrial reform: more abundant supplies of commodities such as cotton, tobacco, and sugar for industrial processing; more, and more varied, food for urban employees to buy with their bonuses; a surge of rural demand for manufactured farm and consumer goods; increased rural savings available for bank loans to industry; and valuable foreign exchange earnings from farm exports.

Yet the most significant contribution of the rural reforms to the industrial reform drive was the less tangible one: as a demonstration of what profit incentives and market competition could accomplish, the rural reform changed the terms of political debate in China.[23] Henceforth, CCP leaders had to make economic arguments for the policies they advocated.

The transformations in agriculture made an excellent case for those who espoused market reforms in industry. The early, sensational results of the rural reforms disarmed leaders like Chen Yun who were skeptical of radical changes in state factories. With the conservative reformers lying low during most of the 1978–85 period, Deng was unimpeded in his drive to implement a radical re-

---

23. On a visit to the Soviet Union in 1991 I was told by several researchers that the success of the Chinese agricultural reform had greatly influenced Mikhail Gorbachev and other Soviet leaders to believe that radical economic reforms were necessary in their own country.

formist line. Not until grain production leveled off in the second half of the decade did Chen Yun and his followers start to make serious trouble for the reforms and the leaders identified with them, namely Hu Yaobang and Zhao Ziyang.

Legalizing and Expanding the Second Economy

Although small collective factories and shops as well as individual peddlers have always existed in Chinese cities, they were officially discouraged as "seeds of capitalism" under Mao Zedong's reign. During the Cultural Revolution decade, urban services and commerce practically evaporated because collective and individual businesses were shut down. It became almost impossible to find someone to fix a bicycle or repair a pair of shoes.[24]

The reform-minded CCP leadership actively encouraged collective and private enterprises after 1978.[25] The main rationale for this policy was the need to provide jobs for millions of unemployed urban youth. Secondary objectives were to improve the provision of city services and enliven commerce. Once legalized, collective and private enterprises flourished because they operated outside the plan and met market demand. The government nurtured them with preferential treatment that gave them competitive advantages over state enterprises: low tax rates, the retention of all their own profits, and no restrictions on employees' salaries.

Legalizing China's second economy and letting it escape from the restrictive regulations applied to the state economy were far easier political tasks than was deregulating the state economy itself. The CCP and government bureaucracy were willing to allow the nonstate sector to operate alongside the state sector because it was an add-on that did not appear to threaten anyone's vested interests in the state sector. The 1983 decision to grant nonstate enterprises a lower tax rate (35 percent) than state enterprises (55 percent) sparked no debate; it seemed only fair given the higher production costs of nonstate firms, which had to obtain their own inputs on the market (author's interviews). While Chinese policymakers tied themselves up in knots over the reforms of state-owned industry,

24. The most comprehensive analysis of Chinese commerce under communist rule is Dorothy Solinger, *Chinese Business under Socialism* (1983).
25. In Chinese usage, an "individual" (*geti*) firm (fewer than eight employees) is distinguished from a "private" (*siying*) firm (eight or more employees). I use "private" to apply to both types.

the legalization and decontrol of collective and private business went much more smoothly.

By 1989 the number of employees in urban collective enterprises had grown to 35 million (from 20 million in 1978) and those in private businesses to 6.5 million (from 150,000 in 1978). An additional 1.3 million were employed by Chinese-foreign joint ventures, state-collective joint enterprises, or state-private joint enterprises (*Statistical Yearbook* 1990, 115). Breaking the state monopoly of retail sales, in 1988 collective shops took 38 percent of the business (up from 7.4 percent in 1978) and private shops 20 percent (up from 2.1 percent in 1978; *Statistical Yearbook* 1989, 601).

Even in industry, the growth of collective and private enterprises was astounding, especially in the countryside, where retired workers and former peasants proved themselves to be excellent entrepreneurs.[26] From 1978 to 1988 the share of total industrial output produced by nonstate firms almost doubled, from 22 percent to 43 percent (*Statistical Yearbook* 1990, 29). In the economy as a whole, by the end of the 1980s less than 40 percent of China's national income originated in the state sector. This trend placed China in a position approaching that of Italy and France, where state-owned firms produce one-third of national output (Lardy 1991, 6).

The explosion of collective and private business shook up state enterprises and made it impossible for them to maintain business as usual. New collective and private businesses leached human, financial, and material resources out of the state sector. Wages and bonuses in state factories were rising, but not as rapidly as those in the nonstate sector. Talented people began to defect from the state sector to private and collective enterprises. State factories had to scramble to find new sources of raw materials, such as cotton and tobacco, after their traditional sources were stolen from them by collective and private upstarts.

The emergence of a vigorous nonstate sector changed the language of debate within the state sector. State factories previously protected from competition by the plan were forced for the first time to compete with collective and private factories. By putting competitive pressure on state firms, the legal second economy turned many industrial bureaucrats and managers into advocates of expanding market freedoms. The dynamism of the nonstate sector,

26.   For a fascinating study of a controversial experiment in nonagricultural private businesses in the Wenzhou district of Zhejiang Province, see Nolan and Dong Fureng 1989.

like the growth generated by the agricultural reforms, not only produced products, services, taxes, and profits that could be plowed
into the state sector but also demonstrated the efficacy of market
incentives. Jealous of the lucrative market sales, concessionary tax
rates, generous profit retention ratios, and managerial autonomy
available to collective and private firms, the managers of state firms
began to pressure the government to extend the same freedoms to
them. By 1991 state managers had received the right to diversify
ownership forms within state firms according to the policy of "one
factory, two systems" (*yi chang liang zhi*). State managers channeled
some of their retained funds into collectively or privately owned
subsidiaries, merged with collective or private firms, or leased existing facilities to groups or individuals.

Enterprise Labor Reforms

Beginning in 1978, Chinese policymakers began to search for ways
to motivate workers to work harder. Past wage and bonus systems
had been based mainly on seniority and provided little incentive
for worker effort. The Maoist belief in the primacy of moral over
material incentives resulted in an egalitarian industrial order in
which wage differentials and piecework bonuses played a less important role than they did in the Soviet Union. During the Cultural
Revolution decade wage increases and bonuses were completely rejected as counterrevolutionary "economism." Workers reacted to
the lack of incentives and stagnation of their living standards by
slacking off on the job. Absenteeism was rampant, and when workers did show up, they worked lackadaisically.

Post-1978 labor reforms rejected "egalitarianism" and turned it
into a term of opprobrium; the labor reforms sought to put into
practice an alternative socialist principle, "To each according to his
work." The goal was to reward workers for the work they actually
accomplished. Although basic wages continued to be set by the
national seniority-based pay scales, bonuses linked to enterprise
profits became a larger share of worker income. This approach to
raising industrial productivity found broad acceptance within the
CCP and government bureaucracy; except for a few doctrinaire
Maoists, hardly a contrary voice was heard.

Bonuses were tied to individual work performance. Independent
workers, such as machine-tool workers, were paid piecework bonuses for exceeding output quotas, and group workers were as-

signed a bonus level according to the evaluation of their work group or group leader. The total amount of money available for bonuses was determined by the profits produced by the enterprise and the share contributed by workshops and work groups.

Wage grade promotions (all wage raises are in the form of wage grade promotions), which occurred in 1971–72, 1977–78, 1978–79, and 1979–80, were determined on a more meritocratic basis than in the past. Whether or not an employee received a raise depended on work performance and technical accomplishment, tested through written and practical examinations, in addition to seniority and work attitude.

Applying the new wage and bonus systems was a difficult process. Face-to-face evaluation in work groups for bonuses and wage raises was so divisive that workers often preferred distribution by equal shares, seniority, or rotation (Shirk 1981). To overcome egalitarian peer group pressures, some managers and work group leaders took over employee evaluation and bonus distribution after 1983–84 (Walder, personal communication). But managers themselves had an interest in keeping their workers contented and therefore tended to hand out bonuses indiscriminately (Walder 1987). During the 1980s workers' income increased dramatically and bonuses represented a larger share, yet egalitarianism persisted: bonuses continued to be universal wage supplements, not rewards for work performance, and income differentials among state workers remained narrow (Zhao Renwei 1990).

Another challenge facing the reformers was the issue of job security. Although economists criticized the Chinese practice of lifetime job security for tolerating lazy workers and putting insufficient pressure on workers, there was little action to break the iron rice bowl. Some new, younger workers were hired as "contract workers" on renewable short-term contracts instead of lifetime tenure, but the majority of the labor force still consisted of permanent employees without risk of ever losing their jobs.

Although Chinese policymakers were reluctant to take any big steps toward an industrial labor market, they did take a few small ones. Some state enterprises began to hire their own employees—particularly technicians and managers—through advertisements and interviews. And although blue-collar workers still were assigned by government labor bureaus, factories were allowed to screen them (and presumably reject them) according to academic recruitment examinations. Collective and private firms and some joint ventures were free to do their own hiring.

On the management side, factory managers acquired more control. In the past administrative control had been shared by the enterprise party secretary and the manager, and in reality the party secretary was dominant. Under the new managerial responsibility system, the party role was supposed to be substantially narrowed to only political education; in production and administration the party was expected to follow and help implement managers' decisions. The managers' powers were expanded, particularly in personnel matters, which previously had been the domain of the party. Managers appointed their own technical and administrative staff. Managers signed a contract with their administrative superiors specifying their responsibilities and their targets for improving enterprise performance; managers' salaries and bonuses were tied to their success in reaching these goals. Managers in turn signed similar responsibility contracts with the heads of subordinate units such as workshops.

In the early stage of the reform drive (1978–80) policymakers toyed with the idea of worker self-management. The Workers' Congress, a representative body elected by the employees in each enterprise, was touted as the instrument of workers' control. In many enterprises the employees were allowed to hold elections for shop heads and even managers. After 1981, in reaction to the political instability caused by an assertive labor movement in Poland, the Chinese backed away from the concept of worker self-management. A few enterprises still elected shop heads and even enterprise managers, but the Workers' Congress, which met only once or twice a year, never became more than an institutional ritual of workers' control, and most managers continued to be appointed by industrial bureaus and local party committees. The national leaders decided to strengthen the hand of the manager instead of the workers, bringing the Chinese firm closer to Soviet-style one-person management than to Yugoslav democratic management.

When conservative elites increased their hold on the CCP after the 1989 Tiananmen crackdown, the CCP reclaimed its leadership role in factories. In 1990–91 economic officials could not keep a straight face when they repeated to me the new official formula for the division of roles between factory managers and party secretaries: "The manager is the center [*zhongxin*] and the party secretary is the core [*hexin*]."

Opening China to Foreign Trade and Investment

Under Mao Zedong's rule, China pursued a policy of self-reliance, engaging in foreign trade only to fill domestic shortages in essential commodities such as grain and to generate the hard currency to import a small number of turnkey industrial plants.[27] Although foreign trade was increased in the mid-1970s, foreign capitalists still were viewed with suspicion, and it was a point of national pride that China could go it almost entirely alone. The prohibition on foreign investment from advanced industrial countries remained in effect.

After Mao's death, Deng Xiaoping and his allies concluded that because no country had ever achieved modernization by "closed door–ism" (Gu Mu 1985), China must join the world economy. Their 1979 decision to expand foreign trade and allow foreign companies to invest in Chinese enterprises—the so-called open policy—was a bold attempt to accelerate China's modernization and catch up with its Asian neighbors.[28]

To attract foreign investment, the government allowed particular geographic areas to offer concessionary customs and tax treatment to potential investors. These privileges were granted to four export processing zones, or Special Economic Zones, located in the provinces of Guangdong and Fujian (1979), to fourteen coastal cities and the South China island of Hainan (1984), and to three coastal river deltas—the Pearl River Delta, Yangtze River Delta, and southern Fujian (1985). The local economies in regions awarded special foreign investment status flourished. Naturally, political leaders in these regions were grateful for the advantages Beijing had showered on them and reciprocated by becoming staunch supporters of Deng Xiaoping and his economic reform drive.

27. "Turnkey" factories are factories in which the contractor completes the work of building and installation to the point of readiness for operation and then sells the factory to the customer at a prearranged price.
28. Although the December 1978 Third Plenum communiqué made no mention of foreign investment, a few days after the plenum closed, the party elder Li Xiannian announced that China would accept foreign investment (Crane 1990). The Joint Venture Law and the creation of the Special Economic Zones were formally approved by the center in summer 1979. For thorough treatment of various aspects of China's open policy, see Crane 1990; Ho and Huenemann 1984; Jao and Leung 1986; J. Mann 1989; Pearson 1991; Vogel 1989.

Economic legislation to govern international business dealings had to be written, and new types of intermediary institutions such as foreign investment and trust corporations established. China's new membership in the International Monetary Fund and World Bank brought it substantial development loans and technical advice. In seeking joint ventures and coproduction arrangements with foreign companies, the Chinese were less interested in finding investment capital than they were in importing advanced technology and managerial know-how from abroad. As of 1989, twenty thousand joint venture contracts had been signed, and eight thousand joint ventures were in operation.

The government promoted exports not only to earn foreign exchange for imports of sophisticated equipment but also to introduce the rigors of international competition into the Chinese domestic economy. To compete in the world market, Chinese manufacturers had to improve the quality of their products and be responsive to the specific requirements of customers, neither of which was necessary in the Chinese planned economy. Despite the problems of Chinese inexperience, international recession, and protectionism in many national markets, China was able to expand its exports from U.S. $9.7 billion in 1978 to U.S. $52.5 billion in 1989. Total trade grew from U.S. $20.6 billion in 1978 to U.S. $111.7 billion in 1989 (*Statistical Yearbook* 1990, 641).

In a pattern reminiscent of the reforms in agriculture and non-state business, the envy of officials in units not yet benefiting from foreign trade and investment reforms turned them into reform advocates. Coastal cities jealous of the Guangdong and Fujian Special Economic Zones demanded and received similar status as Open Cities in 1984. And inland officials, put at a severe competitive disadvantage by the open policy, demanded not that the open policy be rolled back but that it be extended to them. They pressed to create their own special zones or at least to be given greater autonomy in doing business with foreigners.

To satisfy provinces and ministries hungry for the benefits of foreign business and to increase the volume of trade, the Chinese leaders decentralized administration of foreign trade and investment. The monopoly of the central Ministry of Foreign Economic Relations and Trade (MOFERT) was broken to allow industrial ministries, local governments, and some enterprises to negotiate directly with foreigners and keep a share of the foreign exchange they earned.

The decentralization sparked a competitive free-for-all. Localities vied for foreign business by lowering taxes and duties and by price gouging. Ministries set up their own trading companies to take commissions away from the MOFERT trading companies. MOFERT, arguing that all this competition benefited foreign businesses and harmed China's national interests, periodically attempted to reassert control and unify China's international business relations.

Decentralization also stimulated an import-buying spree, which depleted foreign exchange reserves. No longer under MOFERT's thumb, local agencies and enterprises rushed to buy sophisticated foreign equipment and snazzy foreign cars. In the second half of the decade the trade imbalance was exacerbated by the growing domestic demand for manufactured goods and domestic price inflation, which discouraged enterprises from exporting. Only the contraction of the domestic economy that began in late 1988 cut imports and restored a favorable trade balance.

One of the most impressive successes of the Chinese reform drive was the gradual decontrol of foreign exchange. When the reform drive began in the late 1970s, the Chinese domestic currency, the renminbi, was highly overvalued at 1.5 yuan to the U.S. dollar. By 1986 the renminbi was devalued to 3.7 to the dollar. Domestic price inflation after 1986 resulted in the appreciation of the real value of Chinese currency, a trend reversed by a devaluation of over 20 percent in December 1989 (to 4.7 yuan to the dollar), one of about 10 percent in November 1990 (to 5.22 yuan to the dollar), and a smaller one to 5.3 yuan to the dollar in late April 1991. In the mid-1980s the Chinese government also established foreign exchange markets for the use of joint venture and local firms (Lardy 1991, 9, 11).

The decontrol of foreign exchange and the domestic economic retrenchment helped the Chinese government expand exports and cut imports in 1990, when it was faced with heavy foreign debt repayments. As a result, the trade deficit that had existed since 1984 was eliminated.

The open policy was plagued by conservative political attacks as well as by pressures from MOFERT for recentralization. Many inland officials, along with some CCP old-timers and ordinary citizens throughout China, were alarmed by the foreign styles and ideas that rushed in through the open door along with foreign investment and technology. They were particularly repelled by the freewheeling atmosphere of the Special Economic Zones.

The conflicts over foreign trade and investment policies differed from the conflicts over industrial reforms in that the divisions were primarily along regional rather than bureaucratic lines and therefore were potentially more threatening to political stability. The benefits of the open policy fell almost entirely to the coastal provinces, widening the already large economic gap between coast and interior. The CCP, anxious to manage these regional conflicts in a way that maintained the economic advantages of unbalanced growth without threatening national unity, kept many foreign economic policy decisions in its own hands, delegating less discretion to the government bureaucracy than it did in the domestic economic reforms.

Although the foreign dimension of China's economic reform drive made the drive more vulnerable to the threats of parochialism and regional conflict, it also made important positive contributions to the reform drive. Technology imports, the pressure of foreign competition, opportunities for Chinese to travel and study abroad, and World Bank loans were all invaluable stimuli to industrial modernization. Coastal provinces, the primary beneficiaries of the open policy, were strong supporters of the reform drive, and inland provinces, despite their cultural backlash against the policy, demanded more openness for themselves. The support of foreign corporations and foreign governments for the reform drive was a political asset to Deng Xiaoping and his reformist allies and helped sustain the reforms. Whenever the reforms appeared jeopardized by bureaucratic recentralization, reformist leaders could argue that policy changes would cause foreign investors to lose confidence in China. In this way, foreign corporations and governments became part of Deng Xiaoping's reform coalition.

Conclusion

The rapid changes in the Chinese economy stimulated by the reforms in agriculture, nonstate business, labor incentives, and foreign investment and trade provided support for the industrial reform drive. The beneficiaries of these other reforms—including rural entrepreneurs, private businesspersons in the cities, workers making more money, the coastal regions taking off under the open policy, and the foreign corporations and governments with new economic stakes in China—put their weight behind the industrial reform drive. Envy of the success of these other market-oriented models motivated state industrial bureaucrats and managers to press for greater market freedoms for themselves. The open policy in particular gave China's reformist leaders valuable goodies, among them foreign exchange, import opportunities, and joint venture deals that they could assign to subordinates who supported them and the reform drive.

Still, the path of China's industrial reforms was much rockier than the path taken by the reforms in agriculture, collective and private business, and work incentives. Industrial reforms were inherently redistributive and ran up against opposition from powerful central bureaucracies who found nothing objectionable about the other kinds of reforms. The foreign trade and investment reforms were even more controversial than the proposed changes in domestic state industry, but the CCP kept a tight hold on them instead of channeling them through the government bureaucracy.

2

CHINESE POLITICAL INSTITUTIONS

What does it mean, institutionally, to be a communist state? What are the core features of communist political institutions? Although this section focuses on China's political institutions and notes some significant differences between Chinese and Soviet institutions, it can be read as the beginnings of a general framework of communist political institutions. The institutional structures of all communist states are similar because they all are derived from the Soviet Union. When the Chinese communists came to power in 1949, they borrowed their political and economic framework from the USSR, the only available model of a communist state. Soviet-style political institutions also were transferred to the countries of Eastern Europe, North Vietnam, and North Korea.

Charting institutional relationships, incentives, and decision rules in a communist state is much more difficult than it is in a democracy with a constitution, laws, and administrative regulations. Discovering the rules of the game in an authoritarian political setting requires looking for practices established by precedent and norms as well as by written rules. Although there are enough clues to enable us to begin this type of institutional analysis of communism, some features of communist institutions remain ambiguous so that participants and observers may disagree among themselves about what the rules of politics actually are. The task of explicating communist institutions is further complicated by the evolving nature of these institutions and political leaders' strategic design (and continual redesign) of institutions to tilt the system toward particular policy objectives.

Despite these difficulties, in part 2 I sketch a framework of Chinese communist political institutions built on five dimensions of governance: authority relations (chapter 3), leadership incentives (chapter 4), bargaining arena (chapter 5), enfranchised participants (chapter 6), and decision rules (chapter 7). This part is intended as an institutional overview, to help place the economic policy process in a political context. Many (but not all) the pieces of this framework will be used in the account of Chinese industrial reforms presented in the following chapters.

With a clear framework of Chinese political institutions, the pace, sequencing, content, and form of reform policies become explicable. The link between institutional setting and reform policy outcomes is explored in chapter 8. Puzzles such as "Why were the reforms piecemeal instead of comprehensive?" "Why did agricultural reforms and fiscal reforms come early in the reform drive, and why were price and bankruptcy reforms postponed?" "Why were reform policies compromised to protect heavy industry?" and "Why did particularistic contracting formulas always triumph over uniform rules?" can be solved by clarifying the institutional context in which these policy choices were made.

3 Authority Relations

The Communist Party and the Government

To predict policy outcomes in any political system, we must chart the lines of institutional authority. If politicians can be removed from office by popular elections, then we know that politicians operate within the limits set by their expectations of the reactions of voters (Dahl 1956).[1] The same "law of anticipated reactions" (Friedrich 1963) governs the actions of bureaucratic officials who are appointed and fired by politicians. Voters may pay scant attention to politics, and politicians may intervene only rarely in the work of bureaucratic agencies; still, the threat of ex post sanctions creates ex ante incentives for politicians to serve voters and for bureaucrats to serve politicians (Weingast and Moran 1983).

The authority relationship between the communist party and the government is at the core of all communist political systems. The communist party is considered "the organized expression of the will of society" (Schurmann 1968, 110). The party leads the work of the government (called the "state" [*guojia*] by Chinese). Although the party's control over the government is very tight and most government officials are party members, the party and government are nevertheless organizationally distinct.

The language of Western institutional economics is useful for conceptualizing the relationship between communist party and government: it is a "delegation relationship" in which the communist party is the "principal" and the government is the "agent." The party has formal political authority over the government but delegates to the government much of the actual work of administering

1. Of course, if politicians' tenure in office depends not on popular votes but on the approval of military commanders, then politicians will strive to keep these commanders satisfied.

the country.[2] The relationship between party committees and government departments at the same administrative level and between party committees at one level and government departments at a lower level is one of "direct subordination" (Liu Hong 1988).

The party's authority over the government is based primarily on its authority to appoint and promote government officials, what in the Soviet Union is called the *nomenklatura* power (Burns 1987). The party also sets the general policy line (*luxian*) for the government to implement, approves the government budget and plan, and oversees the work of the government. Finally, the party is responsible for the ideological education and evaluation of government cadres and all other members of society.[3]

The crucial difference between communist and democratic systems is the political accountability of the principals. In communist systems the communist party is not formally accountable to its citizens; it claims to reflect the will of the people by leading them toward a communist future but is unconstrained by any institutional mechanism making it accountable to people's preferences. (Current preferences of the masses are disparaged by Marxists as "false consciousness.") In contrast, politicians in a democracy know they will be voted out of office if they enact policies or allow the bureaucrats to take actions that violate their constituents' perceived interests; the voters are the ultimate principals. Popular legislative elections in China for people's congresses (which have lawmaking authority) and people's consultative congresses (which have advisory authority) are widely viewed by Chinese as a charade of democratic oversight; everyone knows that these elections are stage-managed by CCP commit-

2. For an interesting comparison of party-government relations in democratic and socialist systems, see Yan Jiaqi 1988 (42). Yan says that "the ruling party of a country organizes a government and exercises its principles and policies through the government"; therefore, the leader of the ruling party should concurrently serve as the head of state in both socialist and capitalist countries. In his view, "The mixing of the party with the government does not find expression in party leaders concurrently being heads of state but in party organs overriding government departments."

3. "In authoritarian systems without active legislatures, the principal form of control over the bureaucracy has been the mass party, particularly its Leninist variant. The Leninist party exercises control over the bureaucracy by managing appointments and promotions, monopolizing leading posts, supervising the indoctrination of state officials, disciplining party members who hold government positions, and setting the bureaucracy's principal policy guidelines" (Harding 1981, 16).

tees.[4] The Chinese see their system as unambiguously hierarchical with the CCP clearly in charge: "The party committee waves its hand [*hui shou*], the government gets to work [*dong shou*], the people's congress standing committee votes [*ju shou*], and the people's consultative congress claps [*pai shou*]" (Wang Hui 1989, 7).

Although the communist party has ultimate authority in a communist polity, it cannot administer the country on its own. Like any principal in a large organization, it has limited information. The party delegates to the government bureaucracy the authority to make and implement economic policies because the bureaucrats have more expert and specialized information than party leaders have.

Party Oversight of Government: Parallel Rule

Once the party has delegated authority to the government, the problem of oversight arises. How do communist party leaders know whether or not government bureaucrats are carrying out policies that conform with the party's preferences? Bureaucratic agents naturally distort the information they pass up to their political masters in order to place themselves in a good light. In democracies, elected politicians oversee government operations by establishing a system of rules, procedures, and informal practices that enable citizen interest groups to check up on administrative actions. This type of decentralized oversight, which Mathew McCubbins and Thomas Schwartz (1984) call "fire-alarm oversight," is less costly to politicians than is the constant monitoring of administrative actions.[5]

In communist political systems, however, the communist party is unwilling to enfranchise "constituents" to oversee government actions; the party's political monopoly depends on the political demobilization of the population. Communist leaders therefore adopt a more centralized, active, and direct approach to monitoring gov-

4. According to the constitution, top positions in the state bureaucracy are filled by the National People's Congress, but as Yan Jiaqi says, "The political reality is that the candidates nominated or recommended by the CCP are always elected" (1988, 42).
5. Fire-alarm oversight, by enfranchising interest groups to monitor the activities of government agencies, also guarantees that politicians' most influential constituents are satisfied. Democratic politicians do not need to know about all actions of appointed officials; rather, they need to know only those actions that might displease their constituents (McCubbins and Schwartz 1984).

ernment actions; McCubbins and Schwartz (1984) call it "police-patrol" oversight.[6]

Faced with the structural problem of bureaucratic oversight (and the real, immediate problem of supervising officials who had served the pre-Communist regime), Soviet Communist Party leaders in 1919 developed a "police-patrol" method that we now call "parallel rule." The Chinese system of party control over the government is essentially identical to the Soviet system on which it was modeled: the Communist Party selects all government officials; almost all government officials and all top officials are themselves party members; and in each government agency, party members are organized under a party committee that is subordinate to the party committee at the higher administrative level. The hierarchy of government organs is overlaid by a parallel hierarchy of party committees that enables party leaders to supervise party members in the government and lead the work of the government. Party cadres oversee government operations from within the government, not from outside. The system of parallel rule reflects a distinctive characteristic of communist administrative style, namely, leaders' mistrust of the latitude of organizations (Gustafson 1981).

The communist parties in both the Soviet Union and China also established specialized functional departments at central and provincial levels to oversee the work of government economic agencies. Staffed by specialists, these party organs for agriculture, industry, and finance took over many of the administrative functions from the government, especially at the provincial level.[7] The state admin-

6. Without the help of citizen groups, party leaders have a difficult time acquiring information about government actions. Despite their two-thousand-year tradition of bureaucratic authoritarianism, the Chinese are no better than any other communist regime at monitoring bureaucratic behavior. This problem is not remedied by letters to the editor, denunciations to higher-level officials, open meetings with government officials, or any of the other practices vaunted by the Chinese press as evidence of socialist democracy in China. Public opinion polls are a partial remedy to the party's information problem (and, from the perspective of an authoritarian elite, are preferable to elections because they provide information without imposing accountability), but they do not provide sufficiently specific information on the actions of particular agencies. Inquiries by individual members of legislative institutions (people's congresses) and quasi-legislative institutions (people's consultative congresses) at national and local levels do get specific responses from agencies, but lacking the freedom to coalesce into blocs or propose legislation, these individual inquiries have minimal impact on agency behavior.

7. "In the past all levels in the localities set up certain organs as counterparts to the government, and also assigned some industrial secretaries,

istrative apparatus became redundant, a "duplicate administrative structure," as Lin Biao described it in 1969 (Harding 1981, 284). The communist party became the locus of bargaining over economic policies. A 1953 Chinese regulation, "The Decision on the Central Authorities' Leadership over the Work of the Government," formalized this fact:

> All the major and important general and specific government policies, and all major questions concerning the government's work, must first be submitted to the central [party] authorities for examination and approval. And only after the relevant discussions are carried out by the central authorities, and the relevant decisions or approval given by the central authorities, can major and important general and specific government policies begin to be implemented. (Zhou Yi 1987, 18)

The CCP leaders, for reasons not yet entirely clear, took the method of parallel rule even further than the Soviets did.[8] Premier Zhao Ziyang said, "China is one of the socialist countries most seriously afflicted by lack of separation of party and government" (Zhao Ziyang 1987d, 13).[9] "Party groups" (*dang zu*), sometimes called party "fractions" or party "core groups," were established in all government agencies and took over the job of actually administering the work of the agency. Although these institutions originated in the Soviet Union, they came to play a much more significant role in China.

The party group (or fraction) within a government agency is even more powerful than the party committee (Barnett 1967; Burns 1987;

---

agricultural secretaries, standing committee members in charge of finance and trade or culture and education, and so on. They monopolized government work to a greater extent than at the central level, hence the amount of work involved in separating party from government there is greater than at the central level" (Zhao Ziyang 1987, 10).

8. According to one official, the problem was more serious at local levels than at the center. Under Mao, China's central party apparatus was less involved in industry, and the local and enterprise-level party organizations were more involved in industry than were their counterparts in the Soviet Union. According to this official, the party center rarely got involved in industrial policies because Mao Zedong was personally uninterested in industry until 1964, when he felt he was losing control over industry and organized his own "small planning commission" under Yu Qiuli (author's interview).

9. Franz Schurmann (1968) made the same observation twenty years ago.

author's interviews).[10] Central ministry party groups are appointed by the CCP Organization Department, whereas party committees are at least theoretically elected. The party committee supervises the behavior of only the party members within that agency, but the party group has authority over the nonparty bureaucrats as well as those who are party members and plays a decision-making role, setting policy for the entire vertical system (*xitong*) under the ministry as well as for the ministry itself.[11] For example, the party group in the Ministry of Metallurgy makes policy decisions not only for the ministry but also for subordinate provincial and municipal metallurgical bureaus and even for the factories run by the ministry and bureaus. The party group is smaller than a party committee, consisting of only three to five people; its membership overlaps with the top administrative personnel in the ministry (including the minister, several vice ministers, and the party secretary). Although everyone wears two hats, they distinguish between ordinary administrative meetings and meetings of the party group when major policy issues are discussed (author's interviews). In China, the party group essentially appropriated the authority of the official heads of the government agency, creating a confusing system of dual administrative leadership.[12]

At the enterprise level, the CCP also went beyond the Soviet party in playing an administrative role (Ma Hong 1987; Zhao Ziyang 1987d). Soviet party committees always limited their role to super-

10. Schurmann (1968) described the function of the party fraction as more limited than that of the party committee. According to him, the fraction supervised only party members within the agency, whereas the committee had decision-making powers within the agency (160). Either Schurmann, basing his analysis only on CCP rules and handbooks, was wrong, or over time the functions of party fractions and committees have been reversed. Doak Barnett (1967), whose findings were based on interview data, described the party fraction as "the real center of power and authority in the ministry, more important even than the party committee" (24).

11. The Guangdong CCP handbook quoted in Schurmann 1968 (160) may imply the broader authority of the leading group when it states, "Party fractions, in cases where it is necessary to carry out their tasks, may direct the work of the basic-level party organizations in the unit concerned."

12. "In the government setup, the CCP bypasses the government executives at all levels by leading all government departments directly through the 'party groups' in government institutions" (Yan Jiaqi 1988, 42). For example, when the vice minister of finance responsible for tax work proposed a tax reform to a national tax work conference in 1979, his speech had to be approved by the party group within the ministry (author's interview).

vision of party members in the enterprise, allowing the manager full responsibility for production. The Chinese, after the Eighth Party Congress in 1956, put the manager under the leadership of the party committee (Ma Hong 1987). As Zhao Ziyang said in 1987, in China the issue of party control over factory management became a "yardstick for supporting or opposing party leadership. . . . [E]verytime we undertook a campaign, this setup was strengthened, to the extent that the party committees monopolized many administrative matters" (Zhao Ziyang 1987d, 13).

Under this system the CCP not only controlled the government with tight, constant, "police patrol" oversight but actually substituted itself for the government. The organizational lines between the party and government blurred, and the delegation relationship almost entirely disappeared. For example, the head of the CCP committee in charge of all the party groups and committees within the agencies of the central government sat (and still sits) in the State Council, the government cabinet (author's interviews). Some leadership bodies straddle party and government; the most important of these bodies are the "leadership small groups" (*lingdao xiaozu*) in charge of each policy area (finance and economics, foreign policy, etc.; Hamrin 1990). The Finance and Economics Leadership Small Group, five to seven top leaders who make many of the most important economic policy decisions, moves back and forth between government and party depending on which leader is taking charge of economic work.[13]

Despite the blurring of organizational lines, the distinction between party and government never entirely disappeared even in Zhongnanhai, the compound in Beijing where the top national headquarters of both the government State Council and the CCP Central Committee are located. The government headquarters are in the northern part of Zhongnanhai, and the party headquarters in the southern part. When Zhao Ziyang served as premier from 1980 to 1987, the Finance and Economics Leadership Small Group was housed in the northern part of Zhongnanhai; when Zhao moved over to be CCP general secretary, the small group moved with him to the party section in the southern part of the compound

13. Under the reform separating the work of party and government, the Beijing city authorities promised to "determine the affiliation of units which integrate the functions of party and government" ("Beijing CCP Adopts Reorganization Measures" 1988, 63).

(author's interviews).[14] The relocation of this group in 1987 reveals not only the organizational boundaries between government and party but also the ambiguous organizational status of leadership small groups and the continuing link between institutions and individuals in Chinese politics.[15]

The CCP's tight control over the government was achieved at a tremendous cost. The informational advantages of bureaucratic delegation—expertise and specialization—were lost. Poorly educated veteran party officials made policy decisions on the basis of political instincts rather than technical knowledge. Party members serving in government agencies were promoted more for political loyalty than for professional accomplishment (Harding 1981), and government officials would not act decisively for fear of becoming the target of a CCP rectification campaign against officials whose actions were deemed ideologically incorrect.

The Party Puts the Government on a Longer Leash

In the 1980s Deng Xiaoping and his allies decided that, although they wanted to retain the essential elements of the existing political system, they had to modify the party-government relationship if they were serious about improving economic performance and rebuilding confidence in the economic stewardship of the Communist Party.[16] The party had to trade off a degree of control to gain greater economic efficiency.[17] Beginning in approximately 1980, more of the

14. Zhao Ziyang was in charge of economic policy from 1980 to 1988, and the Finance and Economics Leadership Small Group reported to him.

15. Kenneth Lieberthal and Michel Oksenberg (1988) cite as evidence of organizational integration the fact that top party and government organs are both housed in the Zhongnanhai compound. I cite as evidence of organizational boundaries the fact that within Zhongnanhai, party organs are grouped together at the southern end and government organs are clustered at the northern end.

16. Ma Hong made clear that the objective of political reform was improvement of economic performance: "Reform of the political structure is not only for the sake of reform, but is aimed at promoting the operation of the economic structure and the development of productive forces. Therefore to judge whether the political structural reform is successful, the most important thing is to see whether it is conducive to the development of productive forces" (1987, 38).

17. As Alec Nove has said about the Soviet Union, "The party cannot simply seek to 'maximize its power.' It *also* desires results. In economic matters, at least. If the subject is, say, modern art, then control and power can take unquestioned precedence, since the leaders (and most of their followers) simply do not care for or about modern art. Industrial and agricultural production is quite another matter" (1980, 321).

bargaining over specific economic policies was shifted to the government arena. The CCP leadership still set the overall policy line of economic reform, which was approved in Central Committee meetings, and the Finance and Economics Leadership Small Group, which straddled party and government, had to approve the most important economic reform policy decisions.[18] But the Standing Committee of the State Council, meeting twice a week, took charge of deliberating and implementing specific economic policies (author's interviews).

In 1986 Deng Xiaoping made the separation of the work of party and government the core of his modest version of political reform (*Beijing Review*, 18 May 1987). Specialized party departments overlapping their counterpart government departments were abolished at the provincial level, having earlier been abolished at the center (Zhao Ziyang 1987). In enterprises, the party took administrative responsibility from party secretaries and restored it to managers. At the center, the CCP constitution was revised to eliminate gradually the party groups within government agencies ("Draft Revision" 1987). Civil service reforms were proposed to establish a dual structure within the bureaucracy, a cadre of professional civil servants selected by meritocratic examination and promoted on professional criteria alongside the administrative officials appointed and promoted by the party organization departments (Zhao Ziyang 1987; Yan Jiaqi 1988; "New Management System" 1987; Burns 1988).

Party leaders intended none of these changes to destroy the authority of the party over the government, only to improve the quality of decision-making by putting the government on a longer leash. For economic reform to succeed, the party leaders had to retain the power to take policy initiatives. The impetus for bold departures from the status quo had to come from above. At the Thirteenth Party Congress, Zhao Ziyang, even while urging greater autonomy for government, emphasized that the CCP Central Committee would retain its leadership over the government "in political principles and orientation and in major policy decisions" and would continue to appoint leading cadres for central state organs. The powerful provincial party committees would also retain political leadership and personnel appointment powers. The party would

18. As previously noted, during 1980–87, when Zhao Ziyang managed the reform drive from his government post as premier, the Finance and Economics Leadership Small Group acted as if it were a government leadership body, in effect, a specialized standing committee of the State Council.

continue to supervise the work of the government but would no longer substitute itself for the government. As Zhao argued to his party colleagues, many of whom were skeptical, separation of party and government would actually strengthen party leadership of the government: "Leaders must keep very cool; they must stand high and see far, consider things carefully, and avoid getting entangled in a pile of routine affairs. They cannot truly play a leading role if they are entangled in trivia all day long" (Zhao Ziyang 1987c, 13).

The party's control over the government made the economic reform drive possible. Party leaders had the power to prod the bureaucracy to action.[19] With their vested interests in the command economy, the central government planners and ministry bureaucrats were unlikely to take such bold initiatives on their own. The local political entrepreneurs who introduced the first market reform experiments, Zhao Ziyang and Wan Li, were CCP secretaries of their provinces. The political entrepreneur at the top who promoted the popularization of these experiments and masterminded the reform drive was Deng Xiaoping, whose authority was primarily personal, not institutional, and who led from the CCP Politburo, not from his government post as vice premier. By making economic reform the reigning political-ideological line, the reformist party leaders made it impossible for anyone, inside or outside the government, to oppose the reform drive openly. And by replacing thousands of poorly educated or conservative government officials at central and local levels, the party empowered a new cohort of officials, eager and able to promote economic reforms.

Modifying Chinese political institutions to delegate more discretion to the government bureaucracy was an attractive strategy to party leaders facing the political challenges of economic reform. Because government job promotion still depended on pleasing the party and following its line, enhancing the independence of the bureaucracy gave government officials a greater career incentive to be efficient and to take actions that were economically rational but politically risky.[20]

19.   Often project proposals were bounced back and forth among ministries and provinces with little progress until a party leader visited the region, focused his attention on the project, and put it on the agenda of the State Council. For example, see the description of the case of the Datong–Qinhuangdao railway in Zhang Chaowen 1989.
20.   As Tang Tsou has observed, modernization creates pressures for the party to grant all professionals, including government bureaucrats, greater autonomy (1983).

Moreover, the party leadership was divided and conservative party opponents of reforms threatened to subvert them. By shifting more economic policy-making from the party to the government, reformists were able to circumvent party conservatives who still sat in the Politburo.[21] Even though the Politburo retained authority to set the general line and to veto government decisions, it did not debate every particular issue. The shift in bargaining arena from party to government opened possibilities for progress in economic reform.[22] And by broadening the process of economic policy-making to include government commissions, ministries, and provinces, reformist party leaders devised a reform package acceptable to key groups in the state.

It is obvious, especially with the advantage of hindsight after 1989, that the institutional changes designed to reduce the party's interference in economic administration were resisted by elements in the party. Some party officials felt threatened both by what they perceived as the loss of party control and by the economic reforms themselves. Others insisted as a condition of their retirement from the Politburo that their protégés be appointed to high-level government and party posts (Dittmer 1989).

The split within the party over changes in the party-government relationship came into the open in October 1987, when the abolition of party groups in government agencies was proposed at the Thirteenth Party Congress by Zhao Ziyang. In a peculiar twist of Chinese political history, the declared positions of the CCP general

21. Within the CCP, the reformists made an end run around the conservatives in the Politburo by building up the power of the Secretariat, which Hu Yaobang had packed with reform-minded officials. The 1982 CCP constitution gave the head of the Secretariat (that is, the general secretary) the authority to call Politburo and Standing Committee meetings. Hu Yaobang's Secretariat staff and Zhao Ziyang's State Council staff sometimes met together to discuss reform strategy (author's interviews). Hu Yaobang said that he and Zhao presided together over the Secretariat, although only Hu had formal authority ("Deng to Give Up CCP Job" 1982). In 1987, after Hu Yaobang was fired and the conservatives strengthened their hand, the CCP constitution was revised to make the Secretariat subordinate to the Politburo.

22. Robert Bates and Paul Collier (1991) found a similar strategic redesign of institutions in Zambia. Whenever the president wanted to change economic policies, he shifted the policy-making arena between the ruling party (the United National Independence Party) and the government. The president knew that policies made in the government bureaucracy would be market-oriented, whereas policies made within party institutions would emphasize government control of the economy.

secretary and government premier were reversed: Zhao Ziyang, who had just been transferred from premier to party general secretary after Hu Yaobang's purge in January 1987, spoke for the principle of delegation from party to government while acting to keep control over the economic reform in his own (party) hands and out of the hands of the more conservative new premier, Li Peng. From the government side, newly appointed Premier Li Peng spoke out against the diminution of party authority while trying to keep party General Secretary Zhao from continuing to "meddle" in the economic reform. Zhao said in his work report to the congress, "Party groups in government departments should be gradually abolished since the practice of making these groups responsible to the party committees of the next higher level which have approved their establishment is not conducive to unity and efficiency in government work" (Zhao Ziyang 1987, 10). The key words, "gradually abolished," indicate a compromise over whether to eliminate the party groups at all. The revised CCP constitution went only so far as to make party groups optional instead of mandatory ("Draft Revision" 1987).

At a party meeting on party work in central state organs in March 1988, the conservative Premier Li Peng, a member of the Politburo Standing Committee, stressed the necessity of continuing party leadership of central government agencies. He explained that although party groups in central government ministries and commissions would be abolished "step by step," party committees would be retained and become "even more important." He made the conservative position clear: "In the new situation, party work in state organs can only be strengthened and must not be weakened in the slightest degree" (Li Peng 1988, 15). The circular issued by the Central Committee on this issue in July 1988 reflected Li Peng's position, stating that "when party groups have been dissolved, the work of the party committees in government departments should be geared up"; the circular also permitted departments to defer dissolving party groups if it was warranted by the circumstances ("Leading Party Groups" 1988, 29).[23]

The divisions among leaders at the top of the party hierarchy on these institutional issues and the inconsistencies in their positions

---

23. By 1989 Li Peng had resolved the inconsistencies in his position by emphasizing the power of the State Council to formulate economic policy while continuing to support in principle the leadership role of the CCP (Li Peng 1989).

reinforced the reluctance of party cadres to constrict their domain. As a result, the separation of party and government probably was more rhetorical than real. Clearly, the bargaining arena for making specific economic policies had shifted from party to government after 1980. Both documents and interviews with officials indicate that most industrial reform policies were deliberated and promulgated by the government instead of the party.[24] What is less clear is that the party groups within central government agencies actually ceased to lead the agencies or that provinces dissolved the specialized departments under the provincial party committee. At least some provinces reported "stiff ideological resistance" to such institutional changes (Hu Guohua 1988). Local party secretaries probably felt more threatened by loss of function than did the top party leaders, who continued to have important responsibilities for setting the policy line (Nove 1980). Newspaper articles described local secretaries as keenly feeling "the sense of losing powers, positions, and prestige" after the changes (Liao Shixian and Huang Moya 1988, 25). The ambiguity of formal authority relations among local party committees, governments, and people's congresses (according to the constitution of the PRC, both the party and the people's congress have the authority to lead the work of the government) caused constant squabbling (Guan Shaofeng 1988). Articles on local institutional relations, while supporting the general line of separating the work of party and government, always stressed that the party was on top.[25]

When the conservative group within the party leadership strengthened its position after the spring 1989 crackdown on mass protests, there was a clear turnabout in the party's line on the party-government relationship. Zhao Ziyang was blamed for a loss of political control over policy and society, a loss of control that led in turn to turmoil and disorder (*luan*). The party was urged to restore its active leadership over enterprises, local governments, and national government (Li Ximing 1989; "Official Discusses Party Role"

24.   According to Barnett, who interviewed Zhao Ziyang on the delegation issue, foreign policy was also shifted from the CCP to the government (Barnett 1985). Nevertheless, it is clear that policies on culture, education, ideology, and agriculture continued to be formulated within the party. For example, on educational policy-making, see Yang Ruiming 1985.
25.   For example, "On important matters, the party organizations should require the people's congress officials and deputies with party membership to carry out the party's relevant resolutions and to implement the party's principles" (Guan Shaofeng 1988, 16).

1989). Party groups within government agencies were revived (author's interviews). The Standing Committee of the Politburo and the Politburo appeared to take a more active and direct role in economic policy-making in 1990 and 1991 (Li Shangzhi and He Ping 1991).[26]

As a result of top-level party divisions on this institutional issue, throughout the decade of reform the party continued to hold sway over economic policy-making even while most economic policies were made in government settings. As one Chinese commentator explained, while state organs "can choose either to accept or not accept the party's policies," if a state organ refuses to follow the party's policies that are "absolutely correct," "then party organizations and party members within the state organs should supervise and ensure the correct implementation of the party lines and the general and specific policies, by giving play to the exemplary role of the party members within the state organs" (Zhou Yi 1987, 18). In other words, whether or not party groups exist, the party can always use its authority over party members in the bureaucracy to impose its preferences on the government.[27]

26. Interestingly, although the party's control over the policy process was restored, the reform slogan "Separating the functions of the party from those of the government" continued to be used, at least by people on the government side, among them Yuan Mu, chief State Council spokesperson (Dong Yuguo 1991, 12).
27. The frail autonomy of government institutions is illustrated by an example of conflict over agenda-setting in the State Council. (Agenda-setting is a prerogative of the bureaucracy typical of most political systems.) Bo Yibo, a conservative veteran leader, had retired from all official posts and been appointed vice chairman of the CCP Central Advisory Commission, the body created by Deng Xiaoping as a "pasture" where elderly party leaders could retire without loss of face. In February 1988 Bo Yibo came to a regular State Council meeting with a Central Advisory Commission proposal on transportation safety probably designed to embarrass the government bureaucracy over recent accidents. Wan Li, a reformist veteran who had been permitted to keep his government post as vice premier and who was chairing the State Council meeting (Premier Li Peng had left to participate in a Politburo Standing Committee meeting), refused to alter the agenda to allow discussion of the issue. According to the unofficial report of the incident, the State Council leaders had learned in advance about Bo's intention and obtained Deng Xiaoping's support for sticking to the original agenda. State bureaucratic authority had widened but was still fragile and dependent on the support of the preeminent leader (Lo Ping 1988). Another way to look at this incident is as a classic showdown between personal and institutional authority. The party elders challenged the institutional authority of the State Council to set its own agenda. The fact that the State Council could not defend its institutional prerogatives without calling on

To summarize, during the decade of economic reform, party leaders delegated more discretion to the government in economic policy-making. Delegation was intended to improve the quality of economic decisions, to tilt the policy process to favor reform outcomes, and to devise a policy package acceptable to key groups in society. This effort to separate the work of party and government sparked substantial dissension within the party ranks and was carried out only to the extent that economic policy-making was shifted largely to the government arena. Party oversight over the government bureaucracy continued to be of the tight, centralized, police-patrol type, and the party retained the authority to select government officials, propose policy initiatives, and veto policies that emerged from the government side.

What kind of policy-making process is characteristic of this pattern of authority relations?

1.   Based on the "law of anticipated reactions," policies emerging from the government bureaucracy reflect the preferences of party leaders.

2.   If the party leadership is divided and the party's line is changeable, then government reform policies are likely to shift or be inconsistent.

3.   Whenever the composition and preferences of the party leadership change, government policies will change too.

4.   Because of the party's police-patrol oversight from within the government bureaucracy, party vetoes of policies made in the government arena are rare. The heads of government commissions, ministries, and provinces know from their participation in high-level party meetings what party leaders would find acceptable and what they would not; because their careers depend on pleasing party leaders, they will not promulgate policies of which party leaders would disapprove.

In subsequent chapters I show how the economic reform policies made in government settings reflect the preferences of CCP leaders.

Deng Xiaoping's personal authority reveals the continued importance of personal authority in China.

4 Leadership Incentives

Political Succession and
Reciprocal Accountability

Having established that the communist party has ultimate authority in communist political systems such as that of China, I now disaggregate the party and look inside it: Who has authority within the party? How are the preferences of the party formed? Answering these questions requires us to spell out the way leaders of the communist party are chosen and the nature of competition for leadership in the party. In democratic systems the political incentives of politicians are shaped by the electoral connection: politicians take policy positions that will win them votes from their constituents. What is the equivalent of the electoral connection in communist authoritarian systems? Although communist leaders obviously are not popularly elected, neither are they pure dictators, totally exempt from accountability to others. But the lines of accountability in communist regimes are more elusive than are those in democracies; the leadership selection process is less transparent, and the formal rules for selection are not always followed. Despite these pitfalls, to understand the linkage between leadership competition and policy outcomes in communist countries we must try to figure out how their leaders are chosen. The following section sketches out how Chinese Communist Party leaders are chosen. Here, *leadership selection* refers to the selection of the party general secretary and the members of the highest collective organs of the party, the Standing Committee of the Politburo and the Politburo.[1]

1. In Mao Zedong's era the top leader held the position of chairman of the CCP. When Deng Xiaoping succeeded Mao, he eliminated the position of party chairman to reduce the overconcentration of authority within the CCP and encourage collective leadership. Since then the top formal position within the CCP has been the general secretary. However, Deng Xiaoping plays the role of preeminent leader without holding the formal position of general secretary; instead, the general secretary is the presumed

The competition for political leadership in communist states is almost constant. It is not punctuated by fixed terms of office. Even after someone has attained the position of party leader, he has to worry about keeping it. He can never be entirely secure because one of his lieutenants might overthrow him at any time (Tullock 1987). Still, incumbent leaders, especially those of advanced age, are less constrained by career incentives than are those who are hoping to succeed them. Potential successors are always trying to build a coalition of supporters. At the lower level, party and government officials make guesses about which contender will win, test them by pressing policy claims on them, and sometimes throw their weight behind one of them. Naturally, the struggle for power intensifies when the top leader is conspicuously weak (as in the case of Hua Guofeng) or elderly (as in the case of Deng Xiaoping).

Party leaders in a communist system are chosen not by an electorate but by what we might call a "selectorate," a term adopted from British parliamentary politics to define the group within a political party that has effective power to choose leaders. Who constitutes the selectorate in a communist polity? In China (as in the USSR before its demise) the communist party constitution grants formal authority to select party leaders to the Central Committee, which is in turn selected by the party congress.[2] The Soviet system was more institutionalized than is that of China: ever since 1957, when Nikita Khrushchev defeated an effort to oust him in the Standing Committee of the Politburo (Presidium) by winning the support of a Central Committee meeting, and 1964, when the Central Committee removed Khrushchev from his leadership position, the Central Committee had established its actual as well as formal authority to select the party leader.[3]

---

successor to Deng. After Deng, the preeminent leader will probably hold the formal post of general secretary. This arrangement reflects the indeterminacy in the authority and responsibility of the institutional role of party chairman or general secretary in communist polities (Brzezinski and Huntington 1964).

The size of CCP leadership institutions is not specified in party rules. As of 1991, the Standing Committee of the Politburo had 6 members, the Politburo 18 members and 2 alternates, and the Central Committee 175 members and 110 alternates.

2. The Thirteenth Party Congress in 1987 consisted of 1,936 delegates elected by party congresses in localities, central party and government departments, and military departments.

3. As Jerry Hough (1991, 95) writes: "Any serious student of the structure of power in the Soviet Union before the summer of 1990 would have fo-

The rules of the game are the same but less strictly adhered to in China. According to the CCP constitution, the Central Committee has the formal authority to select the Politburo, the Standing Committee of the Politburo, and the party general secretary. In two out of the last three general secretary appointments, the Central Committee at least ratified the appointment. In one instance, however, when Hu Yaobang was fired in January 1987, the Politburo acted on its own.

Informal Authority: The Elders, the Military, and the Preeminent Leader

The authority of the Central Committee to select party leaders has not been definitively established in China because informal power continues to play a more significant role in the Chinese succession process than it did in the Soviet Union. Individuals who are not Politburo or Central Committee members participate in making selection decisions behind the scenes; in the view of many politically knowledgeable Chinese and foreign scholars, the actors on the stage (i.e., those holding formal posts) are merely puppets controlled by the retired party elders who stand behind the curtain.[4] The elders often step from behind the curtain to attend enlarged meetings of the Politburo and Central Committee (a process permitted by party rules) and sometimes even vote in these meetings, in violation of party rules (Kuo Chien 1991, 54).[5] Although many of the party elders hold membership in the CCP Central Advisory Commission and Central Commission for Discipline Inspection,

---

cused on the role of the Central Committee—the plenum of the Central Committee, as Soviets would express it. Although Westerners often said incorrectly that the Politburo was the focus of power in the old system, the only institution that could elect or replace a General Secretary—or any Politburo member—was the Central Committee. Whoever controlled a majority of the voting members of the Central Committee controlled the Politburo and the rest of the political system. Normally the loyalty of the Central Committee to the General Secretary was taken for granted by any potential challenger and, therefore, not tested, but a General Secretary who did not continually worry about that loyalty courted the fate that befell Nikita Khrushchev in October 1964."

4. For example, Lowell Dittmer (1990) describes two leadership groups, one having titles but no real power (i.e., the Standing Committee of the Politburo), the other holding power without official responsibility (i.e., the elders).

5. The elders often are consulted on policy issues pertinent to the department (*xitong*) with which their career was associated. And they sometimes sit in on meetings of leadership small groups (author's interviews).

their influence in high-level decision-making depends not on their formal positions but on their personal stature as revolutionary war heroes and founders of the PRC.[6]

Deng Xiaoping is a member of the older generation of party veterans who had been the targets of the Cultural Revolution. Deng based his political comeback in 1977 on the support of this group of "rehabilitated cadres," and although he was more open to radical economic reforms than most of them, he shared many of their old-fashioned notions about communist politics. Even when he might disagree with them, his own personal stature—unlike Mao Zedong's—was not so much higher than theirs that he could afford to ignore their views. Deng perpetuated the use of informal authority by deferring to the elders and legitimated it by continuing to serve as number one leader even after retiring from all his government and party posts. Presumably, after the founder generation of the CCP dies, the importance of personal authority will diminish (although, of course, not disappear), and formal institutional authority will become more important.

The weakly institutionalized process of leadership selection in the CCP is illustrated in the three rounds of succession competition since Mao Zedong's death in 1976. The decision to fire Hua Guofeng as party chairman and to replace him with Hu Yaobang, who would serve as general secretary (Deng refused to accept the general secretary position but became the preeminent leader when Hua was fired), was made in a nine-day Politburo meeting during November and December 1980; the decision was approved by the Central Committee at a meeting eleven days later.[7] The Politburo meeting reportedly had been preceded by informal discussions in elite circles about asking Hua to step down beginning as early as the end of 1978 (Lo Ping 1981).

The decision to oust Hu Yaobang from the general secretaryship was made in January 1987 by an *enlarged* meeting of the Politburo

6. The Central Advisory Commission was established by the 1982 party constitution as a temporary institution (with only advisory authority) to facilitate the retirement of elderly party leaders from the Politburo and Central Committee. Deng Xiaoping suggested that it be dissolved at the Fourteenth Party Congress in 1992 (Lam 1991). The Central Commission for Discipline Inspection was established in 1978 to replace the old CCP Control Commission and was headed by one of the most influential elders, Chen Yun.

7. The post of party chairman was eliminated; the top leadership post became party general secretary.

that included members of the Central Advisory Commission, two members of the Central Commission for Discipline Inspection, and two other leading comrades (State Councillors Song Ping and Gu Mu), along with the eighteen members and two alternate members of the Politburo.[8] According to one source, everyone present, including the nonmembers of the Politburo, "unanimously agreed" to dismiss Hu, violating party rules that nonmembers may participate but not vote in Politburo or Central Committee decisions (Lo Ping 1987a, K1). Another violation was that the decision was announced without Central Committee ratification. The Politburo meeting was preceded by meetings of the party Secretariat, meetings with Central Committee members from various provinces, and other informal meetings of party elites (*Kyodo* 1987; Lo Ping 1987; Lo Ping 1987a). Hu's opponents may have decided not to call a Central Committee meeting after holding discussions with Central Committee members and discovering that many members still supported Hu. One Hong Kong observer described the event as the elders in the Advisory Commission "seizing power" from the Central Committee (Lo Ping 1987a, K3). No Central Committee meeting was held during the first nine months of 1987; Zhao Ziyang's appointment to replace Hu was not formalized until the Thirteenth Party Congress in October 1987.

Zhao Ziyang lost his job as CCP general secretary at a series of enlarged meetings of the Standing Committee of the Politburo and the Politburo during the political crisis of May–June 1989.[9] In May there was an abortive attempt to hold a Central Committee meeting. Central Committee members were summoned to Beijing, but after talking with them individually, party leaders decided that there was too much disagreement about the way to deal with the demonstrators to risk a meeting. Zhao Ziyang's ouster was not finalized until an enlarged Politburo meeting on 19–21 June (more than two weeks after the armed suppression of the demonstrations) and the long-delayed Fourth Plenum of the Central Committee held two days later. To guarantee that there would be no doubt about the outcome, the Central Committee plenum was packed by a full comple-

8. One source says four members of the Advisory Commission attended ("Hu Yaobang Resigns" 1987); another source says seventeen (Lo Ping 1987a).
9. Sensitive to criticism that the elders' participation in these crucial meetings was illegitimate, Yang Shangkun stressed that the decision to accept Zhao's resignation was made by a majority of the Standing Committee of the Politburo ("Main Points of Comrade Yang Shangkun's Speech" 1989, 20).

ment of the Central Advisory Commission and Central Disciplinary Inspection Commission members along with other "leading comrades from relevant departments," making a total of 557 participants in all (Shambaugh 1989, 853). Even before the outbreak of student demonstrations in April 1989, the elderly conservatives in the party had been pressuring Deng Xiaoping to get rid of Zhao Ziyang. Many informal meetings of the nine most influential octogenarians were held during 1989 to discuss leadership changes.[10]

In the three rounds of succession competition after Mao's death, the elders of the CCP increased their already considerable power in the leadership selection process even though they were gradually retired from official party and government posts. (By the time of the Thirteenth Party Congress in 1987, all of them except for Yang Shangkun had retired from the Politburo.) The apex of their power came after their triumph in engineering the defeat of Zhao Ziyang in 1989. During 1990–91 the octogenarians were emboldened to make more frequent appearances in front of the curtain; Yang Shangkun started to assume the role of public spokesman for the collective concerns of the "old comrades" (He Shaoming 1990), and reports multiplied of the octogenarians delivering instructions (usually read by others because the elderly leaders were too frail to speak in person) to meetings of the Standing Committee of the Politburo and the Politburo (see, for example, Chen Chieh-hung 1991).[11]

The military also plays a more active role in succession decisions in China than it did in the Soviet Union. In the Soviet Union, the

10. As of 1989, the nine octogenarians were (in order of individual rank) Deng Xiaoping (85), former chair of the Military Affairs Committee; Chen Yun (84), chairman of the Central Advisory Commission; Yang Shangkun (82), president of the state and secretary general of the Military Affairs Committee; Li Xiannian (80), chairman of the Chinese People's Political Consultative Congress National Committee; Wang Zhen (81), vice president of the state; Bo Yibo (81), vice chairman of the Central Advisory Commission; Song Renqiong (80), vice chairman of the Central Advisory Commission; Peng Zhen (87), retired former chairman of the National People's Congress Standing Committee; and Deng Yingchao (85). Yang Shangkun, in his May 1989 speech, left out Song Renqiong and Bo Yibo and included two elderly PLA marshals, Nie Rongzhen and Xu Xiangqian ("Main Points of Comrade Yang Shangkun's Speech" 1989, 20). According to Yang's speech, the spring 1989 student demonstrations created such a serious political crisis that the octogenarians got together to discuss central affairs for the first time in many years.

11. If, as some observers believe, the elders are the true principals in Chinese politics, then, as Yang Shangkun humorously suggested, the ultimate authorities may be the medical doctors who are the only ones who can give orders to the elders (Lo Ping 1991, 30).

national government had authority over the military through the Ministry of Defense. In China, however, civilian governmental authority over the military has not yet been established; the People's Liberation Army (PLA) takes its orders only from the Communist Party through the party Military Affairs Commission, which reports directly to the Politburo. Deng Xiaoping attempted unsuccessfully to strengthen the civilian governmental authority over the PLA by creating a Military Affairs Committee (MAC) under the State Council. The membership of the governmental body is identical with the membership of the party body (Yang Baibing 1991), and whenever the group meets, it is identified in government documents and the press as a party organ, not a government organ.

After the Cultural Revolution, when the CCP was decimated by Red Guard attacks, PLA officers stepped into civilian political leadership positions; as of 1971 twenty-two of the twenty-nine provincial first party secretaries were military men (Joffe 1987, 158). Beginning in the second half of the 1970s, however, party dominance was reestablished and military officers were sent back to the barracks. Still, most of the party elders are military as well as party leaders, Yang Shangkun being the most prominent example. And let us not forget that after Mao's death in 1976, his widow, Jiang Qing, and the other three members of the radical Gang of Four were arrested by PLA forces working with moderate elites within the CCP in an action resembling a military coup. Thirteen years later, in 1989, the PLA sided with Deng Xiaoping and the elders in making a tough military response to the protesters; if commanders in the PLA had refused to obey the leader's order (as Soviet military commanders did in the August 1991 coup attempt), Zhao might still be party general secretary. The support of the military appears to be crucial for a victory in party power struggles in a way that the support of civilian party and government officials is not.[12] But the PRC is not a military regime in Leninist clothing: the military, although an indispensable member of any winning coalition, cannot dictate leaders or policies (Joffe 1987).[13]

12. Having demonstrated its political indispensability in Tiananmen Square on 4 June 1989, the PLA demanded and received a big increase in the defense budget, 15 percent in 1990 (Wang Bingqian 1990, 16). Not surprisingly, Li Peng and Jiang Zemin, two of the top contenders to succeed Deng, enthusiastically endorsed the increase (Chen Wei-chun 1991).
13. Timothy Colton (1986) views the Soviet military in much the same way.

It goes without saying that the incumbent leader is the most important member of the selectorate, holding the equivalent of much more than one vote and certainly holding a veto. The incumbent leader is a member of every winning coalition in the succession contest. Nevertheless, the leader cannot guarantee that his chosen successor will actually inherit his mantle.

Communist leaders who want to ensure a smooth transition to their successors face an insuperable contradiction: once a leader chooses a successor, he gives the successor a strong motive to do him in and speed up the succession (Tullock 1987; Rush 1968). It is not surprising that Chinese communist leaders have come to distrust their successors after they have anointed them. Once they have chosen them, they begin finding fault with them and are sensitive to any sign of the successor's impatience to take over (MacFarquhar 1988). One of the reported reasons that Deng Xiaoping fired his chosen successor Hu Yaobang in January 1987 was that Hu had been talking too avidly about rejuvenating the ranks of party leaders and had responded too enthusiastically to Deng's public musings about his own "early retirement" ("Rejuvenation" 1987).

If the leader transfers power to a successor, he gives everyone an incentive to shift loyalties from the leader to the successor; but if the leader doesn't transfer power and remains in charge, he makes the successor look weak. Pseudo retirement by the leader is likely to make the successor the target of the runners-up, who see that the race is not yet over. The "relay model" (MacFarquhar 1988), in which the leader hands over the baton and then continues running for a spell alongside his successor to ensure that the baton has been firmly grasped, encountered this problem in China. When Deng Xiaoping chose Hu Yaobang as his successor, Deng retained the chairmanship of the CCP Military Affairs Committee, the linchpin for party control over the army. Deng's unwillingness or inability to place his successor in this key position weakened Hu and made him vulnerable to the ambitions of his rivals, especially on the conservative side.[14] After Hu's ouster, Deng made Zhao Ziyang party general secretary and appointed him vice chairman of the MAC,

14. An earlier example of fierce competition among rival contenders for the throne occurred in 1953, when Gao Gang apparently tried to bring down Liu Shaoqi, Mao's probable successor. Gao was thwarted by Zhou Enlai and Deng Xiaoping, other possible successors who refused to cooperate with him and who revealed the plot to Mao Zedong ("*Selected Works of Deng Xiaoping*" 1983).

but the number two post in the MAC was not sufficient for Zhao to consolidate power. Zhao met the same fate as Hu Yaobang during the mass protests of spring 1989.

Over the decade one can see Deng Xiaoping grappling with this dilemma: how could he lock in the succession and guarantee the perpetuation of reforms without destabilizing the situation? Deng (and many others in China) believed he was the only fulcrum who could balance the reformists and the conservative old-timers within the party, managing the conservatives so that the reforms could move ahead. Deng placed the two reformists, Hu Yaobang and Zhao Ziyang, at the head of the party and government; he gradually replaced millions of local and central officials, including the majority of the Central Committee members; and he persuaded many of the old Long March veteran leaders to retire from the Politburo to the CCP Central Advisory Commission, which he created in 1982 as a face-saving solution to the retirement problem.[15] Yet neither Hu nor Zhao ever was made head of the MAC, and Deng continued to lead from the Standing Committee of the Politburo until the Thirteenth Party Congress in 1987, after which he retained his position as chairman of the MAC until the Fifth Plenum of the Thirteenth Central Committee in November 1989. Deng himself reportedly said, "It would have been nice if I could have retired in 1985." In 1985 he resigned from the chairmanship of the Central Advisory Commission but remained in his other party leadership posts at the urging of both the reformist successors and the elderly conservatives; each side felt its interests were protected by Deng and that Deng's total retirement would leave them vulnerable to defeat by the other side (Lo So 1989). No doubt Deng himself was just as convinced of his own indispensability.

Only after the political crisis of 1989 did Deng at last insist on leaving the MAC. Having seen both Hu and Zhao defeated by conservative rivals, he finally recognized that a successor without full authority was a sitting duck. To establish the authority of his new

15. A special national conference of party delegates was convened in 1985 to accelerate this process during the long five years between the twelfth and thirteenth party congresses. The conservatives had been sniping at the reforms, and Hu and Zhao were worried that the elderly Deng might die before the Thirteenth Party Congress in 1987. But at the conference, although the Central Committee and Politburo were reconstituted with a more reformist coloration, the Standing Committee of the Politburo remained unchanged and continued to include Deng and two conservative octogenarians, Chen Yun and Li Xiannian (Mu Fu 1985).

successor, Jiang Zemin, he made him head of the MAC as well as party general secretary. Yet even as he was urging the other leaders in the Politburo to unite around Jiang Zemin and insisting that he had retired completely, he was playing power broker, spending hours every day in informal meetings (Lo Ping 1989).

Over the decade Deng Xiaoping's political prestige was significantly diluted by his inconsistent actions, in particular his decision to join with the conservatives to oust Hu and Zhao, whom he had picked to succeed him. Given Deng's weakened position, his efforts to secure the succession of Jiang Zemin may be no more successful than the efforts of Mao Zedong, who also had been enfeebled by age and by political failures, to place Hua Guofeng on the throne.

Formal Authority: The Central Committee

Despite the continuing influence of the revolutionary elders, the military, and the preeminent leader, the younger generation of CCP leaders had reason to expect that the collective institutions of the party, particularly the Central Committee, soon would play a larger role. Deng Xiaoping and the other top party leaders had committed themselves to deconcentrating power and regularizing intraparty decision-making (Teiwes 1984). Deng pushed the party to implement a systematic cadre retirement policy for the first time (Manion 1991). At the Twelfth Party Congress in 1982, delegates were allowed to add names to, and to delete names from, the list of Central Committee nominees provided by the leadership (James Wang 1989, 81). At the Thirteenth Party Congress in 1987, the election rules were further democratized to require more nominations than the number of seats (Oksenberg 1987).

Thus, Hu Yaobang and Zhao Ziyang, potential successors to Deng Xiaoping, did not flout the power of the elders and even continued to consult them periodically (author's interviews); however, they did bet their futures on a broader constituency within the Central Committee by actively promoting reform policies welcomed by local officials and industrial interests within the Central Committee. "Playing to the provinces" with fiscal decentralization (see chapter 9) and the particularistic form of the economic reforms were political strategies premised on the influence of the Central Committee. Having focused their succession campaigns on the Central Committee, Hu and Zhao were apparently caught by surprise in 1987 and 1989 by the continued dominance of the elders.

The empirical evidence that the CCP Central Committee plays the authoritative role in leadership appointment decisions is admittedly weak: there is no case of the Central Committee's overruling the elders or the preeminent leader in succession decisions comparable to the 1957 example in the Soviet Union. However, the evidence of the Central Committee's authority in policy decisions is stronger. Parris Chang's research on the Chinese policy-making process during the 1950s and 1960s indicates that except when Mao Zedong was an active participant in policy-making (1955–59), the policy process was "routine and institutionalized" and the "ultimate organ" for deciding policy issues was the Central Committee (P. Chang 1990, 184):

> Although the Central Committee, as an institution, rarely initiated policy measures, top leadership sought and took into account opinions of Central Committee members. . . . Exactly how the "anticipated reaction" of the Central Committee members conditioned and shaped a decision of the Politburo is hard to gauge; nonetheless, the influence was certainly present, although perhaps indirect or limited. When the top leadership was deadlocked, however, policy conflicts at the top were carried to the Central Committee for resolution; consequently, members of the Central Committee were drawn into participation in settling disputes and making momentous decisions which, at times, changed the political fate of powerful leaders. (P. Chang 1990, 179)

A significant example of the Central Committee's role in shaping policy outcomes in the post-Mao era occurred after 1989, when conservative CCP leaders Chen Yun and Yao Yilin tried to recentralize China's fiscal system. In the work conferences preceding both the Fifth Plenum of the Thirteenth Central Committee in November 1989 and the Seventh Plenum in December 1990, the provincial and municipal officials who constitute the largest bloc in the Central Committee objected to the recentralization proposals. As a result of this opposition, the Central Committee plenums had to be postponed, and when they finally met, the Central Committee acted to retain fiscal decentralization, thereby reversing the original recommendation of the leaders (Lam 1989; Shambaugh 1989; see chapter 9 of this volume).[16]

16. There are also, however, examples of the preeminent leader overruling the Central Committee even in the Deng era. One such example was the

Given the actual political behavior of elites, the evidence that the Central Committee is the final veto gate in policy-making, and the formal party rules giving the Central Committee the authority to select party leaders, it appears that the Central Committee is in the process of becoming the key group in the selectorate in China. Because the Central Committee holds the formal authority for choosing the leader, even if it only ratifies the choice made in a smoke-filled room in Deng Xiaoping's house, the people in that smoke-filled room recognize they must pick someone acceptable to the Central Committee. The maneuvering may take place outside the formal meetings of the Central Committee, but the body is not merely a rubber stamp; the leader chosen must reflect the preferences of the committee.

During this period of institutional transition in China, then, a candidate for appointment as general secretary, Politburo member, or Standing Committee member in China must win the support of an elite selectorate consisting of fewer than five hundred top party leaders, including:

The Central Committee (As of 1992, 175 full and 110 alternate members). There are three main blocs in the Central Committee: Central Communist Party and government officials; local party and government officials; and PLA officers. During the reform decade the largest bloc within the Central Committee consisted of local officials.

The Communist Party elders (most of whom are in the CCP Central Advisory Commission, approximately 175 members, or the CCP Central Commission for Discipline Inspection, approximately 100 members). Probably only a subset of the membership of these two bodies participates in selection decisions.

The leaders of the PLA (some of whom are in the MAC, approximately 20 members). The PLA is also one of the three large blocs in the Central Committee.

The preeminent leader (1).

---

decision, made by a Central Committee work conference in December 1980, to cancel the construction of several large plants (including Baoshan Iron and Steel near Shanghai) being purchased from abroad. At a February 1981 meeting with a Japanese delegation sent to argue against cancellation, Deng Xiaoping unilaterally reversed the work conference decision and said the projects would continue. Party officials and government bureaucrats were taken by surprise (Kokubun 1986).

Although we can identify the groups within the selectorate, we do not know for sure what is the "voting rule" by which the selectorate chooses leaders. CCP institutions such as the Central Committee, the Politburo, and the Standing Committee of the Politburo take votes and make decisions by majority rule, not by consensus. However, the extrainstitutional groups in the selectorate probably make decisions by consensus. Under ordinary circumstances, the preeminent leader begins the leadership selection process by discussing the nominations with the elders and PLA leaders. If they reach agreement on a name, it is then submitted to the Central Committee for approval. If the preeminent leader cannot obtain agreement among the elders and PLA leaders on the nomination, he will not submit it to the Central Committee. (During 1991 Deng Xiaoping reportedly wanted to promote two middle-aged, reform-minded officials, Zhu Rongji and Zou Jiahua, into the Politburo and Standing Committee. When he could not get the elders and military leaders to agree, he did not put forward the nominations [Cheng 1991].)

Reciprocal Accountability: The Leaders Choose the Officials and the Officials Choose the Leaders

In communist political systems the lines of political accountability are more complicated and ambiguous than are the lines of accountability in democracies between voters and elected politicians and politicians and appointed government bureaucrats. One thing that is clear is that under communism, ordinary citizens are excluded from the political game. They cannot control the actions of party and government officials except by the rarely used means of mass protest because the rules of communist political competition prohibit party politicians from mobilizing social support. The political playing field is restricted to the party and government officialdom.

Within the communist state, institutions are hierarchical in that the top leaders of the party appoint subordinate officials of the party, government, and military. Even after the decentralization of the Chinese nomenklatura system in 1984, the party center was authorized to appoint at least five thousand of the country's leading officials, including all provincial governors and party secretaries, heads of central ministries and commissions, heads of central party departments, senior military officers, and even the Standing Committee of the National People's Congress (Burns 1987).[17] The party

17. The civilian officials are appointed by the Organization Department, the

center periodically reassigns provincial leaders and military region-al commanders. Although the officials appointed by the party cen-ter are expected to articulate the interests of their particular regions or agencies, they always look to the party leaders in Beijing because they know their careers depend on satisfying these leaders.

Yet this relationship between party leaders and subordinate offi-cials is not a pure hierarchy: according to the party rules, the Cen-tral Committee has the authority to choose the party leaders, and the Central Committee consists of party, government, and military officials appointed by party leaders. The leaders appoint the officials and the officials in the Central Committee choose (or at least ratify the choice of) the leaders. Government officials are both the agents and the constituents of party leaders; local officials are both the agents and the constituents of central leaders. Officials hold their positions at the pleasure of the party leadership, but party leaders hold their positions at the pleasure of the officials in the selectorate. The lines of accountability run in both directions, turning a hierarchical relation-ship into one of "reciprocal accountability."[18]

Reciprocal accountability is a distinctive feature of communist institutions.[19] Unlike a democracy, in which the people are sover-eign, or an absolute monarchy or dictatorship, in which the leader is sovereign, reciprocal accountability is a relationship in which nei-ther side has a definitive right (Roeder 1990). The lines of authority run in both directions.[20]

---

military ones by the MAC (Burns 1987, 46). A further reform to transfer to power to fill less important government posts from CCP bodies to the State Council was introduced in 1988 but reversed in 1990 (Burns forthcoming).

18. "Reciprocal accountability" is similar to Robert Daniels's (1971) notion of the "circular flow of power" within communist parties.

19. Philip Roeder (forthcoming) has identified the identical pattern in the Soviet Union.

20. Mathew McCubbins has suggested to me that the reciprocal lines of authority in communist states resemble those in corporations: the share-holders (communist party members) elect the board of directors (central committee) and have a veto over corporate policy. The board of directors elects the chairman of the board (general secretary) and the managers who are delegated to run the firm (government leaders). The managers hire the employees (government officials). So the management is an agent of the shareholders and the employees are agents of management. However, managers (government leaders) and employees (government officials) are also shareholders (communist party members) and as such have power to choose the board of directors (central committee). And the board of direc-tors controls the sale of stock and thereby controls the size and shape of the class of shareholders. When division over corporate policy occurs

Power is not shared equally between leaders and central committee under reciprocal accountability, however; top-down authority is
much stronger than bottom-up authority. An important limitation
on bottom-up authority is the communist rule against factionalism
that originated in the Soviet Union and was transferred to China.
Party and government officials are prohibited from coordinating
their actions to form blocs in party decision-making. Officials in
central party and government departments or in the military have
some degree of de facto coordination if they are under the same
higher-level body—for example, industry under the State Economic
Commission (SEC) or the military under the MAC—but this coordination is limited by the vertical divisions within the bureaucracy.
Crossing these vertical lines—for example, someone from the industrial ministries working together with someone from the military to defeat a proposal—would violate the antifactionalism rule.

Unlike industrial sectors or military branches, provinces have no
permanent bureaucratic representation; it is therefore harder for
provincial leaders to coordinate their actions in the Central Committee. The antifactionalism rule puts the provincial leaders in the
Central Committee at a real disadvantage vis-à-vis the center. If the
central party leaders believe that the provincial leaders are coordinating their efforts and forming a local bloc against the center, the
central leaders will dismiss or demote the provincial leaders. A
1950s example of such an event was the firing of the Manchurian
leaders Gao Gang and Rao Shushi; a 1990s example was the firing
of Guangdong governor Ye Xuanping (see chapter 9).

The strength of top-down authority also derives from the fact
that CCP leaders appoint the officials who serve in the Central
Committee and stage-manage the elections for the party congress
that elects the Central Committee.[21] Jerry Hough describes selection
of the Central Committee slate by the party congress in the Soviet
Union: the composition of the slate was worked out informally by
the Politburo or a subset of Politburo members in preliminary discussions with agency and regional officials, but because it had to
be approved by the party congress, it reflected the balance of forces

---

among shareholders or members of the board of directors, proxy fights
(party power struggles) result.
21. The Central Committee instructed that the delegates to the 1982 party
congress be elected by secret ballot in local party congresses and that the
number of nominations exceed the number of delegate positions (James
Wang 1989, 81).

in the congress (Hough and Fainsod 1979). The Chinese method for selecting a new Central Committee slate appears to be the same. Prior to the National Conference of Party Delegates in 1985, the Standing Committee of the Politburo formed a seven-person group headed by General Secretary Hu Yaobang to consult with localities and departments in putting together the slate. The slate was discussed and revised by the Politburo and Secretariat and then submitted to the national conference (Zeng Jianhui 1985).

The leaders' control over the composition of the Central Committee provides an element of flexibility in communist systems. Leaders try to consolidate support by changing the membership of the Central Committee selectorate and by expanding the size of the Central Committee to bring new groups into it. Power struggles and policy innovations involve a search for new constituencies. For example, Mao Zedong, in his battle against the party establishment during the Cultural Revolution, expanded the size of the Central Committee from 97 to 170 in 1969 and increased the proportion of members from worker and peasant mass organizations from almost none to 19 percent in 1969 and 30 percent in 1973 (James Wang 1989, 85).[22]

Although it is possible to describe the changing composition of the Central Committee in terms of age, generation, educational background, regional origin, or other characteristics, the most common breakdown is in terms of institutional position. Historically, the three largest blocs in the CCP Central Committee have been central party and government officials (31.4 percent of the total membership as of 1987), provincial and municipal party and government officials (43 percent in 1987), and the military (19 percent in 1987).[23] Changing the relative membership shares of these three groups enables party leaders to defeat their rivals and initiate new policy directions. Mao overwhelmed his party opponents during the Cultural Revolution by making the military into the largest bloc of members (43 percent in 1969, declining to 32 percent in 1973); Deng Xiaoping overcame the resistance of central bureaucrats to economic reform by making local officials the largest bloc (43 percent in 1987).[24]

22. The Central Committee was expanded again at the start of the reform drive in 1977 to 333 full members.
23. The remaining members are scientific professionals and representatives of mass organizations. The term *bloc* does not imply that the members coordinate their votes.
24. Local representatives dominated the Thirteenth Party Congress in

Chinese leaders have had more control over the composition of the Central Committee than Soviet leaders had because ever since the 1920s CPSU Central Committee seats were allocated according to 106 slots, with the shares of the slots assigned to the center, the governments of the republics, and party and military officials remaining very stable (Daniels 1989). This norm of job-slot representation in the Soviet Central Committee constrained the latitude of Soviet communism. The less institutionalized nature of the CCP Central Committee made the Chinese version of communism more flexible. Even in China, however, once the Central Committee is elected by the party congress, it holds authority for the next five years.[25] Incumbent party leaders, and those aspiring to replace them, must seek support among current Central Committee members.

Policy and Power: How Leaders Appeal to the Selectorate

On what basis does the CCP selectorate choose its leaders? Under communism, because all political competition is waged within the party and government bureaucracies—there is no separate, open sphere of politics as there is in democracies—competition and policy formulation are intertwined in what T. H. Rigby (1964; 1980) has called "crypto-politics." Communist officials cannot openly campaign for leadership posts, and because of the party's official myth of unity, officials cannot openly form blocs or factions. Instead, competitive politics are "predominantly covert and parasitical upon task-oriented activities." And group interests, denied overt channels of expression, are fed into the bureaucratic policy process, where they seek ambitious officials who will take up their cause

---

1987: two-thirds of the delegates were elected by local party organizations, as compared to 16 percent from central agencies and 14 percent from the military (James Wang 1989, 84). I do not have comparative figures from party congresses in earlier periods.
25. In 1985 Deng Xiaoping used the irregular procedure of calling a National Party Conference (Mao established the precedent by using a party conference to bypass the party congress in 1949) to reshuffle the membership of the Politburo and Central Committee before the regularly scheduled party congress. The party congress in 1987 reacted by amending the CCP constitution to limit party conferences to replacing or newly electing no more than one-fifth of the total members of the Central Committee originally elected by the party congress. Li Peng stated in 1991 that there were no plans to convene a party conference before the party congress scheduled for 1992 ("Li Peng, Others" 1991, 20).

(Rigby 1964). As in proxy fights in corporations, the struggle for power goes on concurrently with the struggles over policy. Policies, foreign and domestic, are major weapons in the pursuit of power (Brzezinski and Huntington 1964).[26] Incumbents and challengers construct policy "platforms" designed to build a winning coalition among the groups within the selectorate.[27] Which policies they espouse depends on their estimate of the relative influence of various groups within the selectorate and their sense of the political strengths and vulnerabilities of themselves and their rivals.

Power seekers shift emphasis among the positions in their policy portfolio to appeal to groups within the selectorate. In some instances, one of which was Zhao Ziyang's stance on enterprise finance reforms (analyzed in detail in chapters 12 and 13), contenders for power actually reverse their positions to appeal to different groups. When Zhao Ziyang first arrived from the provinces in Beijing to serve as premier, he promoted the tax method instead of profit contracting. Later, after he perceived his chances to succeed Deng to have been improved by Hu Yaobang's fall from favor, he changed his position to favor profit contracting in an effort to build national support among local officials and managers of large firms. Hu Yaobang's speech on the party's journalism work in 1985 was another example of a shift in policy position. At the time, Hu was under fire from elderly party conservatives for his speeches advocating "freedom of creation" and "freedom of the press"; he tried to defend himself by giving a speech emphasizing the party's control over the press (Lo Ping 1985; 1985a).

Taking a particular policy position can also enable a potential successor to go on the offensive against a rival. For example, by advocating stronger central control over the economy to solve the

26. According to Frederick Teiwes (1991), in the past the CCP chose its leaders more for their revolutionary status than for the policy positions they espoused. Nowadays, however, policy positions have become more important.
27. Members of the selectorate weigh the competence (Breslauer 1982) and integrity of leaders as well as their policy platforms. Doubts about Hu Yaobang's prudence and competence even among the reformers in the selectorate made it easier for the conservatives to defeat him in 1987. Questions about Li Peng's competence have continued to plague him even after he became premier. During 1988–89 Li Peng went on the offensive against Zhao Ziyang by blaming inflation, corruption, and the drop in grain production on Zhao's mismanagement of the economy during his tenure as premier (Li Peng 1989). The issue of official corruption has also emerged as a potent weapon in leadership competition in the post-Mao era.

problems of reduced grain production, inflation, and corruption in 1988–89, Li Peng discredited the economic management of his chief rival, Zhao Ziyang, and endeared himself to the central officials in the selectorate.

The strong link between policy and power in communist systems means that succession struggles create opportunities for policy innovation (Bunce 1981; Roeder 1985; Breslauer forthcoming; Dittmer 1990; Esherick and Perry 1983). These opportunities for innovation are welcome in communist systems, which as a rule can obtain consensus only with conservative policies that preserve every group's original share of the pie.

In a period of elite conflict over leadership succession, the political dependence of party leaders on the selectorate becomes more prevalent, and the ability of members of the selectorate to extract resources is enhanced. When the leadership is unified, the Central Committee can be counted on to simply ratify the leadership's decisions; but when leaders are competing with one another, the Central Committee becomes the arena for resolving policy disputes (P. Chang 1990, 184). Therefore, during a power struggle policymakers become more responsive to the demands or aspirations of subordinate officials because the support of these officials can significantly affect the outcome (Brzezinski and Huntington 1964). Leaders compete by giving, or promising to give, more resources and power to ministries and provinces. By contrast, when the party elite is unified, centralized control is reimposed.[28] In China, succession competition has up to now been mostly "premortem," not "postmortem," as it was in the Soviet Union (Dittmer 1990), so that campaign giveaways occur before the incumbent leader departs the scene.

The decade of reform in China coincided with a period of succession competition. During 1978–1980 Deng Xiaoping campaigned to supplant Hua Guofeng as Mao Zedong's successor. When Deng's authority as the preeminent leader was established in 1982, his advanced age meant that the party leaders just below him began immediately to plan for the next succession. Until 1986 CCP General Secretary Hu Yaobang was universally understood to be Deng Xiaoping's chosen successor. Hu and Premier Zhao Ziyang functioned

---

28. This pattern of higher-ups being more solicitous of subordinates during power struggles fits Avery Goldstein's (1991) analysis of the predominance of factional ties between leaders and subordinates during periods of "balance of power" politics.

as an effective duumvirate, working together on behalf of the reform drive (although they engaged in turf battles). As the presumed heir to the throne, Hu promoted reform policies that helped him consolidate his personal base of support in the provinces and industrial ministries, while Zhao promoted policies that helped build support for reform policies among conservative central bureaucratic interests. When Hu's position as successor began to slip after 1986, the succession competition intensified. Zhao Ziyang began to think like a serious contender for the top leadership role. He shifted his reform policy position to mobilize support for himself from the same groups who previously had supported Hu.

Carrying out economic reforms during a period of leadership succession meant that contending leaders used reform policies to extend new powers and resources to various groups within the selectorate. In addition, they adopted policies in the form of particularistic contracts to claim credit for their generosity to specific individuals and groups—in other words, to generate patronage. They recognized that they won more political support by granting ad hoc contracts to particular organizations and localities than by setting uniform rules. By the same logic, leaders were reluctant to enforce restrictions that hurt particular individuals or groups.[29]

My analysis of the way Chinese party leaders use the policy-making process to win political support from the selectorate does not allow us to determine which is more important in Chinese politics, clientalist politics or bureaucratic interest group politics. Scholars such as Andrew Walder (1986) and Jean Oi (1989) have shown that under communism the monopolistic authority of factory managers and village leaders to distribute career and livelihood benefits to workers and peasants reinforces traditional patterns of patron-client ties. Andrew Nathan (1973) and Lucian Pye (1981) have described the way these clientalistic ties are transformed into political factions as communist officials construct networks for political support. Other scholars (Lampton 1987; Lampton 1987a; Lieberthal and Oksenberg 1988; Hamrin 1990) recognize the existence of clientalism but see bureaucratic units that pursue their

29. The older and less oriented toward a future career a leader is, the weaker is his incentive to appeal to the selectorate. The higher the revolutionary status of a leader, the weaker is his incentive to offer policy promises to the selectorate. These two propositions provide at least a partial explanation for why most of the CCP elders advocate centralization remedies for economic problems, whereas the middle-aged generation of leaders promotes decentralization.

organizational interests as the basic building blocks of Chinese politics.

The notion of reciprocal accountability is compatible with both clientalist and bureaucratic models, which are themselves not mutually exclusive. During a succession struggle, communist party leaders try to build both types of political bases: a coalition of bureaucratic groups within the selectorate and a national clientalist network. The history of Chinese succession and reform politics in the 1980s suggests that politicians push policies that are attractive to key bureaucratic organizations as a group (for example, heavy industrial ministries or provincial governments), but they also advocate particularistic policy formulas over uniform ones because particularistic allocations translate into patronage to help them build and sustain a clientalistic support network. Particularistic policies enable the contenders for national office to claim credit (and personal loyalty) from particular ministry and provincial leaders for giving them special deals and their own patronage opportunities.

To summarize, power and policy are fused in communist polities such as China. There is no open competition for office, and the contest for power is hidden in the bureaucratic policy process. Top CCP leaders in China are chosen by an elite selectorate consisting of the Central Committee, the elders, the PLA leaders, and the preeminent leader. The Central Committee has the formal authority to choose leaders, but in fact, members of the Central Advisory Commission, Central Discipline Inspection Commission, and MAC who are not members of the Central Committee also participate. The relationship between the officials in the selectorate and top party leaders is one of "reciprocal accountability": each must satisfy the other to remain in office. Because party leaders are accountable to a selectorate consisting of bureaucratic officials, they have an incentive to appeal to these officials by offering policy benefits.

In a political system driven by reciprocal accountability between leaders and subordinate officials, the policy process takes a distinctive shape.

1.   Leaders promote policies that appeal to groups in the selectorate.

2.   Potential successors promote policies that conform with the preferences of the incumbent preeminent leader.

3.   Whenever the selectorate is redefined (say, by cutting out the elders or the military leaders not in the Central Committee), government policies will change as well.

4.   Because leaders are chosen by an elite selectorate, not a mass electorate, policy benefits are concentrated on officials instead of ordinary citizens.

5.   When the leadership is unified, the Central Committee normally ratifies the leadership's policy decisions. But when the leadership is divided by succession competition, the Central Committee may become the bargaining arena.

6.   During succession struggles, groups represented in the Central Committee are able to extract more resources than they can during periods when the leadership authority is consolidated and unified. Contending leaders promote policies that transfer authority and resources to groups in the selectorate and avoid policies that retract benefits.

7.   Contenders for power promote policy formulas based on selective allocation, which enable them to build a network of supporters, instead of policy formulas based on universal rules.

My analyses of reform policy-making show how the competition among CCP leaders for the support of the selectorate biased the process toward particularistic policies and against universalistic ones.

5   Bargaining Arena

The Government Bureaucracy

Policies are shaped by the bargaining arena within which they are deliberated. In China during the 1980s most industrial reform policies were hammered out in government meetings. Except for major statements on the overall direction of the market reforms, which were put together by the party Secretariat and approved by the party Central Committee, all industrial reform policies emerged from the government side.[1] The party set the general line and retained the authority to overrule government decisions, but it delegated to the bureaucracy the authority to make particular policies and administer the gigantic state-owned industrial economy. The story of the enterprise reform policy-making told in subsequent chapters of this book takes place almost entirely in government settings and reflects the bargaining among various government organizations with different interests and preferences.

The following three chapters deal with different aspects of the bureaucratic bargaining arena. This chapter describes the organizational structure of the government and the incentives operating on government officials. Chapter 6 considers which groups are represented around the bargaining table. And chapter 7 analyzes the rules by which the government makes policy decisions.

Organizational Structure: Hierarchy, Divisions,
and Coordination

To understand the bargaining process by which reform policies were made requires mapping the bureaucratic terrain. The national government bureaucracy is organized hierarchically. At the top are

1.   The reform document presented to the Third Plenum of the Twelfth Central Committee in October 1984 was actually drafted by a team representing both the State Council and the CCP Secretariat.

the premier, several vice premiers, the State Council, and the Standing Committee of the State Council. The State Council is the cabinet that has authority over all subordinate agencies and provincial governments. It consists of the premier, vice premiers, ministers and vice ministers of commissions and ministries, and a secretary-general, approximately one hundred members in all as of 1988. The Standing Committee of the State Council, which consists of the premier, two to four vice premiers, the secretary-general, and approximately ten state councillors, each supervising a broad area of government, usually meets about twice a week (Barnett 1985).

Directly under the State Council in the hierarchy are a number of comprehensive economic commissions: the State Planning Commission (SPC), the State Economic Commission (SEC), the Science and Technology Commission, the State Commission on Economic System Reform (*Tigaiwei*), and the Education Commission. The commissions have responsibility for the entire national economy; by contrast, ministries and provinces are responsible for particular sectors or regions. Commissions have formal authority over ministries and provinces, but not final authority (Yuan Baohua 1979; Oksenberg 1982). If a ministry or province is unhappy about an SEC ruling, for example, it can appeal directly to the State Council.

Below the commissions are the ministries. The approximately thirty ministries (the number changes with each bureaucratic reorganization) are organized by sector (e.g., agriculture, coal, machinery) or function (education, culture, public security). The economic sectoral ministries can be thought of as divisions in a huge conglomerate called "China, Incorporated" (although the divisions are weaker vis-à-vis the regional authorities than are their counterparts in "USSR, Incorporated").

The formal bureaucratic rank of an organization is extremely significant for the bargaining process and outcomes in China. Organizations of equal rank can sit down at the bargaining table as equals: ministries with provinces; bureaus (*ju*) with prefectures; and divisions (*chu*) with cities and counties.[2] An organization with

2. One aspect of policy-making that needs further clarification is the role of commissions when policies are bargained out. We know that commissions have higher rank and greater bureaucratic power than ministries do and that they act as administrative superiors to ministries and provinces when they are arbitrating interdepartmental conflicts and when they are engaged in vertical bargaining over routine plan and budget matters. But do they sit as equals with ministries and provinces at meetings negotiating policy packages?

higher rank may issue orders to a subordinate organization.[3] Leverage over the policy process depends directly on the formal rank of the organization.

It is no wonder that government officials care intensely about the official rank of their agencies. Assignment of rank to the national corporations created during the 1980s, such as the China National Petrochemical Corporation (SINOPEC), the China International Trust and Investment Corporation (CITIC), and the China National Offshore Oil Corporation (CNOOC), was hotly debated. The founders of the corporations wanted ministerial rank, whereas the already existing ministries wanted to subordinate the corporations to general bureau or bureau rank (Lieberthal and Oksenberg 1988). Some organizations have ambiguous rank; for example, the General Tax Bureau (GTB) was subordinate to the Ministry of Finance (MOF) at the national level and to the Finance Office at the provincial level, but it held equal rank to the Finance Bureau at the city level. Before an ambitious new tax policy could be implemented in 1983, the Tax Bureau demanded a rank promotion for itself at the provincial level. The Ministry of Finance objected. The compromise was to raise the provincial tax bureaus half a rank; they were still under the provincial finance offices, but they could issue decisions and documents on their own ("State Council Approves the Ministry of Finance Circular" 1982).

A particularly significant feature of Chinese government structure is that ministries and provinces hold equal administrative rank below the commissions (Lieberthal and Oksenberg 1988). When CCP leaders adopted their form of government administration from the Soviet Union in 1953, they altered it to enhance the power of geographic regions. In the USSR all-union ministries could issue orders to the republics. Chinese administrative structure reflects a greater degree of decentralization, even in the context of a unitary state. As the Chinese put it, the horizontal regional authority (*kuai,* "piece") is on a par with the vertical ministerial authority (*tiao,* "line"). This preference for a system that gives a stronger voice to local interests is a historical legacy: ministries and provinces were also assigned equal rank under the pre-1949 Republican government (Ch'ien Tuan-sheng 1961).

3. The Chinese distinguish between formal authority relations called "leadership relations" (*lingdao guanxi*) and administrative relations lacking formal authority called "professional relations" (*yewu guanxi;* Lieberthal and Oksenberg 1988).

Three high-level comprehensive organizations, the State Planning Commission, the Ministry of Finance, and the State Economic Commission (which was formally abolished and merged with the State Planning Commission in 1988), played particularly important roles in the saga of economic reform.[4]

The State Planning Commission formulates annual and five-year plans for capital construction investment, production, and material supply, balances output and material allocation figures, and sends down mandatory plan targets through the ministries and the provinces to the enterprises. Because it issues directives to the ministries and provinces, it is the most powerful institution in the Chinese economic system (Donnithorne 1967). The annual national planning conference, to which every ministry and province sends representatives, is an important forum for articulating group demands on economic policy (Lieberthal and Oksenberg 1988; author's interviews).[5]

The SPC's organizational ideology reflects its organizational function, which places the highest value on "balance" (*pingheng*) in the economy. Planners conceptualize economic balance as the provision of material supply and financial funds to match the demands of production and consumption. Balance also means no wide disparities among enterprises or regions. SPC bureaucrats believe that planning is the best way to achieve this balance; unplanned economic activity creates shortages and waste. They think that only the SPC, with its comprehensive view of the national economy, is competent to make investment and production decisions and that decentralization of decisions leads to inequality and chaos (author's interviews).

4. The State Commission on Economic System Reform (*Tigaiwei*) was responsible for drawing up draft proposals but played a less significant role in the bureaucratic politics of reform than did the SPC and SEC. The Reform Commission's basic function was to provide staff work on economic reform to Premier Zhao Ziyang. When commission officials presented proposals to Zhao, they laid out several policy options and discussed the strengths and weaknesses of each. They also made oral presentations to Zhao or Vice Premier Tian Jiyun describing which bureaucratic organizations favored which options and why (author's interviews).
5. Carol Lee Hamrin (1990) has described how planning cycles shape the policy-making agenda in Chinese politics. The reduced length of the meetings, from about one month in the prereform days to ten to fourteen days now, indicates that the planning meetings themselves have become a less important forum for economic decision-making because reforms have reduced the amount of economic activity under the domain of the central plan (author's interviews).

The Ministry of Finance, because of its comprehensive function, sometimes acts as a commission while holding the formal rank of ministry. Its responsibility to guarantee central revenue puts it in the conservative position of the chief defender of the central state. In its organizational ideology the MOF resembles the household head (*jiazhang*) who is always anxious about meeting his family's large and often unavoidable expenses with his limited income. Articles from MOF officials constantly express frustration about people's insatiable demands for funds and their lack of gratitude for what they have already received from the state (Xu Yi 1982). MOF officials are always worried that their revenues will not grow to cover their increasing expenses. Financial officials are "savers," whereas officials in industrial ministries and provincial governments generally are "spenders." On many occasions the MOF has stood in the way of reformist leaders who wanted to shift more resources and authority to enterprises or local governments. Reformist officials complained, "The MOF is shortsighted because it looks only at the accounts on a yearly basis. Spending more might increase state revenue in the long term." According to MOF officials, it is not that they oppose reform but only that they do not approve of "using money to buy reform" (*yong qian mai gaige*) from the lower levels (author's interviews). Although the MOF generally takes a skeptical attitude toward decentralizing reforms, it sometimes supports reforms that reduce its burden by shifting responsibilities, along with funds, to lower levels and that make the flow of central revenues more reliable, even if those same reforms shrink the central share.

The State Economic Commission was established in 1982 to implement the national plan and manage the economy (Zhang Jingfu 1982).[6] Its primary functions were coordination, dispatch, and improvement of enterprise management. The SEC also was in charge of many of the economic reform experiments in enterprises and localities. The SEC broke down the SPC's annual targets into monthly and quarterly targets and monitored the performance of ministries and provinces in meeting them; when there was a shortage in a key sector, such as steel, the SEC made adjustments.

6. The SEC was formed by merging the old Economic Commission (which had a much more limited jurisdiction), the Agricultural Commission, the Machinery Commission, the Energy Commission, the Finance and Trade Small Group, the Construction Commission, and a portion of the Science and Technology Commission.

Most of the work of the SEC involved coordination, or *xietiao*.[7] This term, constantly heard in the halls of Chinese government offices, has meanings that transcend the simple English definition of "coordination."[8] What Chinese officials mean by *xietiao* is bureaucratic conflict resolution, working out agreement among the conflicting positions of different organizations. Centrally planned economies generate countless disputes among enterprises, localities, and administrative bureaus that require resolution; in contrast, the sources of bureaucratic conflict in a capitalist economy, where the government is responsible for only taxation and regulation, are far fewer. To add to the burden, communist governments lack real judiciaries or legislatures that could share the responsibility for adjudication; in communist "mono-organizational" systems (Rigby 1980) the entire load of conflict resolution falls on the bureaucracy. The entity responsible for resolving most of these conflicts on the national level in China was the SEC.[9]

7. The Economic Reform Bureau of the SEC spends most of its time resolving disputes among subordinate units sparked by changes in the economic structure—for instance, the disputes between national ministries and the city of Wuhan over control of factories after Wuhan became an independent planning entity (author's interview).

8. When I interviewed in Taiwan, officials of the ruling Guomindang party said that most of their time was taken up with *xietiao* work among various government agencies and institutions. The political system of the Republic of China (Taiwan), which comprises five branches of government, has no centralized authority to resolve disputes, so the ruling party continues to play that role.

9. When the SEC was abolished in 1988, the *xietiao* burden on the State Council increased to unbearable proportions. The State Council tried to cope by creating in 1990 a new body at the commission level, the State Production Commission (*guojia shengchan weiyuanhui*), which included two former SEC bureaus, the Production Dispatch Bureau (*shengchan diaodu ju*) and the Enterprise Management Bureau (*qiye guanli ju*). Although the new body, like the old SEC, is at the same bureaucratic rank as the Planning Commission, its actual authority may have slipped a bit because its head is concurrently a *vice minister* of the Planning Commission (author's interviews). The Production Commission has replaced the SEC as the prime locus of national *xietiao* work. The Reform Commission's responsibility for resolving conflicts among agencies and regions regarding economic reform measures has also been enlarged ("State Council Circular" 1991). Because of the heavy burden of coordination work, only seven to eight provincial-level units have merged their economic commissions with their planning commissions; most of them, including the three provincial-level cities (Beijing, Tianjin, and Shanghai), retained their separate Economic Commissions (author's interviews). In 1991 central officials were speculating that the SEC would soon be revived (author's interviews).

The SEC strongly advocated reform policies promoting greater enterprise autonomy.[10] SEC officials explained that they supported reform because their work involved seeing the economy from the viewpoint of the enterprises themselves (author's interviews). The enthusiasm of the SEC for expanding managerial autonomy also resulted from a historical accident: the SEC was expanded and the State Commission on Economic System Reform created in 1982, the same year that the Machine Building Commission was dissolved and scaled back to a Machine Building Ministry. Many of the personnel, including the influential party elder Bo Yibo, who were released from the Machine Building Commission took up top staff positions in the SEC and the Reform Commission, where they pushed policies congenial to managers in machine building and other manufacturing industries (author's interviews).

The SEC's advocacy of greater enterprise autonomy often pitted it against other comprehensive bureaucracies. The SEC and the MOF often clashed over how much money should remain with the enterprises and how much should go to the state (author's interviews). The SPC and SEC quarreled over industrial investment priorities. The SPC was responsible for distributing capital construction funds, and the SEC was responsible for distributing technical renovation funds (a much smaller amount than the capital construction funds). The amount of money for technical renovation was supposed to be decided by consultations between them. Naturally, each commission argued that more funds should be allocated to its particular category. Because the SPC and SEC had trouble agreeing, the State Council had to step in. Some ministries and provinces tried to take advantage of the conflict by going to the SPC and calling their project capital construction and going to the SEC and calling it technical renovation (author's interviews).

Bureaucratic Incentives: Why Where You Stand Is Where You Sit

Chinese governmental institutions are structured to encourage expressions of departmental points of view. Of course, ministers and ministry officials are appointed by the CCP and cannot stray too far from the preferences of the party, but the party expects ministers to articulate the interests of their particular sector. When

10. Even before it was expanded in 1982, the SEC was identified as an advocate of reform ("Industrial Management" 1979).

ministers or vice ministers are called together to discuss a policy proposal, they are assumed to represent the perspectives of their ministries, and provincial officials are assumed to represent their provinces (author's interviews).[11] When officials speak in meetings, they always speak on behalf of their organizations, not as individuals (author's interviews).[12] The frequently heard Chinese colloquial version of the Western adage "Where you stand is where you sit" is "Where you squat is where you shit" (*pigu zuo zai na yi bian*; author's interviews).

The structure of the government bureaucracy affords virtual (i.e., nonelectoral) representation to economic groups. Industries promote their preferences not through interest groups that lobby from outside the bureaucracy but through the ministries themselves. Ministry officials represent the needs of their entire sector, including locally run factories as well as the factories run directly by the ministries (author's interviews). As one official said, "In their economic interests, the ministries and the enterprises stand on one line" (author's interview).

Even at the commission level, where interests are supposed to be aggregated, sectoral and regional perspectives are reinforced by the internal organization of commissions. SPC and SEC bureaus are divided by region and economic sector, so that the head of the energy bureau, for example, argues for resource allocations to the coal, petroleum, electricity, and nuclear power industries.[13] Within the State Council the degree of aggregation is greater. Each vice premier and state councillor is assigned responsibility for a set of sectors or functions, such as agriculture, energy industries, or finance, and is called the sector's or function's "channel" (*guikou*; author's interviews; Lieberthal and Oksenberg 1988). Although such divisions of responsibility encourage specialized expertise in policy-making, they also guarantee that sector- and region-based bargaining continue right up to the top of the government hierarchy (Chen Junsheng 1987).[14] The comprehensive agencies have their

11. The same is true of the Soviet Union; see Ellen Jones 1984.
12. The classic example cited by many interviewees was Bo Yibo, who always spoke on behalf of the machinery industry.
13. In 1984 SPC officials said they were planning to replace their sectoral divisions with divisions based on service functions such as information and technical renovation (author's interviews). As far as I know, this change has not been made.
14. Vice chairmen of provinces, cities, and counties are also assigned sectoral jurisdictions and are expected to press for more benefits for their

own organizational viewpoints as well: the SPC represents the macro-economy, the SEC represents the enterprises, and the MOF represents the central state (author's interviews).

The CCP has intentionally created bureaucratic career incentives designed to reinforce organizational allegiances. Officials rise up the career ladder within one ministry or province. Only the top elite are transferred from one province to another or from one ministerial portfolio to another (Hough and Fainsod 1979; Lieberthal and Oksenberg 1988). Most officials spend their entire careers in one organization, absorbing and serving the particular ideology of that organization. The vast majority of promotion decisions are made by party units within particular organizations, the party group in ministries and commissions, and the party committee in provinces and localities. Since 1984 the CCP Central Committee Organization Department has had direct responsibility for filling only five thousand positions (including both party and government posts) out of a total of more than eight million cadre positions. Even before 1984 the Central Committee controlled only 13,000 positions, compared with the 51,000 controlled by the Soviet Central Committee (Burns 1987).

Yet even those officials whose careers depend on the evaluations by the Central Committee do not act as if they believe that strong advocacy on behalf of their ministry or province is frowned on by the party center. All provinces have offices in Beijing. Provinces and even prefectures send high-level emissaries to Beijing to lobby on important issues (author's interviews; "Shaanxi Prefecture" 1985).[15] Although provincial secretaries or ministers are sometimes fired for not carrying out a policy that has already been promulgated, I am not aware of any punished since 1978 for excessive dedication to departmental interests. Officials in China and the Soviet Union feel no need to disguise their commitments to departmental objectives (author's interviews; Hough and Fainsod 1979). Naturally, they ar-

---

sectors. One county cited as an example in the press had one head and thirteen deputy heads: "At the official work meetings they attended the deputy county heads asked the county head for power, material resources, and manpower in the interest of the parts they represented, thus bothering the county head instead of helping him carry out his work" ("Forum Discusses Deng's Speech" 1987, K5).

15.   Provinces sometimes attempt to influence national policy by enlisting the assistance of Beijing officials of local origin ("Visitors of Hunan Origin" 1984).

gue departmental positions in terms of broad national interests, but the same is true of bureaucrats and politicians everywhere. Everyone in China, including party people, takes for granted that bureaucrats articulate departmental interests and perspectives. Therefore, in bargaining over economic policies, government officials believe that they can promote their own careers by promoting the interests of their ministries and provinces.

Bureaucrats undoubtedly feel freer to assert departmental points of view in meetings today than they did when Mao Zedong reigned. Under Mao, officials probably were more cautious because they feared becoming the target of an ideological campaign if they ended up on the wrong side of a policy dispute. Rectification campaigns to criticize the political thought and behavior of officials were frequent, and someone who was too outspoken ran the risk of becoming the object of criticism. Nowadays use of ideological weapons (what the Chinese call "using the big stick") is discouraged in the bureaucratic arena (Teiwes 1991). Although there are still ideological campaigns (e.g., to criticize spiritual pollution or bourgeois liberalization), they are directed primarily at intellectuals and largely kept out of economic policy issues.[16]

By giving ministries and provinces a new stake in the profitability of their subordinate enterprises, the economic reforms have intensified the motivation of officials to press for policies favorable to their enterprises. Ministries and provincial departments generally claim a few percentage points of the retained profits of the enterprises they manage directly as a "scientific research subsidy" (*keyen butie*), "reserve funds" (*jidong jijin*), or some other type of fund (author's interviews). Although these funds are reallocated by ministries and provincial departments to their enterprises (usually in a pattern of egalitarian redistribution, subsidizing the weaker firms by taxing the stronger ones; Walder 1986a), some of the money is converted to bonuses for ministry and department employees. In the mid-1980s the Ministry of Petroleum was famous in Beijing for the lavish bonuses its employees received (author's interviews). Even if officials do not profit directly from their enterprises, they push for policies giving more retained profits to those enterprises. As one ministry official explained, "Enterprises are like the children

16. Whenever these campaigns have spread into the economy and threatened the economic reforms, Deng Xiaoping has reined in the campaigns.

of the ministries. If the children have money and don't have to ask the parents for it, the parents are happy and there is less conflict within the family" (author's interview).

Given Chinese bureaucratic structure and incentives, it is hardly surprising that administrative departments constantly clash over policy issues. The Chinese press is filled with complaints about "departmentalism" ("Resolutely Stop Acts of Wrangling" 1983), "internal battles" ("Henan Governor Cheng Weigao" 1988), and "disputing over trifles" (Jilin Provincial Service 1983). Bureaucrats as a group are frequently condemned for "overemphasizing the rights and interests of their own departments and lacking a concept of overall interests in their speeches and work" ("It Is Necessary for All to Cling to the Goal of Reform" 1986, K11). Disputes at local levels between government agencies of equal rank can persist for years without resolution.[17]

Because policy issues run the constant risk of getting bogged down in interministerial squabbling, when the party leadership identifies a high-priority issue, it often creates an ad hoc office or leading group directly under the State Council to handle it. During the reform decade such ad hoc offices proliferated as party leaders sought to smooth the way for reform initiatives.[18] Although some of these offices, such as the Special Economic Zone Office, are under the direct leadership of the State Council and hold higher rank than ministries and provinces do, they face difficulties in implementing new policies because they have no binding authority over ministries and provinces (author's interviews).

17. One such conflict in Hubei Province between the Songyi Railway Administration and the Zhicheng Port Office lasted two years and three months, seriously disrupting rail transport and shipping; the Hubei government and party committee and even the party group of the SEC were scolded by the party for not stepping in to settle the conflict ("CCP Circular" 1983).

18. For one example, the San Xi (Three West) Areas Agricultural Construction Leading Group, see "State Council Discusses Gansu" 1983. Another temporary high-level organization was the Adjustment Office (*tiaojie bangongshi*) created in 1986 under chief Vice Premier Tian Jiyun. The Adjustment Office, based on a similar unit in Hungary, was a special dispatch office to get extra supplies and solve special problems related to the reforms, a sort of high-level SEC or Reform Commission. Sometimes it also organized coordination among the affected parties to launch new reform initiatives, for example, bringing together Guangdong Province and the State Council Special Economic Zone Office to arrange for the establishment of Hainan Province (author's interviews).

Bargaining over economic policies is vertical as well as horizontal. Vertical bargaining involves superiors and subordinates at various levels of the hierarchy, such as between commissions and ministries. Horizontal bargaining takes place between entities of equal rank, such as between ministries. Economic reform policies were hammered out in a process of horizontal bargaining, but vertical bargaining occurs over routine budgetary and planning allotments. Ministries and provinces plead with the SPC for lower output quotas and more investment funds. Although ministries and provinces are administrative subordinates, like all agents they can claim that they will not be able to perform their functions satisfactorily without more resources. Provinces, which have direct control over land and labor, often demand side payments from the center before they will cooperate in major public works projects within their jurisdiction (Lieberthal and Oksenberg 1988). As Andrew Janos notes about all communist systems, "The margin between minimum and optimum performance becomes a 'marketable surplus' or resource that can be withheld, surrendered, or negotiated (albeit discreetly) by intimating the consequences in Aesopian language. Frequently such bargaining involves references to the possible collapse of departmental morale, or difficulties in fulfilling a work project, without adequate budgetary allocations or favorable response to other departmental demands" (Janos 1976, 21).[19]

Evidence of pervasive bureaucratic politics is abundant in all communist countries. In China, Kenneth G. Lieberthal and Michel Oksenberg (1988), David Lampton (1987a), and my own research provide ample observations of a pluralistic process of bureaucratic bargaining after 1980; Roderick MacFarquhar (1974; 1983), Parris H. Chang (1970; 1990), Lieberthal and Bruce J. Dickson (1989), and David Bachman (1991) demonstrate a similar pattern during the Maoist era, although the party appears then to have been the locus of bargaining.[20] Even under Stalin in the Soviet Union, during 1945–53 when the command economy had reached its height, "the

19. This issue is also called the "incentive compatibility" problem.
20. A serious deficiency in our understanding of Chinese politics is the lack of a baseline with which to compare current political practices. Teiwes (1979; 1984), MacFarquhar (1974; 1983), Oksenberg (1971), and Bachman (1991) suggest that during Mao Zedong's reign the locus of economic policy-making was the CCP instead of the government. It would be valuable to confirm this conclusion with information from retrospective interviewing in China.

leadership could not enforce its most basic priorities of resource allocation due to the power the system effectively allowed to the production branch ministries. . . . the leadership always had to pay due attention to the interests of the implementors, be they regional or departmental. If it did not, its policies would not be carried out" (Dunmore 1980, 5, 94). Jerry F. Hough (1969) and Hough and Merle Fainsod (1979) are replete with examples of Soviet bureaucratic departmentalism from the post-Stalin era. Donna Bahry (1987) found that despite the USSR's high degree of centralization, republic officials were expected to assert local interests and were promoted for doing so.

Yet there is substantial scholarly disagreement about whether bureaucratic politics actually shapes policy outcomes, disagreement that reflects confusion about the nature of bureaucratic incentives under communism. Those who challenge the notion of "institutional pluralism" (Hough 1977) point to the dominant authority of the communist party over government resource allocation and career promotion. Some scholars go so far as to argue that in a communist regime the centralized control of the party over bureaucratic careers makes it impossible for government bureaucrats to articulate the particularistic interests of their units (Comisso 1986). Thane Gustafson's view is that government bureaucrats in communist systems "do not have power, but at most a sort of negative capacity for drag" (1981, 145). Brzezinski and Huntington (1964, 197) also emphasize that the economic or social power of bureaucratic or social groups is not an autonomous political resource but is "on loan from the center."

Critics of the notion of institutional pluralism are right to focus on the dependence of bureaucrats and their departments on the authority of the communist party. They have identified the institutional relationship at the core of communist politics: the party is the principal, and the government the agent. (As noted in the preceding section, there is also a reciprocal dimension to this relationship.) The careers of ministers, governors, and all officials under them are determined by party bodies at the same or higher levels. Government officials always look to the higher bodies of the government and party to anticipate their preferences. They do not want to push for a policy that is good for their agency but will be vetoed by their superiors. They know the way to achieve career success is to satisfy their masters.

But what these critics ignore is the nature of the delegation relationship between the communist party and the government in all communist systems. Party leaders have designed a system that encourages officials to advocate for their organizations, and the leaders believe that the party benefits from such a system. The structure of the government bureaucracy reflects the party's notion of which groups should have a voice in policy bargaining (see chapter 6). By delegating policy-making to government ministries and provinces, the party leaders devise policies acceptable to key economic groups. In most cases, party leaders do not have the information or time to determine which specific policy they prefer. Party leaders find out which policy they want by seeing if the group representatives whom they have allowed to sit around the bargaining table can agree on a policy (see chapter 7). Moreover, making policy by bureaucratic bargaining instead of by party fiat improves the odds that the officials responsible for implementing the policy actually support it, a particularly important consideration when it is a reform policy that involves a radical departure from the status quo.

Certainly Gustafson is right that most of what looks like bureaucratic politics "is in reality no more than the playing out of the leaders' own objectives"; as he says, bureaucratic power is delegated power and is not independent of the center (Gustafson 1981, 145).[21] The post-1989 slowdown in reform policy-making vividly demonstrates the proposition that the party can always retract its grant of decision-making authority from the government bureaucracy and try to run the economy from party headquarters. Yet what Gustafson fails to recognize is that there are real advantages to the party in delegating policy-making authority to the government bureaucracy and encouraging bureaucrats to act as departmental advocates.

Delegation to government agencies, moreover, presents few risks to party leaders. By configuring the bureaucracy, the party determines who gets to sit around the bargaining table. Party power over

21. Thane Gustafson (1981, 145–46) uses a feudal metaphor to conceptualize the monolithic nature of authority in Leninist systems: "There is no evidence that the bureaucratic resources delegated by the suzerains of the command state are appropriable by the vassals (and still less by their clerics), and therefore, unlike land or capital, delegated bureaucratic resources do not engender the basis for power independent of the center. In this sense it is still possible, more than twenty-five years after Stalin's death, to construct a plausible case for calling the Soviet system totalitarian."

bureaucratic careers guarantees that few officials will "cross the shadowy line between advocacy and pressure" (Brzezinski and Huntington 1964, 196) in promoting the interests of their agencies. Parallel rule means that party authorities participate from within the agency in setting agency policy positions. And party leadership bodies can always veto the policy that emerges from the government. No wonder party leaders do not expect any surprises from a policy process structured in this way.

To summarize, specific economic policies in China are made in a bureaucratic bargaining arena with the following structural characteristics: It is hierarchical, with the State Council having authority over the commissions, which in turn have authority over ministries and provinces. Formal administrative rank of organizations is important because it determines who can bargain with whom and who can give orders to whom. Ministries and provinces have equal administrative rank, and conflicts between them can be resolved only at the commission level or above. The government bureaucracy was structured by the CCP to encourage advocacy of agency positions and virtual representation for economic interests. There is no other arena in which economic groups can articulate and resolve their different interests. The career incentives of government officials, while making them dependent on the party, reinforce their commitments to their particular organizational interests.

What patterns of policy-making are characteristic of a government bureaucracy structured in this way?

1.   Officials press for policies that satisfy the interests of their own commission, ministry, or province.

2.   Policy-making is highly contentious. Conflicts between ministries and provinces are frequent and difficult to resolve.

3.   Decision-making is slow and inefficient, especially when policies that involve redistribution are being considered.

More specific statements about policy outcomes depend on who is enfranchised to participate in bureaucratic decision-making and what decision rules they use.

6 Who Is Enfranchised in the Policy-making Process?

The structure of the government bureaucracy reflects the communist party's notion of which group viewpoints should be represented in policy deliberations. Just as a ruling party in a democracy structures decision-making processes so that its most important constituents are well represented, so the leaders of communist parties structure decision-making processes so that the groups on whom they depend for support have a strong voice. The process of establishing a particular set of bureaucratic agencies and organizing collective choice so that individuals represent the preferences of their agencies enfranchises certain groups but not others. (It is striking, for example, that the national labor organization is represented in key economic meetings in Hungary but not in China; Comisso, personal communication.) In China the Ministry of Labor and All-China Federation of Trade Unions do not participate in high-level discussions of economic policy unless labor issues are the main focus of the discussions; otherwise, labor interests are aggregated with those of management at the level of the industrial ministry (author's interviews). It goes without saying that if a group is disenfranchised from the policy process, it is less likely to be satisfied with the policies that are chosen.

The founders of communist states created an institutional structure designed to produce the policy actions they preferred. If their policy preferences change, communist leaders are freer to restructure institutions than are democratic leaders bound to constitutions. Even in communist systems, however, institutional arrangements are "sticky" and constrain radical shifts in policy direction.

The Strong Voice of Industry

CCP leaders set up China's national economic bureaucracy in 1953 to reflect their developmental priorities, industry over agriculture and heavy industry over light industry. The extensive growth strategy adopted by the Chinese from the Soviet Union concentrated investment on the expansion of heavy industry. Chinese leaders established an administrative structure that would give heavy industry the strongest voice and thereby produce policies favoring heavy industry. Only a few ministries were concerned with agriculture, but there were approximately fifteen industrial ministries. Moreover, the bureaucratic structure favored heavy industry over light. A variety of light industrial sectors were combined under one Ministry of Light Industry; only textiles was separated out under its own ministry. Meanwhile, each heavy industry had its own bureaucratic voice in the ministries of chemicals, coal, petroleum, nuclear power, aviation, aeronautics, railways, communications, shipbuilding, electric power, machinery, electronics, and iron and steel. The clout of heavy industrial ministries was enhanced by their intimate ties to the PLA; all but one of the six (later eight) of the machine-building ministries produced military equipment and were administered by the PLA.

Once institutionalized in the configuration of ministries, the pro-heavy-industry bias was perpetuated.[1] The most able cadres from the provinces were recruited into the heavy industrial ministries (author's interviews). From the 1950s on it was recognized that the leaders of the heavy industrial bureaucracies were of superior caliber; many of them were promoted to the top ranks of government and party leadership. In addition, the workers and managers in heavy industry were more numerous (68 percent of the Chinese work force in 1983; *Statistical Yearbook* 1983, 128), were paid more than those in light industry, and had higher status and political influence.[2] The managers of several large heavy industrial plants

1. Mao Zedong considered himself, and the CCP as an institution, the representatives of agriculture and the peasantry. Yet Mao and his party allies established a political and economic structure that consistently favored industry; and even when Mao periodically shifted the policy-making arena from the government bureaucracy to party or mass campaign settings, the interests of agriculture received short shrift. The answer to the paradox of urban bias in a revolutionary regime with a rural base awaits future research on how group interests were represented and bargained out within the CCP, particularly during the formative years of the PRC in the 1950s.
2. In comparing the prestige of the heavy and light industrial work forces, it is noteworthy that light industry is feminized; that is, a large percentage of its employees are women (see *Statistical Yearbook* 1983, 141). Feminized sectors generally have lower social and political status.

(e.g., Anshan, Wuhan, and Capital Iron and Steel Companies) had cadre ranks as high as provincial governors. Heavy industrial ministries ran many of their enterprises directly from Beijing, whereas light industrial and textile factories were locally managed, and farms were collectively owned and managed. Without enterprises directly under their control, officials in the ministries of light industry, textiles, and agriculture were considered political lightweights (author's interviews). Like the Soviet Union, China unbalanced the policy process by making heavy industrial elites far stronger in numbers, talent, and power than other economic elites (Hough 1977).[3]

China's public finance system reinforced the pro-industry bias by creating a "rich industry, poor agriculture" system. Agricultural products and raw materials were assigned low prices, and manufactured goods were assigned high prices. Cheap inputs and expensive products added up to high profits for manufacturing industries. The lion's share of state revenues came from the profits of manufacturing enterprises.[4] This kind of fiscal system institutionalized the dependence of the central state on the financial health of industry. Any attempt to raise the prices of agricultural products or reduce the prices of manufactured goods naturally met the opposition of the MOF. (Changing the pattern of urban bias in Chinese policy-making would require transforming the state's revenue base.)

The system of planning by material balances also placed in a powerful position the heavy industrial sectors that produced materials and equipment for many other parts of the economy. The scale of the planning process forced central planners, who had too many items to handle, to identify some products as priorities (Lyons 1990).[5] Because both the military and much of the economy depended on supplies of coal, steel, chemicals, and machinery, these

3. The disparity in political influence of heavy and light industrial ministries in China parallels the Soviet disparity between all-union ministries (most of which were in heavy industry), which directly managed their own enterprises, and union-republic ministries, which managed enterprises through the republics.

4. Industry's contribution to total state revenues increased from 30 percent in 1950 to 50 percent in 1957, 73 percent in 1965, 77 percent in 1975, 83 percent in 1980, and 86 percent in 1983; Ministry of Finance, *Chinese Financial Statistics* 1989, cited in Wong 1990 (table 3).

5. For a critique of the Chinese planning process for beginning from steel and other key industrial products instead of from the manufactured end products, see *Jingji yanjiu,* 9 July 1979, 1–2.

priority industries were able to extort more resources when bargaining over output quotas and investment allocations with the SPC. And because the central plan never controlled all industrial production, the heavy industrial ministries also had leverage over other ministries that needed their cooperation to provide inputs in short supply directly to them (Dunmore 1980).

The privileged bureaucratic position of heavy industry and weak position of agriculture were reflected in the allocation of resources. During the period 1953–80, 54 percent of total in-plan capital construction investment went to industry; light industry received 6 percent, and heavy industry 48 percent (*Statistical Yearbook* 1989, 487).[6] Meanwhile, agriculture limped along with only 10.6 percent. As part of the rural economic reforms, the government in 1979 promised to increase state investment in agriculture ("Decisions on Some Questions" 1979), but instead it actually cut agricultural investment to 5.1 percent during 1981–85 and to only 3.0 percent in 1986, 3.1 percent in 1987, and 3.0 percent in 1988 (*Statistical Yearbook* 1989, 487). In a system that gave agriculture only a feeble bureaucratic voice and lacked elections, China's 800 million rural dwellers remained a disenfranchised majority.[7] Despite the CCP's ideology of rural populism, urban bias was built into Chinese political institutions and reflected in policy outcomes.

Bureaucratic Reorganizations

The frequent bureaucratic reorganizations since the 1950s were efforts by Chinese leaders to change the structure of interest articulation and aggregation as well as to improve efficiency. Whenever ministries are merged or divided, raised to commission level, or demoted to bureau level, the voices of various sectors are strengthened or weakened. When a sector or function is losing out in ministry- or province-level bargaining, one ploy is to transform the ministry to a commission. The elevation of education from ministry to commission status in 1987, for example, was designed to give education more clout in the competition for government resources in addition to enhancing coordination of educational activities under different ministries.

6. During the period 1952–78 the amount of capital construction funds received by the Chinese iron and steel industry was 4.83 times that received by light industry and 5.4 times that received by textiles (Zhao Chunxin 1981).
7. Just as Robert Bates's work on Africa would predict (Bates 1983).

Mergers of ministries sometimes are designed to force sectors that constantly burden the SEC or State Council with their unresolved disputes to work them out at the ministry level instead. One consequence of ministerial merger, of course, is a loss of bargaining power for each component in the merger; this complaint was heard from the Ministries of Water Resources and Electric Power when the two were merged first in 1958 and again in 1982. The objections of the Ministries of Railways and Communications and the Civil Aviation Administration prevented their proposed merger into a Ministry of Transportation in 1988 ("NPC Presidium Holds Fourth Meeting" 1988). When the Ministry of Urban and Rural Construction and Environmental Protection was abolished in 1988, some officials worried that the consequences would be a neglect of environmental protection; they were reassured that the Environmental Protection Bureau previously under the ministry would be elevated to become an independent bureau directly under the State Council ("NPC Presidium Holds Fourth Meeting April 5" 1988).

One particularly significant merger was the 1988 takeover of the SEC by the SPC to form a supersized State Planning Commission (*Xinhua*, 9 April 1988). This reorganization, which occurred when Premier Li Peng was hitting hard at Zhao Ziyang's reforms, was no doubt partially motivated by the conservatives' desire to throttle the reformist entrepreneurship of the SEC. The SEC had led the effort to expand enterprise autonomy since 1979, whereas the SPC had defended the authority of the plan. When the SEC ceased to exist and became only a set of bureaus under the SPC (some of the SEC bureaus also were transferred to the Reform Commission and, in 1990, to a new organ called the Production Commission), the reforms lost their highest-ranking bureaucratic advocate.

Policy Work Conferences: Enfranchising Provinces in the Policy-making Process

It is worth highlighting the obvious fact that communist government bureaucracies are organized by sector and function, not by territory, as legislatures are. Under the system transferred to China from the Soviet Union, the members of the State Council are heads of ministries and commissions, not the heads of provinces. Although provinces can petition the State Council on matters of particular concern, in routine governmental policy-making and implementation, territorial perspectives are expressed only through the regional bureaus of the commissions. Provinces and large cities have offices in Beijing, but these offices do little lobbying (author's interviews).[8] Although provinces send delegations to annual planning, budget, and other meetings and can directly petition the State Council, they do not have permanent formal membership in the bureaucratic arena.[9] Their representation in the National People's Congress (NPC), a body that is only slowly beginning to exercise policy initiative, does not yet compensate for their lack of formal representation in the bureaucratic arena where most economic policies are made.

The disenfranchisement of provinces in State Council policy-making is an institutional anomaly in China, where provinces play a powerful role within the CCP and where there is a considerable degree of de facto delegation of authority and resources to the provinces.[10] The lack of provincial representation was a problem for the reformist leaders of the CCP, who sought to use provincial officials as a political counterweight to the central bureaucracy. How were the vested interests in the status quo of the central commissions and ministries to be balanced if the provinces did not sit at the bargaining table?

The solution was to expand the bureaucratic bargaining arena by increasing the frequency of economic policy work conferences to which provincial representatives were invited. The practice of holding work conferences bringing together provincial and central officials began in the 1950s and 1960s under Mao Zedong (Lieberthal and Dickson 1989; P. Chang 1970).[11] Party central work conferences usually were scheduled before the formal meetings of the Central Committee and were also held during the summer, when officials met at the seaside resort of Beidaihe. In addition to these large party central work conferences, at which important policy issues

8. As an SPC official explained, the heads of the provincial representative offices were of too low bureaucratic status (section [*chu*] heads) to contact a high-level body such as the SPC. Provinces sent vice governors or heads of provincial planning commissions to lobby the SPC in Beijing (author's interview).

9. In the Soviet Union the heads of the republics are ex officio members of the Council of Ministers, reflecting the federal structure of the USSR. Chinese provinces are not represented in the State Council.

10. One Chinese official observed, "The localities are strong in the party, and the ministries are strong in the government" (author's interview).

11. Parris Chang (1970) asserts that work conferences became important only after 1960, but Kenneth G. Lieberthal and Bruce J. Dickson (1989) show that this trend began in the 1950s.

were discussed, the party and government held a variety of conferences focused on particular policy areas (e.g., agriculture, finance, industry), including telephone conferences among provincial officials (using the primitive telecommunications technology of 1950s and 1960s China).

Although policy work conferences are not a new practice, in the 1980s they became the main arena for bargaining out economic reform policies. The formulation and implementation of economic policies are based on extensive consultation with all concerned groups, including technical think tanks, central agencies, and provincial governments. Each new reform policy was discussed at a series of national work conferences, which gave provincial officials as well as central officials an opportunity to sit around the bargaining table. These work conferences were not pro forma consultations; real bargaining took place and policies were revised or abandoned. By expanding the decision-making arena, reformist leaders enfranchised provinces, got around the vested interests of central bureaucratic organizations, and gave economic reforms a fighting chance.

The widening of bureaucratic consultation was a matter of principle to Deng Xiaoping. Deng, in his important 1980 speech "On the Reform of the System of Party and State Leadership," argued that the overconcentration of power in the hands of a few individuals in the party had produced the Great Leap Forward, the Cultural Revolution, and other excesses of Mao Zedong's rule (Deng Xiaoping 1980). He urged that more groups be consulted in decision-making to prevent overconcentration. Therefore, every reform policy was debated in a series of meetings to which a large number of agencies, both local and central, and technical experts were invited.[12]

The work conference has some special characteristics as a bargaining arena. First, a variety of organizations can organize a policy conference or meeting; by contrast, the meetings of permanent organizations can be called only by the formal heads of the organi-

12. "An examination of the policy-making process in the post-1978 period does reveal a more elaborate procedure involving the review of future policies by many qualified officials in different functional areas, and thereby presumably forestalling the kind of off-the-cuff decision making by a single autocrat that apparently led to the formation of the People's Communes" (Dittmer 1984, 366).

zations. By calling national meetings, organizations such as the State Commission on Economic System Reform or the SEC could act as political entrepreneurs promoting the cause of industrial reform.

Second, the set of participants in any of these conferences is not formally laid down, giving much latitude to the officials who call them. As noted in chapter 3, this flexibility extends even to participation in the meetings of formal party bodies such as the Politburo and Central Committee. In the past as well as today, meetings of these party leadership bodies are often "enlarged" to include non-member participants whom the leaders want to attend, no doubt to pack the meetings with political allies. As Lieberthal and Dickson note, the Chinese meeting system never was "closely constrained by organizational boundaries and formal rules" (Lieberthal and Dickson 1989, xxxviii).

Finally, policy work conferences, while allowing provinces to join central ministries at the bargaining table, give provinces equal formal representation despite obvious disparities in their populations, wealth, level of industrialization, and so on. A representation formula that invites to a meeting, say, one official from Sichuan and one from Qinghai, even though Sichuan is the equal of more than twenty Qinghais in population and industrial output, obviously disadvantages Sichuan.[13] As a result, although work conferences strengthen the voice of provinces vis-à-vis the central bureaucracy, they may favor the less populous, backward provinces over the more populous, developed ones.[14]

To summarize, the structure of the Chinese government bureaucracy enfranchises some groups but not others; among the disenfranchised groups are labor and women. The number and formal

13. This paragraph is highly speculative. I do not have information on the actual size of provincial delegations to policy work conferences or on whether or not these conferences make decisions by voting. And, as Michel Oksenberg pointed out to me (personal communication), the relative influence of provinces at meetings depends on the seniority and party rank of their representatives as well as the number of representatives.

14. As provinces acquire more de facto control over resources, the most economically dynamic provinces are likely to cease to be satisfied with this kind of nonrepresentative, noninstitutionalized participation in policy-making and press for a stronger, permanent voice at the center. One approach would be to demand a strengthening of the national legislature, the National People's Congress; another, less probable approach would be to shift economic policy-making from the State Council, where provinces are not represented, back to the CCP Central Committee, where they are the largest bloc of votes.

rank of bureaucratic agencies assigned to various sectors (as well as their institutional ties to the military and the central state's degree of financial dependence on them) give them more or less influence in the policy process. By this principle, Chinese industry has more clout than agriculture, and within industry, heavy industry has more clout than light industry. Although sectoral interests are represented at the State Council through ministries, regional interests are not. To enfranchise provinces and bring regional interests to bear in the policy process, party leaders rely on work conferences.

What kind of policy-making characterizes a bargaining arena with this pattern of group enfranchisement?

1. Policies hammered out without the participation of certain groups do not incorporate the preferences of these groups. (No wonder Chinese economic reform policies do not include protections for the rights of women or labor.)[15]

2. Underrepresented sectors (such as agriculture) receive a relatively small share of resources, while overrepresented sectors (such as heavy industry) receive the lion's share.

3. If the bureaucratic configuration remains the same, then the shares of resources will also remain the same.

4. Bureaucratic reorganizations will change the pattern of resource allocation.

5. Policy innovations occur when bureaucratic reorganizations enfranchise or strengthen the representation of new groups and disenfranchise or weaken the representation of groups favored by previous policies.

6. Party authorities can also achieve policy innovations by shifting policy-making to a different arena (e.g., work conferences, legislatures, party bodies) or, more rarely, by imposing the innovations over the heads of the bureaucracy.

As I argue in subsequent chapters, economic reforms in China were strongly influenced by the powerful voices of heavy industry and provincial officials.

15. In fact, policies encouraging enterprises to maximize profits without stipulations to protect fair employment practices have caused managers to hire fewer women because the managers do not want to provide expensive maternity leaves or day-care facilities. And after an initial flirtation with the idea of Yugoslav-style worker self-management in 1978–80, bureaucratic policymakers dropped the idea, and all subsequent reform policies were aimed at strong managerial control of enterprises.

7 Decision Rules

Delegation by Consensus

The Chinese government makes policy according to a decision rule of "delegation by consensus."[1] The CCP delegates to the State Council the authority to make specific economic decisions. The State Council leaders at the top of the bureaucratic hierarchy delegate to their subordinates the authority to make decisions *if* the agents can agree. If the agents reach consensus, the decision is automatically ratified by the higher level; if the agents cannot agree, then the authorities step in to make the decision, or the matter is dropped or tabled until consensus can be achieved. Delegation by consensus is practiced at each level of the organizational hierarchy, State Council to commissions, commissions to ministries and provinces, ministries and provinces to bureaus and cities, and so on.

The Logic of Delegation by Consensus in Bureaucracies

The rule of delegation by consensus—"If the agents agree, let it be"—is followed by most hierarchical organizations, including business corporations and political systems.[2] Delegation of consensually

---

1. This decision rule is identical to what management specialists call "management by exception" (Lawler 1976).
2. Parliamentary systems such as those of Japan or France may appear to be dominated by their bureaucracies, but they are actually ruled by parliamentary party majorities who have effectively used delegation by consensus to allow their bureaucratic agents to work out policy packages. If the politician principals seem invisible and rarely intervene to overrule a bureaucratic decision, it is because they have structured the bargaining game to produce outcomes satisfactory to them and to their most influential constituencies. The rare exception to delegation by consensus is the American political system. Bureaucratic agencies make their recommendations directly to the president or Congress, and the locus of bargaining is the congressional committee, not the bureaucracy. The reason for this difference between presidential and parliamentary systems is the separation of

exercised power is so widespread in hierarchical settings that it could be called "the bureaucratic method." From the standpoint of the principals, delegation by consensus offers many advantages. As noted earlier, delegation of policy choice to bureaucratic agents exploits the superior information of these agents and relieves the principals of the costs of constant intervention in the policy process. And it gives all the agents who will implement a policy a voice in its formulation.

The risks of delegation by consensus are minimal because the bureaucratic authorities, and ultimately the political authorities (in China, the CCP leaders), can veto any policy they oppose. (Overrulings are rare, however, because in pure hierarchies leaders are loath to lose the advantages of delegation, and in systems of reciprocal accountability, such as communist states, leaders do not want to alienate their bureaucratic constituents.)[3] Because the political authorities have set up the government bureaucracy to represent the groups of officials on whom they depend for political support, policy decisions made by the bureaucracy are likely to be acceptable to these groups and therefore to the political authorities. The consensus rule, which guarantees that the leaders will find out if any group is unhappy with a policy, is a kind of "fire alarm" (McCubbins and Schwartz 1984): a veto by an agent sets off a bell to let the leaders know that one of their core groups is not satisfied.

---

powers characteristic of presidential systems. Congress and the president, as dual principals, share authority over the bureaucracy; Congress is reluctant to shift the decision-making process to the bureaucracy for fear that the president might strengthen his influence over policy (Kiewiet and McCubbins 1991). In parliamentary systems, and in the Chinese communist system at the present, the ruling party has no rivals for control of the bureaucracy and therefore can delegate to it decision-making authority. We may speculate that if the National People's Congress someday becomes a genuine legislature exercising authority over the bureaucracy, the party might retract its generous grant of authority to the bureaucracy, unless the party is able to dominate the NPC like a ruling parliamentary party in a democracy.

3. If the central government faces an emergency situation, it may impose a decision on a recalcitrant bureaucracy. One example cited in an interview dealt with a foreign financial obligation. In 1979 the State Commission on Economic System Reform proposed a special tax on petroleum to encourage its conservation. The Ministry of Petroleum objected, and the State Council did nothing. Several years later, however, the government had a long-term contract to supply petroleum to Japan that had to be met; in 1982 the State Council imposed the tax after repeated "consultations" (*shangliang*) with the Petroleum Ministry (author's interviews).

Delegation by consensus also provides information at an early stage of the process about each group's "price" of support for the policy. When China's State Council calls work conferences to let ministries, commissions, and provinces work out a new policy, the leaders as well as the bureaucratic advocates of the policy learn early on each group's "price" of support for the policy and can estimate whether it will be possible to meet the sum of all these "prices" through compromise and side payments. (In a choice situation requiring consensus, we would expect the "prices" to be higher than they are in a situation decided by majority rule.)

The Chinese government has been making economic policies according to delegation by consensus at least since the early 1980s,[4] as research by Kenneth G. Lieberthal and Michel Oksenberg (1988) and by David M. Lampton (1987a) has shown.[5] The difficulty of overcoming minority vetoes has been noted by numerous Chinese observers. The secretary-general of the State Council complained, "Many problems remain unsolved for a long time simply because of the objection from a minority. . . . Too many people exercise veto in our public organs" (Chen Junsheng 1987, K33). A *Liaowang* commentator complained about the same phenomenon: "Even if the majority of departments agree on a matter, it cannot be implemented because of unreasonable objections from a certain department or leader. Consequently, the problem is perpetuated. In this way, the so-called right of veto is exercised" ("On 'Wrangles,'" 1986, K17).[6]

Achieving bureaucratic consensus on economic policy in a country such as China can be a long, tortuous process. Ministries and

4. We have some information about bureaucratic pluralism during the Maoist era, but no information about the choice rules by which government meetings and bodies made decisions.
5. Ellen Jones (1984) describes consensus decision-making in the Soviet Union.
6. Although we know that during the last decade the Chinese government chose economic policies by consensus, not by majority rule, we don't have a formal definition of consensus. It is unlikely that consensus requires strict unanimity. Some agencies may be able to exercise a blocking veto whereas others cannot. Agencies that generate revenues, have control over a large number of enterprises, and have ties to top party leaders have more clout than do agencies without these resources. If everyone knows that an agency is weak and that its position will not be sustained by the upper level, it will be unable to block the measure or force a compromise when a stronger agency could succeed in doing so. More case studies of policy-making are needed before we can speak with any certainty about the differential ability of agencies to veto measures under delegation by consensus in China.

provinces have a say even when the policy issues are not relevant to their particular jurisdiction. And bureaucratic choice, like legislative choice, runs up against the Arrow's Paradox problem of intransitivity of social choice: groups are unable to make up their mind because every time one option is adopted, it can be quickly replaced by another (Schwartz 1987; Hammond and Miller 1985).[7] (Legislatures solve the cycling problem by the use of institutional innovations such as committees [Shepsle 1979] or implicit contracts agreeing not to reconsider issues already decided by the group [Schwartz 1988].) Bureaucracies usually cope by shifting attention from one activity to another over time (different departments care about different activities; Cyert and March 1963) or by selecting and socializing their members so that fragmentation is overcome by commitment to the organizational ideology. Communist systems appear to rely heavily on inculcating ideological commitment (Harding 1981).

Decisions such as the national plan or national budget are brought to closure relatively easily because the sequence of decision gates is well institutionalized and must meet definite deadlines. Other types of decisions can be kicked around at lower levels for years without being resolved. If the upper-level leaders do not know what position they want to take on the issue or do not want to bear the costs of imposing a decision on a divided bureaucracy, the issue can wander indefinitely in bureaucratic purgatory. With a change in leadership or objective circumstances, it can be revived.[8]

Some observers might say that the process of bureaucratic deliberation is cumbersome and costly for a political leadership in a hurry to put economic reforms in place. Others might argue that

7. The Arrow Paradox describes legislative decision-making by majority rule under conditions of nondictatorship. Communist bureaucracies make decisions by consensus and party leaders may act as dictators. Therefore, cycling is not as pervasive a problem in communist systems as it is in democratic ones. Empirically, cycling is a problem, albeit a less pervasive one, in communist systems. Theoretically, I am aware of no models of cycling under consensus rules.
8. An infamous example is the massive Three Gorges Dam on the Yangtze River in Hubei Province, which has been debated within the bureaucracy since the 1950s (Lampton 1987a; Lieberthal and Oksenberg 1988). The project was very "lumpy," and there were no side payments large enough to compensate the groups who would bear its social and economic costs. Long-time observers of the controversy were surprised to hear in early 1990 that conservative leaders such as Li Peng, having strengthened their control of the CCP, were breathing new life into the project.

delegation by consensus is merely a smoke screen for top-down authoritarianism: if even one official knows the leaders' preferred outcome, then that outcome can win approval by consensus.

The answer to both objections is that bureaucratic authorities usually lack the information to know what specific policies they prefer; the same is even more true for the political authorities. The authorities certainly know the general direction they want policies to take—in the Chinese case, in the direction of reforms that improve economic performance—but they have few definite ideas about how to achieve this goal. Having made sure that the right agencies are represented around the bargaining table, they rely on these agencies to work out a specific policy. In other words, the authorities derive their preferences from the policy consensus of their agents.

By contrast, whenever the authorities know exactly what they want and can agree on it, lower-level bureaucrats want to give it to them. If the leaders' preferences are unified and clear, they provide a focal point for bureaucratic consensus. In most bureaucratic settings, however, including China, the people at the top only rarely send a clear, unified signal about their specific policy preferences.

Even when such a clear signal from the authorities is absent, hierarchical control contributes to coordination of bureaucratic policy choice by giving agents an incentive to resolve their differences and come to agreement. Chinese ministry and province officials are not just the representatives of their agencies; they are also employees of the State Council and CCP. Every agency representative must decide whether to agree to a lower-level decision that does not entirely satisfy agency preferences or to hold out and force the intervention of the higher levels. To make this decision, the agency representative seeks information about the preferences of the higher-level leaders to anticipate their decision.[9] Unless the agency representative has reason to believe that the higher levels would make a decision more favorable to the agency's interests, the representative will compromise to reach agreement at the lower level. After all, a bureaucrat who consistently refuses to compromise certainly will not be popular with upper-level leaders and may be punished by

9. This type of information is often obtained through personal connections (*guanxi*) with higher-level leaders. One of the greatest values of clientalist ties to the client and to the patron is information about the preferences and likely outcomes at the other end of the bureaucratic ladder.

nonpromotion or demotion.[10] Therefore, in most circumstances an agency will settle for a less-than-optimal decision at the lower level instead of gambling on a better decision at a higher level.[11]

When Delegation by Consensus Breaks Down: Escalation of Coordination

From the standpoint of the principal, delegation by consensus works well when it allows key groups to articulate their interests but creates incentives for them to compromise their differences without forcing the principal to intervene. By this standard, Chinese delegation by consensus has not worked well during the 1980s. From the perspective of the top leaders of the government (articulated by Chen Junsheng, then secretary-general of the State Council), the work of the government has been impeded by constant arguing and "the escalation of coordination [*xietiao*]." Problems that once were solved at lower levels are now being pushed up to the State Council (Chen Junsheng 1987, K33). The Standing Committee of the State Council spends much of its twice-weekly meetings resolving interministerial differences over relatively minor issues (author's interviews).

After the SEC was merged with the SPC in 1988, the SPC gained in power but failed to perform the coordination function effectively; that burden fell directly on the State Council, "increasing the pressure of work on the State Council and leaving the differences of opinion unsettled for a long time because of a lack of coordination" ("State Economic Commission May Be Restored" 1989, 31). In the early 1980s the SEC had held primary responsibility for resolving conflicts among ministries and provinces. As Chen Junsheng explained, "When a solution to a certain issue is impossible through the negotiation of departments, coordination by a comprehensive commission is necessary" (Chen Junsheng 1987, K38).

10. There is no evidence that uncooperative behavior is punished by cutting an agency's budget, which is the case in democracies run by delegation by consensus.
11. Agencies that frequently had dealings with one another also found it easy to reach agreement on disputes. For example, whenever the Ministry of Water Conservancy and Electric Power (MWCEP) and the Ministry of Machine Building (MMB) clashed over the MMB's protectionist stance toward imports of equipment—the MWCEP wanted to import the equipment, but the MMB wanted it to use its domestically produced equipment—they easily resolved it because the MWCEP was the MMB's "old customer" (author's interviews).

Even before the SEC was abolished, the decision-making machine appeared to be breaking down. Controversies festered for years without resolution as agencies dug in their heels and refused to compromise. Reaching agreement required "a process of repeated negotiation, in which all parties concerned may argue, each holding its ground" (Chen Junsheng 1987, K34). Policy decisions were not permanent because a leader who did not like the outcome of one work meeting could call for another with a different set of participants. Sometimes agencies rejected the judgment of the SEC, holding out for better terms. In one infamous case, the Ministry of Light Industry (MLI) and the Ministry of Machine Building (MMB) waged war for five years over which one of them would be authorized to produce refrigerators and washing machines, which had become very lucrative consumer items. The SEC thought it had worked out a compromise whereby the MLI would assume responsibility for overall management of household electrical appliances, with the MMB having the right to produce some of the more sophisticated models. The MMB refused to accept the outcome; it insisted that the SPC rather than the MLI be put in charge and argued that otherwise the MLI officials would put unfair restrictions on the output, export, and technology imports of their competitors ("Breaking with Departmental Bias" 1984; author's interviews). Chinese officials I interviewed related many interministry disputes that the SEC had difficulty resolving, such as the fight between the Material Supply Bureau and the MLI over who would be granted the right to sell scrap metal; between the Ministry of Chemicals and the MLI over the right to import the equipment to manufacture light-sensitive paper; among the MLI, the Ministry of Electronics, and one of the military industry ministries over the right to manufacture electronic watches; and among the Ministries of Commerce, Textiles, and Light Industry over garment manufacturing (author's interviews). Some of these disputes were deadlocked at the SEC level and finally had to be settled by the Finance and Economics Leadership Small Group or the Standing Committee of the State Council.[12]

When an agency was dissatisfied with the ruling of the upper level, it sometimes argued for a special exception or just refused to obey ("On 'Wrangles'" 1986).[13] Sometimes upper-level departments

12. As Chinese industry becomes more competitive, these disputes over monopoly manufacturing and trade rights should diminish.
13. Another option was to appeal to the Presidium of the National Peo-

in conflict mobilized their subordinates to resist, creating bureaucratic feuds that meant that "none of the decisions are put into effect in the end" (Chen Junsheng 1987, K34). Economic reform policies were plagued by the problem of bureaucratic noncompliance. As one reform economist described the problem,

> At present, reform measures are mainly worked out and decided by administrative departments. The administrative officials have rich administrative experience, but their experience has limitations. It is difficult for them to free themselves from being bound by departmental or local interests. So they reach compromises through bargaining and then each one still goes his own way. (Luo Liewen and Ruan Jiangning 1989, 2)

Why was delegation by consensus in China working poorly during the 1980s? The most important reason is that divisions within the party leadership encouraged intransigence among subordinates. When the party leadership was unified and committed to a policy, it was easy for it to win bureaucratic consensus on the policy. Conflicts among principals, however, increased uncertainty for agents and led them to hold out instead of give in, gambling on a higher-level resolution of the issue.

For most of the past decade bureaucrats have perceived the CCP leaders as divided. By 1981–82 the conflicts between the two most influential elders, Deng Xiaoping and Chen Yun, were readily apparent. Party Secretary Hu Yaobang and Premier Zhao Ziyang, although allies in the drive for economic reform, were in competition to succeed Deng Xiaoping and advocated different approaches to industrial reform. After elderly party conservatives pressured Deng to fire Hu Yaobang in January 1987, it was obvious that party elites were divided by even more fundamental disagreements over the direction of reform; as Zhao Ziyang reportedly complained to Deng Xiaoping in May 1987, "If there are two different views at the higher level, it is impossible to act in unison at the lower level" (Lo Ping 1987b, K10). Reading the signals from Zhongnanhai (the compound where party and government leading organs are housed), many agency representatives calculated that their chances of obtaining

---

ple's Congress; in one case the Presidium overruled the Ministry of Agriculture's ruling in a fishing field dispute between a county in Hebei Province and a county in Shandong Province and ordered the State Council to resolve the dispute ("Wan Li Chairs Second Presidium Meeting" 1989).

more favorable treatment in a policy package would be enhanced by refusing to compromise and kicking the decision up to the higher level; some of them also figured that they could get away with not carrying out the policy.

Even when subordinates lacked specific information about the preferences of particular leaders, because of reciprocal accountability they had reason to expect more generous and lenient treatment when there was leadership conflict. During power struggles party leaders seek supporters among central and local officials, especially those who sit in the Central Committee selectorate. Leaders welcome opportunities to appeal to particular officials by pressing their interests when policies are decided, and they are loath to antagonize potential supporters by forcing them to accept too painful an outcome. From this perspective, bureaucratic recalcitrance and noncompliance can be seen as reflecting not a reduction in the authority of central party leaders but their reluctance to alienate potential supporters by pushing them too hard. When the principals are divided, the agents can get away with more (as every child knows).

Another reason why delegation by consensus was operating poorly was that the economic reform policy agenda placed the government bureaucracy under intense strain. A transformation of the economic structure involves redistributing authority and rewards among sectors, bureaucratic agencies, and regions. As Vice Premier Tian Jiyun pointedly remarked to a 1986 meeting of central government agencies,

> The overall reform of the economic structure is in a sense, a readjustment of power and interest, in which a large amount of contradictions exist. Among them, there are contradictions between the central authorities and the localities; between the state, the collective, and the individual; between one department and another; between one locality and another; between departments and localities; and so on. (Tian Jiyun 1986)

Theoretically, by increasing efficiency these changes in the economic system should benefit everyone. But as economic theorists have observed, the redistributive effects of changes in the rules of the economic game are bound to create group conflict (Pratt and Zeckhauser 1985). The groups who were favored and protected by the old command economy and who feel threatened by changes in the economic system resist the reforms or fight to retain as much of their original privileges as they can. Even those who stand to benefit from market reforms may not recognize the potential gain.[14]

The redistributive ramifications of reform policies presented a serious political challenge to the Chinese system of decision-making, which operates to preserve the status quo. As a rule, communist bureaucracies operating by consensus decision-making usually produce only incremental change (Hough 1977; Bunce 1981). Drastic changes in policy direction or massive shifts in the allocation of resources are inhibited by the requirement that all agencies agree to them. The consensus rule produces policies under which everyone benefits or at least no one loses too much. As one high-level policy adviser in China put it, "We must use all our policies to 'coordinate' [*xietiao*] interests among agencies and localities" (author's interview).

In China the normative reflection of consensus decision-making is an ideology one might call "balancism" (*pinghengzhuyi*; see chapter 5). According to this ideology, the function of the state is to balance interunit inequities created by arbitrary policies, especially administratively set prices. Fairness (*gongping*) requires that no unit lose too much because administrative prices make them less profitable than other units or because the legacies of past decisions (such as investments in fixed assets) work against them under current formulas. Government bodies are expected to adjust policies to prevent large disparities in benefits among units. The expression *ku le bu jun* (disparity between sadness and happiness) is frequently used by government bureaucrats to explain that a particular policy modification was necessary to guarantee equity—that is, to prevent some unit from suffering through no fault of its own. Representa-

14. As Albert Hirschman (1958, 59–61) has observed, in a planned economy the managers and ministers of an industry are likely to identify themselves with existing firms and are unlikely to favor disruptive changes that would interfere with the plans for these firms: "In this respect then, a planned economy is likely to behave much like the guild system; the process of 'creative destruction' is constitutionally alien to it because destruction here means self-destruction rather than destruction of somebody else." Hirschman goes on to say that decisionmakers in a planned economy tend to overestimate the prospective losses of any innovation because "it is in the nature of most innovations that its beneficiaries are anonymous, inarticulate, and unaware of the benefits-to-accrue (they include among others the consumers that are yet unborn), while those who stand to lose from the innovation are highly vocal vested interests."

tives of ministries, localities, or enterprises who are in a strong competitive position to benefit from economic reforms (because their products are in demand in the market, because the irrationalities of the price system work for them, or because they are more efficient and productive in their operations) often complain that government organs worry too much about taking care (*zhaogu*) of the weak and not enough about promoting the strong (author's interviews).

The conservative bias of delegation by consensus makes the political challenge of economic reform formidable. Introducing a market through a bureaucracy, especially one operating under delegation by consensus, is extremely difficult. Under the consensus rule even a minority of ministries or provinces who prefer the status quo to the proposed changes can obstruct progress in reform.

Economic reform, by creating new financial interests among bureaucratic and regional agencies, also made bargaining among them more intense. Policies designed to improve economic incentives by allowing ministries, provinces, local industrial bureaus, and so on to retain a share of their renminbi and hard-currency earnings make bureaucratic agencies more profit conscious. They fight more fiercely to obtain preferred policies and refuse to compromise their disputes with other agencies over which one has the right to produce lucrative products because now there are big profits at stake. With some issues, especially at the local level, it is possible to work out a compromise by giving all affected parties a financial share in the deal. Many potentially profitable joint ventures and other projects are approved only because every agency with approval authority is given a percentage of the profits (Lieberthal and Oksenberg 1988). But this new mode of resolving differences by dividing the profits encourages agencies to press their demands in the bargaining process. They recognize that assertiveness can pay off in several percentage points of a profitable venture. As the secretary-general of the State Council notes, "A profitable undertaking invariably draws the intervention of many departments, with every department demanding a slice of the cake, and none will make any concession. Sometimes this ends in a confrontation" (Chen Junsheng 1987, K33).[15]

15.   Another commentator complained that "since people want to have a hand in profitable things, they confront and vie with one another for a bigger share of profits. They mess up a perfectly good undertaking, either by dividing the profits before they materialize, or by not yielding even an inch in vying for profit or power" ("On 'Wrangles'" 1986, K17).

The expansion of the bargaining arena to include more groups also placed decision-making institutions under strain. During the reform decade the number of administrative organizations proliferated and the overall size of government staff increased. Although policy work conferences were nothing new in China, they grew more frequent (and probably larger) during the reform era, expanding the bargaining table to accommodate a larger number of organizations. However, inviting more groups to the bargaining table complicates the process of building consensus. Instead of a small, stable group of central officials who are willing to trade votes on one issue because they trust others to pay them back on the next issue, there are larger, ad hoc groups that find logrolling and agreement much more problematic.

To summarize, the Chinese government bureaucracy makes decisions by a system of "delegation by consensus." Party leaders delegate the authority to subordinate government agencies to work out economic policies. If everyone agrees, the leaders simply ratify the policy. If some agencies disagree, then the proposal is either sent upstairs to the higher levels for resolution or is tabled. Hierarchical control gives bureaucratic agents an incentive to compromise rather than exercise their veto if the political authorities are unified and their preferences clear. During the 1980s Chinese leaders were divided, delegation by consensus appeared to be working poorly, and many bureaucratic conflicts had to be resolved at the State Council level.

What can we say about policy-making under a system of delegation by consensus?

1. Policy decisions are more difficult and time-consuming and require more side payments than they do under majority rule.

2. Policies emerging from this kind of system tend to be incremental because participants will veto proposals that make them substantially worse off than they are under the status quo.

3. Highly redistributive issues are postponed or fail to pass unless the authorities impose them on bureaucratic subordinates.

4. The larger and less stable the set of participants, the more elusive is policy consensus.

5. When the authorities are divided and their preferences uncertain, agents are less willing to compromise and agreement on
policies is more difficult to achieve.

Delegation by consensus presented a formidable challenge to CCP
economic reformers. The combination of divided leadership and
consensus decision-making resulted in compromise and expansionary versions of reform policy and a gradual introduction of reforms.

8 Chinese Political Institutions and the Path of Economic Reforms

Deng Xiaoping's decision to retain China's authoritarian, bureaucratic political institutions and to introduce economic reforms through them set the course for the reform drive. Every policy bore the marks of being hammered out in Chinese communist institutions: the CCP delegated specific economic policy decisions to government bureaucracies; party leaders used reform policies to compete for power by appealing to the officials in the selectorate; bureaucrats articulated the interests of their economic sectors and geographic regions; regions as well as sectors sat around the table; industry had a stronger voice than agriculture, and heavy industry a stronger voice than light industry; and decisions were made by consensus. The pace, sequencing, content, and form of industrial reform policies from 1979 on reflect this institutional context.[1]

Pace

Chinese reform was *gradual and piecemeal*. Instead of rushing ahead with a comprehensive, radical transformation of the entire system that would threaten the vested interests of many groups, Deng Xiaoping and his reformist lieutenants were extremely cautious, "taking one step forward and looking around before taking another" (author's interviews). The party leaders did not impose a big-bang transformation from above but instead incorporated bureaucratic groups in the design of reforms and thereby prolonged the

---

1. As one Chinese commentator observed, the actual pattern of economic reform did not reflect economic theories so much as it did "the conflict of various kinds of interests, that is the conflict, coordination, and balancing of interests between various trades and industries, between urban and rural areas, between localities, and between localities and the central authorities" (Wang Depei 1991, 39).

period of transition.[2] Zhao Ziyang, who as premier and later as party general secretary was the operational leader of the reform drive, recognized that many political risks were inherent in economic reform and that therefore the leaders were "required to act carefully in reforms, like wading across a river on rocks [*mozhe shitou guohe*]" ("Reforms Must Be Carried Out Step by Step" 1985, K26). He understood that "the reform of the economic structure is actually a process in which various interests and relations are readjusted and redistributed" and that if the interests of a particular department or locality were harmed by a particular reform, it would oppose the reform ("Fully Understand the Long-Term Character and Difficulty of the Reform" 1987, K13). As one of Zhao's chief economic advisers explained, "We try to protect everyone's vested interests. This has negative as well as positive consequences. It means it's slow. As a rule, we have two years of fermentation for every reform policy. But it means people support the reform" (author's interview). Gradual reform might be a long-term process, requiring as long as several generations ("Fully Understand the Long-Term Character and Difficulty of the Reform" 1987, K13), but no other strategy had a chance of success in the context of a political system such as China's.

To minimize the threat to central economic agencies, the powerful SPC in particular, Zhao Ziyang decided to *expand the market sector gradually while maintaining the plan sector* instead of replacing plan with market at one shot. The policy allowing enterprises to sell their above-quota output on their own at market prices created an economic incentive for managers and ministry officials to press for more market opportunities while allowing central planners to save their function and their face. Stimulated by the new incentives, the economy grew rapidly, mainly in the market sector. This strategy of "letting the economy outgrow the plan" (Naughton 1986, 622; 1990a, 13; forthcoming) created a transitional two-track economy, with numerous accompanying economic problems, but it was politically very successful. Managers and industrial bureaucrats were protected by the security of the old system—the government continued to bail out enterprises operating in the red—while gaining access to the profitable opportunities of the market.

2. This approach contrasts with the way Mao Zedong imposed radical shifts in policy from above.

In a similar fashion, party leaders *freed collective and private businesses* and encouraged them to grow by offering them generous tax and profit retention arrangements. The policy of fostering nonstate businesses was justified by the necessity of creating jobs for unemployed city youth and surplus rural labor. Policies legalizing and stimulating the second economy were unobjectionable to the ministry, commission, and province officials sitting around the bargaining table in Beijing. Their interests were directly and immediately affected by policies regarding state enterprises but were affected in only a diffuse and long-term way by policies regarding nonstate enterprises.

Given the conservative bias of delegation by consensus, the gradual creation of new forms of economic activity alongside the traditional planned economy was politically more feasible than a direct attack on central planning and state ownership would have been. And over time the new economic forms and practices became not just the sideshow but the main event in the reform drive. The market track and nonstate sector began to drive the reforms not because they gained new political clout and overwhelmed the bastions of conservatism; in fact, they have almost no representation in the bureaucratic bargaining arena, which is still dominated by planners and industrial ministries.[3] Instead, the force of the second economy derived from its influence on the *learning* of officials, managers, and workers in planned state industry. Having been forced to compete with nonstate enterprises that operate entirely in the market, people in the state sector came to accept the risks and appreciate the advantages of greater economic freedoms.

Sequencing

The sequencing of reforms reflected the difficulties in achieving bureaucratic consensus. *Redistributive policies that created the most intense conflict within the bureaucracy were continually postponed and never got off the ground because it was impossible to achieve consensus on them.* One such redistributive measure was the "hard

3. Although the reformist leadership created new bureaucracies such as the State Council Economic System Reform Commission, the State Council Economic Zone Office, and the China International Trust and Investment Corporation to get around the entrenched bureaucracies wedded to central planning, the new bureaucracies do not appear to carry much weight in the bargaining process (author's interviews).

budget constraint" (i.e., bankruptcy). Forcing enterprises to take sole responsibility for their own profits and losses (*zi fu ying kui*) is an essential component of market rationality, but it was politically infeasible in the Chinese system. From the perspective of "balancism" it was considered unfair to punish enterprises that could not make profits because of external, "objective" (*keguan*) causes beyond their control (prices, demands of planners, fixed assets, etc.). The burden would fall mainly on a few sectors (coal, steel, heavy machinery) and the inland provinces where these sectors are concentrated (author's interviews).

Another highly redistributive issue that the Chinese system found difficult to handle was price reform. Zhao Ziyang began talking about price reform in 1981. He set up a group under Xue Muqiao to prepare price reform policies and announced in early 1985 that the State Council would soon take action on price readjustment in industry as well as agriculture ("Zhao Comments" 1985). The fact that the overall adjustment of industrial prices (e.g., raising the prices of raw materials such as coal, iron, and steel) was repeatedly postponed while food prices were liberalized suggests that intense bureaucratic conflict rather than the potential of negative public reaction to inflation prevented the government from pushing ahead with industrial price reform.

Unequal bureaucratic representation for different economic sectors helps explain why *agricultural reforms were introduced before industrial reforms and progressed more rapidly and successfully*, becoming a model to inspire industrial reform. As one Chinese official said, "Reforming agriculture before industry wasn't a self-conscious strategy; it just went faster because it is not as complicated as industry" (author's interview).[4] In contrast to the stop-start rhythm of the industrial reform drive, agriculture reform progressed continuously and smoothly. When problems arose, national leaders addressed them by extending the scope of reform instead of by backpedaling. For example, because the incentive of farmers to increase production was weakened by the monopoly of state-run supply and marketing cooperatives over rural commerce, in 1983 the authorities broke the monopoly and gave farm households the right to engage in private transport and marketing of farm commodities. Because farmers were investing in their own houses but not in pro-

---

4. The Chinese word *fuza*, translated as "complicated," connotes political conflict as well as technical complexity.

ductive assets, in 1984 the authorities clarified and strengthened their property rights over the land; leases were extended to fifteen years and made renewable and transferable. When the dramatic increases in farm output overburdened the central treasury with price subsidies, the authorities eliminated state mandatory purchases of grain and widened the commodity market to include grain in 1985.

Agricultural reform was easier to pull off in the Chinese political system than was industrial reform because, although originally there were strong *ideological* objections to dismantling collective agriculture (reflected in the prohibition on household contracting included in the December 1978 plenum document), agricultural reform faced less *bureaucratic* resistance and could find bureaucratic consensus.[5] Fewer central agencies are concerned with agriculture (the Ministry of Agriculture, Animal Husbandry, and Fisheries, the Ministry of Grain, and the All-China Federation of Supply and Marketing Cooperatives), and they have little political clout. Agricultural agencies generate deficits rather than revenues, have less control over collective farms than the industrial ministries do over state-owned factories, and tend to set only broad policy guidelines over their subordinate provincial departments. All these qualities are sources of weakness in bureaucratic politics as played in Beijing. When the shift from mandatory purchases to long-term contracts of basic agricultural commodities drastically transformed the operations of the Ministry of Grain, and the liberalization of rural marketing smashed the monopoly of the Supply and Marketing Cooperative, the agencies were unable to mount an effective challenge.

Moreover, the CCP continued to play a more active role in agriculture than in industry, as it has always done.[6] Agricultural policy decisions were made in party bodies whereas industrial reform issues were delegated to the State Council. When a party leadership group committed to raising rural living standards attained dominance, it was able to sustain the agricultural reform drive without any significant bureaucratic opposition.

---

5. For some of the economic reasons why agricultural reform was more successful than industrial reform, see Shirk 1989.
6. The CCP has a Rural Policy Research Center but no equivalent organization for industry. Whereas all important agricultural policy decisions are issued by the party, most industrial policy decisions are promulgated by the State Council.

Probably most important, agricultural reform was unobjectionable from the perspective of the industrial ministries. Decollectivization put more money in the pockets of farmers, so they could purchase more manufactured goods and contribute more revenue to the state. To exploit this new market, manufacturers of farm equipment and other inputs were permitted to raise their prices. Agricultural reform improved the supply of cotton, sugar, and other commodities used as raw materials for industry. There was no contest when it came to allocating investment funds from the central budget; even though agriculture contributed more to the treasury than it had in the past, its share of investment was reduced, not increased. City dwellers received subsidies to cover the increases in food prices. In other words, rural reforms in no way threatened the political or economic preeminence of urban industry.

In the sequence by which Chinese reforms were introduced, *one of the first reforms was a fiscal decentralization to provincial governments,* designed to appeal to the large bloc of local officials in the Central Committee. In 1980 a policy called "apportioning revenues and expenditures between the central and local authorities while holding the latter responsible for their own profit and loss," colloquially called "eating in separate kitchens" (*fen zao chifan*), was promulgated ("Temporary Provisions" 1980). This policy allowed provinces to fix for five years the amount of revenues they were required to remit to the center and to keep a proportion or all revenues over that amount. Provinces were assigned to five different categories of treatment, ranging from Guangdong and Fujian, which retained 100 percent of their above-quota revenues, to the three municipalities of Beijing, Shanghai, and Tianjin, which retained none. In addition, provinces and lower-level governments were permitted to keep all profits from the enterprises controlled by them (Donnithorne 1981; Fujimoto 1980; Han Guochun 1982).

The "eating in separate kitchens" fiscal reform was the core element of the party leadership's effort to "play to the provinces" (see chapter 9). As a political strategy to win provincial support for the reform drive and for individual reformist leaders, it was extremely successful. And once local authorities were given an incentive to expand their revenue base by developing local industry, there was an impressive burst of entrepreneurial energy. But the decision to change the financial incentives of local governments early in the game had negative consequences for the way the rest of the game was played. A local investment drive, with most of the funds going into profitable but redundant and wasteful processing plants, generated inflation, supply shortages, budget deficits, and foreign exchange deficits. The national market became balkanized as local officials erected blockades to protect their markets. Local officials fought any proposed reform that would shift resources or authority from local governments to the enterprises themselves. The fiscal decentralization successfully created new vested interests in reform, but these new vested interests were an impediment to moving beyond partial reform to more complete marketization.

Content

Two clear patterns in the content of Chinese industrial reform policies of the 1980s reflect the difficulties of introducing a market through a communist authoritarian bureaucracy that makes decisions by consensus.

First, reform policies were highly *expansionary*. As noted in chapter 2, it was easy to stimulate the Chinese economy to grow rapidly under partial reform conditions. From an economist's perspective rapid growth is desirable only if it is produced by increased efficiency. If growth is not achieved by using resources more efficiently, then all parties may think they are better off, but in real economic terms they are not. But to the Chinese political leaders who were out to promote reform and their own careers, high growth rates were valued no matter how they were achieved. They preferred policies that could show conspicuous good results—defined mainly in terms of growth rates—in a short time.[7] After all, no one knew when the next round of leadership succession would occur.

Economic expansion also made it easier to keep everyone happy, to give every group a reason to welcome reform, and thereby to accomplish what Albert Hirschman (1958) describes as the most difficult trick of economic reform, namely, turning a process that is

7. One Chinese economist was highly critical of "the theory of quick success" underlying China's economic reform drive. He said that the theory produced not only an overheated economy, with all its accompanying problems, but also "a sense of comfort and contentment among our people" that made it impossible to reach a consensus on any policies requiring hardship. Moreover, "excessively high hopes resulted in greater disappointments." Because quick successes could not be attained, pessimist sentiments increased abruptly. "Despite notable and considerable achievements made in the past 10 years of reform, complaints and curses were heard everywhere" (Xiao Jiabao 1989, 42).

inherently redistributive into one in which everyone wins. Zhao Ziyang acknowledged that the benchmark of a successful reform was providing benefits for everyone: "When adopting a reform measure, we must do our best to benefit all quarters concerned so that our reform will always have the support of the broad masses of the people and its success will be guaranteed" (Zhao Ziyang 1987c, K1).

The industrial reforms carried out during the 1980s were essentially a package of giveaways, dispersing funds and authority widely to bureaucratic agencies, localities, and enterprises. The reform economist Liu Guoguang, looking back from the vantage point of 1990, complained that "in the ten years of reform, we mainly delegated powers, shared benefits, and used material incentives to arouse the enthusiasm of enterprises, localities, and workers" (Liu Guoguang 1990, 22). Loose control over the money supply and what Westerners might call "political Keynesianism" (incumbent leaders increasing government spending to build political support for themselves) caused inflation and other economic problems, but from the political standpoint, their logic was overpowering.[8] Workers got big raises and bonuses; from 1978 to 1987 the average wage of workers in state enterprises increased by 140.1 percent while labor productivity increased by only 49.8 percent (Liu Yiqun et al. 1989, 57). Along with wage raises and bonuses, managers handed out to their employees free lunches, Western-style suits, furniture, bicycles, and any other consumer goods the managers could get their hands on (Dai Yuqing 1985). Managers, local politicians, and ministry bureaucrats all got to keep a share of the profits, and with the economy growing at 8–10 percent per year, the sense of new economic power was exciting. The local industrial construction boom created jobs and wealth. It was as if reform had put China on a nationwide spending spree. Financial discipline was discarded: with the exception of the MOF, no one, certainly none of the party leaders contending for power, wanted to be the party pooper.

A major element in the expansion was the growth of the government. The average increase in the number of government cadres reached 330,000 per year, compared with an average increase of 110,000 per year before 1980. By the end of 1986 the total staff of government offices and organizations was 7.34 million, 78.2 percent

8. Barry Ames (1987) found that in military authoritarian regimes in Latin America, incumbent leaders pump up government spending not prior to an "election," as in democratic regimes, but after seizing power.

higher than it was in 1978. Administrative expenditures increased between 1978 and 1988 by 388 percent and claimed a larger share of the budget, from 5.1 percent in 1978 to 9.0 percent in 1988 (*Statistical Yearbook* 1989, 666, 668). The growth in the administrative apparatus at a time when economic reforms were supposedly reducing the government role in the economy was undoubtedly a side payment to propitiate government bureaucrats whose interests were threatened by market reforms.[9] Swelling the ranks of the bureaucracy may also have been a way for party reforms to bring in new officials more committed to reform goals than were veterans wedded to the command economy.

The reform policies that passed successfully through the Chinese bureaucratic bargaining machine were not just expansionary; they were also *compromises designed to leave no one worse off than before.* Reform policies bear the mark of consensus decision-making. One important example, analyzed in chapter 12, was the decision to create a new tax system for industrial enterprises with a policy called "substituting tax for profits" (*li gai shui*). The goal of this policy was to place the financial relations between enterprises and the central government on a stable, institutionalized basis. Instead of each enterprise bargaining for a particular profit retention rate, all enterprises producing the same product would have to pay a uniform tax rate. When the tax-for-profit policy was originally proposed in 1983, the MOF recommended a moderately high tax rate and a long list of specific taxes including local taxes. At a series of meetings called to discuss the proposal, representatives of heavy industrial ministries and inland provinces complained that under such a heavy tax burden their many unprofitable enterprises would be forced to close. To achieve consensus it was necessary to revise the policy. After the product tax rate was reduced and the list of taxes pared down, the MOF came into the work conference with simulations showing that the revised formula would reduce state revenues. The revenue gap was filled by tacking on a so-called adjustment tax (*tiaojie shui*), which was applied only to the most profitable medium and large state enterprises (most of them in

9. According to the Chinese press, administrative departments still believe "there is strength in numbers" and try "every possible means to set up new organs and increase staff" ("Resolve Must Be Great" 1987). Although Tang Tian (1987) does not report how this expansion was divided between central and local levels, I suspect that the largest part was at the local level.

coastal cities such as Shanghai). The adjustment tax was set on an individual enterprise basis, thereby violating a fundamental principle of market competition but creating the compromise necessary to win approval of the policy (author's interviews).

Reform policies always included a "grandfather clause" to protect groups benefiting from current policies, and charges always were set at the level of the previous year. Nothing less would win consensus approval. For example, the tax-for-profit regulations guaranteed enterprises that they would pay in taxes no more than the profit they had remitted the year before.

Particularistic contracting, which replaced tax-for-profit, enabled decisionmakers to keep the balance among ministries, provinces, and enterprises. Tax rates, profit retention rates, foreign exchange retention rates, revenue-sharing rates, and product prices were fungible; if a bureaucratic entity lost a little with one reform, it could be compensated by giving it a little more with the next reform. For example, if the tax-for-profit policy resulted in a loss of revenues to a particular province, the central government paid the province back by reducing the total revenue it was required to remit to the center (Lieberthal and Oksenberg 1988).

Unfortunately, not every policy could be designed to make no one worse off. Chinese officials have always agreed that the only politically feasible approach to price reform was to compensate those who were hurt by it—for example, by wage subsidies to urban consumers in the case of food prices and by tax exemptions for manufacturing enterprises in the case of raw materials prices. One reason that industrial price readjustment grew more intractable over the course of reform was that it became increasingly difficult for the already strained central treasury to come up with the financial side payments necessary to make the package universally acceptable (see chapter 13).

The policies that emerged from the bureaucracy after 1980 suggest that the progress of economic reform was sustained only by *compromises to appease the powerful heavy industrial ministries*. When reform proposals were first introduced, heavy industrial interests, the prime beneficiaries of the command economy, expressed open opposition (Solinger 1982). By replacing some ministers and making reform its ideological line, the party discouraged outright opposition from the heavy industrial ministries. And over time, especially after the shock of readjustment (see chapter 10), the bureaucrats in these ministries came to recognize that they could do better by demanding a larger share of the benefits of reform than by opposing all reforms.

In exchange for supporting various reform policies, the heavy industrial ministries received valuable side payments, such as "departmental contracts" (*bumen chengbao*). The departmental contracts were aid programs for the ministries in charge of fuels, raw materials, and transportation, which felt they were falling further and further behind under the two-track economic system. Industrial sectors with many enterprises operating under low (or no) quotas could make a killing selling on the market, while their own enterprises had to continue to produce almost entirely for the plan. The petroleum, coal, metallurgy, railroads, and communication ministries and the airline, petrochemical, and nonferrous metals corporations demanded and received special departmental contracts with the SPC under which they received a certain amount of investment and inexpensive inputs in exchange for delivering a certain output for the next five years. The ministries and their subordinate enterprises were free to sell excess production on the market at higher prices ("Metallurgical Conference's New System Approved" 1985; "Different Types of Contracted Managerial Responsibility Systems" 1987). The contracts guaranteed access to the market and higher profits to these particular agencies, which in turn allocated the plan burdens and market opportunities to the enterprises under them. The departmental contracts were very popular both with the SPC— because they helped guarantee plan procurement (the lure of the market sector had made this task increasingly difficult)—and, naturally, with the ministries that benefited from them (author's interviews). The departmental contracts violated the reform principle of increasing enterprise autonomy from administrative control but were politically expedient for obtaining the consensus necessary to continue the reform drive.

The need to obtain the support of the influential heavy industrial ministries for the package of economic reforms probably also explains the striking stability of the shares of central budgetary investment allocated to economic sectors during the period of economic reform. Heavy industry, which had claimed the lion's share of state investment under the old system, found its investment allocation cut drastically in 1980–81 when top leaders sought to improve proportional balance by shifting resources to light industry. The blow to heavy industry was so severe and its representatives complained so loudly that its share was increased again after

1982 (*Statistical Yearbook* 1989, 487). Since that time heavy industry has continued to receive favored treatment by the center, and light industry has increased its share of *total* investment only because most investment is now controlled at the local, not central, level.

Form

A striking pattern running through all Chinese industrial reform policies is a preference, driven by leadership incentives, for *particularistic contracting over uniform rules*. Party leaders, competing with one another to win power by appealing to bureaucratic groups and individual officials within the selectorate, design policies to allocate benefits selectively to particular units. "Look what I did for you," says the party politician, who naturally expects to receive political support in return for his patronage.

Economists and officials who advocated the contracting approach to marketization dubbed it "Chinese-style economic reform."[10] (The *New York Times* columnist William Safire [1990] called it "a fake market system in which the government sells power," demonstrating that you do not have to be a China specialist to grasp the essence of Chinese politics.) The fiscal contracts between the center and the provinces; the original profit retention experiments in enterprises; the selection of certain cities as reform experiments; the profit contracting system for enterprises; contracts between ministries and the SPC; the foreign trade contracts between the center and the provinces; and the Special Economic Zones and fourteen Open Cities—all of these programs have the same form. A program offering favorable treatment, usually involving access to high-priced market sales and retention of a larger share of the earnings, is extended to particular provinces, cities, ministries, or enterprises. The central leader promoting the program wins the gratitude and support of the units selected for special treatment. Often the program involves authorizing officials in some provinces, cities, or ministries to select the lucky enterprises and thereby to build local patronage machines for themselves.

Although many of these programs are called reform "experiments" for testing the results of various types of reforms, in fact they are not true experiments but rather "Potemkin village" models for convincing people to support reform. They are not experiments because the units operating on the special program are bolstered

10. Such a label implicitly damns any contrary proposals as *not* Chinese style, in other words, as influenced by foreign ideas. This rhetorical device of calling up nationalism is common in Chinese policy polemics.

with other forms of "preferential treatment" (*yuhui tiaojian*), including cheap material inputs, electricity, bank loans, and so on. There was no way an experiment could fail. If an experimental enterprise somehow turned in a disappointing performance, it was dropped from the program and never mentioned again. This mode of building political support for economic policies was first developed by Mao Zedong, who designated particular factories or collective farms as "models," a more accurate label than "experiments."

Once the value of the reforms was demonstrated by the success of the "experiments," other units clamored to participate. Enterprise managers and provincial, municipal, and ministry officials all pressured the government to extend the programs' benefits to more units. Leaders were happy to comply because they won credit for the reforms and for themselves from a larger number of subordinates. Even after a reform program was popularized, it took the form of particularistic contracting, with the terms of the program bargained out for each unit, enabling officials at all levels of the system to build political support.

Chinese reform pork-barrel politics had a distinct spatial dimension. The party leaders in Beijing granted special favors to the coastal provinces, particularly Guangdong and Fujian, to develop their foreign economic ties. Broadened authority to conduct foreign trade and to approve foreign investment projects, the right to offer preferential terms to foreign investors, and an especially generous share of foreign exchange earnings were offered first to four Special Economic Zones and then, in response to political pressures from local officials, to fourteen Open Cities. Guangdong and Fujian also had a very cushy fiscal contract with the center, making them objects of envy by Shanghai, which still felt exploited by Beijing.[11] When the coastal provinces were granted special policies to move "one step ahead" (in Ezra Vogel's [1989] term) toward the world market, less privileged coastal areas and the inland provinces demanded the same policies for themselves.[12] After Li Peng became a

11. When I interviewed the mayor of Shanghai, Wang Daohan, in 1984, he answered my question about the slow pace of economic reform in Shanghai by saying, "Of course we're behind Guangdong on reform. If the center gave us the same financial deal they gave Guangdong, we would be moving faster on reform."

12. The issue was not just fairness but also the externalities from the more market-based economies in the vanguard coastal regions. For example, when Guangdong had a price liberalization, all the goods produced in neighboring regions flowed to Guangdong (author's interview). Another pork-barrel policy designed to broaden support for the economic reform

serious contender to succeed Deng Xiaoping in 1987, he tried to build his own base of regional supporters by supporting the creation of Pudong, a major new foreign investment zone for Shanghai, and giving preferential status as "advanced and new technology development zones" to inland provinces and cities.[13]

Selective allocation of the benefits of reform was a hugely successful device for Chinese leaders to generate enthusiasm for the reform drive and political support for themselves. Chinese economic experts criticized the particularistic form of reform policies, but the political logic of particularism was overwhelming.[14]

The dynamic of particularistic contracting between levels of government and between government and enterprises is essentially one of "administratively generated rent" (Krueger 1974).[15] When the government grants a special privilege to a unit (a local government or an enterprise), it in effect lowers the price of producing earnings to the unit. Because the privilege is scarce, units are willing to pay more for the privilege than they theoretically would if they were bidding for it in a market. The difference between the market clearing price and the price people are willing to pay for the privilege is the administratively generated rent. In other words, factory managers and lower-level government officials are competing for favorable treatment from government officials and are willing to pay well for it.

In this way, administrative intervention in the market creates resources that officials can consume or use in various ways. Government officials can appropriate the value of the rent in the form of bribes (financial corruption) or political support (patronage). Or

---

drive was the establishment of new universities. Officials of established universities complained in 1984 that, whereas they were expected to raise about one-fifth of their own funds, money was being "frittered away" on more than four hundred new universities founded all over China since 1980 (author's interviews).

13. The technology development zone policy is designed to generate patronage opportunities for both central and local officials: that is, some zones will be approved by Beijing, and others will be approved by provincial and municipal governments (Chen Jianping 1991).

14. "There is a saying: 'We want policies [*zhengce*] rather than money.' In fact, policies are usually the equivalent to money. The many preferential methods in various fields constitute an essential reason for economic confusion, a loss in financial resources, and expenses exceeding revenue. It also hinders the deepening of reform. It is probably hard to say how many preferential policies there are now" (Wang Mengkui 1990, 3).

15. This paragraph draws on the analysis in Bates 1981 (96–99).

they can decentralize the power to distribute favors to subordinate officials in exchange for political backing; the subordinate officials in turn distribute favors to generate bribes or patronage. The administratively generated rents help the government create grateful clients who expand the ranks of the reform coalition and stand behind the leader who instituted the program of privileges.[16] During a period of transition from plan to market, such as China is experiencing, when economic rules of the game are uncertain and when officials control access to lucrative market opportunities, economic policy-making comes to be dominated by patronage politics.[17]

The rent-generating dynamic explains why at several critical junctures Chinese leaders, regardless of their different predispositions, all came out for reform programs based on the selective allocation of benefits instead of universal rules. When Zhao Ziyang first came to Beijing in the early 1980s, he advocated the replacement of enterprise profit contracts with a uniform tax code; several years later he switched to profit contracting after he started thinking like a potential successor to Deng and discovered the value of contracts for building a base of political support (see chapter 13). Even Li Peng, who played mainly to the bloc of central officials in the selectorate and stressed the plan over the market, came out in favor of retaining fiscal contracts for provinces and enterprises after becoming premier in 1987. Li Peng did slam previous reform experiments for giving "special or preferential treatment to these units to ensure good results being achieved there," but he supported the continuation of financial contracts. Even more, he could not resist the temptation to generate patronage with his own new pork-barrel policies, specifically, enterprise joint-stock system "experiments" (Li Peng 1989) and technology development zones.[18]

16. Administratively generated rents obviously are not a new phenomenon in China. A command economy is also a rent-seeking society. Every annual plan is a collection of particularistic bargains between the central leaders and subordinate units, generating valuable political resources for the leaders to consume or distribute.
17. Jeremy Paltiel (1989, 271) finds this pattern in both Mexico and China. He points out that subordinates are as hungry for patronage as officials are eager to provide it. He attributes the pervasiveness of patronage in semi-marketized economies to the absence of property rights: "To substitute for the protection of property based on law, the economic actor must seek the protection of political patrons. Uncertainty about potential party intervention guarantees the persistence of clientalist *guanxi* or connections."
18. The political advantages of particularistic treatment may also explain what appears to be selective enforcement of anticorruption measures. De-

Conclusion: Evaluating the Record of Economic Reform

The political challenge of economic reform in communist states is to devise policies that build a coalition of support for the reform drive while improving economic efficiency. The Chinese industrial reforms were extremely successful by the first measure but less successful by the second. "Chinese-style reform" produced bureaucratic consensus but only modest improvement in the economic performance of state-owned firms. State-owned factory losses increased, especially after 1985.[19] State industry expanded but made little progress in modernizing its technology or management. Toward the end of the decade inflation rates soared to over 25 percent, not high by international standards, but the highest anyone in China had experienced for forty years. Budget deficits persisted, and perceptions of widespread corruption sullied the reform drive in the eyes of the public. The conspicuous economic problems produced by partial reform provided ammunition for conservatives to reclaim power at the top reaches of the party.

Measures to enforce financial discipline on enterprises and to establish rational prices would have made more sense in economic terms but were politically unattainable. Stable, rational prices that improve efficiency or fair, uniform taxes are collective goods that benefit everyone in general, but no one in particular, and achieving them inflicts harm on some particular groups.[20] The political logic

spite all the talk about corruption, party and government leaders have punished few corrupt officials. Laxity toward official corruption can be viewed as a side payment to officials to give them a personal stake in reform or at least in the halfway version of reform currently in effect in China. Because an individual official knows that higher-ups could charge him with corruption at any time, lack of exposure is in effect special treatment for which the official gratefully exchanges his political support.

19.   Enterprise losses increased from 3.4 billion yuan in 1984 to 11.6 billion yuan in 1988; 1989 was an even worse year for industrial performance, with 19 percent of state factories operating at a loss, compared with 13 percent in 1988 (Chen Yun and Zhang Guimin 1990).

20.   As one group of reform economists explained, even when the leaders of reform knew that measures such as increases in interest rates would be effective at curtailing demand and curbing inflation, they hesitated to press forward with them because they had not yet worked out how to deal with objections from state financial departments and industrial circles. As they summarized the dilemma, "In the work of improvement and rectification [of the economy], there is a contradiction where objectively there is the need to pay a price but subjectively people are unwilling to pay that price

of Chinese institutions meant that such measures were consistently defeated, overwhelmed by policies that were expansionary give-aways. Compromises were designed to make no group worse off by providing contracts allocated on a particularistic basis.

The institutional context meant that instead of economically optimal comprehensive reform, China ended up with a second-best, gradual, piecemeal reform that created new markets and nonstate firms alongside the old planned economy and state firms. The gradual two-track approach proved to be surprisingly successful at raising living standards and sustaining the momentum of the reform drive. Even when the political system was deadlocked over comprehensive reforms of state-owned industry, progress continued in the nonstate sector and marketization proceeded apace. During the gradual transition, the dynamism of the nonstate, market track was a powerful attraction to state industrial firms, tilting the economy further and further away from the plan.

---

and hope that the crisis will be resolved without their having to lift a little finger" (Dai Yuanchen et al. 1989, 3).

3

ECONOMIC REFORM POLICY-MAKING

9 Playing to the Provinces

*Fiscal Decentralization
and the Politics of Reform*

The cornerstone of the CCP leaders' political strategy to build support for economic reform was a fiscal decentralization popularly called "eating in separate kitchens" (*fen zao chifan*). A Chinese account called fiscal reform "the breakthrough point for the entire economic reform" (Caizheng Bu Caishui Tizhi Gaige Zhu 1989). Experiments with revenue-sharing contracts between the central government and provincial governments were introduced in Jiangsu and Sichuan in 1977, and the method was extended to all provinces beginning in 1980. Putting an expansion of financial autonomy for provincial governments into the reform package gave provincial officials a vested interest in promoting and sustaining the reform drive. Such a policy package was the best way to create a political counterweight to the central bureaucracy and achieve market reform while preserving China's communist institutions.[1]

Fiscal decentralization was an attractive solution to the political challenge of economic reform in China given the nature of its political institutions. China's fiscal authority is controlled by the national leaders in Beijing and is not formally shared by center and provinces. Central leaders can delegate fiscal authority to particular provinces or not, as they wish. Because the central party apparatus appoints provincial leaders, the military, and the mass media, and because central planners allocate key materials and capital for big development projects, the center has little reason to fear that dele-

---

1. The strategy of achieving market reform by devolving authority and resources to local officials (and thereby allowing them to build up local political machines) made the Chinese and Yugoslav reform drives surprisingly similar. Of course, the reform experiences in China and Yugoslavia differed in other respects. For example, in Yugoslavia the national legislature became the main policy-making arena, whereas in China policy-making remained within the party and government bureaucracy.

gations of fiscal authority to the provinces will lead to a loss of central control or national disintegration.[2]

Under reciprocal accountability within the CCP, however, any radical change in policy direction presents grave risks to the leader who initiates the change. Presumably, the members of the Central Committee, the key institution in the selectorate that chooses party leaders, were originally chosen to support the previous policies or have acquired vested interests in these policies; they have the authority to replace a leader who abandons these policies. The solution for the leader who believes that policy innovation is necessary is to reconstitute the membership of the Central Committee and thereby bend the party line in a new direction. By increasing the proportion of provincial leaders in the Central Committee and making them the largest bloc in that body (43 percent in 1987; if regional military officers are included, more than 50 percent), Deng Xiaoping and his allies enabled the reforms to go forward despite the vested interests of central government and party officials in the status quo. Provincial officials were already influential within the CCP, and once they became the largest group in the Central Committee, it was in the personal interests of each ambitious central politician to build a base of support among this group by giving power and money to the provinces.

Once the provincial representatives in the Central Committee put the weight of the party behind the reforms, the government bureaucracy would follow party orders to formulate and implement the reforms. To make sure that the provinces were enfranchised to participate in reform policy-making, party leaders held frequent policy work conferences at which provincial representatives as well as ministries were represented. By playing to the provinces, proreform

2. My hierarchical conception of center-local relations contradicts David Granick's (1990) claim that local governments were principals with their own property rights. In my view, central party officials hold all formal authority and delegate some of it to lower levels of government for three reasons: to improve incentive compatibility; to divest itself of sole responsibility; and to win the political support of lower-level officials. Granick's observation that legacies of past investments in enterprises give different levels of government a normative claim to a share of enterprise products and profits is correct and important. However, his evidence for continuity in the relationships of levels of government and enterprises to demonstrate the validity of the hypothesis concerning property rights is not completely persuasive. Moreover, the strongest evidence for hierarchy is one he ignores, namely, the power of the central party authorities to appoint and dismiss territorial officials.

party leaders were able to change the direction of China's economic policies without altering its fundamental political institutions.

Chinese reformist leaders learned to play to the provinces by observing Mao Zedong, who had pioneered this strategy. In the Great Leap Forward (1958) and the Cultural Revolution (1966–69) Mao sought to overcome the resistance of stodgy central bureaucrats to his vision of accelerated growth and revolutionary collectivism and egalitarianism by appealing to provincial officials and building up their power within the Central Committee. Now Deng Xiaoping and his lieutenants were promoting a very different vision of change, but the essence of the strategy was the same. And, ironically, the progressive diffusion of funds caused by Mao's decentralization efforts during the Cultural Revolution decade now made the Ministry of Finance, typically a proponent of fiscal centralization, receptive to the idea of fiscal decentralization. The MOF was sympathetic to any fiscal scheme that would prevent the further deterioration of its control and would shift responsibility along with resources to the local level.[3]

The form of fiscal decentralization policies, namely, particularistic contracts negotiated by the center with each provincial government, gave central politicians the opportunity to win the gratitude and the political support of officials from the provinces. Sharing formulas tilted toward the provinces left the central treasury short of funds. The solution was to close the central revenue gap by politically innocuous solutions that widely spread fiscal burdens— specifically, making some industries central fiscal preserves under state corporations, extracting loans from all provinces, and shifting more budgetary responsibilities to all provinces. Chinese fiscal reform followed the winning formula of concentrated benefits and diffused costs.

This fiscal reform formula did not make the local governments as a whole better off. The central government shifted many of its spending responsibilities to local governments—including public works expenditures and subsidies to food and consumer goods (Naughton 1990a)—and took substantial funds from local governments in the form of state corporations and loans.

Over the course of the reform drive, government budgetary revenues declined as a share of GNP from 35 percent in 1978 (higher

3. Throughout this book, when I refer to "local" or "locality," I mean provinces, autonomous regions, and provincial-level cities as well as large municipalities.

than the figure for other developing countries but below that of the communist governments of Eastern Europe and the Soviet Union in that year) to 20 percent in 1988 (the average for low-income and lower-middle-income countries was 19 percent in that year; Naughton 1990a). Budgetary revenues at both central and local levels were squeezed by changes in relative prices, competition from the non-state sector, and enterprises retaining a larger share of the revenues; on the expenditure side, government budgets at all levels were strained by the need to subsidize the growing losses of state enterprises. Prior to the reforms, Chinese state industry contributed 75 percent of budgetary revenues and, after netting out all industrial investment, contributed 5.9 percent of GNP to the budget (1978 figures). Compared to state enterprises in other developing countries (a typical example is India, whose enterprises constituted a 5.0 percent net burden on the budget), Chinese enterprises made a significant budgetary contribution. By the end of the decade, however, the system of collecting revenues through industrial enterprises was simply not working any more at either the central or the local level (Naughton 1990a; Wong 1990).[4] The net budgetary surplus provided by state enterprises had declined to only 0.4 percent of GNP (Naughton 1990a). Central and local governments were fighting over a smaller and smaller piece of China's economic pie.

Even though fiscal contracting did not leave provincial and city governments better off than before, local officials had no interest in abandoning contracting for either a return to fiscal centralization or some new method that separated central and local taxes. Fiscal contracting was perpetuated because it created patronage benefits for both central and local officials. Provincial officials fiercely opposed any effort to recentralize revenues, and because the provincial budgets were just as strained as the central budget was, it was hard for the central authorities to justify taking any funds away from the provinces. On the contrary, as the fiscal burdens on provinces grew heavier, provinces were able to win increasingly generous revenue-sharing contract terms.

The consequences of playing to the provinces by means of fiscal decentralization and other forms of administrative decentralization were contradictory. The strategy was very successful at enhancing the political clout of provincial officials and putting it behind the

4.   As of 1987 the revenues of more than 40 percent of provinces, cities, and regions did not cover their expenditures, and two-thirds of the counties had to rely on subsidies (Dai Yuanchen and He Suoheng 1987, 27).

reform drive. A Central Committee in which the largest bloc was local officials strongly committed to dismantling the centralized command economy helped sustain the momentum of reforms.

At the same time, however, local officials, who enjoyed the patronage opportunities afforded them by partial reform, became obstacles to carrying reform through to full marketization. As one Chinese account explained, because the financial system reform devolving funds to localities was one step ahead of other reforms, each new reform initiative threatened the financial interests of localities (Tian Yinong et al. 1988). Local officials helped block important measures, such as the replacement of profits with taxes, that would have expanded the financial autonomy of factories while shrinking the financial control of local governments over factories (see chapter 12). Having taken advantage of their new financial authority to build political machines for themselves, the local politicians fought off any attempt by the center or the enterprises to change the rules of the game back to central control or forward to market freedom.

The economic consequences of creating a system that strengthened the financial incentives of provincial officials also were mixed. True, the officials responded to the new incentives with zeal, promoting local industry like natural entrepreneurs. To observe provincial officials touting their local investment climate to foreign businesspeople was to realize that more than thirty years of communist rule had not destroyed the Chinese aptitude for commerce, even among communist bureaucrats, a group generally thought to be sluggishly conservative. Once they had their own funds, coastal provinces such as Guangdong, Fujian, and Jiangsu, whose economies were backward and depressed because of decades of neglect by central authorities (who had concentrated investment on inland provinces), were dramatically revived. Another positive consequence was that putting more of the revenues in the hands of local officials stimulated the construction of "nonproductive infrastructure"—housing, roads, telephones, town gas, and so on—that the central government had long ignored in favor of industrial expansion.[5]

However, in an economic environment still characterized by irrational prices and lack of risk, the revenue-maximizing behavior of

5. It would be interesting to compare the national budgetary allocations in the prereform era with provincial and city budgetary allocations after reform to see whether in fact the local governments spend less on industry and more to satisfy other public needs than the national government did.

local officials produced some perverse results. First, local governments engaged in investment and construction binges. They built mostly processing plants that were profitable because of irrational administratively set prices but were nonetheless wasteful. The local investment booms created supply shortages, inflation, and deficits. Second, now that they had a direct stake in local industry, provincial officials moved to protect local firms from competition by firms from other provinces. Local protectionism segmented the national market.

The decision to maintain the traditional bureaucratic political system and promote reform by creating a bloc of proreform local officials created vested interests in halfway reform and impeded progress to more thorough reform. Determined to protect what the Chinese call their "partial interests," local officials blocked or diluted crucial reform initiatives that would have improved the efficiency and self-regulation of the economy. And local bureaucratic entrepreneurs continued to stimulate economic overheating, causing inflation and other problems that discredited the reform drive and allowed conservative CCP elders to subvert it. Yet even when the conservatives increased their power within the party in 1988, they were unable to impose a new financial system on the provinces. During a period of succession competition, to flout the wishes of provincial politicians would have been political suicide even for conservative leaders whose primary base of support was the central bureaucracy.

This chapter begins by explaining why fiscal reform made sense in the Chinese historical context. I go on to describe the evolution of the fiscal system over the course of the reform decade and show how it reflects the political value of provincial officials to central politicians. After a brief note on other reform policies aimed at enhancing the power of localities, I discuss the consequences of fiscal decentralization. The chapter concludes by showing that the political logic of fiscal contracting to the provinces overpowered the centralizing instincts of Li Peng and his conservative party allies when their power increased in 1988.

The Financial Relationship Between Center and Localities in Prereform China

In 1951, shortly after the communist takeover, the basic shape of the PRC fiscal system was laid down. Although it later was subject to frequent tinkering, it essentially persists to the present day

(Caizheng Bu Caishui Tizhi Gaige Zhu 1989; Hsiao 1987; Guojia Caizheng Gailun Bianxie Zu 1984). The center monopolized formal financial authority and shared fiscal responsibilities and resources with lower levels. The system of fiscal decentralization was called "unified leadership, level-by-level management" (*tongyi lingdao fen ji guanli*). "Unified leadership" meant that the central government determined provincial expenditure budgets and that provincial governments had little freedom to make their own spending decisions.[6] Because there was no national revenue collection bureaucracy, no Chinese Internal Revenue Service, local officials collected profits and taxes as the agents of the central government.[7]

"Level-by-level management" meant that the profits of enterprises run by central ministries went to the central government, and the profits of locally run enterprises went to local governments. Revenue flows were determined by the quasi-ownership relations (what the Chinese call "subordination relations" [*lishu guanxi*]) between different levels of government and the enterprises. If a locality's revenues were insufficient to meet its expenditures as determined by the center, then the locality was given a share of the industrial-commercial tax and other taxes generated by local economic activity that were categorized as "shared" revenues. If revenues from local enterprises exceeded local expenditure needs as defined by the center, then the locality remitted a surplus to the center. Most provinces gave the center more than they received from it. Light industry, on which profits are high, was controlled largely by local authorities, whereas centrally controlled enterprises were concentrated in less profitable heavy industry (Donnithorne 1981).[8] After just one year of total centralization in 1950, the Chinese leadership in 1951 moved to a system that linked local revenues to locally administered enterprises.

The PRC fiscal system reflected China's tradition of centralized formal authority with a significant degree of de facto decentralization to the provincial level and below (although specific arrangements were not identical with earlier ones [Ch'ien Tuan-sheng 1961;

6. As Granick (1990) points out, local governments had greater control over the material products of local factories than over financial profits.
7. For a proposal to put local tax collectors under the direct control of the central tax department, see Dai Yuanchen et al. 1989.
8. As Audrey Donnithorne (1981) points out, the Chinese national government was able to draw on the taxable capacity of light industry only by taxing local governments, which was politically much harder than taxing firms.

Kuhn 1970; S. Mann 1987; Waldron 1990; Zelin 1984]). The central government relied on local agents to collect central revenues and gave these agents a share of the revenues as an incentive. Influenced by this historical tradition, China's communist leaders initially sought to strengthen central authority but soon returned to the historical pattern of decentralization.

The PRC's administrative and fiscal structure was much more decentralized than was the Soviet Union's even during the 1950s.[9] The horizontal authority of territorial governments over enterprises (called *kuai* by the Chinese) was more on a par with the vertical authority of the central ministries over enterprises (called *tiao* by the Chinese) than was the case in the USSR. The bureaucratic rank of provincial governments was equal to the bureaucratic rank of ministries in the PRC, just as it had been in the Guomindang's Republican government (Ch'ien Tuan-sheng 1961). The power of appointment was also less highly centralized in China than it was in the Soviet Union, with the party center responsible for filling only 13,000 posts on its nomenklatura list, as compared with 51,000 in the Soviet Union (Burns 1987). Although the heads of provincial finance departments were appointed by the party authorities in Beijing (the central nomenklatura included all positions one and two steps down in the hierarchy), lower-level financial officials were chosen by party authorities at the provincial level and below.

The more prominent role of provincial officials in the PRC than in the USSR reflected contemporary factors as well as Chinese tradition. Because the technical capacity of Chinese central planners was inadequate to the task of planning the entire economy, Beijing's economic commands never had the scope that Moscow's did. Chinese central economic authorities from the beginning relied on local help for industrial planning, finance, and administration. Also, provincial officials played a more prominent role in the Chinese Communist Party than they did in the Communist Party of the Soviet Union, whose provincial communist party organizations had been decimated by Stalin (Schurmann 1967).[10]

9.   Research by Donna Bahry (1987) shows that in the federal Soviet system, although the republics' share of the budget increased after Stalin, central control over planning and budgeting remained tight.
10.   Chinese provincial authority was also closely tied to the military, especially during the 1970s after the Cultural Revolution. Many provincial CCP secretaries served simultaneously as PLA officers.

The greater weight of Chinese provincial officials in the financial system also stemmed from differences in the Chinese and Soviet government-set price systems. In the Soviet Union planners set prices so that heavy industry, which was under centralized administration, was highly profitable. Under Chinese prices, however, heavy industry was much less profitable than light industry. Chinese relative prices forced the center to depend on revenues generated by light industrial plants, most of which were small and locally run.

On the expenditure side, the prereform PRC fiscal system was nearly as centralized as the Soviet one. Until the early 1970s (except during the Great Leap Forward in 1958) ministries handed down compulsory expenditure levels to provinces and had budgetary control over enterprise expenditures (Oksenberg and Tong 1990; author's interviews). Just because a province generated more funds did not mean it could spend them. If a province fulfilled its revenue collection targets and spent within the expenditure target, it was permitted to retain a small share of above-budget revenue, but its uses still had to be approved by the center.

Even on the revenue side, although the profits of locally run factories were earmarked as local revenues, the center was very much in command. Revenue-sharing contracts were renegotiated annually by central authorities. Year-by-year contracting caused haggling between center and provinces and made it difficult for provincial governments to accumulate funds for investment; whenever a province retained a substantial revenue surplus, the central government changed the terms to claim a larger share (Caizheng Bu Caishui Tizhi Gaige Zhu 1989). Annual contracts, although time-consuming, enhanced central authority by forcing provinces to compete with one another to obtain a good deal by demonstrating compliance with central instructions. By transferring funds through Beijing to backward regions, the center used the system to promote income redistribution and equalization of social services (Lardy 1979; Oksenberg and Tong 1984).

The Chinese fiscal system evolved in the direction of greater decentralization for two reasons. First, given the center's essential dependence on the light industrial profits produced by local factories, it made economic sense for the center to create a system that was more "incentive compatible." Allowing provinces to retain a larger share of revenues, especially above-quota revenues, and granting them the discretion to spend them strengthened the motivation of provincial officials to promote profitable enterprises and conscientiously collect revenues from them. Deng Xiaoping, who when serving as minister of finance during the early 1950s had laid down the basic principles for the financial system, stressed the incentive effect of allowing provincial governments to retain surplus revenues (Zuo Chuntai 1982; Oksenberg and Tong 1987).

Second, in view of the political influence of provincial officials within the CCP, it made political sense for party leaders to play to the provinces. The structure of PRC institutions made provincial officials a natural counterweight to central officials. Whenever Mao Zedong felt his political dominance threatened by rival party leaders and his policy initiatives obstructed by central government bureaucrats, he turned to provincial leaders for support. Mao's rhetoric of playing to the provinces linked the assertion of provincial authority, or *kuai*, to party leadership and politics in command, as pitted against the narrowly economic and partial interests of the ministries, or *tiao* (Unger 1987). Whenever he played to the provinces, Mao simultaneously used the center's nomenklatura power to replace provincial leaders not solidly in his camp with those he could count on (Teiwes 1966; P. Chang 1990). During the 1950s and 1960s Mao played to the provinces to overcome the resistance of central planners and ministry officials to his program for accelerating economic growth and social transformation and to defeat his party rivals.[11]

The first wave of decentralization began in 1955–56 with a critical reassessment of the performance of the Soviet economic model during the first five-year plan undertaken to prepare for the Eighth Party Congress. Mao was impatient with the slow pace of economic modernization and social transformation. From December 1955 until May 1956 he and other CCP leaders (including Chen Yun and Deng Xiaoping) conducted a comprehensive review of national eco-

---

11. Even in the Soviet Union, with a more centralized institutional setup, leaders with ambitious reform agendas have sought to enlist provincial leaders against the conservative central bureaucracy. Nikita Khrushchev tried to play to the provinces to weaken his rivals and disarm the powerful central ministries. The support of republic allies in the Central Committee saved Khrushchev when the Presidium (Politburo) tried to get rid of him in 1957 (Bahry 1987, 27). Of course, in the end the central apparatus overwhelmed Khrushchev's local supporters and brought the leader down. Mikhail Gorbachev also built a coalition of support for reform by building a base among republic party officials (Colton 1986).

nomic performance, ministry by ministry, province by province (Bo Yibo 1991). In February 1956 Nikita Khrushchev's speech at the Twentieth CPSU Congress criticizing Stalin's rule reinforced Mao's doubts about the wisdom of the Soviet economic model. Mao's conclusions from this reassessment were summarized in his speech "On the Ten Great Relationships," first presented in April 1956 to the Politburo.

The essence of Mao's judgment was that the Soviet model had failed to provide effective incentives for economic effort. To accelerate economic development China must more effectively mobilize people's initiative. The higher people's enthusiasm and initiative, the greater, faster, better, and more economical results production would yield (Wu Jinglian 1990).

Mao made common cause with provincial governments and large enterprises that complained about the restrictions central ministries placed on their financial autonomy. "If the power of localities is too small, it will not be advantageous to socialist construction," he said (Bo Yibo 1991, 26). "We must not follow the example of the Soviet Union in concentrating everything in the hands of the central authorities, shackling the local authorities and denying them the right to independent action" (Wu Jinglian 1990, 26). In other words, the fiscal and administrative system must be decentralized to stimulate local enthusiasm and initiative.

After the 1956 congress Mao sped the pace of agricultural cooperativization and launched the Great Leap Forward by mobilizing the support of provincial leaders at meetings in 1956–57 (P. Chang 1970; MacFarquhar 1974; Lieberthal and Dickson 1989; Goodman 1984).[12] An integral part of the campaign to collectivize agriculture, industrialize the countryside, and speed up economic modernization was a package of policies delegating greater fiscal and admin-

12. David Goodman (1984) challenges Parris Chang's (1990) assertion that the provincial leaders promised to support Mao's policies in exchange for greater provincial autonomy by presenting evidence that the provincial leaders were not in complete agreement: although some advocated greater financial autonomy, others demanded more central aid to provinces for projects such as water conservation. To argue that provincial officials have political influence in the policy process and that Mao Zedong tried to win their support does not require that they always agree on policy; in fact, given the very different situations faced by their regions, it would be surprising if they had unanimous policy preferences. Moreover, provincial leaders probably find no inconsistency in their calls for greater financial autonomy and more state aid for particular projects such as water conservation; they wish to have both.

istrative power to the provinces. Provinces were granted a larger share of their revenues, greater discretion over tax rates and expenditures and planning authority, and the "ownership" of almost all central enterprises.[13] Theoretically, the new sharing arrangements were to be fixed for three years to enable provinces to make long-term plans, but in 1959, when the Great Leap Forward had proved to be a national economic disaster, the arrangements were adjusted. When economic failure caused Mao Zedong to lose prestige and the central economic organs to reassert themselves, the fiscal system was recentralized. It was impossible to put the cat back into the bag, however. Funds and financial authority remained more dispersed than they had been before the Great Leap.

Mao stirred up a second wave of decentralization in the mid-1960s, when he reclaimed power from central bureaucrats and party moderates by launching the Cultural Revolution. In 1964, provinces were authorized to set aside a portion of their revenues as extra-budgetary funds, creating a financial cushion to win the support of provincial subordinates for Mao's national policy initiatives.[14] In 1968, enterprises were allowed to retain approximately 10 percent of their profits to use for local projects (Sun Yun 1982). From 1965–66 on, provinces won authority over construction projects under a certain limit and a share of their budget surplus for their own use (Oksenberg and Tong 1987).

The fiscal system introduced in 1970 by Mao's radical supporters tilted even more toward the provinces. A program of regional self-sufficiency, justified by the threat of war, was introduced, involving a massive transfer of central enterprises to provincial control and a shift of most revenue sources and expenditure categories to the provincial level (Naughton 1988a). Provincial governments were granted authority to set their own budgets and, after transferring a lump sum to the center according to contract, were able to keep and use all remaining revenues (Oksenberg and Tong 1987). The decentralization slogan was "Delegating powers to lower levels is a revolution; the more you do, the more revolutionary you will be" (Wu Jinglian 1990, 5). After Deng Xiaoping returned to power in 1975, he attempted to restore central control over budgetary authority and funds, provoking a political struggle in which the

13. For a detailed description of the fiscal system of the Great Leap Forward, see Oksenberg and Tong 1987.
14. Richard Cyert and James March (1963) would call extrabudgetary funds a form of "organizational slack."

radical Gang of Four took the side of the provinces (Unger 1987; J. Tong 1989).[15] At the time of Mao's death in 1976, financial authority and resources were still highly dispersed, and provincial authorities, especially from the industrialized provinces that remitted a large proportion of their revenues to the center, were pressing for even more fiscal decentralization.[16]

The history of the 1949–76 fiscal system provides the context for the decision to lead off the post-Mao economic reform drive with fiscal reform. As one economic official said, the "eating in separate kitchens" reform was the "result of history; . . . there was no other rational solution" (author's interview). The legacy of the prior system explains the political logic of fiscal reform:

A tradition of revenues divided according to the quasi ownership of enterprises by different levels of government. Centrally run enterprises provided revenues for the center and locally run enterprises provided revenues for provinces. Different levels of government assumed proprietary financial rights over their own enterprises.[17]

A trend of dispersion of financial resources that had accelerated during the Cultural Revolution. Provincial governments ran a large proportion of industrial enterprises, retained a substantial share of budgetary revenue, and controlled sizable extrabudgetary funds, equal to three times the 1965 amount (Sun Yun 1982). Provincial officials had come to view these resources and powers as entitlements.
The central treasury could not be supported by the taxes and profits of central enterprises and was dependent on profits and taxes generated by locally run (mostly light) industry (Guojia Caizheng Gailun Bianxie Zu 1984). As Audrey Donnithorne (1972) put it, the Chinese central government was in the position of a medieval king who was not able to live off his own and who therefore had to extract funds from feudatories.

15.   In early 1976 a decision was made to recentralize a proportion of depreciation funds, but later that year Deng Xiaoping was purged again, and at a central work conference in June the recentralization was reversed (Naughton 1987).
16.   Chinese planning was also much more decentralized than Soviet planning. The volume of interprovincial trade in China was depressed because provincial planners sought independent balances. This argument is presented in Lyons 1987.
17.   During most periods the same method of differentiating revenues by the subordination relations of enterprises was used in the Soviet Union, but a much smaller proportion of enterprises was "owned" by local governments (Bahry 1987).

A pattern of playing to the provinces in elite political competition. Mao Zedong, by playing to the provinces during the Great Leap Forward and Cultural Revolution, had turned provincial officials into a key constituency within the party. After 1958 almost all the provincial party first secretaries were either full or alternate members of the Central Committee, and a significant number (approximately half) of Politburo members were concurrent or former provincial first secretaries (Goodman 1984). Provincial leaders were important members of the selectorate that chose the party leader. To extend Donnithorne's metaphor, the feudatories sat in the council that selected (or at least ratified the selection of) the king. The central government and CCP had formal authority over provincial governments, but the political incentives of individual party leaders were not to use this authority against provincial officials—to exercise self-restraint (Granick 1990)—and to keep good relations with them instead.

No division of authority and responsibility between central and local governments. Funds had been decentralized, but fiscal responsibility had not. The system remained one of "eating from the big pot" (*chi da guo fan*). The center was considered responsible for guaranteeing the original level of local revenues even when the economic situation changed (Guojia Caizheng Gailun Bianxie Zu 1984). Whenever unexpected economic developments landed provinces in financial straits, the MOF was expected to bail them out. According to the same principle, if the central budget was hard-pressed, the MOF could reclaim funds from the provinces by renegotiating the terms of annual sharing contracts. There was no institutionalized link between revenue and expenditure, between power and responsibility.

The Initiation of Post-Mao Fiscal Reforms

The initiative to expand fiscal autonomy with the "eating in separate kitchens" reform came from both the bottom up and the top down. Several provinces proposed revenue-sharing experiments during 1976 and 1977. The boldest was Jiangsu, an economically developed coastal province that proposed a package of decentralizing reforms in planning, material allocation, and fiscal management. Jiangsu's proposed fiscal arrangement, the "fixed-rate responsibility" system (*guding bili baogan*), was a variant of the "sharing total revenues" arrangement implemented nationally from 1959 to 1970 and in 1976. Total provincial revenues were split between center and province (Jiangsu's share was set at 42 percent), with the percentages remaining unchanged for four years. The province decided its own expenditures (central ministries ceased to issue spending targets to the province) and was responsible for balancing its own budget. Jiangsu's experiment was introduced in 1977 and by 1980 was judged a success in motivating the province to expand production and revenue and to contribute more revenue to the center (Oksenberg and Tong 1987). Two other types of contractual sharing schemes that were tried out on an experimental basis in sixteen other provinces beginning in 1977 were suggested by Minister of Finance Zhang Jingfu (Oksenberg and Tong 1987).

Surprisingly, the move to popularize fiscal decentralization was proposed in 1979 by the MOF itself (author's interviews). The immediate context of the move was the inability of the MOF to meet its financial demands because the fiscal system had become so dispersed (*fensan*) during the 1960s and 1970s. Provincial officials had pursued their own interests, and the flow of central revenues had dwindled. When describing the position of the MOF, officials often used the family metaphor: as family head (*jiazhang*), the MOF had a hard time managing the family without enough money. Ministries and local governments, like prodigal sons, spent recklessly.[18] The children argued among themselves and complained that the family head mistreated them. In that situation, it was better for the family head to divide the family and put the children off on their own.[19] Hence, the family metaphor of the decentralization policy: dividing the family by splitting up the kitchen (literally, the stove).

From the viewpoint of the MOF, the advantage of eating in separate kitchens was that it clarified the responsibilities as well as the resources of each tier of government and guaranteed central income at current levels. The reform would stem the progressive deterioration of central revenues and force localities to share financial risk with the center. Minister of Finance Zhang Jingfu diagnosed the problems with the previous system at the National People's Congress in June 1979:

> The current system of public finance administration, in terms of the relationship between central government finance and regional finance, is still in a state in which true "administration by separate levels" is unimplemented, the authority and

18. The notion of "prodigal bureaucracy" was suggested by Fred Riggs 1964.
19. According to interviews, the SPC proposed decentralizing capital construction at the same time (1979) and for the same reason, that is, to divest itself of responsibility.

duties of the various levels with regard to public finance are not clearly defined, what should be concentrated is not concentrated and what should be dispersed is not dispersed. (*Renmin ribao*, 30 June 1979, quoted in Fujimoto 1980, 3)

Another official expressed the MOF viewpoint in more pointed language: "Financial power had become so dispersed during the Cultural Revolution that the 'eating in separate kitchens' system was the only way the Finance Ministry could fix [*guding*] its level of state revenue. After the Cultural Revolution this was the only way the Finance Ministry could get its hands on the money" (author's interview). When advocating the scheme to the bureaucracy, MOF officials stressed its incentive advantages in arousing local economic activism, but in their own minds they viewed the scheme as a move in the direction of tightening up (*shou*), not letting go (*fang*). As one Chinese account put it, "The original intention of 'eating in separate kitchens' was to 'share down' [*xia fen*] the burden in a situation of financial stringency, not to share benefits" (Macroeconomic Management Project Group 1987, 16).

Who were the CCP leaders urging the MOF to decentralize the fiscal system? Interview accounts disagree. Some officials said that the decision was made by a small group of top party leaders including Zhao Ziyang, who had just come from Sichuan. One MOF official said that this group "decided to give power and money to provincial leaders, which made them happy and made them support reform." According to this interpretation, Zhao, having just come from Sichuan, understood the perspective of provincial officials and convinced Deng Xiaoping to play to it. In fact, Zhao was not appointed premier until 1980, after the key 1979 meetings deliberating fiscal arrangements, but he may nonetheless have been an influential participant at the meetings. Deng Xiaoping's role in initiating the reform is also questioned. Some officials said the policy actually was originated by Hua Guofeng, then CCP chairman.[20]

The pressure from provincial officials for greater fiscal autonomy in 1979 was palpable to central party and government officials. Some officials I interviewed said that the provinces left the center little choice but to pursue fiscal decentralization. As one official said, "They couldn't *not* do it at that time; the provinces wouldn't

20. Hua had already played to the provinces with his 1978 Twelve-Year Plan.

have agreed."[21] The provincial leaders "forced a showdown" (*tan pai*) with the center and insisted on a fiscal scheme that would be fixed for several years, that allowed them to decide how to spend their revenues, and that gave them a larger share of their revenues.[22] In the context of the succession contest between Deng Xiaoping and Hua Guofeng, the provincial leaders could not be denied. Hua Guofeng may have been the original high-level author of "eating in separate kitchens," but after Deng Xiaoping had defeated him and become the dominant leader, he embraced the policy as a way to consolidate his authority and build support for the reform drive. Deng's right-hand men, Hu Yaobang and Zhao Ziyang, did the same.

The meetings discussing the fiscal system reforms gave provincial leaders ample opportunities to voice their demands. At a central work conference in April 1979 fiscal decentralization was discussed and one form of decentralization chosen. A conference of provincial party secretaries in October 1979 decided to adopt a different form (Tian Yinong et al. 1988; Oksenberg and Tong 1987). The final formula and the timetable for implementation, as well as each province's sharing contract (including base figure, percentages to be remitted and retained, or amount of subsidy), were determined at the National Planning Conference attended by representatives of provinces and ministries in December 1979 ("State Council Notice on Carrying Out the Financial Management System of 'Apportioning Revenues'" 1981).

The implementation of the reform was supposed to await the return of several thousand large enterprises to direct central government subordination, but this condition was never met as both the managers of the enterprises and provincial leaders objected (author's interviews).[23] Instead, at the December 1979 conference a sense of urgency, particularly on the part of provincial participants, compelled a decision to rush ahead to implementation without recentralizing the enterprises (Tian Yinong et al. 1988, 76; Naughton

21. Backward provinces and national minority provinces that operated at a deficit opposed financial decentralization (author's interviews).
22. Some provincial advocates pressed for an approach to reform called "local planned economy" that would shift all economic authority from center to provinces. They held up American federalism as the model to emulate (Fang Weizhong 1979).
23. One interviewee estimated that five hundred large enterprises had been slated for recentralization.

1987). As Barry Naughton observes, "Local governments got greater operational autonomy without having to sacrifice any of their revenue sources" (1987, 71–72).

At the time the "eating from separate kitchens" reform was introduced, few critical voices were heard. Some economists identified the potential problems with the method at policy research conferences in 1979–80 (author's interviews; Guo Daimo and Zhang Zhaoming 1979; Fang Weizhong 1979). A paper criticizing fiscal decentralization came out of the Economic Reform Small Group, the precursor of the Commission on Economic System Reform (author's interviews). But the policy had such a compelling political logic, from the perspectives of the reformist party leadership, the MOF, and provincial officials, that any doubts about its wisdom were swept aside.[24]

The 1980 Fiscal Reforms: Eating in Separate Kitchens

The reforms introduced in 1980 expanded the fiscal authority and resources of provinces. Although the contractual sharing form of the new fiscal arrangements resembled that of the past, the new arrangements were fundamentally different in three respects:[25] (1) Revenue shares were fixed for five years so that provinces could profit from increases in revenue and plan ahead. (2) Provinces were responsible for balancing their own budgets by adjusting their expenditures to match their revenues; they could no longer rely on bailouts from the center. (3) Provinces had budgetary authority to arrange the structure and amount of local spending; they ceased to receive mandatory fiscal targets from the central ministries.[26]

24. According to Tian Yinong et al. 1988 (75), despite the original intention in 1979 to reform other aspects of the economic structure before tackling financial reform, the clamor from all quarters for more financial power was so deafening that financial reform was undertaken first.
25. This summary description draws heavily on Oksenberg and Tong 1987.
26. The ministries must have been reluctant to give up their control over local enterprise expenditures. In a 1979 document on fiscal decentralization the State Council emphasized that although the central ministries would no longer have authority to hand down local expenditure targets, they still were to "guide the direction, approve the work program, carry out supervision and urging, sum up experiences, and help local enterprises in their sector" ("State Council Notice on Carrying Out the Financial Management System of 'Linking Revenues' " 1979, 803).

The new system was applied flexibly to the thirty provincial-level governments, establishing different rules for different regions.[27] The reform included five separate arrangements:[28]

1. Guangdong and Fujian, the two provinces where the national government was concentrating its efforts to attract foreign investment, were granted the most generous plan, "lump sum transfer." Almost all revenue sources were turned over to the provinces. Guangdong would give the center 1 billion yuan per year, and Fujian would receive as a subsidy 150 million yuan per year. The amounts were fixed for five years. The provinces could keep everything above these amounts.

2. The metropolises of Beijing, Tianjin, and Shanghai, which provided the lion's share of central revenues, were placed on the most restrictive plan, despite their objections. Their plan, a version of the Jiangsu "sharing total revenues" arrangement, fixed a percentage of total revenue they were required to remit to the center each year; in 1980 Shanghai remitted 88.8 percent, Beijing 63.5 percent, and Tianjin 68.8 percent (Oksenberg and Tong 1987). Because the funds they generated were vital to the central government, their percentages were revised every year, in contrast with the Jiangsu scheme, which fixed percentages for four years.

3. Jiangsu continued its experiment in "sharing total revenues" with the percentages fixed for four years. With the exception of the profits and taxes of centrally controlled enterprises, which in all schemes continued to be channeled directly to the central treasury (*Liaoning jingji tongji nianjian* 1987), all taxes and profits were lumped together and then divided by percentage between center and province.

4. Sixteen provinces were put on a "sharing specific revenues" system, which resembled the sharing arrangement in effect from 1951 to 1958. Revenue sources were divided into four categories: central fixed income, local fixed income, fixed-rate shared income, and income shared by adjustment. Central fixed income was obtained mainly from the profits and taxes of centrally run enterprises. Local fixed income was derived mainly from the profits of

27. There were originally twenty-nine provinces; Hainan became the thirtieth. Provincial-level governments include provinces, autonomous regions, and the municipalities of Beijing, Tianjin, and Shanghai.
28. The system was described in "State Council Notice on Carrying Out the Financial Management System of 'Apportioning Revenues'" 1981.

locally run enterprises. Fixed-rate shared income came mainly from large enterprises that had devolved to local management during the Cultural Revolution and that the center had wanted to reclaim (the center received 80 percent of their profits, the province 20 percent). The only revenue included in the category "income shared by adjustment" was the industrial commercial tax, the most important tax revenue. The contract fixed the sharing rate for shared income, adjustment shared income, and the local remittance to the center for five years.

The "sharing specific revenues" system was chosen over the Jiangsu "sharing total revenues" system for the majority of provinces by provincial party secretaries at their October 1979 meeting.[29] The "sharing specific revenues" arrangement earmarked the profits of local enterprises as local revenues and thereby strengthened the local government's sense of proprietorship over these enterprises. During a period of economic expansion and optimism, most local officials preferred this form of revenue sharing.

5. Eight national minority provinces and autonomous regions that had previously received subsidies from the center to cover their chronic deficits were put on the "sharing specific revenues" system with their subsidy fixed for five years and increased annually by 10 percent. These provinces could retain the total amount of revenue collected above the budget.

The Evolution of Fiscal Sharing Systems, 1980–87: Satisfying the Provinces

The evolution of fiscal sharing schemes reveals the ability of provincial officials to win concessions from the center because central party leaders needed their support for the reform drive and for their own political careers. Provincial officials could make a strong case

29. In July 1979 the State Council had made a preliminary decision to implement a version of fiscal decentralization called "linking revenues and expenditures, sharing total revenues, contracting for percentages, fixed for three years" (shouzhi guagou, chuan e fencheng, bili baogan, san nian bubian); this plan was essentially the Jiangsu "sharing total revenues" system. The "apportioning revenues and expenditures while contracting responsibility according to levels" (huafen shouzhi, fenji baogan) or "sharing fixed revenues" system was introduced on an experimental basis only in Sichuan because it was said to require reforms in other aspects of the economy ("State Council Notice on Carrying Out the Financial Management System of 'Linking Revenues'" 1979). After the October meeting of provincial party secretaries and the December National Planning Conference, the State Council announced a change to the "sharing fixed revenues" system.

to keep more revenues because they were taking on more budgetary responsibilities and the reform environment created new uncertainties for their enterprises.

The terms of each revenue-sharing contract were set in bargaining between provincial officials and the budget department of the MOF. The contract had to be approved by the office of the minister of finance and by the State Council ("State Council Notice on Carrying Out the Financial Management System of 'Linking Revenues'" 1979). A province dissatisfied with the terms of its contract could appeal to the minister of finance and even to the State Council (author's interviews). In effect, the responsibility for each contract was appropriated by the State Council, whose members were sensitive to political direction from the top levels of the CCP. The revenue-sharing contract was a political document, and the politicians in the State Council wanted to claim credit for it.

When the sharing rates between the center and the provinces were negotiated at the 1979 National Planning Conference, the provinces came out ahead of the center.[30] The MOF conceded to lower its revenue targets and increase central appropriations by 3 billion yuan, reducing the provinces' expenditure burden by 10 percent and providing an additional several billion yuan as subsidies; it had to absorb a budget deficit of almost 13 billion yuan (Tian Yinong et al. 1988; Oksenberg and Tong 1987). This pattern of fiscal bargaining between center and province—that is, setting sharing rates that were generous to the provinces but left the center with insufficient funds—was observed by several officials I interviewed. It had occurred in the case of the Jiangsu experiment in 1977; after one year the center's share was adjusted up from 57 percent to 61 percent, only in part because of a change excluding enterprise depreciation funds from the local revenue base (Oksenberg and Tong 1987). One official explained that the center usually gave in to provinces when negotiating base numbers and percentages. The center always felt it had to take care of the localities, especially because its reform policies were responsible for squeezing local enterprises.

Although the original intention was for fiscal contracts to remain fixed for five years, the economic and political environment interfered. On the economic side, the reform of other aspects of the

30. In an earlier document the State Council had stressed that in the fiscal contract negotiations, stability of central revenues and national financial balance had to take priority ("State Council Notice on Carrying Out the Financial Management System of 'Linking Revenues' " 1979).

economic system failed to keep pace with fiscal reform.[31] Prices were still administratively controlled so that whenever a product's price was revised, provinces whose revenues were affected demanded and usually received an adjustment in their fiscal sharing contract (author's interviews). For example, when textile prices were changed, textile-producing localities came to the center for compensation. And whenever the subordinate relations of an enterprise were altered, say, by shifting a factory from local management to central management, there was a battle to get the center to recalculate revenue and expenditure shares (author's interviews).[32]

The environment was particularly perilous during the initial period of fiscal reform, which coincided with the 1981–82 retrenchment. Especially hard hit were provinces that received most of their income from heavy industry, which bore the brunt of contractionary policies. In Liaoning, for instance, the center agreed to help by raising the province's revenue retention rate but made it wait a year because of heavy central deficits; it extended a loan to Liaoning in the meantime (author's interview).

In an uncertain economic environment, the system of fiscal contracting became a method for maintaining the center-provincial balance. One article from the MOF praised fiscal reform for "maintaining relative stability in the distribution relationship between the central administration and local administrations and reducing the pounding on the budget management system resulting from changes in economic factors" (Caizheng Bu Caishui Tizhi Gaige Zhu 1988, 35). In 1983 there was a major readjustment of contract terms to compensate provinces for 1980–82 changes in the subordinate relations of enterprises, changes in interest rates, changes in the prices of such items as soybeans and petroleum for agricultural use, and unexpected expenses to demobilize soldiers (Tian Yinong et al. 1988, 84). The provinces treated their original financial position as an entitlement that they expected the center to preserve by compensating for economic perturbations.

31. "The failure to achieve a complete set of reforms has affected the implementation of fiscal reforms" (Caizheng Bu Caishui Tizhi Gaige Zhu 1989, 232).
32. According to the 1980 regulations, a change in the subordinate relationships of enterprises or the levying of new taxes constituted grounds for a renegotiation of contract terms, whereas price changes, wage increases, and tax rate changes did not ("State Council Notice on Carrying Out the Financial Management System of 'Apportioning Revenues' " 1981).

The central government was never able to shift fiscal responsibility to the provinces even though that had been the aim of the 1980 reform: the kitchens were not entirely separate after all, and provincial officials still expected the center to feed them. As one MOF assessment concluded, "While in name there is separate responsibility at different levels, this is not really implemented and the problem of eating from the big pot has not been fundamentally solved" (Caizheng Bu Caishui Tizhi Gaige Zhu 1988, 35). An MOF official complained in an interview that the reform system that was called a "guarantee for doing" (*baogan*, "contract") was in reality a "guarantee for not doing" (*bao bu gan*).[33]

The center's continuing solicitousness toward the provinces reflected China's institutional context of delegation by consensus (see chapter 7). Keeping the provinces satisfied and on board the reform drive was an important consideration for reformist party leaders. Another political consideration was succession politics. The "eating in separate kitchens" reform was a set of particularistic deals for provincial officials designed to win their support for individual party leaders as well as for the reform drive. The only provinces that were clearly dissatisfied were the three metropolises whose revenues were too crucial to the center to allow political considerations to dominate.[34] Zhao Ziyang tried to appease officials from these metropolises by periodically raising their revenue share, but still in a context of high rates of transfer (author's interviews).[35]

Fiscal contracting served the collective interests of party leaders in building support for reform and their individual interests in building support for themselves, but it left the central treasury too poor to meet its obligations for price subsidies, infrastructure construction, and the like. Therefore, Beijing officials devised several politically innocuous approaches to meeting central needs for revenue.

33. The continued existence of the big pot is illustrated by the widespread "chicken game" between local and central governments over grain procurement funds during 1989–90. Local governments spent their grain procurement funds for other purposes and then asked the center to bail them out to prevent peasant unrest.
34. That is not to say that fiscal reform didn't aggravate regional tensions. For one thing, many provinces were jealous of Guangdong's special financial privileges (author's interviews).
35. Shanghai's share was increased from 12.1 percent in 1984 to 24 percent in 1985. Tianjin's share was raised from 46 percent in 1984 to 58 percent in 1985 (J. Tong 1989, 28).

First, they appropriated the earnings of several of the most profitable industries by organizing them into national state corporations. State corporations for automobiles, tobacco products, petrochemicals, nonferrous metals, and shipping were established during 1982–83.[36] The creation of these corporations, which was urged on Zhao Ziyang by his adviser Ma Hong, was supported unanimously by the party leadership (author's interviews). Central corporations were considered a matter of fiscal necessity even though they flew in the face of market reform principles. As monopolies they discouraged competition, and as administrative entities they constrained the freedom of subordinate enterprises. Enterprises chafed at the restrictions imposed by corporations and often complained about them to the SEC, but there was little the SEC could do. Beginning in 1984 the Reform Commission and State Council held meetings to discuss how to restore competition and enterprise autonomy to the sectors controlled by corporations, but little progress was made (author's interviews). As of 1985, although some steps had been taken to encourage competition—for example, by dividing the automobile corporation into two—the revenues generated by these corporations, as well as by all enterprises under the Ministries of Petroleum, Coal, and Electric Power, had become the preserve of the center (Wong 1990).

Most of the industries affected by the creation of central corporations were widely dispersed. To appease the provinces and ministries that lost revenues to the new corporations, Beijing offered side payments including a 20 percent share of the taxes and profits of the enterprises they gave up.[37] Corporations were a more feasible way to increase central revenues than was hitting up particular provinces. Even so, central implementation of these cash-cow corporations was lax. In the case of the tobacco corporation, for example, many localities refused to give up their cigarette factories, and no one forced them to do so. The automobile corporation had less than a complete monopoly as well (author's interviews).

36. One of these corporations, the Chinese National Petrochemical Corporation, was granted the bureaucratic status of a ministry; all the others were made subordinate to ministries.
37. In the case of the Chinese National Petrochemical Corporation, the cities of Beijing and Shanghai, although they had no financial claim over the profits of their petrochemical factories, did obtain depreciation funds from them. When the corporation was founded, the cities were allowed to keep their original share of the factories' depreciation funds for three years (author's interview).

Second, "temporary" shortfalls in central revenue were met by ad hoc extractions applied universally. Provincial governments lent the center eight billion yuan in 1980 and another four billion in 1981; the center wrote off the loans in 1982 (Oksenberg and Tong 1987; Hsiao 1987). In 1983 a 10 percent tax (later raised to 15 percent) on extrabudgetary funds was slapped on all provinces to generate central funds for infrastructure projects, and a 10 percent tax on construction projects financed by extrabudgetary funds was added at the end of 1983 (Oksenberg and Tong 1987). In 1987 all budgetary expenditures were slashed by 10 percent, and local officials were required to lend this amount to the center (Wang Bingqian 1987). Throughout the decade local governments, enterprises, and individuals were pressured to purchase treasury bonds "voluntarily." Of course, these extractions proved that eating from the big pot worked both ways: the provinces were expected to bail out the center just as the center was expected to bail out the provinces.

Finally, the central government shifted more budgetary responsibilities to all the provinces, handing over virtually all responsibility for price subsidies, housing and urban infrastructure construction, education, health, and many other budget items calculated according to uniform formulas.

The universal approach for generating central revenues was politically safer for party leaders than leaning hard on particular provinces. Everyone paid a little, and no one felt the pinch too severely.[38] With the combination of particularistic sharing contracts tilted toward the provinces and a few sectoral preserves, universally applied extractions, and uniform, formula-based expenditure obligations to pay back the center, party leaders had found a politically winning formula of concentrated benefits and diffuse costs.

The evolution of revenue-sharing arrangements after 1980 reflected central officials' continued deference toward provincial interests. The State Council often justified policy modifications as measures to

38. In one exception to the universal application of these extractions, the center asked Guangdong and Fujian for loans in 1981 (1.6 billion yuan from Guangdong, 154 million yuan from Fujian) and again in 1982; the loans were written off in 1983 and never repaid (J. Tong 1989, 19). Officials in Guangdong and Fujian probably calculated that it was worth their while to pay off the center to keep their special privileges (which included capital construction and foreign investment approval authority, planning authority, a separate labor market, and foreign exchange retention as well as fiscal autonomy). From their point of view, the loans were protection money to the organization boss to preserve their profitable franchise.

strengthen central financial control ("State Council Notice on Improving the Financial Management System of 'Apportioning Revenues'" 1982). Conservative party elders and leaders of the central economic bureaucracies were certainly worried about protecting central revenues and keypoint capital construction. But in fact, shifts in fiscal arrangements were impelled more by changes in the situation at the lower levels than by the needs of the central treasury.

In 1982, two years after the reforms were introduced, ten of the fifteen provinces originally on the "sharing specific revenues" system shifted over to the Jiangsu "sharing total revenues" system, and by 1983 all provinces except the three metropolises, Guangdong, and Fujian were on the Jiangsu system ("State Council Notice on Improving the Financial Management System of 'Apportioning Revenues'" 1982; Caizheng Bu Caishui Tizhi Gaige Zhu 1989; Oksenberg and Tong 1987; Wong 1990). With the exception of centrally run enterprises whose profits and taxes still went directly to the center, the profits and taxes of all enterprises were pooled, with the center and province dividing the total.

The reason for the change was that readjustment, wage increases, and enterprise profit retention had cut into the profits of local enterprises, and local governments were hurting (Tian Yinong et al. 1988, 83). Under the "sharing total revenues" system, local governments got a larger share of industrial-commercial tax revenues, which were more stable, in exchange for giving up a share of the profits of local enterprises. During a period of expansion local governments preferred the "sharing fixed revenues" system because local enterprise profits were growing and their claim on these profits was complete. The "sharing fixed revenues" system also made their proprietorship of local factories more direct. But when contraction and structural reform were threatening the profits of local factories, they preferred to spread their risk with a system that put their finances on a broader base. As one 1982 account explained, while the "sharing fixed revenues" method seems more attractive to localities, "as a matter of fact, when the local fixed income increases slowly or even decreases because of various reasons, while the supplementary income from the revenue of industrial and commercial tax increases relatively sharply or does not decrease, the localities will be willing to accept the method of sharing total revenues" (Zuo Chuntai 1982, 16). In other words, provincial officials will opt for whatever sharing scheme will maximize short-term returns. In 1982–83 provinces obtained not only a beneficial change in the fiscal sharing method but also new sharing rates that were computed to compensate them for the loans they had provided to the center ("State Council Notice on Improving the Financial Management System of 'Apportioning Revenues'" 1982; Oksenberg and Tong 1987).

The primacy of provincial interests was demonstrated once again when in early 1983 MOF officials and Zhao Ziyang's advisers proposed to replace fiscal contracting and enterprise profit contracting with a new financial system that involved collecting revenues from the enterprises in the form of taxes instead of profits (the tax-for-profit reform). Two of the objectives of the tax-for-profit proposal were (1) to reduce the negotiability of enterprise and local government financial obligations by formalizing them in the form of taxes; and (2) to weaken the financial linkage between enterprise "ownership" and budgetary revenues by creating local and national taxes that all enterprises, regardless of their subordination relations, would pay (Wong 1990).

Provincial officials resisted the effort to replace the easily manipulable and politically useful system of financial contracting with a uniform, legalized tax system. Admittedly, they wasted time and energy haggling over the terms of the financial contracts with the center above and the enterprises below; under contracting, their fiscal relations with both in the short term were zero-sum (Guojia Caizheng Gailun Bianxie Zu 1984; Caizheng Bu Caishui Tizhi Gaige Zhu 1989). And the formal authority of the center gave it the upper hand in bargaining over fiscal sharing contracts with provinces because provincial officials competed to win good terms. Yet the center rarely used its leverage over the provinces, preferring to bend toward them because, under reciprocal accountability, they were politically dependent on them. And, most important to provincial leaders, the power to bargain profit retention contracts with local enterprises offered them opportunities to collect political rents and build local machines.

Provincial officials also disliked the proposed tax system because they wanted to maintain their proprietary financial rights over local enterprises. The shift to the "sharing total revenues" system from the "sharing specific revenues" system in 1982–83 had diffused but not broken the financial linkage between provincial governments and provincial enterprises. Local party and government leaders enjoyed the political and economic benefits of their role as corporate heads of the local economy and were loath to give up the role.[39] One MOF official said, "An objective of the tax-for-profit reform was to break the administrative relationship of enterprises with localities, but it was not possible to do it. Some people's thought on this issue had not yet changed, and it also was a question of power" (author's interview).

In a series of meetings to discuss replacing profits with taxes, provincial officials expressed their doubts and succeeded in modifying or delaying elements of the plan that they opposed (see chapter 12 for details). The tax-for-profit reform was introduced in two stages. The first, begun in 1983, required enterprises to pay only an income tax and allowed them to continue to retain and remit to local governments after-tax profits at the same level as 1982. The second stage, begun in 1984, converted all profits to taxes but did not eliminate negotiability or financial linkages based on the subordination relations of enterprises, although that had been the original intention. An adjustment tax was bargained out with individual enterprises in seven-year contracts granting one rate on current profit levels and another lower rate for incremental profits (Wong 1990). Most important of all, because of the objections of provincial governments, separate local taxes were never implemented, and center and provinces continued to share the same tax base. The State Council declared in 1985 that all provinces would "temporarily" follow the system of "revenue sharing on the basis of dividing up tax revenues," which essentially replicated the Jiangsu "sharing total revenues" system (Wong 1990).[40]

Thanks to an effective defense by provincial officials, provincial financial interests were left intact. Although all revenues from enterprises were called taxes instead of profits, little else had

39. One group of Chinese reform economists argued that the emergence of problems such as local administrative interference and market blockades could not be blamed entirely on the decentralized fiscal system. They were the result of introducing fiscal decentralization into a system characterized by "unified local party and government leadership and the role played by local party and government authorities in functioning as the acting owners of enterprise assets under the system of public ownership" (Hua Sheng et al. 1988, no. 9:13).

40. Although formally all provinces were on a system of "sharing fixed revenues," "because conditions were not ripe" the "sharing total revenues" system was "temporarily implemented" (Caizheng Bu Caishui Tizhi Gaige Zhu 1989).

changed. As one official said, "It is the same regardless of whether we call it profits or tax; it is all revenue anyway."

Not surprisingly, CCP leaders did not intervene in the bureaucratic policy-making process to impose a thoroughgoing fiscal reform over the objections of provincial officials. The provincial officials were too important a bloc within the party to push around. Moreover, from the standpoint of individual leaders at the top levels of the party, tax-for-profit would have impeded their career-building strategies. Party politicians took advantage of the particularism of fiscal contracting to win political support for themselves and therefore were not enthusiastic about abandoning it.

Even the MOF, which was undoubtedly the agency most strongly committed to tax-for-profit, was basically satisfied with the current fiscal contracting system. MOF officials acknowledged the negative unintended consequences of "eating in separate kitchens"—from their point of view the most serious was the central budget deficit—but they always defended it as an improvement over the pre-1980 system. They complained that the income of central authorities was only one-third of national financial income while central expenditure was two-thirds of national financial expenditures (Caizheng Bu Caishui Tizhi Gaige Zhu 1988). And it galled them that the center always ran deficits while provincial governments sat on surpluses.[41] But the combination of fiscal contracting with national state corporations and loans from local governments had increased the central share of total budgetary income from 13.8 percent in 1972 and 14.3 percent in 1979 to over 20 percent in 1982, over 30 percent in 1985, and 35.3 percent in 1988 (Tian Yinong et al. 1988; "Minister of Finance" 1988). The good thing about fiscal contracting, according to MOF officials, was that "it could guarantee the center's financial income while at the same time arousing the activism of the localities." MOF officials were generally proud of their authorship of the 1980 fiscal reform, claiming that it proved they were more reform-minded and less conservative than everyone thought. One official said, "The Finance Ministry has to think about the interests of the localities as well as about the center. Some people who aren't familiar with our work think we care only about the center, but it is

41. During the period from 1979 to 1987 the center accumulated deficits totaling more than 64 billion yuan, while local governments ran surpluses totaling more than 7 billion yuan (Caizheng Bu Caishui Tizhi Gaige Zhu 1989, 232)

not so." Another MOF official said, "The Ministry of Finance supports reform. What we don't approve of is using money to buy reform from the lower levels."

Officials at all levels in China were unanimous in their public commitment to introduce the "system of divided taxes" whereby "on the basis of setting down the responsibility of central and local authorities, and in accordance with the principle of unifying responsibility and financial power, the income from different taxes is allocated to either the central administration or local administrations." They could agree on the advantages of the system of divided taxes over the system of sharing total revenues in breaking down localism, eliminating the constant wrangling between center and localities, and preventing the center and localities from having to bail out one another (Caizheng Bu Caishui Tizhi Gaige Zhu 1988, 35). Yet because individual central and local officials had a political incentive to stick with the current system, nothing was done to change it. Zhao Ziyang put the system of divided taxes in the comprehensive reform package he tried to introduce in 1986 (see chapter 13). The defeat of the package was in large measure due to the objections of local officials to the system of divided taxes.

Other Administrative Decentralization Policies

The "eating in separate kitchens" fiscal reform was not the only policy designed to enhance the power of local governments. Over the course of the decade the central government promulgated a number of different measures intended to improve the economic incentives of local governments and shift more responsibility to them in such matters as approving capital construction projects and foreign joint ventures, planning and material supply, retention of foreign exchange earnings, and many others. The CCP Central Committee declared its intention eventually to send down (*xiafang*) all industrial enterprises under ministry management to be run by local governments ("State Council Decision on Measures" 1984). The central government never abrogated its ultimate authority over the provinces; local budgets still had to be approved by the center, and the center could always reclaim control over capital construction, as it did during the economic contraction of 1989–90. Yet, thanks to various decentralization policies, provincial officials assumed day-to-day control of the local economy and took advantage of this control to build up local industry and local political machines.

One of the most significant decentralizing measures of the reform decade was the 1984 devolution of nomenklatura authority to CCP officials in provinces and ministries. The CCP retained its overall authority to appoint all government personnel, but the scope of each tier's appointment authority was cut back to include only positions at the same level and one level down instead of two levels down. The effect was to reduce the number of posts directly managed by the CCP Central Committee from 13,000 to 5,000 and to transfer two-thirds of the posts to province and ministry party committees; provincial party committees in turn decentralized nomenklatura control to prefectural, city, and county party committees (Burns 1987). The reform did not reduce the total size of the nomenklatura but expanded the patronage opportunities of local party officials.

The "central cities" (*zhongxin chengshi*) reform was another decentralizing measure with far-reaching consequences. The idea of giving cities provincial-level economic power was advocated by reformist party leaders as a method of improving the coordination of the economy. "Eating in separate kitchens" (itself originally proposed as a method to improve coordination) had provoked conflict between central ministries and provinces because the provinces had become more powerful and more assertive. Many enterprises labored under the dual rule of ministry and province. Their managers complained about having "too many mothers-in-law [*popo*]" who interfered in their operations. Shifting power to cities seemed like a good way to free enterprises from the constant strife between ministries and provinces.

The central cities notion was first proposed in 1979 by Chongqing, a regional economic city that had long felt exploited by the Sichuan provincial government (author's interviews).[42] Zhao Ziyang promoted the idea at the Fifth Session of the Fifth National People's Congress in 1982. The best way to restore effective coordination of the economy, according to Zhao, was to put all enterprises except those important to military security under regions with cities as their center (Xue Muqiao 1983).

City officials, who had for years chafed at restrictions and extractions imposed by provincial governments, welcomed the central cities idea. Naturally, though, provincial officials hated to give up

---

42. Chongqing is the largest city and the economic hub of southwest China, but Chengdu, not Chongqing, is the capital of Sichuan Province.

control over a major industrial city. Zhao Ziyang, who had only recently moved to Beijing from Sichuan, knew what he was doing when he made Chongqing the demonstration point for the central cities reform. The Sichuan authorities, who had benefited tremendously from Zhao's initiative making them the vanguard of comprehensive reform, could hardly argue publicly with their patron. Other provinces had no choice but to follow suit. And although Zhao Ziyang may have lost some popularity with the officials in provinces forced to give up power to central cities, he gained points with the officials in the cities.

From 1983 to 1987 the Central Committee and the State Council extended provincial-level economic authority to nine cities—Chongqing, Wuhan, Shenyang, Dalian, Guangzhou, Xian, Harbin, Qingdao, and Ningbo (Tian Jia et al. 1987; "State Council Decision to Improve the Method of Local Financial Contracts" 1988). As of 1991 the number had increased to fourteen and included Xiamen, Shenzhen, Nanjing, Chengdu, and Changchun ("*Xinhua* Policy Terminology Series" 1991). Although these cities were not granted the full authority of provinces—for one thing, the provinces still managed personnel appointments in the cities—they were full-fledged entities under the national plan (*jihua danlie*) and the budget.[43] The proliferation of subordinate units complicated the work of national planning and financial officials. Yet pressure from other cities jealous of the privileges of central cities forced central and provincial officials to extend special treatment, not as extensive as the powers granted to central cities but valuable nonetheless, to more and more so-called experimental cities.[44]

Special powers were granted to cities on a particularistic basis, enabling politicians to claim credit. The central cities reform, originally sold as a rationalizing measure, resulted in a proliferation of local government entities that engaged one another and the ministries in fierce competition. Many reformist economists and officials in Beijing who had originally been sympathetic to the central cities idea came to view it as simply a new form of localism, or *kuai-kuai* (author's interviews).

43. For an argument on behalf of giving full provincial-level legal status to central cities, see Tian Jia et al. 1987.
44. By 1984 one account listed fifty-two experimental cities in China ("Fifty-two Cities" 1984); in 1985 there were fifty-eight ("State Council Office Issues a Circular" 1985).

The competition among cities, provinces, and ministries was more bureaucratic than economic. Instead of ending jurisdictional conflicts, the central cities reform multiplied them. The Reform Bureau of the SEC was swamped with a multitude of disputes that arose in the process of shifting enterprises and powers from provinces to central cities. Negotiations over the division of revenues and responsibilities were as protracted and acrimonious as treaty negotiations between countries engaged in war. Provinces and central cities fought to keep profitable enterprises and divest themselves of unprofitable ones such as coal mines (author's interviews). Material supply issues were also relevant. For example, when Wuhan became a central city, the Ministry of Post and Telecommunications offered to send down to city jurisdiction the Wuhan factory that produced telephone equipment; the city refused because it lacked the ability to provide the factory the raw materials the ministry could provide (author's interview). In another jurisdictional dispute, Wuhan wanted to take over several pharmaceutical plants that had previously been administered directly by the national Pharmaceutical Bureau. Hubei Province and the Pharmaceutical Bureau both objected, arguing that medicines were special in character because their quality had to be maintained by unified management. The SEC ruled in favor of ministry-level management (author's interview).

The Effects of Fiscal Decentralization

The "eating in separate kitchens" reform, combined with other decentralizing measures, gave officials at the provincial level and below the incentive to develop their local economies and the wherewithal to do it. Given the lack of financial risk, it made sense for local officials to expand local industry. When the national government tried to restrict the production of some item by increasing its tax rate, the local officials were eager to expand production because it earned them more tax revenues (Zhu Mingchun 1990a). From the standpoint of local officials, expansion was desirable because it increased their revenues. As one Chinese analyst put it, "The financial system of eating in separate kitchens objectively gives rise to an economic mechanism that causes the expansion of the scale of investment" (Song Tingming 1985, 2).

Local government and CCP leaders responded to the new incentives with a burst of entrepreneurial energy. They founded new local industries and pitched the merits of their provinces to foreign investors. Stimulated by local initiatives, local and national growth rates skyrocketed.

Yet in the context of an only partially marketized command economy, local efforts to maximize revenues also had negative results, the most serious of which were (1) economic overheating accompanied by inflation, shortages, and budget and trade deficits; (2) segmentation of the national market by local protectionism; (3) competition among local governments for foreign trade and investment; and (4) local administrative interference and rent-seeking in enterprise management.

THE INCENTIVES OF LOCAL GOVERNMENT OFFICIALS

Local officials acted rationally to maximize their revenues, but the incentives in the reform environment were perverse. Because of irrational prices and lack of real financial risk, local government heads built new plants instead of improving the efficiency of existing plants. They invested more in high-profit processing plants than in infrastructure construction. And they protected their infant industries by excluding goods from rival plants in other provinces.

Voices from Beijing called for subordination of local interests to the national interest (Jing Ping 1983). But after fiscal decentralization and the loosening of central economic control, national policies actually sent the opposite message.[45] China is a unitary and not a federal state, and the center hands down powers and resources to local governments in a "nonstandardized manner" and may retract them at any time. Because their economic rights are not guaranteed by law, local officials have a short time horizon; it makes sense for them to think about immediate financial gains (Wu Minyi 1990).

The only way for local governments to keep up with their budget obligations was to accelerate local industrial growth (Wong 1990; Han Guochun 1982).[46] MOF officials liked to portray provincial of-

45. As one article acknowledged, "If we properly curtail the construction of ordinary processing industry projects in our locality or department and concentrate our financial and material resources on supporting the state in the construction of key projects and the development of energy sources and transport in our country, we eventually will benefit, although our immediate earnings will be smaller" (Hua Xing 1983, K11).
46. By law, local governments were not allowed to run deficits or go into debt.

ficials as enriching themselves at the expense of the central state, but in fact provincial revenues under the post-1980 system hardly covered essential expenditures. Industrial revenues contributed three-fourths of provincial revenues, and the profitability of factories had declined over the decade of reform. As one economist explained, "Local finances were propped up simply by the economic growth rate. . . . Had it not been for a 20 percent or even 30 percent industrial growth rate, some localities could not have made ends meet, and many localities would even find it impossible to pay workers and staff their wages" (Rui Jun 1988, 44). Estimates of the relationship between industrial growth and local revenue varied from a 5 percent increase in revenue, requiring an increase of more than 10 percent in industrial output (Shen Liren 1986, 5), to a 5–10 percent increase in revenue, requiring a 20–30 percent increase in industrial output (Rui Jun 1988, 44).

Revenues were not the only value of industrial growth to local officials. New factories also meant local control over more materials, always an advantage in a shortage economy, and generated jobs for local unemployed workers and administrative positions for the supporters and cronies of local officials.

The career incentives of local officials as agents of the central government reinforced their progrowth stance. Pressure for high growth from the center, characteristic of command economies, did not abate in the reform era. Party leaders still looked for high growth rates to prove that their economic policies, now the policies of structural reform, were correct. And, as in the past, local officials strove for high growth rates to promote their careers by demonstrating that they were enthusiastically and competently carrying out the center's policies. Many economists and a few party leaders, the most prominent being Chen Yun,[47] condemned this fetish for growth.[48] Nevertheless, growth targets were promoted by reformist

---

47. Chen Yun pointed out in the 1950s that excessive industrial expansion destabilized the economy: "The scale of construction must match the financial strength and material power of the state. Whether or not they match determines whether there will be economic stability or instability. In this large country of ours, with a population of 600 million, economic stability is extremely important" (quoted in Wei Lichun 1985, 35).
48. "In 1981, it was pointed out that the development strategy had to be transformed from development in terms of quantity and speed to development in terms of economic results and from the extensive form of development to the intensive form of development. However, under the demand for excessively high targets of development, transformation has not been

leaders using campaign methods similar to those of the past.[49] While this striving for growth was a "deep rooted leftist habit" left over from the Great Leap Forward and the Cultural Revolution (Li Rui 1985), the content had become reformist. Now "a higher output value serves to prove the emancipation of the mind . . . while a low output value means the mind is not emancipated" (Wang Min 1985; Wu Jinglian, Li Jiange, and Ding Ningning 1985).

Local officials not only had strong incentives to expand industry but also had access to the resources necessary to accomplish the expansion. The reduction of the scope of central planning, the establishment of a dual-track market-plan system, and the expansion of foreign trade meant that local managers could obtain materials if they had money (or items to barter). It was impossible for the center to control local investment because, as the director of the Material Supply Bureau complained, there were insufficient material resources under state control (Li Kaixin 1983).

Financial resources as well as material ones were available locally. Local extrabudgetary funds, including enterprise-retained profits, depreciation, the revenues of government agencies, and revenues from local surtaxes, mushroomed from 31 percent of budgetary funds in 1978 to 59 percent in 1981, 81 percent in 1984, and 90 percent in 1987 (*Statistical Yearbook* 1989, 674). The share of capital construction investment contributed by extrabudgetary funds doubled from 20 percent in 1978 to 40 percent in 1987 (Deng Yingtao and Xu Xiaobo 1987).

The shift from government investment grants to bank loans and the decentralization of bank administration also made it easier than ever for local political leaders to find funds to build new factories. In 1984 the various bank systems—the Agriculture Bank, the Industrial-Commercial Bank, the Construction Bank, and the Bank of China—were allowed to compete in making loans, and local branches were granted more autonomy. Without objective price criteria to evaluate projects or meaningful interest rates to ration credit, local bankers found it almost impossible to turn down the pet projects of local officials.[50]

---

achieved yet. All levels, from upper to lower levels, have the impulse to concentrate on output value" (Liu Guoguan 1989).

49. Provinces with high growth rates were lauded as "surpassing the past" provinces. Provinces that repeated this performance were praised as "three year champions in succession" or "five year champions in succession" (Shen Liren 1986).

50. Yugoslav banks were dominated by local interests under a similar decentralized fiscal system (Tyson 1983).

LOCAL INDUSTRIAL GROWTH AND ECONOMIC OVERHEATING

With strong incentives to expand local industry and the resources necessary to do it, local officials constructed new factories and thereby stimulated national economic growth, setting off a series of economic cycles during the decade of reform. Introduced during the Hua Guofeng expansion in 1978, the reforms enlarging enterprise autonomy and decentralizing government finance accelerated the expansionary trend. Readjustment measures had little effect until 1981, when industry still grew at a respectable 4.3 percent. The second surge of growth began in 1984, when industry grew at a rate of 16.3 percent, rising to 21.4 percent in 1985. Contractionary policies reduced industrial growth to 11.7 percent in 1986, but re-stimulative macroeconomic policies brought it back up to 17.7 percent in 1987. The 1987–88 contraction was ineffective, and industry grew at a rate of 20.8 percent in 1988. Contractionary policies instituted after Tiananmen were more effective, reducing industrial growth to 8.9 percent in 1989 (all growth rates from *Statistical Yearbook* 1990, 415).

Each surge of growth created overheating and caused shortages, deficits, and inflation. Over the decade the inflationary pressures intensified. The rise in the urban consumer price index reached a peak of 30 percent in November 1988 (Naughton 1989). The apparent inability of the central government to control the investment behavior of local officials and regulate the economy began to discredit the reforms among elites and masses. Each time the economy went out of control, conservative elites within the CCP went on the attack against the "chaos" created by the reforms. Inflation and overheating provided ammunition for them to increase their influence in party decision-making. As a result, periods of economic contraction coincided with periods of retrenchment in ideology and culture as Deng Xiaoping sought to protect the economic reforms by appeasing the conservatives with symbolic compensation.

LOCAL PROTECTIONISM

While central authorities kept talking about coordinating the national economy like one big chessboard (Liu Lixin and Tian Chunsheng 1983), local authorities in pursuit of revenue were dividing it up. Fiscal decentralization encouraged local officials to protect local markets for their own factories by erecting administrative blockades.[51] Especially in less developed provinces, officials nurtured their infant consumer-goods industries by excluding high-quality, brand name merchandise from Shanghai and other traditional manufacturing centers. (To make matters worse, local infant industries robbed the brand name factories of their usual sources of material inputs.) Provinces also hoarded their raw materials to reap the profits from processing them themselves. Local energies were focused more on fighting bureaucratic battles (often at the SEC) to restrict competition than on competing in the national marketplace. The balkanization of the Chinese market, which had begun under Mao Zedong's policies of regional self-reliance, was exacerbated greatly by the 1980 fiscal reforms.

The pervasiveness of local protectionism is indicated by the fact that when in 1990 Beijing mayor Chen Xitong declared that Beijing would stop practicing local protectionism, it was front-page news. According to the press report, local governments' protectionist strategies included stipulations that a portion of the earnings derived from the price disparity of color televisions purchased from outside be turned over to local coffers; orders to commercial enterprises specifying the amount of local products to be sold each month; the earmarking of loans for the purchase of local goods; and lists of products forbidden to be "imported" from other regions (Chen Yun and Zhang Guimin 1990).

Many Chinese economists criticized fiscal decentralization for returning the country to a feudal economy, with each locality walling itself off like a feudal manor (Luo Liewen and Ruan Jiangning 1989; Wang Jinjia 1989). The gains in interregional trade from specialization and scale were lost as the national market was segmented by administrative barriers.[52]

COMPETITION FOR FOREIGN TRADE AND INVESTMENT

Local officials were spurred by the new revenue-sharing system to compete with one another for foreign business in ways that central

51. The problem of local protectionism emerged soon after the fiscal reform was introduced. In April 1982 the State Council issued a regulation prohibiting regional blockades in purchasing and marketing industrial products ("State Council on Marketing Industrial Products" 1982, K10–11; see also Qi Xiangwu and Hou Yunchun 1982). Press complaints about protectionist practices persisted over the decade (Ying Guang 1983; "Do Not Put Up New Blockades" 1984).
52. Provinces such as Jiangsu and Guangdong that pursued more open domestic trading policies prospered (Wu Minyi 1990).

authorities viewed as detrimental to national interests. Local firms engaged in price-gouging competition for export markets, and provinces and cities tripped over one another to entice foreign investors by offering concessionary terms. Foreign joint ventures were sought after for their hard-currency export earnings, in which local governments could now share, as well as for their new technologies, which could give localities the edge in domestic competition. Local officials, in their eagerness to make a deal, ignored the urgings of the center not to undercut the national interest by luring joint ventures with excessively low tax rates or promises of access to the domestic market (Shirk 1988). (Once they locked in a foreign investor, however, local governments often imposed restrictions to protect local firms from the competition of the joint venture.) Profit-seeking local officials, eager to outdo one another, rushed to import production lines to manufacture color televisions, photocopying machines, and radio-cassette recorders, so that production capacity exceeded domestic demand.

ADMINISTRATIVE INTERFERENCE AND RENT-SEEKING

Another negative effect of fiscal decentralization was increasing administrative interference in enterprise management. The "eating in separate kitchens" system intensified local officials' sense of proprietorship over local enterprises, creating what the Chinese call "the local ownership system" (*difang suoyouzhi*).[53] This trend of strengthening the financial stake of bureaucratic entities in their subordinate enterprises, while motivating officials to support their enterprises, also encouraged them to interfere in enterprise operations. When a firm's bureaucratic masters were off in Beijing, the manager could easily ignore them; when they were close by, the manager was forced to listen. One reformist economist complained, "The central leaders, especially Zhao Ziyang, took too strong a line on fiscal decentralization and fundamentally confused the difference between economic market-oriented decentralization and administrative decentralization. There is a contradiction between the two. Provincial officials meddle in local enterprises and stifle their economic autonomy" (author's interview). The managers of strong,

53. The financial link between local governments and their subordinate enterprises was more direct under the "sharing specific revenues" version of the reform than it was under "sharing total revenues." But even under the latter scheme local revenues were tied to the performance of local enterprises.

profitable local firms frequently complained that local officials subverted them by appropriating their earnings to redistribute to weaker firms.

As Christine Wong (1990) points out, the local government had become both a player and the referee in local economic competition. Administrative interventions in economic activity by and large were not conducive to enterprise autonomy or efficiency. The particularism of reform policies created a situation in which both local officials and enterprise managers concentrated on rent-seeking rather than economic returns. A World Bank analysis diagnosed the problem:

> In China, the treatment of every enterprise and problem as a special case leads to collusion between local governments and enterprises, with the local governments acting as patrons rather than regulators. The lack of universally applicable rules diverts the energies of enterprises to bargaining from improving efficiency and product quality. Enterprises seek rents rather than profits. (Tidrick and Chen 1987, 198–99)

Decentralizing reforms had granted local officials the authority to regulate access to the market and to redistribute fiscal benefits and burdens, investment funds, access to foreign investment and trade, and so on. These economic powers created new opportunities for local officials to collect rents from bureaucratic subordinates and enterprise managers. Naturally, like their counterparts in Beijing, local officials built up political capital by allocating benefits selectively and imposing costs uniformly.[54]

Provincial party and government authorities chose to collect rents in various forms and put them to various uses. The most common strategy was to build up an industrial empire by reinvesting funds into industrial expansion. A more populist strategy involved using the funds to make dramatic improvements in roads, housing, and other public works (the best example of this kind of local populism was the record of Li Ruihuan as party secretary of Tianjin).[55] The corruption strategy was to slip funds into the pock-

54. The press criticized local officials for forgiving or reducing taxes for particular enterprises on the one hand, and for imposing extra taxes (such as the so-called local energy and transportation construction tax) on all enterprises on the other hand ("Immediately Stop Additional Levies" 1984).
55. Because the Chinese system lacks elections, we would predict that officials would use rents more for industrial empire building, which trans-

ets of the politicians and their relatives and friends. Province and city heads also were expected to return a share of the rents in the form of political loyalty to the central party politicians who had been their benefactors. And local party secretaries took at least some of the rents in the form of political loyalty from their own bureaucratic subordinates, establishing local political machines by exchanging economic favors for political loyalty.[56] These machines, linking party leaders with government bureaucrats, bankers, and managers, then became the engine of local economic development.

Decentralizing reforms changed the career incentives of provincial officials. In the past the focus of their ambitions had been the central party-state bureaucracy in Beijing. But after 1980 so much of the economic action occurred at the provincial level and provincial leaders exercised such national influence that some politicians from the most dynamic regions chose to remain in the provinces instead of climbing the ladder to Beijing. One well-known example was Ye Xuanping, governor of Guangdong province, who turned down attractive job offers in Beijing (one to be a vice premier of the State Council) to stay in Guangdong; he was fired in 1991. Another example is Jia Qinglin, deputy party secretary of Fujian, who turned down a ministry post in Beijing in the hopes that he would become provincial governor instead (Kuan 1990). To the degree that the allure of national position has faded, the center has lost some leverage over the behavior of provincial officials.

Under the post-1980 incentive structure, the political ambitions of individual local officials became closely identified with the economic accomplishments of their domains. As one press commentary noted, "Leaders one-sidedly consider and stress the partial interests of their departments, localities, and units in total disregard of overall interests. To show off their personal achievements in their

---

lates into bureaucratic power and prestige, than for popular public works, which translate into votes. The fact that a few officials such as Li Ruihuan have experimented with the populist strategy hints that they are gambling on a change in the political system occurring in the future.

56. On local political machines in other communist countries, see Hough 1969 and Woodall 1982. We as yet have little empirical information about how these local industry-based political machines work in China. For example, is the party secretary the power broker in Chinese provinces and cities as he was in the Soviet Union, or is the broker role played by government leaders instead? Did the delegation of more financial authority to localities create new conflicts of interest on the local level?

official careers, they do not hesitate to infringe upon the fundamental interests of the state and the people" ("Reducing the Scale of Capital Construction" 1988).

Whether officials aimed to climb the ladder of success to Beijing or to become leading figures on the local scene, their reputation was enhanced by industrial growth and local building projects. A press commentator linked the local investment drive to the Chinese political structure: "Judging historically, those who dare not boldly build several more factories, enterprises, office buildings, auditoriums, and hotels will appear to be 'right,' will make only average achievements in their official career, and will have no capital to serve as officials and vie for leadership positions" ("What Is Unnecessary Should Be Given Up" 1988, 34). The center might preach local self-restraint in growth rates and construction, but in reality, local officials in rapidly growing areas with a lot of construction were more likely to move up than were those in sleepy backwater areas.

The cumulative effect of the economic and political incentives structured by post-1980 fiscal and administrative decentralization was dynamic economic growth distorted by shortages, inflation, and deficits as well as by local protectionism and administrative meddling. These economic maladies provided ammunition for conservative CCP leaders, who wanted to stem the tide of marketization and restore central financial control. As the economic problems, inflation in particular, worsened over the course of the decade, the political strength of conservative party elites increased. The "eating in separate kitchens" reform generated political support for the reform drive among the provincial officials who served in the Central Committee; yet the overheating and inflation largely caused by fiscal reform provided ammunition for its conservative opponents to challenge the reformers in succession politics at the top reaches of party power.

Reciprocal Accountability and Playing to the Provinces

The strategy of playing to the provinces involved granting provincial and city officials greater freedom of action in their local arenas and encouraging them to play a greater leadership role in the national arena. The Thirteenth Party Congress reserved permanent seats in the Politburo for the three metropolises, Beijing, Shanghai, and Tianjin. Provincial party secretaries constituted the largest bloc in the Central Committee, 43 percent of the full members of the Eleventh Central Committee (1977), 34 percent of the Twelfth Central Committee (1982), and 38 percent of the Thirteenth Central Committee (1987; James Wang 1989).[57]

The presence of provincial advocates in these party bodies provided high-level support for sustaining economic reform, as Deng Xiaoping, Hu Yaobang, and Zhao Ziyang had intended. Government officials knew that the Central Committee would be reluctant to approve any policy rolling back reforms and retracting local authority. As one Chinese official commented, "Local officials used the slogans of reform such as 'enlivening the economy' [*gaohuo jingji*] to fight against financial recentralization" (author's interview).

The evolution of fiscal reforms after 1987, when the conservatives staged a comeback in elite politics (Hu Yaobang was purged, Zhao Ziyang replaced him as CCP general secretary, and Li Peng became premier), demonstrated the influence of provincial officials within the party. Even during a period of conservative resurgence at the top, fiscal policies were constrained by provincial preferences and the political incentives of succession contenders to play to the provinces.

When they increased their influence at the top of the party after 1987, conservative leaders from the older generation, among them Chen Yun and Yao Yilin (Yao became head of the SPC and a member of the Standing Committee of the Politburo), wanted to change the fiscal rules to weaken the incentives for local construction and put more funds under central control. As Yao Yilin expressed this view,

> Our economy is now excessively decentralized and proper centralization is called for. . . . The central finance suffers huge deficits every year; efforts must be exerted to cut deficits back each year until they are basically effaced. Under such circumstances, localities should contribute more to the central coffers in addition to the central finance's practice of economy. (Chao Hao-sheng 1989, 24)

Chen Yun and Yao Yilin expected their protégé Li Peng, who had been elevated to the premiership and membership in the Standing Committee of the Politburo in 1987, to support fiscal recentralization by abolishing fiscal contracting and establishing a system of

57. The inclusion of locally based PLA officers would bring the proportion to over half.

divided taxes (separate systems for central taxes and local taxes), as the tax-for-profit policy had originally proposed. Instead, they found that Li Peng was unwilling to impose unpopular policies on provincial officials.

The split in the conservative ranks was caused by differences in the political incentives operating on individuals from different generations. Chen and Yao were too old to be governed by political ambition; at the end of their political careers, they were free to promote their policy preference for financial centralization without regard to its appeal among members of the selectorate. Li Peng, by contrast, was young enough to aspire to succeed Deng Xiaoping as China's top leader. When taking a policy stance, he had to take into consideration the views of the selectorate, including the members of the Central Committee as well as the elders.

Li Peng's reluctance to antagonize provincial leaders helps explain the 1988 State Council decision to retain fiscal contracting and to renegotiate individual sharing deals with the provinces, a decision that left the central government with even less revenue than before. What Li Peng came up with was a package of particularistic giveaways that enabled him to claim credit with provincial officials. First, the State Council began to emphasize the contractual form of revenue-sharing arrangements. The term *contracting* (*baogan*) had acquired great reformist cachet, derived from the dramatic success of the agricultural reform and introduction of the enterprise contract system in 1987.[58] Then the council asserted that according to these contracts, provinces would be fully responsible for their expenditures (except in the case of natural disasters).[59] Last, it diversified the revenue-sharing system into at least six different arrangements, two of which were forms of "progressive contracting" (*dizeng baogan*) that gave incentives for local governments to "have greater initiative to invigorate their economies" ("Li Peng Chairs State Council Executive Meeting" 1988; "State Council Decision to Improve the Method of Local Financial Contracts" 1988).[60]

58.   The original financial agreements between center and provinces introduced in 1980 had been described as contracts sharing responsibility as well as resources, but in 1988 the contract notion was reemphasized.
59.   The original 1980 system had intended to eliminate the "eating from the big pot" phenomenon, but in fact, center and provinces continued to eat from one another's plates.
60.   The contracting methods were specified as revenue-progressive increase contract (*shouru dizeng baogan*), dividing total revenues (*zonge fencheng*), dividing the total plus dividing the increase (*zonge fencheng jia*

Li Peng made a point of sympathizing with the economically strongest regions, which, even while eating in separate kitchens, had been required to contribute a large share of their revenues to the center.[61] He had the State Council identify thirteen "high revenue areas which have to deliver a larger percentage of revenues to the state [and] have little enthusiasm for increasing revenues"; this set of powerful provinces included Jiangsu, Liaoning, Beijing, and Chongqing ("Li Peng Chairs State Council Executive Meeting" 1988). The State Council granted these provinces three-year revenue-progressive increase contracts (*shouru dizeng baogan*) that would rouse their enthusiasm by allowing them to retain a big chunk of the revenues they generated above the base level.[62] In another decision Li Peng and the State Council responded to the jealousy of the high-revenue, high-contribution provinces by changing the terms of Guangdong's cushy deal. Beginning in 1988, for three years Guangdong would increase its remittance to the center at a rate of 9 percent per year instead of keeping 100 percent of revenues above a very low base (Lin Ruo 1988).[63] Li Peng also promoted plans for Pudong, a new Special Economic Zone for Shanghai. Li challenged Zhao Ziyang, who had a base of support in the coastal areas of Guangdong, Fujian, and the fourteen Open Cities, by building his own support base in the economically dynamic parts of China that had so far received less preferential treatment by the center, including Shanghai, Beijing, Chongqing, Jiangsu, and Liaoning.

---

zengzhang fencheng), remittance-progressive increase contract (*shangjie e dizeng bao gan*), fixed-amount remittance (*dinge shangjie*), and fixed-amount subsidy (*dinge buzhu*; "State Council Decision to Improve the Method of Local Financial Contracts" 1988).

61. Appealing to powerful political actors who felt they had been put at a competitive disadvantage by Zhao Ziyang's version of economic reform was a consistent theme in Li Peng's succession strategy. He took up the cause of large state factories as well as high-revenue provinces (see chapter 13).

62. The State Council meeting announcing the contracts for these thirteen high-revenue areas also announced that from then on the terms of all provincial contracts would be made public ("State Council Decision to Improve the Method of Local Financial Contracts" 1988). This measure probably was designed to satisfy the high-revenue provinces that still turned over to the center a high proportion of their revenues. These provinces wanted everyone to recognize their own contributions to the public good and wanted to show up the free ride of other provinces.

63. Guangdong officials denied the widely held notion that Guangdong was trying to buy autonomy from Beijing by contributing more to the state treasury (Yeung 1991).

Central authorities admitted that the 1988 version of fiscal contracting would reduce central revenues and cause short-term profit-seeking on the part of the provinces ("State Council Decision to Improve the Method of Local Financial Contracts" 1988).[64] In theory, they continued to advocate a system dividing taxes between levels as the best alternative, but as one article put it, "The contract system is more readily acceptable to different circles" (Zhang Zhenbin 1988, 25). In other words, it was more politically feasible. Li Peng's actions indicate that the influence of provincial officials within the CCP had grown to the point that no contender to top leadership stood a chance of winning without the support of at least some provincial officials.

When the political balance within the party elite shifted even more to the conservative side after the Tiananmen crackdown and the purge of Zhao Ziyang in June 1989, the conservatives again proposed eliminating provincial revenue contracts and strengthening central financial authority. During the work conferences proceeding the Fifth Plenum of the CCP Thirteenth Central Committee in November 1989, Yao Yilin spoke in favor of the proposal, but provincial party secretaries and governors argued vehemently against the proposal and in the end rejected it (Lam 1989; Shambaugh 1989). The minister of finance had to announce at the 1990 meeting of the National People's Congress that the system of fiscal contracting would continue, with only a few local experiments in divided taxation (Wang Bingqian 1990).

This issue of fiscal recentralization again was hotly contested during the 1990 drafting of the Eighth Five-Year Plan and Ten-Year Plan. At a November 1990 meeting of provincial leaders, Ye Xuanping, the governor of Guangdong, strongly articulated the provincial demand for continued financial autonomy ("Proposals of the CCP Central Committee" 1991). The cleavage between the interests of center and localities was more obvious than ever before. Provincial leaders were reported to have put aside their squabbling

64. One financial specialist predicted optimistically that "if we fixed an appropriate base figure for the contracted budget and a contracted growth rate, at least the financial revenues on the part of the central financial authorities would not decrease, according to normal predictions. Even if the increase in the local financial revenues is higher than the increase in the financial revenues of the central financial authorities, there will not be a serious imbalance between the revenue and expenditure of the central authorities since both the revenue and expenditure budgets are contracted" (Zhang Zhenbin 1988, 25).

over relative gains to present a unified front against the center (Cheung 1990). As a result of the conflict, the date for the Seventh Plenum of the Thirteenth Central Committee, originally planned for October 1990, was postponed until late December, and the enlarged Politburo meeting that usually precedes a Central Committee plenum was not held (Ho Po-shih 1991).

The vehemence of the provincial opposition to fiscal recentralization impressed Li Peng, who came out for a compromise that would retain the fiscal contracting system for the entire five-year period and introduce the system of dividing taxes on an experimental basis only.[65] Li's position was adopted by the Central Committee and was incorporated in the long-term plans. By showing his sympathy with the local officials' views, Li hoped to keep the support of at least some of these officials and prevent them from siding with one of his political rivals.

The provincial leaders within the Central Committee succeeded in blocking the center from retracting its grant of financial authority to the provinces. Soon after Ye Xuanping spoke out openly against the center's proposals in late 1990, however, he was forced out of his position as Guangdong governor and given a purely ceremonial post as vice chairman of the Standing Committee of the Chinese People's Political Consultative Congress.[66] At the same time, the head of the Communist Party Organization Department emphasized the need for the center to reshuffle officials periodically from one place to another (Lu Feng 1991). The message was clear: the center will defer to the views of the officials in the selectorate when making policy, but the center holds the power to appoint officials, and any official who challenges party leaders by organizing a bloc will be dismissed (see chapter 4).

The "eating in separate kitchens" reform was a successful political strategy for building a coalition of support for the reform drive among provincial officials. Once provincial officials were the largest group within the Central Committee and were committed to the

65. "Originally, a proposal was made to change the local financial contract system and exercise a tax apportioning system to raise the proportion of revenue to national income, and the proportion of central finances to the entire revenue. But taking account of the difficulties of localities and enterprises, the financial contract system will continue to remain implemented next year and during the Seventh Five-Year Plan, whereas the tax apportioning system will be exercised on a trial basis" (Li Peng 1990, 20).

66. Ye Xuanping retained his local power base by refusing to move on a full-time basis to Beijing and continuing to live in his Guangdong home.

current situation of partial reform, it was unthinkable for ambitious central politicians such as Hu Yaobang, Zhao Ziyang, and even Li Peng to attempt to roll back the reforms. Some of the economic problems produced by decentralization produced an elite conservative backlash against the reform drive and provided ammunition for the conservatives to strengthen their influence at the highest reaches of party leadership. But even when the conservatives strengthened their hand after 1987, the incentives produced by reciprocal accountability operated on the younger generation of conservative leaders, discouraging them from antagonizing the provincial representatives in the Central Committee by pushing recentralization.

Of course, while local officials draped themselves in the mantle of market reform, what they meant by reform was, in fact, the perpetuation of the hybrid, partially reformed system, not a genuine market economy. They preferred to maintain their quasi-ownership rights over local factories and to exploit these rights to collect rents for themselves rather than playing only the role of referee in market competition.

10 Creating Vested Interests in Reform

Industrial Reform Takeoff, 1978–81

The decade of economic transformation in China began in 1978 with Deng Xiaoping's effort to defeat CCP Chairman Hua Guofeng and win the position of preeminent leader for himself. By the end of 1980 Deng had defeated Hua by mobilizing support behind his platform of industrial enterprise reform. The early reform experiments promoted by Deng, which allowed enterprises to sell their above-quota output on their own at higher market prices and to retain a share of their profits, were a clear political success. In marked contrast to the sluggish start (or nonstart) of the Soviet industrial reforms, the Chinese industrial reforms took off rapidly. Beginning as a local experiment, in less than a year the reforms grew into a national movement welcomed by ministry, locality, and enterprise officials. The experiments turned them away from dependence on the plan and reoriented them toward earning profits by selling on the market. In this way, the early reforms created new vested interests in their continuation and extension. Implemented as particularistic experiments, with each enterprise or locality having its own special treatment, the early reforms generated political support for Deng Xiaoping and other leaders who could claim credit for them.

Once the industrial reforms built up a head of steam, party conservatives had a hard time stopping them. Despite a 1979 budget deficit that was the largest in the history of the PRC, the enthusiasm of the "spenders" overwhelmed the warnings of the "savers." Given the weight in the selectorate of local and industrial ministry officials who were benefiting from decentralization, the attempts of central bureaucracies such as the Ministry of Finance or of influential individuals such as Chen Yun to recentralize economic control and slow the growth stimulated by the reforms were ineffectual. When subordinates perceived divisions among the top leadership over economic reform, they refused to comply with contractionary policies detrimental to their own interests. They knew that so long as the leaders were divided, no central leader would be able to enforce a tough policy on them.

Industrial Reform Takes Off from Local Experiments

In 1978 it looked as if post-Mao leaders intended to return industrial finance and management to the golden age of the 1950s instead of creating something new. The most important 1978 document on industrial management, the "Thirty Articles" (or "Decisions Concerning Some Problems on the Acceleration of Industrial Development") drafted by the State Planning Commission, took the restoration line.[1]

The 1978 policies were intended to recentralize industrial financial and administrative authority after the chaos of the Cultural Revolution. Key enterprises were to be returned to central control; the number of enterprises under direct control of the center more than doubled from 1,260 in 1978 to 2,681 in 1981 (Zhou Taihe et al. 1984, 160). The Ministry of Finance attempted to strengthen its control over local tax policies. And particularly significant for enterprise finance, the Cultural Revolution rule concerning depreciation, which allowed 100 percent of depreciation funds to remain with the enterprise and the local bureau supervising it, was replaced with a plan returning 30 percent to the central authorities, leaving only 50 percent for the enterprise and 20 percent for the local authorities (Zhou Taihe et al. 1984, 160). (The depreciation rule of the traditional Soviet-style command model, which China had followed until 1967, required that all depreciation funds be remitted to the center.)

Completely in keeping with the policy direction of restoring the pre–Cultural Revolution system was the MOF's proposal to revive the enterprise fund (*qiye jijin*) that had existed in 1953–57 and 1961–67 (P. Lee 1986; Richman 1969).[2] State enterprises meeting all eight plan targets (output; variety; quality; raw material, energy, and electric power consumption; labor productivity; cost; profit; and cir-

1. The Thirty Articles incorporated most of the provisions of the Twenty Articles, a policy proposal to rationalize industrial management drafted under Deng Xiaoping in 1975 but vetoed by Gang of Four members; see P. Lee 1987 (128).
2. The revival of enterprise funds was Article Nine of the Thirty Articles; P. Lee 1987 (178).

culating capital) were allowed to create a fund equal to 5 percent of their total wage bill (3 percent for those achieving only quantity, quality, variety, and profit) to be distributed as collective welfare and individual bonuses (Zhou Taihe et al. 1984, 161; P. Lee 1986, 50). The proposal was approved in November 1978 (Fang Weizhong et al. 1984, 608). This type of enterprise fund had been a fixture of the Soviet command economy for many years.

The initiative to move beyond the enterprise fund to a genuine profit-retention system came from a political entrepreneur in Sichuan Province named Zhao Ziyang. Despite the conservative bias of the bureaucratic Chinese system, genuine policy innovation sometimes emerged from the provinces. In the second half of 1978 Zhao Ziyang, the Communist Party first secretary in Sichuan, joined with other provincial leaders to investigate industrial management problems in local factories. Zhao Ziyang reportedly traveled abroad at the time to observe different models of management (Su Wenming et al. 1982, 91). The provincial officials observed that collective and private enterprises functioned more efficiently than did state-run ones. The Soviet-style practice of centralizing all earnings and expenditures of state-owned industry in the hands of the national government (the *tongshou tongzhi* system) robbed factory managers and employees of any incentive for efficient or profitable operation. The path to economic modernization was to improve enterprise motivation, and the key to motivation was to give the enterprise a profit incentive. Therefore, in October 1978 the Sichuan officials selected six industrial firms to experiment with expanded enterprise autonomy, including profit retention.

The Sichuan experiments were a high-risk strategy that paid off for Zhao Ziyang, who moved up to the CCP Politburo in September 1979, the Standing Committee of the Politburo in February 1980, and the government premiership in September 1980. Because of his longtime personal relationship with Deng Xiaoping, Zhao may have heard that economic policy innovation would be well received in Beijing. Personal ties are invaluable sources of information about the preferences of leaders at the top of the hierarchy for lower-level leaders calculating what policy position to take. Zhao also may have been encouraged by a July 1978 speech by President Hu Qiaomu of the Chinese Academy of Social Sciences, who advocated greater reliance on economic laws and suggested that enterprises would benefit from less reliance on administrative methods and greater attention to profit incentives (Hu Qiaomu 1978); also, by spring

1978 articles in economic journals were arguing that "profit" should no longer be considered a "symbol of capitalism" (Ji Chongwei and Wang Zhenji 1978; Sun Ru 1978).[3] Or perhaps Zhao simply gambled that the uncertain political environment of a succession period created an opening for a new face with new ideas. A simultaneous (but apparently not coordinated) gamble was made by Wan Li, first secretary of Anhui Province, who encouraged county-level experiments with an agricultural household responsibility system and who also was later promoted to Beijing by Deng Xiaoping.[4]

Deng Xiaoping reacted favorably to these provincial experiments and began to build his own national reform platform on them. He started to mobilize support for reform from among industrial and local officials by arguing that power was overconcentrated in the Chinese economic system. In a speech of 13 December 1978 ("Emancipate the Mind, Seek Truth from Facts, and Unite") Deng said, "At present the most pressing need is to expand the decision-making powers of mines, factories, and other enterprises and of production teams, so as to give full scope to their initiative and creativity" (Deng Xiaoping 1984, 157).[5] The Third Plenum of the Eleventh Party Congress, which followed in mid-December and marked the beginning of the reform drive, approved a communiqué that adopted Deng's view and made the overconcentration of power the main theme ("Communiqué" 1978). Following the Third Plenum the Sichuan authorities expanded their management reform experiment to one hundred enterprises, and Yunnan Province placed fifty enterprises on the new system (Zhou Taihe et al. 1984, 166; Reynolds 1982).

The Sichuan experiment was picked up and popularized by the SEC, the central bureaucracy most sympathetic to the plight of factory managers constricted by the administrative controls of the command economy.[6] The SEC's strategy of political entrepreneur-

3. Hu Qiaomu's economic ideas were influenced by those earlier proposed by economic theorist Sun Yefang.
4. According to Su Wenming et al. (1982), there were also early experiments in Yunnan.
5. During the winter of 1978 Deng Xiaoping also acted as political entrepreneur to stimulate demand for political reform. He encouraged critics of the political system to express themselves in wall posters on "Democracy Wall" in Beijing. One obvious objective of Deng's promotion of democratization was to prevail over Hua Guofeng in the competition for leadership succession. See Halpern 1989.
6. Father Ladany, editor of *China News Analysis*, was the first foreign an-

ship was to authorize local experimental projects to "test" the proposed policy. The selective authorization of projects to particular provinces and cities won support for the reform drive from these fortunate local officials. The officials not only benefited from the national publicity and the revenues generated by successful experiments but also gained political resources by granting a few local managers permission to launch these experiments. Managers of both experimental and nonexperimental enterprises reported that there was stiff competition to be named an experimental enterprise because the title carried with it "preferential treatment" (*yuhui tiaojian*). Experimental firms not only could keep more of their own profits but also were favored in the distribution of materials, electric power, and bank loans (author's interviews). Both the SEC and the local officials favored experimental enterprises because the future of the reforms depended on their success. The strongest firms were selected to be pilot projects, and those that floundered were dropped from the "experiment."[7] This mode of building political support for economic policies was pioneered by Mao Zedong, who designated units such as the Daqing oil fields or Dazhai agricultural production brigade as "models," surely a more accurate representation of the actual function of these enterprises than "experiments." Even SEC officials admitted that reform experiments were not true tests of changes in the rules of the game but served primarily political and propaganda functions (author's interviews).

The experiments were an effective way to tie the interests of local officials to the fate of the industrial reform drive. As one official said, "If you are an experimental point, the center takes special care of you. So the conditions are preferential, and you cannot popularize the method. It's hard to tell if the experiment works because it is a good method or because the state has paid you special attention. In the beginning this was a good way to get people to support the reform" (author's interview).

In March 1979 the SEC convened a meeting to review the results of the Sichuan experiments and in May selected another eight enterprises in the cities of Beijing, Shanghai, and Tianjin to "test" expanded autonomy and profit retention (P. Lee 1986, 52). Among

alyst to perceive that the SEC was the main bureaucratic advocate of enterprise reform ("Industrial Management" 1979).
7.   Factories were dropped from experiments if their economic results were poor. Factories chosen to become replacement experimental sites were those that already had good economic results (author's interviews).

these eight early experiments were Capital Iron and Steel in Beijing, which later was to become the leader of the campaign to spread the profit-contracting system (see chapter 11). The terms of the expanded autonomy and profit-sharing experiment were so attractive to enterprise managers and employees, and so many ministries and provinces wanted to set up their own experiments on the same model, that in July the SEC held a national meeting in the Sichuan capital of Chengdu to authorize more ministries and provinces to implement it (Zhou Taihe et al. 1984, 176). The SEC chose some of the experimental enterprises itself and selectively authorized some provinces to choose enterprises (author's interviews). Out of 3,358 experimental enterprises, 1,982 were directly approved by the center, and 1,416 were authorized by local governments.[8] By sharing the political benefits of allocating the scarce and widely coveted designation of experimental enterprise, the SEC generated lower-level support for the reform drive. The July decision was confirmed by the State Council, which also announced five regulations governing the enterprise autonomy experiments, including one on profit retention (Fang Weizhong et al. 1984, 629).

Enterprises and local governments were eager to benefit from the program. Although the central government directed that profit-retention experiments be limited to the small number authorized in 1979 ("State Council Approves the State Economic Commission and Ministry of Finance Directive" 1980; Tidrick and Chen 1987, 3), by 1980 the number of experiments had grown to more than 6,600, constituting 16 percent of the nation's state-owned enterprises (Su Wenming et al. 1982, 93). As a rule, the larger, more profitable firms were chosen to be experimental enterprises. The experimental firms, which made up less than 20 percent of all state enterprises, contributed 60 percent of total national output value and about 70 percent of enterprise profits. The experimental firms were even more financially dominant in China's largest cities, providing 80 percent of total profits in Shanghai and Tianjin and 94 percent in

8. The statistics are from Yuan Yu-sheng, "On the Essence and Principle of Profit Retention," *Kuaiji yanjiu* (Accounting research), no. 3 (1980): 56–57, cited in P. Lee 1987 (278). Lee infers that each province, major city, and autonomous region was authorized to select approximately one hundred enterprises to carry out the profit-retention experiment, but my interviews with officials who were involved with the decision indicate that not all provinces were picked to participate and that some ministries were also allowed to participate.

Beijing ("Report of the Opinions of the State Economic Commission" 1980, 420).

The national version of the experiment was somewhat more restrictive than was Sichuan's, reflecting the caution of the SPC and the MOF. Under Sichuan's rules (the Fourteen Articles) enterprises were allowed, after meeting their plan output quotas, to sell additional production on their own at flexible prices, obtaining inputs for this above-quota production on their own as well. But in the national experiment enterprises had first to offer their above-quota products to state commercial and material supply agencies; only then could they sell them on their own. The national regulations also said nothing about price flexibility or direct procurement of inputs.

As for profit retention, the Sichuan scheme had made profits the key enterprise objective and the source of the enterprise fund. Profits were divided into two parts: the firm could retain 5 percent of the planned profit (determined by the past year's actual profit), plus 15, 20, or 25 percent of profits above that level. The July 1979 national regulations simplified the procedure, allowing enterprises to retain a set percentage of their total profit for the current year. This revision weakened an enterprise's incentive to surpass its planned profit target. However, the national version of the experiment increased the enterprise's share of depreciation funds from 60 percent (in Sichuan) to 70 percent. In both the Sichuan and the national regulations, the enterprise could decide for itself how to spend its retained profits (Reynolds 1982, 126–27).

The profit-retention scheme was extremely popular with enterprises and local governments. Several sources note that profit retention was the only feature of the enterprise reforms that was implemented widely (Xue Muqiao 1982a; "Report of the Opinions of the State Economic Commission" 1980; Naughton 1985). One author described local governments and enterprises as being "preoccupied with profit retention" (P. Lee 1986, 51). Some local authorities modified the national profit-retention rules to enhance local government financial benefits and control. For example, Shanghai experimented with making the city industrial bureau as a whole, and not merely the enterprise, the unit of calculation; Beijing also tried out this method on a smaller scale. This method allowed bureau officials to adjust the distribution of profits among the enterprises it supervised; taking the bureau instead of the enterprise as the accounting unit diluted the incentive effect of profit retention on the individual firms (P. Lee 1987). With local officials and factory managers both seeing advantages in profit retention, it was an unbeatable way for political entrepreneurs at the provincial and national levels to build momentum for reforms. As Barry Naughton says, "The profit retention system changed virtually overnight from a limited experimental program to the predominant financial·system in large and profitable state enterprises" (Naughton 1985, 230).

The Ministry of Finance Fails to Restrict Profit-Retention Experiments

The Ministry of Finance, always worried about maintaining the flow of revenues to the central treasury, took an ambivalent attitude toward profit-retention reforms. On the one hand, the MOF recognized the need for a method to reduce enterprise losses and make enterprises more profitable. In 1979 the losses incurred by state-owned enterprises totaled ten billion yuan, an amount almost five times that of 1966 and equal to 3 percent of the net material product (Zhang Zhuoyuan 1981, 79).

On the other hand, the MOF was alarmed by the 1979 budget deficit of over seventeen billion yuan, the largest deficit since the founding of the PRC.[9] The MOF joined with the SEC in late 1979 to work out a profit-retention scheme that would guarantee that the central treasury got a fair share of the financial returns while still having a positive incentive effect on enterprises. In January 1980 the two agencies announced that experimental firms should shift from the "total sum method," in which they retained a share of total profit, to the "circular comparison method," which differentiated between the planned or baseline profit and the incremental part of the profit, the retention percentage being set higher for the incremental part ("State Council Approves the State Economic

9. Some central officials viewed the 1979 deficit as a temporary dip caused by the expenses of China's war with Vietnam and the costs of terminating projects begun during the 1976–78 Hua Guofeng expansion (Naughton 1985, 231). Minister of Finance Wang Bingqian, in his report to the August 1980 National People's Congress, took a reassuring tone: "China's financial deficit last year did not cause any big increase in the issue of paper money, nor did it bring serious difficulties to the economy" (*FBIS*, 2 Sept. 1980, cited in Solinger 1982, 1238). But when the minister spoke with Michel Oksenberg about the deficit in 1980, he expressed greater concern about the economic harm caused by the deficit (Oksenberg, personal communication).

Commission and Ministry of Finance Directive" 1980). The new scheme, which was similar to the one originally employed in Sichuan, placed additional pressure on enterprises because the baseline was raised every year (P. Lee 1987, 179). To satisfy the demands of the central planners, the new rules also required that the enterprise satisfy all its plan targets in order to keep a share of its profits ("State Council Approves the State Economic Commission and Ministry of Finance Directive" 1980).

Nevertheless, the evolution of the profit-retention rules indicates that the "spread the wealth" reform strategy dominated fiscal concerns during 1979–80 even in the face of the huge deficit. Although circular comparison was preferred by the MOF because it allowed it to claim more of the newly generated profits as state revenue, it was opposed by the larger, more profitable enterprises. After circular comparison was introduced in early 1980, the experimental enterprises (evaluated by output value, realized profit, and remitted profit) did not register as much improvement as they had in 1979 and even declined in Sichuan and Shanghai (P. Lee 1986). The SEC, responsive to enterprise interests, complained that under circular comparison the enterprises' share of profits was too low and that stronger, more profitable enterprises found their profit targets continually raised with little to show for it. The SEC document used the Chinese expression "beat the fastest oxen" to describe the unfair financial exploitation by the state of the stronger firms. To shift more benefits to enterprises, the SEC introduced a plan to allow the implementation of the "fixed comparison method" (a fixed baseline for a number of years and higher percentage retained for above-baseline profits). In November 1980 the State Council approved the change in the rules, trading central financial control for a stronger enterprise profit incentive ("Report of the Opinions of the State Economic Commission" 1980, 422).

The MOF also was thwarted in its efforts to minimize the center's financial risk by limiting the spread of profit-retention experiments. When the first experiments were being authorized during 1979 and 1980, the SEC and the MOF locked horns in the first of many disagreements about reform strategy. The SEC favored authorizing a large number of experiments in larger cities and larger firms; the MOF instead urged that experiments be introduced in a small number of smaller cities and smaller firms (author's interviews). At the beginning of 1980 the MOF tried to limit the number of enterprises introducing profit retention to the approximately 1,600 that had already been approved (*Finance and Accounting* 3 [1980]: 16, 18, cited in Naughton 1985, 230). The MOF's caution was ignored, and the number of experiments was expanded to 6,600 by June 1980. During the National People's Congress of August 1980 it was announced that profit sharing would be expanded to all state enterprises by the end of 1981 (*People's Daily*, 20 Aug. 1980, cited in Naughton 1985, 231; "Report of the Opinions of the State Economic Commission" 1980, 423).

Readjustment Makes No Headway Against Reform until December 1980

The more conservative version of industrial reform proposed by senior leaders such as Chen Yun as an alternative to the rapid expansion of profit-retention schemes was called industrial "readjustment." Since the 1950s Chen Yun had consistently advocated a version of central planning less rigid and less skewed toward heavy industry than the Soviet version was. (During the period 1952–78 the shares of total capital construction were heavy industry 48.7 percent, light industry 5.7 percent, and agriculture 10.7 percent; *Statistical Yearbook* 1990, 157, 166.) In 1956 and again in 1961 he unsuccessfully promoted the idea of readjustment: reducing the scale of capital construction and lowering the growth rate to one that put less strain on the economy; shifting the relationships among sectors to give more emphasis to light industry and agriculture and less to heavy industry; and putting more stress on consumption and less on accumulation (savings and investment). Having being politically rehabilitated by Deng Xiaoping after the Cultural Revolution, Chen Yun was extremely influential, and his early, principled criticisms of the command economy earned him great credibility. Chen was put in charge of economic work as the chair of the newly established Finance and Economics Commission in early 1979 (Lardy and Lieberthal 1983, xxxvi), and he proposed the readjustment idea at a Politburo Standing Committee meeting in spring 1979.

Chen Yun's notion of readjustment was supported by Deng Xiaoping and many reformist economists. The economic rationale was to solve the economic problems created by Hua Guofeng's Great Leap Outward; the political agenda was to discredit Hua as a leader. A Central CCP Work Conference in April 1979 took up the question of readjustment and generated the eight-character slogan "Readjustment, reform, consolidation, and raising standards," putting the priority on readjustment over reform in economic policy. The argument for readjustment rested on the 1978 economic statistics, all blamed on Hua Guofeng's policies: the accumulation rate had soared to an all-time high of 36.5 percent, and heavy industry's share of capital investment was the highest ever at 55 percent (light industry received only 5.7 percent). Investment in nonproductive construction (schools, housing, urban infrastructure) was the lowest ever at 17.5 percent. Overly rapid growth was creating shortages of energy, transportation, and materials; 20 percent of industrial capacity was idle because of energy shortages (Zhou Taihe et al. 1984, 178). Clearly, although the economy was growing fast, the Chinese consumer was not benefiting from growth.

Although readjustment became formal policy from April 1979 on, little was done to implement it until the end of 1980 (Solinger 1982), when Hua Guofeng was removed from his position as premier and Yu Qiuli was fired as head of the SPC. Before that time government bodies initiated no action to take tough readjustment measures. Enthusiasm for the expansionary approach to economic reform—stimulating growth by introducing profit incentives and spreading the new wealth—overwhelmed the caution of Chen Yun. There was a "bitter debate" between the pro-adjustment forces and the industrial and local officials who favored continued high-speed growth (Xue Muqiao 1981). Perceiving the divisions between Deng Xiaoping and Chen Yun and the contradictions between their policies of reform and readjustment, government officials mouthed readjustment slogans but carried out reforms.

In a March 1980 speech Zhao Ziyang expressed some concern that the funds generated by enterprises under profit-retention schemes might contribute to an overstretching of capital investment (Zhao Ziyang 1980). As a provincial-based reformer newly arrived at the capital, Zhao may have been trying to establish himself with the central government and party establishment by demonstrating his concern for national economic stability and balance. As the Chinese might put it, he needed to show that he could speak "Beijing talk" (*Beijing hua*) as well as "local talk" (*difang hua*). Nevertheless, Chinese economists have always credited Zhao with a sincere desire to find policy solutions that were economically sensible as well as politically feasible. In any case, no one followed up on Zhao's speech. Instead, the political logic of distributing reform experiments and revising the terms of the experiments to make them increasingly generous to the enterprises continued to dominate.

Throughout 1979 and 1980 the SEC and the State Council continued to promote expansion through reform. As one Chinese author looked back on the first two years of reform, he said that policy-makers continued to make "leftist mistakes." They did not follow the readjustment principle "in real earnest" because they "still lacked a proper understanding of it" (Su Wenming et al. 1982).

December 1980: The Leadership Unifies and Readjustment Is Implemented

The shift in priorities to readjustment from reform came at the December 1980 CCP Work Conference that was the climax of the conflict between Hua Guofeng and Deng Xiaoping. In November and December 1980 the CCP Politburo met to criticize Hua Guofeng and remove him from his posts as CCP chairman and chairman of the MAC. He was replaced as CCP general secretary by a longtime ally of Deng Xiaoping, former Young Communist League head Hu Yaobang. (The post of CCP chairman was abolished.) Deng Xiaoping himself took over as leader of the MAC. A few months earlier Hua had been replaced as premier by Zhao Ziyang, the political entrepreneur plucked from Sichuan by Deng. The December 1980 Central Party Work Conference occurred after the Politburo meeting that relieved Hua Guofeng as party secretary and replaced him with Hu Yaobang but *before* the Central Committee meeting that would formally ratify the succession.

The timing of the policy shift from reform to readjustment during the climax of the succession contest (between the Politburo and Central Committee rounds of the contest) confirms the linkage between policy and power in communist systems. To discredit Hua Guofeng and win support for the new leadership team (Deng, Chen Yun, Zhao Ziyang, and Hu Yaobang) the problems of expansion, which in reality were caused not only by Hua's 1976–78 Great Leap policies but also by the post-1978 enterprise reforms, were blamed wholly on Hua's mismanagement, and a clear policy departure—readjustment—was promoted instead.

At the work conference the new team of leaders consolidated its authority by shifting from a strategy of outbidding Hua for the support of industrial and local officials with reformist giveaways to one of unifying the party leadership by discrediting Hua's "leftist mistakes in economic work" (Lo Ping 1981). This effort involved bringing Chen Yun into Deng's team and embracing Chen's policies of readjustment.

At the work conference Chen Yun, Zhao Ziyang, Deng Xiaoping, and Li Xiannian gave speeches on the necessity for readjustment.[10] The theme of all the speeches was the need for the party to unify its thinking on the basis of economic readjustment (Chen Yun 1980; Lo Ping 1981). The work conference was Chen Yun's triumph. His cautious perspective on reform finally prevailed; Zhao Ziyang's speech took Chen Yun's ideas as his starting point (Lo Ping 1981).

The Deng team tried to unify the party behind it by stressing the theme of political stability. To build a broad political coalition among the party elite, the political tone of the work conference was clearly conservative. The Democracy Wall activists, who had earlier been encouraged by Deng, were criticized, and socialist spiritual civilization was emphasized. Hua Guofeng's economic mismanagement was criticized for jeopardizing political stability by stimulating inflation.[11] Currency in circulation had increased 30 percent in 1980, retail prices had gone up 6 percent, and prices for nonstaple food had risen 13.6 percent (Su Wenming et al. 1982; Zhou Taihe et al. 1984; Naughton 1985).[12] Unlike the budget deficit, which was an issue mainly for the MOF, inflation was a source of worry for all Chinese leaders, regardless of their other disagreements.[13] They remembered that the Guomindang government had lost power when it was unable to control runaway inflation during the 1940s.

Once the top party leaders unified and gave a clear message that they wanted readjustment, the government responded promptly and forcefully. By the February 1981 meeting of the National People's Congress Standing Committee, SPC Chairman Yao Yilin (a close ally of Chen Yun) was able to report that the 1981 plan had been revised midstream, slashing state capital construction invest-

10. Li Xiannian's speech was a self-criticism because as a longtime ally of heavy industry, he had identified himself with Hua's expansionary policies (Lo Ping 1981).
11. This line of argument presaged the conservatives' criticism of Zhao Ziyang in 1987–89.
12. Barry Naughton (1985, 312) says that the leadership's view of the inflation threat was mistaken because all of the increased currency in circulation could be accounted for as an increase in individuals' cash income.
13. Although the 1980 deficit was smaller than the one in 1979, it was more clearly a consequence of current economic policies than it was a legacy of the past or the temporary bill for waging war. Stimulated by the industrial reforms, industrial profits in 1980 rose 7.3 percent over 1979, but profits remitted to the government began to decline (by 0.3 percent; Ren Tao 1982, 31). According to Naughton (1985, 231), the decline in profit remittances began in June 1980.

ment by nearly one half (from 55 billion to 30 billion yuan) and cutting the output quotas for heavy industry to divert energy and transport to light industry (Yao Yilin 1981, 14). In addition, some enterprise bank deposits were frozen and the reform channeling fixed investment through bank loans was halted. At a national conference on industrial reform in January–March 1981 the reform advocates from the SEC and the newly established State Council Office for Economic Reform admitted that "some units do not have an adequate understanding of the positive meaning of the guideline of readjustment, and readjustment has been encountering certain resistance" (quoted in P. Lee 1987, 181). They announced that there would be no further extension of the enterprise autonomy policy ("State Council on Ensuring Financial Balance" 1981).[14] During the first half of 1981 the State Council took additional measures to reassert central control over enterprise actions, including a ceiling on bonuses, controls over new construction projects, a freeze on bank loans, and other financial controls ("Joint Report" 1981; Zhou Taihe et al. 1984). And the center leaned on local governments and enterprises to purchase "voluntarily" four to five billion yuan in treasury bonds to reduce the budget deficit (Yao Yilin 1981).

Although there was some dissension over the shift from reform to readjustment from the heavy industrial ministries (Solinger 1982), the unified position taken by the communist leadership muted any serious objections. Light industry naturally welcomed readjustment, as did both the MOF, which recognized that the shift in priority from heavy to light industry would generate more taxes and profits per yuan of investment,[15] and the SPC, which wanted

14. Three reasons were given for subordinating reform to readjustment: (a) To improve the proportions within the economy, many enterprises will have to be consolidated and restructured, but enterprises operating under reform experiments "may try out whatever is possible to enlarge their scope of production" instead. (b) To set right national economic imbalance, "it is necessary to carry out centralized leadership over economic work," including some administrative intervention in allocation of materials and funds and approving construction projects. (c) "In the process of reform, there will be clashes of interests between enterprises and the state. Whenever this happens, the former must be subordinate to the latter" (Su Wenming et al. 1982).

15. On an average based on statistics from 1950–80, for every yuan the state invests in the light and textile industries, it gets 12 yuan profit in return; for every yuan it invests in heavy industry, it gets only 70 *fen* profit in return. The return on capital is also faster in the light and textile industries than it is in heavy industry. In the light and textile industries the state can recover its investment in just 1 year and 10 months; in heavy industry,

to reassert central controls over investment in order to promote construction of key energy and transportation projects (author's interviews).

The 1981 readjustment had real teeth. Many heavy industrial enterprises found their plan targets and investment funds cut to almost zero while profit targets remained high. The reduction of output quotas cost enterprises in the machine-building, steel, chemical, and railroad industries two billion yuan in profits, according to one estimate (Ren Tao 1982, 31).

Readjustment Reorients the Interests of Industrial Managers

An unexpected consequence of readjustment was that it converted many managers of heavy industrial plants to the cause of economic reform. Faced with real economic pressure for the first time, these managers were shaken out of their dependence on the plan and forced to compete in the market.[16] Under the rules of reform they were permitted to sell on their own any product the plan did not claim. The reforms had opened new market possibilities for heavy industry. Consumers had more money in their pockets and were hungry for modern appliances. Farmers also had more money to spend and were eager to buy production equipment and consumer goods. Abandoned by the plan, heavy industrial managers turned to the market and learned to produce what buyers wanted. Because the plan targets were cut and supplies of producer goods were plentiful, for the first time there was a real buyers' market.

---

recovery requires 5 years and 7 months. Light industry also earns more foreign exchange through exports than does heavy industry ("Accelerating the Development of Light Industry and Textiles" 1981; see also Solinger 1988). Another source estimates that in 1978, for every 100 yuan of investment funds, light industry realized 62.8 yuan in taxes and profits; textiles, 68.16 yuan; and iron and steel, 13.86 yuan. Moreover, investments in textiles and light industry are recovered approximately four times faster than they are in all heavy industry, two times faster than in electric power, and almost twenty times faster than in coal (Zhao Chunxin 1981, 11–12). Nevertheless, the reduction in industrial production during readjustment hurt the central treasury; taxes and profits declined by 2.4 percent during 1981 (Ren Tao 1982, 31).

16. The results were felt even in 1980, when their plan targets were first cut. Plants in the machine-building sector went from 13.9 percent of output handled on their own in 1979 to 46 percent in 1980. The 1980 percentage of output sold by enterprises themselves was 7.7 percent for all industry, but 11 percent for steel and 33 percent for machine building (Zhou Taihe et al. 1984, 179).

The Chinese machine-building industry, particularly hard-hit by cuts in construction projects, adapted with striking resilience and ingenuity.[17] When central planners canceled their orders for industrial-use electrical generators and other large-scale equipment, machinery factories survived by developing new products for farmers, light industries, and consumers. Some machinery factories created advisory boards composed of potential customers to advise them on what new products were needed. One machinery plant, by taking such an approach, survived a cut in its plan quota to only 1 percent of its normal output and dramatically increased its output and profits in subsequent years.[18] Even the large Number Two Automobile Factory joined with other enterprises to produce ambulances and fire trucks when it could not sell its trucks (author's interviews). The performance of the enterprises under the Ministry of Machine Building tells a story of remarkable managerial flexibility: during 1981 the enterprises' plan quotas were worth a total of 10 billion yuan, only one-quarter of their total production capacity; even so, the enterprises earned 27.3 billion yuan and handed over to the state profits worth 3 billion yuan (Gao Jie 1982, K7).[19]

The Ministry of Machine Building wrote numerous reports digesting the lessons of readjustment (author's interviews). The industry leaders concluded that the machinery sector had been excessively oriented toward large-scale basic construction and had neglected the potential market in agriculture, light industry, consumer goods, and exports; if the ministry directly controlled the enterprises, the enterprises lacked the flexibility to meet market demand (Kobayashi 1981; author's interviews). Once abandoned by the plan, the machinery industry weakened its identification with the command economy and began to see the advantages of new market-based economic arrangements. As a result of its readjustment learning experience, the Ministry of Machine Building became the first ministry to divest (*xiafang*) all its directly affiliated enterprises to local control during 1984–85. The ministry also became

17. The iron and steel industry responded more slowly because it took longer for them to convert to producing new products.
18. Even though the plan claimed an increasingly larger share of the factory's output after 1981 (16 percent in 1982, 40 percent in 1983, and over 80 percent in 1984), its profits multiplied because even within the plan, factories can raise prices if the products are new or of exceptional quality (author's interviews).
19. Another account says the 1981 plan quotas were less than one-third of capacity ("Bo Yibo on Machine Building Industry's Advance" 1982).

one of the first to demand and win the right to deal directly with foreign businesses (Li Anding 1983).

Readjustment Is Short-Lived and Accelerates the Pace of Reform

The evolution of economic policy during 1981 indicates that although the readjustment line provided the policy basis for a leadership coalition to depose Hua Guofeng, it contradicted the political logic of expansion that underlay the reform drive. Readjustment pleased the MOF, the SPC, agriculture, and light industry, but it hurt heavy industry, local governments, and many state enterprises. Political pressure from this latter group was responsible for the weak implementation of the enterprise consolidation aspect of readjustment and for the reversal of central investment proportions after only one year.

An important readjustment strategy for shifting the priority away from heavy industry and improving the financial performance of all industry was the consolidation of unprofitable heavy industrial enterprises. Closing, stopping, merging, or converting (*guan, ting, bing, zhuan*) such plants would lighten the center's financial burden, shift capacity to the production of light industrial consumer goods, and improve overall efficiency. To eliminate inefficient small-scale factories, strengthen centralized coordination of production, and guarantee central revenues, the government also established national corporations for petrochemical, automobile, and tobacco production (see chapter 9). Provinces and cities were encouraged to consolidate firms into their own local corporations. National statistics report that during 1981 provinces and cities established 470 corporations and 647 economic associations ("Achievements in Restructuring Industry Noted" 1982). Another report claimed that more than two thousand industrial corporations and general plants had been set up by January 1982 and that almost one-third of the enterprises in Beijing, Tianjin, and Shanghai were part of such organizations ("Progress Made in Industrial Reorganization" 1982).

The top-level support for the consolidation thrust of readjustment was substantial.[20] Not surprisingly, large state enterprises supported the elimination or takeover of the smaller firms that competed with them and viewed corporatization as a way to free themselves from the heavy hand of industrial bureaus and ministries.

20. For a dissenting voice from a reformist economist, see Li Ling 1983.

The industrial ministries favored industrial integration into large corporations because they believed it would enhance their control (except when it meant losing firms to an independent national corporation such as the Chinese National Petrochemical Corporation). The central planners believed it would be easier to plan for fewer big units than many small ones, and the MOF saw consolidation as a way to shift the burden of subsidizing enterprises operating in the red to the industrial sectors themselves (author's interviews). Even the reform-minded SEC promoted integration because it was supported by the managers of large state factories; the National Leading Group for Enterprise Consolidation was led by SEC head Yuan Baohua.

Despite this top-level support for consolidation, the policy was poorly implemented. Many enterprises consolidated only on paper, as "nothing but a gesture" ("Documents Urge Enterprise Consolidation" 1983). Some wrote fraudulent reports of successful consolidation in order to pass their consolidation inspection (Wang Jijiang and Zhou Baohua 1983). Yuan Baohua complained in 1983 that enterprise consolidation was not just slow but actually "at a standstill" in many areas ("Yuan Baohua Speaks on Enterprise Consolidation" 1983).

Resistance to consolidation derived partly from managers of small firms, who did not want to lose their power. Many of them viewed consolidation as a punishment. Factory managers were loath to be demoted to mere workshop managers (author's interview).[21] Although the center continually called for enterprises to undergo stringent consolidation inspections and be punished for failure to comply, many inspections still were described as perfunctory and indicative of ineffective leadership in many localities. Local officials were responsible for the laxity because they were reluctant to give up their pet local plants (especially chemical fertilizer, steel, and cement plants, which were prime targets for consolidation). To the local politicians who controlled hiring labor and allocating the valuable commodities produced by these plants, their political utility was more compelling.

21. "The majority of comrades of second level plants are biased toward decentralization and demand further delegation of power; some of them even want their plants to possess the same power of independent enterprises. Some comrades in the [company] offices are, on the other hand, biased toward centralization and demand the recovery of the delegated power in order to have highly centralized power" (Zhang Jianming 1982, 45).

Political pressure from heavy industry and from local governments and enterprises also was responsible for the brief duration
of the tough readjustment cuts in heavy industrial investment. The
1981 midstream plan and budget deviated markedly from heavy
industry's previous high share of capital construction investment.
Such sharp breaks with tradition are very unusual in bureaucracies
operating according to delegation by consensus: incrementalism is
the rule, and "balancism" is the ideology. Whenever some sectors
or regions find their share cut, they have a strong claim for compensation in the future to restore the equilibrium.

An appreciation of this strong pressure to maintain original
shares helps explain why as early as mid-1981 the ministries and
provinces representing heavy industry began demanding more resources (Solinger 1982). The central authorities were responsive because the midyear statistics showed that adjustment had created a
severe recession: industrial growth was only 0.8 percent, when it
had been planned as 3 percent; heavy industrial output fell 8.2
percent (cited in Solinger 1982, 97). Because the financial system
depended on profits from heavy industry (approximately 38 percent
of financial revenues came from heavy industry; Zhao Chunxin
1981, 11), the recession also jeopardized the improvement of financial balance. The political risks of persisting in a policy strongly
opposed by the influential heavy industrial ministries, by provinces
such as Shandong, Liaoning, and Shanxi, and by the managers of
many large state enterprises apparently worried the top leaders,
especially Deng Xiaoping, who still needed to shore up his authority after defeating Hua Guofeng, and Hu Yaobang and Zhao Ziyang, who were looking toward the post-Deng succession. During
the latter part of 1981 these three moved to bolster heavy industry
and revive the reform drive, choosing to minimize the warnings of
Chen Yun, who as an elderly leader at the end of his career was
the most insulated from pressure (Chen Yun 1981). At midyear the
State Council decided to loosen up bank loans (Xue Muqiao 1982a),
and around September plans were readjusted upward and the expansion of heavy industry resumed (Naughton 1985). As a consequence, during the fourth quarter of 1981 the industrial growth rate
was 12 percent, with heavy industry growing at 4.5 percent after
three quarters of decline (Xue Muqiao 1982a, 94). Heavy industry's
share of capital construction investment for 1981 as a whole held at
39 percent, only 1.2 points lower than the previous year (its share

was 38.5 percent in 1982 and 41.0 percent in 1983; *Statistical Yearbook* 1990, 166).

At the end of the year Premier Zhao Ziyang, in his speech to the Fourth Session of the Fifth National People's Congress, optimistically reported that readjustment had succeeded in achieving basic economic balance and that the time had come to revive the reform drive: "We must not, on account of financial difficulties, abandon reforms that not only help release the initiative of local authorities, enterprises and workers and staff members, but also contribute to the overall interest" (quoted in Solinger 1982, 1265). Rather than cut heavy industry's investment and targets, the government should strengthen the sector by reorienting its production toward export and consumer goods. Reflecting this decision to revive economic growth and bolster heavy industry after less than a year of contraction, total capital construction, after dropping from 55.8 billion yuan in 1980 to 44.2 billion in 1981, rose again to 55.5 billion in 1982 (Zhou Taihe et al. 1984, 182).

The return to progrowth policies restored the leading place of heavy industry in central priorities. In 1982 heavy industrial output increased at a rate of 9.3 percent, compared to 5.6 percent for light industry (Yu Zuyao 1983). The central government's Sixth Five-Year Plan (1981–85) increased planned investment in heavy industry by 140 percent, whereas planned investment in light industry did not increase at all; however, extrabudgetary local investment in light industry increased dramatically. Thanks to the center, heavy industry's position was protected despite the locally driven boom in light industry. Over the first period of economic reform (1980–85) the total output ratio between light and heavy industry remained basically stable at 47 : 53 (*Statistical Yearbook* 1990, 59).[22]

A historical irony of the Chinese economic reform is that the brief episode of tough deflation during 1981, which conservatives expected to provide the rationale for recentralization, actually accelerated decentralization (Naughton 1985). Industrial managers and the ministry and province bureaucrats who represented them argued that reform was necessary for recovery. The only way to heal the damage caused by readjustment was to give enterprises more autonomy and more profits. Under the hardship conditions created

22. This ratio is about the same as many years before 1970 but reflects a shift away from heavy industry compared with 1971–79, when heavy industry contributed approximately 56 percent of total industrial output (*Statistical Yearbook* 1990, 59).

by readjustment, central policymakers felt compelled to "release water and keep the fish alive" (Lu Baifu 1988). "Releasing the water" meant spreading profit-retention "experiments"; by early 1982 more than 80 percent of all industrial enterprises used one of the various profit-retention methods (Jin Renxiong and Yuan Zhenyu 1983).

"Releasing the water" also meant shifting most enterprises to a profit-retention method called "profit contracting" (*lirun baogan* or *yingkui baogan*),[23] which was even more generous to enterprises than previous methods had been. Each enterprise negotiated a "base figure" of profits that it was required to deliver to the state; it was permitted to retain a proportion of profits above this base. The retention ratio was often very high, and the base figure was not based firmly on the previous years' performance but was negotiable, most commonly to the benefit of the enterprise. The rationale for profit contracting, according to Naughton, was that "since the center was the immediate cause of the instability in the economic environment, it was unfair to ask the enterprises to bear the risk; as a result rewards were increased for those who fulfilled their targets" (Naughton 1985, 234).[24]

Another provision of "releasing the water" allowed enterprises to repay bank loans directly from their profits before they paid taxes or remitted profits. This policy was originally intended as a temporary measure to ease enterprises through the financial difficulties created by readjustment, but as of 1991 it had still proved impossible to retract even though it stimulated irresponsible construction almost as much as the free allocation of investment under the old, prereform system had (Lu Baifu 1988).[25]

The policy emphasis on "enlivening" (*gaohuo*, sometimes translated as "revitalizing") enterprises through reform experiments cer-

23. This method is also sometimes called *yingkui chengbao*. The terms *baogan* and *chengbao* are used interchangeably to mean "contracting."

24. According to one authoritative account, profit contracting began during readjustment in spring 1981 as a desperate move on the part of some localities to meet their financial obligations to the center (Zhou Taihe et al. 1984, 187).

25. Before the 1965 economic reforms in the Soviet Union, interest on bank loans was included in an enterprise's costs (*chengben*), but after the 1965 Soviet reforms the interest on loans was taken from the enterprise's retained profits so it would encourage rational use of loans (Jin Renxiong and Yuan Zhenyu 1983, 20). Chinese economists knew that the policy treating loan repayment as part of enterprise costs (*chengben*) created perverse incentives, but they felt politically impotent to change it (author's interviews).

tainly had a credible economic rationale. Profit sharing was a way to strengthen enterprise incentives to be productive and efficient, and in the long term it would thereby increase state revenue (Zhao Ziyang's speech to the Fourth Session of the Fifth National People's Congress, December 1981, quoted in Solinger 1982). But the terms of the sharing arrangements implemented during 1982–83 were particularly generous to enterprises because Deng, Zhao, and Hu felt it was in their political interests to ease the pain of readjustment and get the economy growing again.

Another ironic consequence of the brief 1981 readjustment was that it reoriented the preferences of many bureaucrats and managers of heavy industry toward economic reform. When they were abandoned by the plan and forced to compete on the market, the industrialists who survived, and especially those who prospered, realized for the first time that the market offered opportunities as well as risks. After that experience heavy industry no longer viewed reform as directly antagonistic to its interests. Instead of trying to block reforms and preserve the traditional command economy—its strategy in the early days of reform (Solinger 1982)—spokespersons for heavy industry began to demand that it get its fair share of the benefits of reform. Machinery Commission head Bo Yibo was a leading proponent of the reform route to reviving heavy industry in 1981 (Paltiel 1985), and after readjustment the machine-building sector was widely acknowledged as having an especially "flexible" (*linghuo*) attitude toward management reforms.

Another legacy of readjustment was the existence of the quasi-administrative corporations, standing between industrial bureaus and enterprises, established to promote enterprise consolidation during readjustment. (Similar corporations or trusts have been a feature of economic reform efforts in many of the countries of Eastern Europe.) In the context of economic hardship produced by readjustment, these corporations, along with industrial bureaus, were allowed to claim a share of enterprise profits, which they could redistribute to balance the financial situation of their subordinate enterprises. To prevent the gap between the successful and unsuccessful firms becoming too wide (*kule buzhun*—literally, "unequal pain and happiness"—is the Chinese term used to justify egalitarian redistribution by bureaucratic authority), the corporations and bureaus were authorized to subsidize the weak enterprises with the profits of the strong ("Joint Report" 1981). These readjustment measures authorized corporations and bureaus to meddle in the financial affairs of enterprises and weakened the incentive effect of profit sharing on enterprise managers. When economic experts and factory managers finally realized after 1984 that the financial authority of corporations had become an obstacle to genuine autonomy at the enterprise level, it proved very difficult to weaken or abolish the corporations.

The First Stage of Industrial Reform Creates New Vested Interests in Reform

All in all, the first period of industrial reform (1978–81) was successful in creating new "vested interests in reform." The central leaders generated support for the reform drive and for themselves by selectively distributing profit-sharing "experiments" to an increasingly large number of enterprises. And from 1980 on, the center devolved fiscal resources and economic authority to provinces and municipalities on a case-by-case basis (see chapter 9). The political logic of this "spread the profits" strategy was overpowering; of all the various aspects of enterprise autonomy reforms, only profit retention was widely implemented. By giving managers and local politicians the incentive and wherewithal to seek profits, the strategy stimulated economic expansion. High growth rates had the additional advantage of creating the illusion of what Albert Hirschman has called "non-antagonistic reform" (Hirschman 1963, 251), or reform that is perceived as making all groups better off: all industrial sectors, including the politically influential heavy industry, grew rapidly, and both workers and peasants increased their income. The brief but painful episode of contraction and readjustment in 1981, by teaching industrial officials the potential benefits offered by the market and by giving them a recovery rationale for demanding more profits and more market freedoms, actually accelerated the process of expansionary reform. By the beginning of 1982 more than 80 percent of state enterprises were operating on some sort of profit-retention scheme (Naughton 1985).

The only worried voices came from the MOF, the SPC, and some cautious reformist economists (such as Xue Muqiao), who pointed out that the profit-retention "wind" had not brought improvements in efficiency or increases in central revenues. Managers and local politicians were fiddling with the rules to keep more profits for themselves instead of turning them over to the financial authorities (see, for example, "Yao Yilin Attends Forum on Enterprise Management" 1981). Many managers and local officials unilaterally raised the profit-retention percentage or switched from one profit-sharing scheme to another; they spent most of their retained profits on employee bonuses and relied on unsecured, low-interest bank loans to finance their investments. Moreover, they were all rushing to produce the same high-profit products (made profitable because of irrational, administratively set prices), which was wasteful and socially unproductive. Administrative and fiscal decentralization encouraged local bureau and corporation officials to continually interfere with enterprise management, obstructing the growth of genuine enterprise autonomy. An industrial reform that was limited only to profit retention could not solve the problems of China's old economic system and created a host of new ones.

Despite these worried voices, the central leaders chose not to retract the financial benefits they had spread selectively among enterprises and localities; the political support generated by particularistic giveaways was too valuable. As a result, the ratio of central state revenue to national income dropped every year: it was 37.2 percent in 1978, 31.9 percent in 1979, 28.3 percent in 1980, 25.8 percent in 1981, and 24.5 percent in 1982 (Jin Xin 1983, K10). The MOF was allowed to dun enterprises and local governments to buy central treasury bonds in 1981; and in 1983 it taxed 10 percent (raised to 15 percent later in the year) of all local extrabudgetary funds and 10 percent of extraplan capital construction. These stop-gap measures spread burdens equally among all units. However, no reform experiment that increased benefits for a particular unit was ever retracted.

Thus, by 1982 a clear political strategy of reform had emerged. The top leadership generated support for themselves and reform by selectively allocating lucrative reform experiments to enterprises, localities, and even (later) to ministries, while the costs of reform (from inefficiency and inflation to bond purchases and taxes on extrabudgetary funds) were diffused to everyone.

11 Leadership Succession and Policy Conflict

The Choice Between Profit Contracting and Substituting Tax-for-Profit, 1982–83

After an impressively rapid takeoff, Chinese industrial reforms encountered turbulence during 1982–83. Experts and officials argued over two alternative approaches to enterprise reform: the particularistic approach of profit-contracting and the standardized approach of replacing profit remission with tax payment (*li gai shui*, or tax-for-profit). The debate between these two approaches began to divide the ranks of proreform economists and officials. Discussions of price reform initiated in 1981 by Premier Zhao Ziyang went nowhere, and market reforms came under ideological fire from CCP conservative leaders.

Divisions over reform policies and lack of progress in extending reforms stemmed from three factors. First, experts engaged in technical debates about which policies would work better in economic terms. The transition from plan to market represented uncharted waters to Chinese economists, who lacked theoretical models or empirical examples that could serve as navigation aids. Second, bureaucratic agencies became embroiled in conflicts concerning whose financial and jurisdictional interests would be affected by various policy proposals. Government organizations such as the Ministry of Finance, the State Economic Commission, and the industrial ministries had much at stake in the choice between profit-contracting and tax-for-profit. Because they recognized that CCP leaders were divided on this question, they stubbornly held to their preferred positions and refused to compromise.

That brings us to the most important reason for the lack of progress on industrial reform during 1982–84. The two leaders right under Deng Xiaoping in China's political hierarchy, General Secretary Hu Yaobang and Premier Zhao Ziyang, split on the issue of profit-contracting versus tax-for-profit. This disagreement was embedded in the natural political competition between Hu and Zhao, the two most likely successors to Deng. During 1982–83 the succession contest was not yet out in the open. As CCP general secretary, Hu Yaobang was the presumptive heir, and Zhao Ziyang did not publicly challenge Hu's claim. Yet Hu and Zhao's disagreement on enterprise reforms and their turf fight over who had the authority to lead the reforms were unusually sharp and open. With the party leadership divided on economic questions, the government bureaucrats had little incentive to compromise.

After considerable debate the State Council finally decided in 1983 to choose tax-for-profit over profit-contracting. This decision was surprising in that fiscal conservatism and technocratic caution appeared to prevail over the political logic of distributing benefits to selected localities and enterprises. The choice was an exception to the generally expansionist thrust and particularistic form of economic reform policies from 1979 to 1989.

Hu Yaobang's failure to gain approval for his profit-contracting approach and the victory of the tax-for-profit approach favored by Zhao Ziyang reflected the strength of Chen Yun and other conservative party elders in the selectorate during 1982–83. These party conservatives had signaled their strength in a series of ideological critiques of market reforms published in the *People's Daily* and other national papers during late 1982. On the other side, support for profit-contracting within the selectorate, from the provincial officials and industrial ministry officials in the Central Committee who would have benefited from it, was not yet firm.

The Competition Between
Hu Yaobang and Zhao Ziyang

During the period 1982–83 Zhao Ziyang and Hu Yaobang, the main contenders to succeed Deng Xiaoping, pursued two different approaches to industrial reform. Both leaders were enthusiastic reformers, and both used economic reform policies to win support from key groups in the world of Chinese officialdom. Their different policy preferences reflected their political strengths and weaknesses.

As a longtime provincial leader newly arrived in the capital, Zhao presumably already had the support of many fellow locals in the Central Committee, although they did not constitute a personal following comparable to Hu's. What he lacked was the support of central officials, and he therefore took a cautious, procenter approach to decentralization. His qualms about profit-contracting, expressed as early as January 1982 ("Zhao Ziyang Talks on Responsibility Systems" 1982), and his sympathy for the MOF's position that tax-for-profit would guarantee a steadier increase in central revenues ingratiated him with party and government officials in Beijing. He showed them that he had already stopped speaking the language of the localities (*shuo difang hua*) and started speaking the language of Beijing (*shuo Beijing hua*).

Zhao Ziyang's advocacy of tax-for-profit was influenced by his position as challenger to Hu Yaobang in the succession contest. As CCP general secretary and a longtime member of the Beijing political elite, Hu had to be considered the front-runner for the top position. To be taken seriously as a contender, Zhao had to demonstrate to Deng Xiaoping and the rest of the selectorate that he could lead the economic reform and make it work. As premier he was in the best slot to prove his competence in running the economy. By pushing tax-for-profit, which he and many reformist economists considered the most rational framework to raise enterprise efficiency, Zhao hoped to claim credit for improving overall economic performance.

Hu Yaobang already was well known in Beijing and could count on a huge national network of personal supporters he had built when serving as head of the Young Communist League. Hu had a reputation for being impulsive, much like Mao Zedong. A political agitator during the Anti-Japanese War, his forte was rousing people to action. Although he had shown no interest in economic issues in the past, after becoming party general secretary Hu turned into a "born-again economic reformer." His policy pronouncements frequently reflected an eagerness for rapid results. At the Twelfth National Party Congress in 1982 he promoted the goal of quadrupling China's national industrial and agricultural output from 710 billion yuan (1980) to 2.8 trillion yuan by the year 2000 (Hu Yaobang 1982). Although this target translated into an annual growth rate of 7.2 percent, not an excessively high rate, Hu's emphasis on growth and mobilization were reminiscent of the Maoist era. His newfound enthusiasm for reform extended even to Chinese social mores: he advocated wearing Western-style clothing and replacing the Chinese style of eating from common plates with the Western style of eating from individual plates ("Eating from Individual Plates Urged" 1984).[1]

---

1. My own theory about the political fall of Hu Yaobang is that any Chinese politician who tries to tell the Chinese people how to eat is doomed

Hu's greatest political resource was his national network of clients. He needed to keep this faction well-fed by distributing patronage. Particularistic contracting was a kind of Chinese "pork," special favors that politicians such as Hu could hand out to their followers. Replacing profit-contracting with the standardized method of tax-for-profit would hurt Hu much more than it would hurt Zhao, who lacked a personal faction.

The Conservatives Signal Their Strength in an Antimarket Ideological Campaign

Party conservatives launched a serious ideological attack on the idea of market reform at the end of 1981; the attack became even more prominent during the fall of 1982. The main theme of the attack was the claim that reformers were deviating from socialism by trying to replace planning with the market. According to the conservatives, the defining characteristic of socialism was mandatory planning. Therefore, the only acceptable formula for economic reform was that planning must be primary (*wei zhu*), and the commodity economy (a euphemism for the still ideologically tainted term *market*) must be secondary (*wei fu*).

Chen Yun launched the campaign to limit reformers by reemphasizing the primacy of planning in speeches in December 1981 and January 1982 (Chen Yun 1981; 1982). During fall 1982 a string of articles appeared in key party periodicals such as the *People's Daily* and *Red Flag* criticizing the ideas of reformers for being ideologically incorrect. These articles, written by the special commentator for the *People's Daily*, high officials in the SPC, and the head of the CCP Secretariat Policy Research Center, among others, frequently quoted Chen Yun. Although the debate was ostensibly theoretical and the top CCP leaders did not get publicly involved, the reformist economists understood that Chen Yun, the elders, and the CCP Propaganda Department were behind the attacks (author's interviews).[2] The articles criticized the notion that reformist economists had learned from Eastern Europe of replacing mandatory plan targets with indicative (guidance) targets as not real socialist planning. The central message of each of the articles was that the reformers' proposals violated the core tenet of socialism, the

---

to fail. Another example was Mao Zedong's attempt to replace family meals with collective mess halls during the Great Leap Forward.

2. The industrial enterprises and the SEC did not come out to defend the reforms against these theoretical-ideological attacks (author's interviews).

planned economy ("Establish a System of Planned Management" 1982; Wang Renzhi and Gui Shiyong 1982; Fang Weizhong 1982; Lu Xiansheng 1982).

In fact, the reformers had tried to protect their proposals for market reforms by proposing them in ideologically acceptable terms; articles written by reformers such as Liu Guoguang and Xue Muqiao always used the slogan "The planned economy is primary, and the commodity economy is secondary" (see, for example, Xue Muqiao 1982).[3] Even though both sides used the same slogan, the ideological conservatives still attacked the reformers and their ideas.[4] As Lucian Pye has pointed out, ideological debates often serve a symbolic function, demonstrating the relative strength of different political factions (Pye 1981). The fact that the elders could go after the reformers in the official party press using such politically loaded language was a statement of their increasing influence.

Other important party events and documents during 1981–82 telegraphed a similar message of continuing and increasing conservative influence within the CCP. An ideological campaign criticizing Bai Hua's screenplay *Unrequited Love* for promoting bourgeois liberalization was launched by the PLA in April 1981 and supported by Deng Xiaoping in July 1981. In June 1981 the CCP's reassessment of Mao Zedong's reign, "Resolution on Some Questions in the History of Our Party Since the Founding of the PRC," bent over backward to pay respect to the achievements of the Civil War period and the 1950s, when many of the elders were in charge. The documents of the September 1982 Twelfth Party Congress treated the 1950s as a golden age in China's economic development; the congress also decided to retain the elders in the Politburo and Politburo Standing Committee. During 1982 a major movement against "economic crimes"—corruption—identified the main threats to Chinese social virtue as bourgeois liberalization and peaceful evolution (from socialism to capitalism) promoted by the open policy and market reforms.

These signals of the strength of the conservative elders, many of whom were still in the Politburo and Standing Committee, influenced Deng Xiaoping's decision to intervene in the reform policy

---

3. Ma Hong, one of Zhao Ziyang's chief economic advisers, wrote an article on the subject identifying himself with Chen Yun's position; see Ma Hong 1982a.
4. One of the authors of these ideological attacks on reform, He Jianzhang, was at the time at the SPC research organ. In 1991, after the conservatives increased their hold on party power, He was appointed to head the Economics Institute of the Chinese Academy of Social Sciences, replacing the well-known reformist economist Zhao Renwei.

debate to back Zhao Ziyang's tax-for-profit approach, which was more compatible with the procentralization preferences of the old guard than was profit-contracting.

The Origins of Tax-for-Profit and Profit Contracting

Both profit-contracting and tax-for-profit originated during the early stage of enterprise reform, when central agencies were encouraging various experimental modes of enterprise finance. In August 1980 an SEC document, approved by the State Council, authorized experiments in various varieties of both profit sharing and substituting tax-for-profit ("Report of the Opinions of the State Economic Commission" 1980). The justification for flexible methods for profit retention (including methods similar to profit-contracting but not yet called profit-contracting) was twofold. First, so long as the price and tax systems remained irrational, flexible methods were needed to balance the lack of uniformity in the objective factors affecting enterprise earnings, that is, factors external to the firm that management could do nothing to change, such as administratively set prices of inputs and products (Xiang Yuanpei and Du Linfeng 1980). Second, enterprises suffering from reduced plan quotas and cuts in investment funds caused by the 1981 readjustment needed special consideration to survive. A 1981 State Council document authorized a method explicitly called "profit-contracting" (and "loss contracting") for enterprises that were making very low profits or operating at a loss because of the shock of readjustment ("Joint Report" 1981; Jiang Yiwei 1983).

Profit contracting allowed each enterprise to negotiate an individual profit-sharing contract with the state: the enterprise promised to deliver to the state a base amount of profits and retained a set proportion of all profits above that amount. Industrial profit contracting was inspired by the dramatically successful system of agricultural contracting at the household level. The method that emerged during late 1981 to help enterprises recover from readjustment was essentially a continuation and elaboration of the early profit-retention experiments.

The idea of substituting enterprise tax payments for profit remission (*li gai shui*) originated in the 1980 SEC document authorizing various types of experiments. The SEC allowed each province, municipality, and autonomous region to pick one or two enterprises to carry out experiments converting profit remission into taxes. The experimental enterprises chosen by localities had to be approved by the SEC and the MOF, but central and local officials shared the political advantages of distributing to subordinate enterprises the privilege of being an experiment.

Various new tax systems had been tested since 1979. The Sichuan method required enterprises to pay three types of taxes—industrial and commercial tax, a fixed-asset tax, and income tax—in lieu of profit remittance. The Shanghai method required enterprises to pay five taxes and two fees—industrial commercial tax, an earnings adjustment tax, real estate tax, vehicle and ship license tax, income tax, and fees for the use of fixed and working capital. The Liuzhou method, sponsored by the General Tax Bureau of the MOF, required enterprises to pay value-added tax, natural endowment tax, differential earnings adjustment tax, income tax, and fees for the use of fixed and working capital.

After paying taxes, experimental enterprises achieved complete financial autonomy and were fully responsible for their own profits and losses, making these original versions of tax-for-profit a more advanced form of enterprise autonomy than profit sharing was (and certainly more advanced than the tax-for-profit policies implemented on a national scale after 1983). From 1980 to 1981 approximately 270 enterprises carried out tax-for-profit experiments (Yang Ximin, "Some Observations of the Substitution of Taxation for Profit Remittance," *Caijing kexue* [Finance and economics science], no. 2 [1983]: 57, cited in P. Lee 1987, 204).

The same 1981 State Council document that explicitly authorized profit-contracting also declared that for the time being the tax-for-profit experiments should not be expanded beyond those already authorized ("Joint Report" 1981). According to the document, one problem with the tax-for-profit method was that experimental enterprises were bargaining for lower tax rates from local authorities and were calculating various types of fees (including employees' welfare, bonuses, and fixed and circulating asset fees) as part of their cost (*chengben*) and paying them out of pretax profits. Because enterprises were devoting themselves to manipulating the system instead of making their operations more efficient, state revenues were lower than expected.

As of 1981 the political lines of support for profit-contracting and tax-for-profit methods had not yet been drawn. The SEC was supporting both methods as ways of promoting management autonomy and winning political support for reform.[5]

5. The Industrial Economic Institute of the Chinese Academy of Social Sciences, which worked closely with the SEC in promoting the interests of

The 1981 limitation on tax-for-profit experiments suggests that the MOF was not yet firmly committed to the tax approach, although there were reports of "some people" who feared that profit-retention was reducing industrial profits turned over to the state ("Do a Still Better Job" 1981). The MOF was overwhelmed with the administrative burden of negotiating with thousands of firms over their profit-retention contracts and wanted to lower transaction costs by fixing uniform tax rates; the MOF also desired a steady, guaranteed flow of central revenues. But the MOF was uneasy about embarking on a full-fledged tax system because it was completely uncharted territory for a bureaucracy used to collecting profits (author's interviews).[6] The shift to taxes would also entail expanding and strengthening the General Tax Bureau, which was only weakly and ambiguously subordinated to the MOF (author's interviews; see chapter 5).[7]

Moreover, as a bureaucracy concerned at least as much about achieving predictability in the revenue flow as about maximizing revenues, the MOF at first may have viewed profit-contracting and the tax method as equally attractive. Profit contracting was originally called a "responsibility system" because it committed the firm to remit a certain amount of revenue to the government and assigned specific responsibilities for generating this revenue to each subunit within the firm. Under profit-contracting, enterprises committed to remit a certain amount to the state for a period of three

---

the enterprises and was later a major promoter of profit contracting (and which was in 1981 headed by Ma Hong), held a national conference in April 1981; the conference's concluding statement claimed that the tax-for-profit scheme was "an objective demand and inevitable tendency of economic reform" (quoted in P. Lee 1987, 203). In the same month, however, SEC head Yuan Baohua made a speech to the national conference on industry and transport in which he urged industrial enterprises to carry out an economic responsibility system like the rural responsibility system ("Industrial Production, Transport Conference Opens" 1981).

6.   Robert H. Bates and Da-hsiang Donald Lien (1985) point out that one important reason for the development of tax systems is that both monarchs and taxpayers prefer collectively imposed taxes to the transaction costs and uncertainties of individual bargaining.

7.   At the central level, the Tax Affairs General Bureau (*shui wu zong bu*) is subordinate to the MOF, but it is the only MOF bureau with the authority to issue decrees. At the municipal level the Tax Bureau is separate and equal to the Finance Bureau. At the provincial level the Tax Bureau is subordinate to the Finance Bureau, but not a whole level down, only half a level down (author's interviews).

to five years, whereas the amount of taxes and fees paid under tax-for-profit depended on how much enterprises earned each year.

Profit contracting also appeared to be an attractive solution to readjustment revenue shortfalls from the standpoint of central and local government officials. City and provincial officials struggling to meet their financial obligations to the center because of the readjustment recession could use the contracting method to squeeze the funds out of subordinate enterprises (Jiang Yiwei 1983).

From the standpoint of enterprise managers, although any profit-sharing experiment was preferable to the old system, which one they liked best depended on their economic situation, their attitude toward risk, and the specific terms of their profit-contract or tax package. The profit-contracting system gave enterprises most of the profits of growth, but also, at least as the system was supposed to work (with contracts fixed for three to five years), all of the risk. In the context of hard times in 1981 the requirement to pay the state a fixed amount every year regardless of changes in demand and prices might have appeared more dangerous than paying taxes, most of which fluctuated with firm performance. In actual implementation, however, profit-contracting probably afforded managers greater flexibility because they could bargain with their industrial bureau bosses for favorable terms. Dynamic enterprises particularly favored the contracting method because most of the profits from growth would accrue to the enterprise instead of the government.

Industrial ministries and local governments generally favored profit-contracting over tax-for-profit because contracting granted them, rather than financial officials, the authority to allocate financial burdens and benefits to subordinate enterprises. This authority gave ministry and local government officials control over favors to exchange with managers and also allowed ministries and local governments to skim off a share of the profits as administration funds or technological development funds.

By 1982, however, the MOF was complaining that profit-contracting was being exploited by the enterprises to rob the state of revenue. In 1981 remitted taxes and profits declined 2.4 percent over the previous year even though total profits increased; finance officials blamed profit-contracting. According to them, revenues began to decline during the second half of 1981 after the profit-contracting system (then called the enterprise responsibility system) was introduced (Ren Tao 1982). Four provincial-level governments that had widely implemented profit-contracting, Shandong, Liaoning, Beijing, and Tianjin, fell short of their revenue targets by more than one billion yuan (Sun Xuewen, "We Must Correctly Carry Out Enterprise Responsibility Systems," *Caimao jingji* [Finance and trade economics], no. 2 [1982]: 33, cited in Naughton 1985, 236).

Managers failed to treat the contract as a legal commitment and constantly bargained to revise the terms of the contract to get more benefits for their enterprises. Managers also inflated their costs and hid their profits; the latter was more difficult to carry off even though state audits were sloppy (author's interviews). If enterprises performed poorly, managers argued that the cause was "objective factors"—that is, changes in prices or demand—and pleaded to have their profit remittance obligation (the base figure) revised downward. The so-called responsibility system actually made enterprises responsible for profits, but not losses. Meanwhile, the burden of subsidizing enterprise losses continued to fall on the MOF.

Commentators, both Chinese and foreign, have noted a Chinese pattern of managers bargaining with government officials for preferential terms under types of partial reform arrangements such as profit-contracting (Walder 1986a; Huang Yasheng 1988). It is commonly assumed that any sharing rule that is not fixed but is negotiated with each individual firm works to the benefit of the enterprise rather than the government. In fact, such an assumption is unfounded without examining the institutional foundations of government-enterprise relations. Although government officials depend on the products and profits generated by enterprises, they also have formal authority over enterprises; they "own" them and appoint their managers. In a growing economy, why shouldn't the government be able to impose a higher profit remittance figure on enterprises every year?

The answer, at least in the case of profit-contracting in China, was that local government authorities had a financial incentive to collude with managers.[8] Enterprises negotiated profit-contracts with the financial officials *at the level that administered the enterprise.* Local industrial bureaus bargained hard on behalf of their subordinate enterprises and sometimes were themselves the unit that contracted to deliver profits and taxes to the state; the better the deal they could obtain for their enterprises, the more funds they could siphon off for their own use (Lin Ling 1983). Most important, under

8. Both Andrew G. Walder (1986) and Huang Yasheng (1988) recognized the shared interests of local officials and enterprise managers.

fiscal decentralization local financial officials were happy to accommodate enterprise and bureau demands because such flexibility meant more revenues kept at the local level instead of being sent to Beijing. Under contracting, local governments and enterprises made a "tacit mutual agreement . . . to dilute the center's interests and strengthen the interests of the local government and enterprises" (Xu Jian 1989, 26).

Bureaucratic Conflicts over Enterprise Reform

Support and opposition for profit-contracting crystallized during 1982, when the redistributive implications of the policy—that is, enterprises, ministries, and localities kept more money and the central treasury received less—became clear.[9] Many firm managers became profit-contracting enthusiasts; the economy was beginning to grow again, and given the flexibility of contract rules and the incentives that local officials had to bend them, there was no way for enterprises not to gain from the arrangement.

The SEC, as always the advocate of managerial and financial autonomy for enterprises, took up the cause of profit-contracting. In October 1981 and August 1982 the SEC (along with the State Commission on Economic System Reform, which was not as firmly in the contracting camp; author's interviews), held two national meetings to discuss the results of profit-contracting experiments (Zhou Taihe et al. 1984, 187).

Beginning in 1982, the SEC became a larger, more powerful force in the central bureaucracy because other economic commissions (Agriculture, Machine Building, Energy, and Capital Construction) were abolished, and all of them except Agriculture were absorbed by the SEC (Zhang Jingfu 1982).[10] This reorganization left only the SEC, the SPC, the State Science and Technology Commission, and the State Commission on Economic System Reform (and the MOF, which held commission status in actuality if not in formal authority) at the commission level over the ministries and provinces.

The SEC's close ally in promoting profit-contracting was the Institute of Industrial Economics of the Chinese Academy of Social

9. Chinese enterprises favoring the method of "progressively increasing profit contracting" (exemplified by the Capital Iron and Steel Corporation) disputed the assumption that such a contracting method resulted in diminishing income for the national treasury as compared with a fixed sharing rate; see, for example, Feng Zonghao 1984.
10. Some parts of the commissions went to other bodies, but most parts went to the SEC.

Sciences (CASS), headed after 1982 by Jiang Yiwei, who became the foremost spokesperson for the contracting approach. The Institute of Industrial Economics publishes a widely read journal, *Economic Management*, which Jiang used to advocate profit-contracting. Both the SEC and the Institute of Industrial Economics had close ties with the top managers of China's largest corporations, and they used those ties to build support for contracting.

Although the SEC and Jiang Yiwei's Institute of Industrial Economics were the leaders of the profit-contracting movement, the two bodies were not in full agreement over the rationale for the policy. Jiang Yiwei propounded the theory of "enterprise self-interest" (*qiye benwei lun*), which he contrasted with the previous system, in which enterprises were merely the administrative appendages of the state ("state self-interest," or *guojia benwei lun*). Jiang argued that enterprises had to be freed to pursue their own financial interests, which essentially were the financial interests of their employees. Under the theory of enterprise self-interest only the employees of the enterprise could make a financial contract with the state; the employees would be represented by the enterprise workers' congress and the manager (Jiang Yiwei 1981; 1983). SEC officials believed that profit-contracting was an effective scheme to motivate enterprises while increasing state revenue, but they were not willing to go as far as Jiang Yiwei in flirting with enterprise self-management and distanced themselves from his theory (author's interviews).

The most famous experiment in profit-contracting, promoted nationwide by the SEC and the Institute of Industrial Economics, was the Capital (Shoudu) Iron and Steel Company in Beijing. Capital Iron and Steel is one of China's industrial giants, having more than 70,000 employees and producing annually, as of 1983, over 3 million tons of iron, 1.5 million tons of steel, and 1 million tons of steel products. In 1979 it was selected to carry out a profit-retention experiment. It switched over to a tax-for-profit system in 1980, and in the second half of 1981 the SEC authorized Capital to shift again to a profit-responsibility system called "progressively increasing profit remission contract system" (*shangjiao lilun dizeng baogan*). The company committed to a base amount of profit it would remit to the state every year (270 million yuan, the amount remitted in 1981) and a certain percentage annual increase in this amount (6 percent) for five years. Anything over that amount would be kept by the company. Jiang Yiwei and other supporters of this method argued that it was the best way to achieve the two goals of guaranteeing the state a steady increase in its revenue and motivating the enterprise to increase profits.[11]

Capital's economic performance received extensive publicity by officials promoting profit-contracting. In most accounts the firm's record during the four years before reform was contrasted with its record during 1979–82 (profits increased by 109 percent, and profits handed over to the state increased by 76 percent);[12] the firm's dramatic transformation was credited to the "economic responsibility system," thereby blurring the differences among the various financial incentive systems Capital had practiced during 1979–82 (CCP Committee of Shoudu Iron and Steel Company 1983; Li Haibo 1983). No matter: the advocates of profit-contracting were glad to claim credit for their preferred form of economic responsibility even though Capital had implemented it only after 1981.

In any case, the statistics for the second half of 1981 and first nine months of 1982 confirmed the positive financial results of the "progressively increasing profit remittance contracting system" (progressive contracting, for short). Average monthly profit greatly increased over the previous year and the amount turned over to the state also increased, although at a slower rate ("How Shoudu Steelworks Has Become a National Success" 1982; "How Shoudu Boosts Profits" 1982). Capital's management was particularly impressed with the results of progressive contracting because it produced increased profits even during the toughest period of readjustment in the second half of 1981, when their plan quotas were cut and their output fell by 360,000 tons. And although many people claimed that Capital's spectacular success was due to the "tricks" usually asso-

11. Opponents pointed out that the 1981 base figure for profit remission was extremely low, a concession to the enterprise to ease the pain of readjustment. Therefore, the dramatic increase in the firm's above-base-figure profits was just an artifact of the readjustment context and a policy gift to the experimental firm, not a true measure of the efficacy of the profit-contracting method (author's interviews).

12. The Capital Iron and Steel authorities didn't report the 76 percent increase in remitted profits (because it was lower than the rate of increase of total profits) but chose instead to report the 297 percent increase in the amount of remitted profits augmented by the amount of reduction in state investment allocations to the company. By using this larger figure, the authorities could claim that because their firm implemented the economic responsibility system, the growth of state income was higher than the growth of the profits of the enterprise (CCP Committee of Shoudu Iron and Steel Company 1983).

ciated with Chinese economic models or experiments, officials from the relevant upper-level agencies investigated and certified that the company had "gained proper efficiency through appropriate ways and measures" (CCP Committee of Shoudu Iron and Steel Company 1983, K10).

The Institute of Industrial Economics visited Capital Iron and Steel in mid-1982 to investigate progressive profit-contracting and in April 1982 wrote a report to Premier Zhao Ziyang proposing that this method be extended to other large enterprises, particularly large, key national enterprises whose products were urgently needed and enterprises that needed to spend large sums to modernize their equipment (author's interviews). In May and June of the same year the SEC held a national meeting in Beijing to which it invited representatives of 131 industrial enterprises (located in every province but Tibet), who were taught how to carry out the Capital-style profit-contracting system (He Zhuoxin 1983). In addition to these national progressive profit-contracting experiments, which had to be approved by the SEC and the MOF, various provinces and cities also selected their own local factories to try out progressive profit-contracting.

The 1981–82 initiatives by the SEC and the Institute of Industrial Economics stimulated a fierce national debate over which type of economic responsibility system should be popularized, profit contracting (including progressive profit-contracting) or tax-for-profit.

In the debate among economists about which method would best promote enterprise efficiency, no one recommended continuing the traditional Soviet-style system, in which all enterprise profits were remitted to the central government. The only two policy alternatives considered both involved granting enterprises greater financial independence. The advocates of profit-contracting argued that their preferred method, by effectively linking the authority, material interest, and financial responsibility of the firm, as had been done in the agricultural household contracting system, created the best incentive for efficiency. Tax-for-profit supporters countered that contracting was largely a way to cater to the material interests of enterprises; that setting contracts by bargaining between the state and individual enterprises allowed enterprises to evade their responsibilities; that only a uniform tax system with the force of law would move enterprises toward full economic responsibility for profits and losses; and that such full economic responsibility was essential for managers to have an incentive to cut costs and strive for efficiency. The technical arguments for the superiority of the tax method were made not just by MOF experts such as Xu Yi but also by well-known reformist economists such as Xue Muqiao.

On the side of profit-contracting were the SEC, the Institute of Industrial Economics and Jiang Yiwei, many managers of large enterprises (particularly heavy industrial ones), and many ministry and local officials. According to the press, during the second half of 1982 everyone wanted to have their own Capital-type profit-contracting experiment (Zhou Taihe 1983). Local officials, particularly but not solely in the most economically dynamic coastal areas, supported profit-contracting ("*Hunan ribao* on Enterprise Responsibility Systems" 1981; "Beijing Speeds Up Reform" 1983; "Ren Zhongyi's Talk" 1983 [on Guangdong]).

The profit-contracting campaign was greatly strengthened by the top-level support of General Secretary Hu Yaobang. Articles on profit contracting often took their inspiration from Hu, either linking profit-contracting with the accomplishment of Hu's target of quadrupled economic growth by the year 2000 (Zhou Taihe 1982) or quoting Hu's statement, "We must change the malpractices in industrial enterprises of not differentiating between the diligent and the lazy and all eating from the same big pot. We must link the immediate personal interests of employees to how good is the management of their enterprises, to stimulate the socialist activism of employees and increase the liveliness of enterprises" (Li Huifen 1984, 19).

One of the main arguments for profit-contracting offered by its supporters was that it gave enterprises the financial resources to undertake the technological renovation of their equipment (Zhou Guanwu 1984). The SEC, the bureaucracy most active in promoting profit-contracting, was also responsible for distributing government funds for technological renovation to enterprises (several years before, the SEC had grabbed these funds away from the capital construction funds allocated by the SPC). The problem of how to find funds for replacing technologically obsolete equipment weighed heavily on the managers of large, heavy industrial firms.[13] Capital Iron and Steel had thoroughly upgraded its production technology after implementing progressive profit-contracting. The argument that profit-contracting would relieve the center of the expensive responsibility for modernizing industrial enterprises should have

13. A survey of firm managers conducted by the Chinese Economic System Reform Research Institute found that technological transformation was their second most important objective (Reynolds 1987, 113).

found a warm reception at the MOF, but the actual reaction was hostile. Although profit-contracting, especially the progressive variety employed at Capital Iron and Steel, might in theory have provided a mechanism for generating more total revenues and reducing the fiscal burden of the central government, the financial authorities in Beijing saw it as a threat to central revenue collection.

The fight between profit-contracting and tax-for-profit was not only a technical debate about the economic merits of each approach. It was also a bureaucratic conflict between the MOF and the SPC, which were bent on conserving central administrative control over the economy, and the SEC, which shared the viewpoint of enterprise managers. The MOF relied on facts about diffusion of revenues, budget deficits, and pressing infrastructure needs to argue for the tax-for-profit alternative.

The main complaint of financial authorities against profit contracting was that it left the largest share of new profits (those above the base figure) to the enterprise, so that over time the state would get the lesser share of the total profit. One article written from the MOF point of view presented the hypothetical case of an enterprise on the progressive profit-contracting plan. During the base year of 1980 the enterprise earned one million yuan of profit, remitting 850,000 yuan to the state and retaining 150,000 for its own use. If its profits increased 10 percent per year and it contracted with the state to give it 4 percent more per year of these additional profits, then the enterprise's retained profits would increase by more than 10 percent per year. After only ten years the state would be receiving only 48.5 percent of the total profits. If the enterprise's profits increased 15 percent per year and the state's share of the additional profits rose 6 percent per year, then the state would be left with less than a majority share in only seven years (Yang Qixian 1983, 22). Such a scenario horrified central financial authorities for practical reasons—their financial responsibilities for capital construction, price subsidies, administrative expenses, and national defense would remain stable or grow while their share of revenues would shrink—and for reasons of principle as well. Even in capitalist countries such as the United States, Great Britain, and Japan, the state claims more than half of companies' growth in profits; corporate tax rates are over 50 percent. In the eyes of the MOF, if this was true under capitalism, then it should certainly be true under socialism (Yang Qixian 1983).

From the MOF's perspective the contract system in industry was a much greater threat than was the contract system in agriculture.

Whereas the central state depended heavily on fiscal revenues from industry, more than 90 percent of agricultural earnings were retained by collectives and individuals. It had always been the case that the largest piece of rural profits went to collective farm members, the second largest to the collective, and the smallest to the state. The MOF's stake in the rural reform was therefore much weaker than its stake in the industrial reform. Spokespersons for the MOF's point of view made these points in arguing that management models from agriculture were inappropriate for industry (Tian Jiyun 1983a).

By 1982 MOF officials were publicly critical of policies, such as profit-contracting, that delegated too much financial authority to enterprises. According to one article expressing the MOF perspective,

> The delegation of authority to enterprises now means, after all, the use of state funds to "fatten" enterprises. If state funds are exhausted and the enterprises have more funds than they know how to use, does this mean any advancement of social welfare? I don't think so. It may even turn out to be a social evil, because the state will be powerless to do anything for the good of the people. (Ma Daying 1982, 6)

As a rule, the MOF's attitude of fiscal conservatism rarely prevails in economic policy-making, although the ministry's influence is sufficient to ensure that the fiscal ramifications of proposed policies are always seriously considered. Most of the time, however, the political advantages of spending outweigh financial considerations; this was true under both the partial reform and the command economy. The MOF always urged that partial interests be subordinated to the interests of the whole, but the political logic of the system encouraged the selective allocation of resources and authority to particular enterprises, localities, and bureaucracies. Chen Yun, as a defender of the financial interests of the central state, complained about this tendency toward particularism: "Comrades doing economic work are liable to give way to partial and local interests and departmentalism and neglect certain important issues" ("The Whole Party" 1983, 1).

The Economic Situation and the Victory of Tax-for-Profit over Profit Contracting

The victory of the MOF's viewpoint in choosing the tax-for-profit approach over profit-contracting in 1982–83 was an exception to the usual dominance of spenders over savers. One factor in the decision

was the actual economic situation at the time. By 1982 state enterprises were keeping 17 billion yuan of profits, a massive increase
over the 2.1 billion they retained in 1978 (Naughton 1985). During
the five years from 1978 to 1982 enterprises retained a total of more
than 42 billion yuan ("A Major Principle" 1983). The central budget
deficit of 1982 was 2.9 billion yuan, not nearly as large as the huge
1979 and 1980 deficits (17 billion and 12.7 billion yuan, respectively), but larger than the 2.5 billion yuan deficit of 1981 (*Statistical
Yearbook* 1985, 523). Under the pressure to limit the size of the deficit, the central government's investment in vitally necessary infrastructure construction had been cut; comparing 1982 to 1978,
central capital construction in the energy sector had shrunk by 10.9
percent and in transportation by 16 percent (Bo Yibo, "Several Problems Concerning the Planned Proportional Development," cited in
P. Lee 1986, 65).

Even so, the economic situation was not as alarming as it had
been a few years earlier, say, in 1979–81. Yet in 1980 the MOF had
been willing to promote fiscal decentralization to provincial governments. The 1980 "eating in separate kitchens" devolution of fiscal
authority to provinces was supported by the financial authorities in
Beijing. In the context of massive budget deficits in 1979 and 1980
the MOF was willing to decentralize funds to the provinces to reduce the fiscal responsibilities of the center.

The major difference between 1980 and 1982–83 was that in 1980
the national economy was still dominated by central planning, and
MOF officials believed fiscal decentralization could help them relieve the strain on the central budget while not surrendering Beijing's overall direction of the economy. In 1982–83 officials from the
MOF and SPC felt much less confident of their control. The combination of fiscal decentralization and enterprise profit retention had
dispersed financial resources and drastically reduced the center's
access to funds (Li Jianli 1982). As of 1982, the MOF complained,
the ministry was responsible for almost two-thirds of total national
financial outlays but had only one-fifth of total national revenues at
its disposal (Ma Daying 1982). The financial base for the authority
of the central state appeared to be eroding. And in view of the clear
expansionary trend of the partially reformed Chinese economy, to
accept profit-contracting, a policy that essentially guaranteed the
center its current level of revenues but gave enterprises most of the
rewards of growth, would have meant accepting a central state that
was permanently weak, a prospect that disturbed many Beijing of-

ficials, not just those in the MOF. A related worry of central officials, especially those in the SPC, was diminishing central control over large enterprises. If big firms such as Capital Iron and Steel had contracts that allowed them to retain most of their increased profits, would they still listen to the state? Would they leave the plan (author's interviews)?[14]

Other Beijing bureaucracies gave credence to the MOF's qualms about the revenue consequences of profit-contracting because by 1982 worries about the political risks of inflation were intensifying. Many government and party people saw that urban workers were growing dissatisfied with consumer price increases stimulated by partial marketization (author's interviews). Zhao Ziyang, in a March 1982 speech, highlighted the link between deficits and inflation as the main risk China faced during the coming year: "If we can't achieve balance between financial revenues and expenditures, and the budget deficit grows larger and creates an expansion of currency in circulation, then it will affect the basic stability of market prices and affect the prospects for (social) peace and unity" (Zhao Ziyang 1982a, 10). As a rule, most party and state leaders and bureaucrats prefer to spend on their pet projects rather than enforce financial stringency, but their minds can be changed by the specter of urban unrest caused by price inflation.

Leadership Competition and Policy Choice

By November 1982 the controversy between the two policy approaches had begun to reveal the clash of opinions within the top leadership between the premier, Zhao Ziyang, and the general secretary, Hu Yaobang. On 8 November the State Council approved a joint report from the Economic Reform Commission, the SEC, and the MOF raising critical questions about profit-contracting (Zheng Derong et al. 1987). On 15 November the *People's Daily*, the official organ of the CCP, ran an article praising the achievements of profit contracting as practiced at Capital Iron and Steel (Zheng Derong et al. 1987). The minister of finance responded on 26 November with a *People's Daily* article stressing the urgent need to centralize funds (Zheng Derong et al. 1987).[15] Zhao Ziyang, at a speech to the Fifth

14. The ownership status of assets bought by enterprises out of their retained profits also worried conservative officials in Beijing, who saw state ownership of industry eroding.
15. A mid-September State Council discussion of the SPC's draft of the Sixth Five-Year Plan was "warmly supported by departments and localities"

Session of the Fifth National People's Congress on 30 November, announced his support for the tax-for-profit approach to concentrating funds (Zheng Derong et al. 1987).

From 20 December 1982 to 17 January 1983 Zhao Ziyang made a state visit to Africa. While Zhao was out of the country, Hu Yaobang intensified his efforts to promote profit-contracting. Hu advocated industrial enterprise profit-contracting at a national conference on industry and commerce.[16] He traveled widely trying to mobilize enthusiasm for the 1983 "year of urban reform" by pointing to the dramatic success of household contracting in agriculture. He urged that contracting "enter the city" and stirred up a strong "contract wind," or *baogan feng* (author's interviews). When Zhao returned and learned of Hu's activities, he was furious. In Zhao's eyes Hu had violated the informal rules for division of responsibility between party and state. According to these rules, the party delegated economic policy-making (with the exception of agriculture) to the state and the premier, while the party and the party general secretary handled educational, cultural, and political-ideological affairs. Zhao strongly objected to Hu's attempt to usurp his responsibility for economic policy-making and subvert his decision to replace profit-contracting with the tax approach. Zhao complained to Deng Xiaoping, who continued to play the role of ultimate arbiter of conflicts within the Politburo and Standing Committee of the Politburo. Deng supported Zhao by privately reprimanding Hu, telling him to stick to politics and leave economics to Zhao (author's interviews).

Deng's intervention effectively tilted the outcome in favor of tax-for-profit. Deng's decision to weigh in on the side of Zhao Ziyang was probably motivated both by Deng's desire to clarify the delegation relationship between the party and the government and his awareness of the political pressure from the conservative wing of the selectorate for reforms that enhanced central economic control instead of destroying it.

---

because it preliminarily decided not to change enterprise profit retention but to concentrate funds for infrastructure construction by taxing extrabudgetary funds instead; the national financial meeting in October "smoothly solved" the problem of raising funds (Wang Zhaodong and Shi Xichuan 1983).

16. A *Hongqi* article published when Zhao was out of the country advocated continuing to implement profit contracting and quoted Hu Yaobang (Zhou Taihe 1982).

The significance of leadership conflicts for economic reform policy is highlighted by the fate of profit-contracting after tax-for-profit became official policy in April 1983. The bureaucratic advocates of profit-contracting, namely, the SEC and the Institute of Industrial Economics, refused to consider the matter closed. Perceptions of a divided leadership and recognition that Hu Yaobang, as party general secretary, held formal dominance over Premier Zhao Ziyang encouraged the SEC and the institute to persist in their campaign to promote contracting.

Of course, the official promulgation of tax-for-profit changed the rhetoric of the contracting campaign. The advocates of profit contracting had to accept the MOF's definition of the situation, namely, that all financial policies must promote concentration of financial resources. Even by this definition profit-contracting was superior to tax-for-profit, according to the supporters of contracting. They argued that if one figured in the self-investment generated from an enterprise's own retained profits as a savings for the central treasury, then the center would in effect receive the largest share even of the new, additional profit (Hao Zhen et al. 1983).

In a point that surely was not lost on local officials, they also argued that the revenues generated by profit-contracting enterprises would enable localities to meet pressing needs without turning to the central treasury; for example, because of Capital Iron and Steel's outstanding performance Beijing had the funds to meet central party directives on civil construction and pollution reduction (Hao Zhen et al. 1983). Finally, appealing to the centralization priorities of the SPC, contracting advocates pointed out that by including additional plan targets in the contract, planners could use contracting to enhance their enforcement of the plan (Zhou Taihe 1982). Moreover, enterprises using contracting would not present problems of uncontrolled capital construction because all their expansion and modernization projects would have to be approved by the authorities as usual (Chen Yongzhong and Li Xiaoping 1984).

The advocates of profit-contracting also had to adjust the scope of their proposals, abandoning the hope of spreading contracting to every state factory. Now they argued that it was wrong to put all enterprises on the same financial regimen; that key enterprises and sectors should be allowed to use profit-contracting; and (again appealing to local officials) that the provinces and cities should have the authority to pick which enterprises qualified for this special treatment (Hao Zhen et al. 1983). Contracting advocates urged that the method be retained for large and medium-sized enterprises faced with expensive tasks of modernizing their equipment, enterprises producing key products that were in short supply (specifically, raw materials and machinery, especially metallurgy, automotive vehicles, and chemicals), or enterprises producing high-quality brand name products to help them eliminate the weaker competition (Chen Yongzhong and Li Xiaoping 1984). Another suggestion was that enterprises implement both approaches, paying product tax and local tax but dividing the after-tax profit by progressive contracting (Chen Yongzhong and Li Xiaoping 1984).

Despite these efforts, when the tax-for-profit policy was implemented in June 1983, the Institute for Industrial Economics and the SEC were forced to scale back the number of enterprises using profit contracting to a mere fifteen (a total of fifty-five factories were included in these fifteen enterprises) from the one hundred they had pushed for (author's interviews). Only those enterprises already practicing profit-contracting with the approval of the State Council, the MOF, or the SEC were permitted to continue until the end of the term of their contracts (Wang Bingqian 1983).[17] Enterprises whose contract systems had been approved at the local level were required to abandon them, although they were allowed to appeal to one of the three central agencies for a special exemption ("Specifics on Shanxi Tax Payment System" 1983).[18]

Yet a hard core of supporters stubbornly continued to promote profit-contracting even when the national policy was firmly against them. The manager of Capital Iron and Steel made practically a full-time job of speaking at meetings organized to promote contracting (Zhou Guanwu 1984). One national meeting held by Capital Iron and Steel in January 1984 brought together the fifteen enterprises practicing progressive contracting, spanning industries including steel, rolling stock, chemicals, radio, and paper ("National Meeting

17. Military industries, posts and telecommunications enterprises, grain handling organizations, foreign trade corporations, agricultural and animal husbandry enterprises, and enterprises for reforming prisoners were also exempted from the requirement to convert to tax-for-profit.
18. In July 1984 the State Council instructed enterprises operating under contracting with the approval only of local governments to submit to a review; if their contract was still in effect and had obtained good results and maintained "a rational relationship with the state in financial distribution," then they could continue to the end of their term. This instruction suggests that at least some locally approved enterprises did not immediately switch over to tax-for-profit when ordered to do so in 1983 ("State Council Issues Notice" 1984, K4–5).

of Enterprises" 1984; "Summary of the National Meeting" 1984). At this meeting they announced the achievements of their enterprises, which surpassed the performance of national state industry as a whole, and contrasted the excellent performance of particular contracting firms with the less outstanding performance of particular tax-for-profit firms. Their agenda was explicit: to expand the practice of progressive profit-contracting.

Contracting efforts found support among some large and medium-sized state factories, especially in heavy industry, and from some localities. Press articles praising the tax-for-profit policy often referred to enterprise fears that converting from profits to taxes would reduce their income and impede their enlivening ("A Major Principle" 1983; "Prepare Well" 1983a). One article from Sichuan said that it took "well-conducted ideological work" to get enterprises practicing contracting to convert to tax-for-profit ("Important Matter" 1983, Q1). Vice Premier Tian Jiyun, in a speech praising tax-for-profit, openly acknowledged that some localities were not conscientiously implementing tax-for-profit and were still pushing contracting. One claim of the contracting diehards was that tax-for-profit was "breaking a promise to the people" (Tian Jiyun 1983a).

In October 1984 the Communiqué of the Third Plenum of the Twelfth Communist Party Central Committee, a major document presenting a comprehensive summary of the direction of reform policies, appeared to kill all hopes for expanding profit-contracting when it stated that industrial enterprises should not adopt management models inspired by the agricultural responsibility system. At that point the Institute for Industrial Economics and the SEC, along with the large state enterprises pressing for greater financial autonomy, accepted defeat. They shifted their efforts to an alternative, output progressive contracting (*chanliang dizeng baogan*), which would commit enterprises to progressively increasing amounts of output delivered to the state plan in exchange for allowing them to self-market (at higher prices) everything above that amount (author's interviews). Although this approach never got anywhere, it was inspired by the same concept as the ministry contracting system (*bumen baogan*), which established a similar output contract between several heavy industrial ministries (oil, coal, metallurgy, railroads, petrochemical) and the state (see chapter 8).

The story of the 1982–83 controversy between the tax-for-profit approach and profit-contracting highlights the importance of competition for leadership succession in the course of economic reform policies. In China, debates between the savers (financial conservatives such as the MOF) and the spenders (growth advocates such as the industrial ministries) are normally resolved in favor of the spenders. The unexpected victory of the MOF and tax-for-profit in 1982–83 reflects not only economic problems, especially inflation, but also Zhao Ziyang's interests in gaining credibility with central bureaucrats and conservative party elders who were powerful groups within the selectorate and Deng Xiaoping's decision not to challenge these conservative groups on this issue. The split between Zhao and Hu Yaobang on enterprise finance also explains why the contracting advocates persisted in their promotion campaign even after tax-for-profit had become the official policy. When the nature of the succession competition changed in 1986, the political logic of profit-contracting became irresistible, and the policy experienced a miraculous revival.

12 Building Bureaucratic Consensus

Formulating the
Tax-for-Profit Policy, 1983–84

The tax-for-profit policy was formulated during 1983–84, a period of buoyant optimism when Chinese and foreigners alike hoped that China would soon achieve a real socialist market economy. Having enterprises start to pay taxes instead of remitting their profits was considered by many economists a crucial step in the transition from plan to market, from an overly centralized, arbitrary command economy to a market environment in which factories competed under fair conditions and took full responsibility for their profits and losses. The State Council's passage of the tax-for-profit policy—the first stage in 1983 and the second stage in 1984—was heralded as a momentous step in creating a competitive environment with equal opportunities for all enterprises.

Yet only a few years later, in 1986, the policy substituting profit remission with tax payment was scrapped and replaced by profit contracting in all enterprises. The move away from tax-for-profit involved abandoning the quest for a self-regulating, state-owned market economy based on standardized rules, genuine competition, and financial risk and returning to the path of particularistic contracting.

The failure of the Chinese political system to come up with a lasting tax reform was profoundly disillusioning to many young economists in China. Several of them (Hua Sheng, Zhang Xuejun, Luo Xiaopeng 1988, no. 9:26–27) described the setback as "shattering illusions that without completely abandoning the old system a fair and effective competitive environment could still be established for enterprises through ingenious technical arrangements." The radicalizing lesson they learned from the failure of tax-for-profit was that it was impossible to achieve genuine reform within the framework of the traditional system.

Why did the tax-for-profit policy have such a short life? The answer is the problem of making decisions by consensus on a redistributive policy. The final version of tax-for-profit was very different from the original vision of reformist economists, reflecting an uneasy compromise among conflicting bureaucratic interests. As the young economists discovered (Hua Sheng, Zhang Xuejun, Luo Xiaopeng 1988, no. 9:26–27), within the traditional system policies do not emerge exactly resembling their original intentions. Obtaining consensus necessitates making sure that no one loses too much under the new policies. The only way to achieve consensus is to protect the vested interests of the ministries, the localities, and the enterprises under them. As one government economic adviser explained, "Political realism requires protecting vested interests [*baohu jide liyi*]. If we don't, they will make a lot of noise and ruin the reform" (author's interview). From the viewpoint of another, more traditionally minded economic official there was a socialist rationale for being solicitous of industries threatened by reforms: "In a state-owned economy the relations among enterprises are internal relations. We must take care of [*zhaogu*] the enterprises" (author's interviews).

Reconciling conflicting bureaucratic interests to reach a consensus on tax-for-profit was particularly difficult because the top CCP leadership was divided on the policy, with Zhao Ziyang, backed by Deng Xiaoping, supporting it and Hu Yaobang supporting profit contracting instead. Because the people in authority were divided, their subordinates were less flexible in the bargaining over the specifics of the policy at work conferences.

Predictably, opposition to a new, strictly enforced tax obligation emerged mainly from the weaker, less profitable enterprises; such enterprises were concentrated in heavy industries and in inland provinces. The only way to obtain agreement was to divide the switch from profits to taxes into two stages, reduce tax rates, leave out some of the most significant taxes, retain many of the particularistic features of the old profit-sharing system, and fill the central revenue gap with an additional "adjustment tax" (*tiaojie shui*) on the most profitable enterprises. The final package not only failed to achieve many of its original economic objectives but also alienated some of the strongest and most powerful interests in the Chinese system, namely, big state factories and local officials, especially those in coastal regions.

Another important feature of the political context of the deliberations over tax-for-profit was Zhao Ziyang's eagerness to accelerate the implementation of the policy and the pressure he put on subordinates to agree to it. The decision to go ahead with tax-for-profit was imposed on the bureaucracy from above by the top leaders of the CCP. No CCP conferences or formal directives on the policy were recorded, but Zhao Ziyang, as premier and member of the Politburo Standing Committee, announced the policy in his November 1982 speech to the National People's Congress, a speech that must have been approved by the Politburo. And although the original intention was to wait until 1985, when prices were to be rationalized, to launch the second stage of the reform, Zhao pushed up the schedule by more than one year. The second-stage plan was introduced by Zhao in his speech (approved by the Politburo) at the National People's Congress in May 1984 and was implemented in October 1984.

Zhao's approach to enterprise finance reform was backed by Deng Xiaoping and favored by Chen Yun and other conservative elders in the party because it guaranteed a steady increase in state revenues. With Hu Yaobang continuing to promote the competing approach of profit contracting, Zhao was anxious to put tax-for-profit in place as soon as possible. He wanted to take the air out of the contracting wind stirred up by Hu and demonstrate to the selectorate the effectiveness of his own approach to reform. Because Zhao Ziyang was in such a hurry to implement tax-for-profit and pressured government officials to agree to a final second-stage package in 1984, industrial and local officials signed on to a policy they did not really support. The 1984 compromise was not an equilibrium policy, and soon after it was implemented, disgruntled factory and local officials began to subvert it.

The moral of the short, unhappy tale of tax-for-profit is that introducing redistributive reforms through a communist bureaucracy is particularly difficult if the political principals are divided. Reforms intensify conflicts of interest among bureaucratic institutions and their subordinate enterprises by granting them their own financial interests. At the same time, market reform policies such as tax-for-profit are inherently redistributive, creating losers as well as winners. The only way to achieve bureaucratic consensus on such policies is to distort them beyond recognition by protecting those who are weak in the face of market competition.[1] Once reform pol-

---

1. Hua Sheng, Zhang Xuejun, and Luo Xiaopeng (1988, no. 9:26) describe this dilemma as a contradiction between *"fang quan gao huo"* (decentralizing

icies are modified to become politically acceptable, they lose their bite, relieving the pressure on enterprises to become more efficient.

Moreover, in a system requiring consensus decisions, even small changes in the balance of group interests or in the distribution of power among the political principals can destroy a policy equilibrium. The 1984 tax-for-profit compromise protected weak industry in the inland provinces by imposing costs on strong industry along the coast. But this equilibrium was not stable. Partial reform stimulated the dynamism of the coastal industry and widened the gap between the coastal and inland economies. Factories in Shanghai, Tianjin, and other coastal cities were no longer willing to tolerate discrimination against the strong in the name of regional equality. Divisions among the top leaders of the party created the opening for big coastal enterprises to fight tax-for-profit with profit contracting.

The Original Vision of Tax-for-Profit

The Chinese policy economists in the State Commission on Economic System Reform and officials in the Ministry of Finance who promoted the original tax-for-profit experiments and advocated the tax-for-profit approach to enterprise reform believed that the reform would accomplish several important objectives.[2]

First, tax-for-profit would *put the financial relations between state and enterprise on a legal footing and guarantee the flow of central revenues.* Whereas profit-remission arrangements were specific for each enterprise and were bargained out among different levels of industrial administration, taxes were objective, impersonal, standardized, and universal. Taxes had the force of law behind them. As one MOF official said, "Enterprises pay more attention to taxes than remitting profits. They take taxes seriously because it is a matter of law and can be punished" (author's interview).

From the standpoint of revenue collectors, taxes were easier to enforce than was profit remission; it was easy to see if enterprises paid too little or not at all (author's interview). By setting the tax

---

authority and resources to enliven the enterprises) and the problem of "*ku le bu zhun*" (unequal sorrow and happiness). Once the enterprises have independent interests, they start to worry about allocative unfairness and fight fiercely for egalitarian protections.
2. On the advantages of tax-for-profit over profit contracting, see Jin Renxiong and Yuan Zhenyu 1983 (42–74); Zhou Taihe et al. 1984 (200–201); Tian Jiyun 1983 (9); "Ministry of Finance Report" 1983; "Tax-for-Profit" 1983; "Finance Official Interviewed" 1983 (K8).

rates high enough, the MOF could guarantee that the central government would get the largest share of enterprise revenues.[3] From the standpoint of enterprise managers, clear knowledge of their tax obligation would make it easier to plan long-term investments. And from the perspective of both state and enterprise, there would be less acrimony generated and less time and energy wasted in bargaining over financial shares; the tax system would put relations between them on a more businesslike basis.

The legalization of enterprises' financial obligations to the state and the guarantee of the flow of central revenues were undoubtedly the most positive features of the tax-for-profit reform from the perspective of MOF officials and conservative party leaders such as Chen Yun. Although they sold the policy as a decentralizing reform, in their own eyes it was primarily a centralizing (*shou*) policy (author's interviews).

Second, the tax-for-profit reform would *enhance the independence of state enterprises*. After paying taxes, enterprises would bear full responsibility for their own profits and losses. Firms operating at a loss would receive no more subsidies, no more government bailouts, no more "eating from the same big pot." Enterprises would face real financial risk. Although the requirement that state enterprises be responsible for their after-tax losses was included in the original tax-for-profit experiments in Sichuan and other provinces,[4] it disappeared from the final national versions of the policy (except for small enterprises). Because the national versions of the tax plan were compromises that did not yet put all enterprises on an equal footing, officials from ministries and provinces with large and medium-sized enterprises operating in the red argued that it would be unfair to punish them for losses that were no fault of their own but were caused by irrational prices and other objective factors.

Third, the tax-for-profit reform would *reconstitute the financial relations between center and locality*. Enterprises would no longer remit funds to different levels of government according to their subordination relations (*lishu guanxi*), with locally run plants paying local

3. The main MOF criticism of progressive profit contracting was that over time the state could end up with less than half of total revenue profits. Tax-for-profit accorded with the MOF slogan "The state gets the biggest part, the enterprise gets the middle part, and the individual gets the smallest part" ("Ministry of Finance Report" 1983, 469).
4. The slogan for the original Sichuan tax-for-profit experiments was "Independent accounting, state levies taxes, and sole responsibility for profit and loss" (*duli hesuan, guojia zheng shui, zi fu ying kuei*; author's interviews).

governments and plants run by ministries paying the central government (with the money still collected by local officials, however). Instead, local governments would be given their own tax base; they would collect local taxes from all enterprises no matter which level ran them. All enterprises would pay national taxes as well. This change was intended to break the proprietary interest of local governments and ministries in the enterprises they administered—the so-called local ownership system (*difang suoyuzhi*) and ministry ownership system (*bumen suoyuzhi*)—and shatter administrative barriers between enterprises. Once local governments had their own tax base, there would be no need for financial contracting between center and localities; the "eating in separate kitchens" scheme would be superseded by a system assigning different taxes to different levels.

Fourth, the new tax system would *create a level playing field for economic competition*. Various taxes would compensate for irrational prices and other factors outside the control of managers that differentially affected enterprise profits. Profits derived from factors such as the administrative price structure, past state investments in fixed assets, the value of urban land, and natural resource endowments would be taxed away so that only profits earned by good management and hard work remained. The tax mechanism would substitute for a full-fledged market to establish an environment for fair competition.

Fifth, the tax system could serve as *an instrument of national industrial policy*. By adjusting product tax rates, Beijing authorities could discourage the production of some goods and encourage the production of others. What policymakers had in mind was deterring organizations from investing in wasteful, redundant processing plants and encouraging them to invest in the production of materials and equipment in short supply instead.

The actual tax-for-profit policy that emerged from the bureaucratic bargaining process bore little resemblance to this vision. Under the rules agreed on, an enterprise's financial obligations were still subject to bargaining, and an enterprise could still rely on state subsidies to cover its losses. Although the subordinate relationship of enterprises to bureaucratic organs was slightly attenuated by the second stage of tax-for-profit, the "eating in separate kitchens" fiscal system still prevailed because local taxes were not implemented. Of the three taxes designed to equalize the basis for enterprise profits, two of them, the fixed assets tax and the natural resources tax, were abandoned; and because the third, the product tax, still left too much "unearned" profit in the hands of some enterprises, an ad hoc adjustment tax was tacked on to the most profitable enterprises.

The final tax-for-profit package certainly had no clear economic logic. To explicate its political logic we need to review the institutional path the policy package traveled from beginning to end.

The First Stage of Tax-for-Profit

The decision to choose tax-for-profit over profit contracting was made in a centralized fashion by China's top leaders at the end of 1982. It was not a matter delegated to large bureaucratic work conferences to decide. Numerous national and local meetings in the last quarter of 1982 discussed the results of the more than four hundred tax-for-profit experiments throughout China and gave the leadership ample opportunity to hear the diverse opinions of various enterprises, sectors, and regions. Reaction to the experiments was mixed, with many reports criticizing specific features of different tax-for-profit arrangements and one report from Hunan going so far as to claim that tax-for-profit was no better than profit sharing (Mo Huilin and Zhu Congguang 1983, 44). Yet in the end Zhao Ziyang came down on the side of tax-for-profit. He proclaimed in a speech of 30 November 1982 before the National People's Congress that tax-for-profit would be the direction taken during the Sixth Five-Year Plan. According to some officials I interviewed, Zhao was persuaded by the MOF and the State Commission on Economic System Reform that tax-for-profit was the superior method for achieving enterprise efficiency. Zhao may also have calculated that siding with the MOF on enterprise finance reform would gain him the valuable political support of Chen Yun and other conservative party elders who had signaled their strength in the theoretical campaign of fall 1982 emphasizing the primacy of planning over markets (see chapter 11). The support of the conservative wing of the party was crucial for sustaining the forward movement of the reform drive and for Zhao's own political future.

But the CCP leadership was not united on this issue. Hu Yaobang persisted in his advocacy of profit contracting even after Zhao had announced the tax-for-profit policy in his November speech. Deng Xiaoping backed Zhao, but bureaucratic subordinates may have believed that Deng's position was strategic, designed to avoid alienating the conservatives, and could change if the balance among party elites shifted.

The uncertainty created by the conflict between the premier and the party general secretary over contending approaches to enterprise finance reform shaped the process of making the tax-for-profit policy and the final policy outcomes. Zhao Ziyang pushed hard to accelerate the implementation of the policy to head off Hu Yaobang's drive to mobilize support for profit contracting. Bureaucratic actors fought stubbornly to protect their interests, although they would have compromised under a unified leadership with clear preferences. Divisions at the top raise the probability that a bureaucracy can obtain a better outcome by holding out and kicking a decision upstairs than it can by settling on a compromise at lower levels. As a result, consensus becomes more elusive. To move ahead under conditions of divided leadership, Zhao Ziyang and his allies had to devise a plan that would make no bureaucratic interests unhappy; he had to perform the political magic trick of turning an inherently redistributive reform into a nonredistributive reform.

Moving from an individualized profit-sharing system to a standardized tax system seemed to threaten almost everyone's interests. According to Vice Premier Tian Jiyun, who was Zhao Ziyang's right-hand man on financial issues, the bottom line for any tax reform policy was that it had to protect state revenue, protect the activism of the enterprises, and be simple and convenient (Tian Jiyun 1983, 13).

Protecting state revenue was, of course, the reason why the MOF was the strongest proponent of tax-for-profit. Reports from discussions on the tax-for-profit experiments around the country indicated that the system effectively enabled the center to obtain a steady increase in revenue (Zhou Taihe et al. 1984, 200). Even so, the MOF had some qualms about implementing tax-for-profit because it was afraid of losing power to the General Tax Bureau (author's interviews). The lines of authority between the MOF and the GTB were ambiguous (see chapter 5). Switching from collecting profits to collecting taxes would inevitably reduce the power of the MOF's Industrial Enterprise Finance Bureau and increase the power of the GTB. The suspicion and administrative friction between finance and tax officials muted MOF's enthusiasm for tax-for-profit and caused problems in implementation.[5] Finance officials were also worried

5. A special Tax-for-Profit Office was established within the MOF in April

that an overly complicated set of tax rules would create an administrative nightmare. They were used to a system of revenue collection that was individualized but simple. A tax system with too many different taxes and different rates would strain their limited administrative capacity. Therefore, the MOF insisted that any new tax system be simple and convenient.

Most of the apprehension about tax-for-profit came from industrial enterprises and their bureaucratic overseers. Protecting the activism of the enterprises with a standardized tax scheme was not going to be easy. Officials described the enterprises as "suspicious" of tax-for-profit (author's interviews). Managers suspected the new rules might cause them to receive less profit than they had under the old rules and might put them at an unfair disadvantage vis-à-vis their competitors. They were confident that under an individualized system they could negotiate a fair deal for themselves. But tax rates that were standardized and legally enforced could work against them and for rival firms. For this reason, industrial enterprises and ministries, especially heavy industry, favored profit contracting (author's interviews).[6]

The central dilemma in moving toward a standardized tax system was how to deal with differences in enterprise profitability caused by objective factors such as irrational prices. Managers and industrial bureaucrats would never stand for a set of rules that forced firms to take responsibility for their own profits and losses if these profits and losses were caused by factors beyond their control. This dilemma was evident in the early tax-for-profit experiments, which were riddled with particularism designed to prevent unfairness. Guangdong's tax-for-profit experiments used a different tax rate for each enterprise (*yi hu yi lu*) to resolve disparities. Provincial officials argued that to have forced enterprises to be responsible for themselves without individual tax rates would have been "irrational": it would have produced results that violated "socialist principles of distribution" by "rewarding the lax and punishing the diligent"

1984 to overcome these internal conflicts and coordinate implementation work.

6. According to interviews, small enterprises welcomed tax-for-profit: although it forced them to be accountable for their own losses, it subsidized them with low tax rates. And, unlike the managers of medium-sized and large factories, who were constrained by the prices, supplies, and output quotas imposed on them by planners, the managers of small factories had the freedoms necessary to cope with financial risk.

(*jiang lan, fa qin*), "widening the gap between suffering and plea-sure" (*ku le bu zhun*), and "beating the fastest oxen" (*bianda kuai niu*; "Opinion on Eight Enterprises" 1983, 27).

It was not just irrational prices and disparities in natural re-sources and previous investments in fixed assets that gave some enterprises an unfair advantage. The continued existence of man-datory planning was itself a source of unfairness. No matter how well a manager ran a factory or how hard the factory's workers worked, they could not make much money if they could not obtain material supplies or freight transportation from the planners. And their profits would remain low so long as the planners claimed a hefty share of their output at low plan prices. Enterprises still dom-inated by the plan and allowed little participation in market activity were severely handicapped. Some experimental Beijing firms com-plained that they were caught between the state planners' demand for a particular variety of products and the local officials' demand for their profits ("A Discussion on the Question of Tax-for-Profit" 1983, 29).

By the time the MOF and the State Council were ready to intro-duce tax-for-profit on a national scale at the end of 1982, they had digested the results of the prior experiments and were familiar with all the technical and political problems raised by the transition to a standardized tax system. Enterprise managers expressed their opin-ions in written reports to the State Council and through meetings with ministry and local government representatives, who were asked explicitly to survey and report these opinions (author's inter-views). Numerous joint research investigations undertaken by con-cerned departments with financial officials and meetings to evaluate the tax experiments gave various bureaucratic groups a chance to express their points of view beginning in late 1981 and continuing throughout 1982 (Wang Bingqian 1983, K5; author's interviews).[7] The annual national tax meeting in February 1982 was another fo-rum in which different tax-for-profit formulas were discussed (au-thor's interviews).

It became obvious that if the State Council converted all profits to taxes in one giant step, too many enterprises would be forced into the red and too many ministries and localities would object. Given the irrational features of the economic environment, it would

---

7. There were experiments in 456 enterprises in 18 provinces using more than 30 different methods (author's interviews).

have been impossible to take account of the interests of both the state and the enterprises or to solve the problem of the gap between sorrow and happiness (Jin Renxiong and Yuan Zhenyu 1983, 77). Therefore, the MOF and State Council decided to divide the transition into two steps. This decision was made early at the State Council level and announced by Zhao Ziyang in his speech of 30 November 1982 (Zhao Ziyang 1982, 31). It was not a bureaucratic compromise worked out from the bottom up.

In a January 1983 article Vice Premier Tian Jiyun explained how the two-stage implementation of tax-for-profit would work (Tian Jiyun 1983, 9). In the first stage only small enterprises would switch over to paying all of their financial obligation to the state in the form of an eight-grade progressive income tax. Large and medium-sized enterprises would convert part of their financial obligation to a standardized 55 percent income (profits) tax but would retain an individualized profit-sharing system for the remaining part. The total obligation would be set to guarantee that the enterprise kept as much money as it had kept in 1982. Tian urged that during the first stage at least half, and preferably three-fifths, of the enterprise obligation be paid in taxes, but the final regulations did not stipulate this point. The retention of individualized profit sharing was justified by the big gaps in profitability and profit levels caused by irrational prices.

The second stage of tax-for-profit, when all obligations would be converted to tax payments, would await the rationalization of prices (Zhao Ziyang 1982; Tian Jiyun 1983; Jin Renxiong and Yuan Zhenyu 1983, 103–4). In the second stage the income tax would become progressive (Zhao Ziyang 1982), and the fiscal system would be changed from center-provincial fiscal contracting to assigning different taxes to each level of government (Tian Jiyun 1983). Although Zhao Ziyang assured people that there would be no comprehensive price reform during the 1983–85 period, he announced plans to adjust upward the excessively low prices of raw materials and fuels and allow prices of minor (third-category) products to float on the market (Zhao Ziyang 1982, 31). Top policymakers apparently expected that these price adjustments would make prices sufficiently rational to enforce a full-fledged tax system because they clearly intended to begin the second stage no later than 1985.[8]

8. Tian Jiyun said that the second stage of tax-for-profit would begin by 1985 at the latest (Tian Jiyun 1983, 9). The first-stage rules stated that en-

By delaying all the really tough features of tax-for-profit until the second stage after price adjustments, Zhao Ziyang preempted opposition from industrial enterprises, ministries, and local governments to moving ahead with the first stage. The first stage protected vested interests among enterprises, retained particularistic profit sharing, and was simple and convenient to carry out. Localities accepted it because it left in place the system of enterprises paying taxes and profits according to subordinate relations and the "eating in separate kitchens" fiscal system and because it delegated to local officials crucial distributive decisions such as the limits of different categories of small enterprises. Industrial ministries and bureaus liked it because they continued to have the authority to negotiate sectorwide profit-sharing arrangements and rates with finance officials and then to carry out internal redistribution among their factories to narrow the gap between sorrow and happiness (Jin Renxiong and Yuan Zhenyu 1983, 81; "Ministry of Finance Regulations for Implementing Tax-for-Profit" 1983, 475–76). The enterprises were guaranteed their 1982 level of retained profits, continued to use various profit-contracting methods to divide the profits, and still received subsidies for their losses.[9] Military industries, posts and telecommunications enterprises, grain handling organizations, foreign trade corporations, agricultural and animal husbandry enterprises, and enterprises for labor reform were exempted from changing over to the tax system at all ("Ministry of Finance Regulations for Implementing Tax-for-Profit" 1983, 476). The MOF could live with the plan because it established the principle of paying taxes and guaranteed under law that at least 55 percent of enterprise earnings were paid to the state treasury.

The MOF and State Council advisers succeeded in drafting a tax plan that turned a highly redistributive issue into one that preserved the status quo and was completely noncontroversial. The State Council approved the draft plan on 1 March 1983 ("Tax-for-Profit" 1983). Later that month, when the National Work Confer-

---

terprise profit-sharing rates would remain fixed for three years, from 1983 to 1985 ("Ministry of Finance Regulations for Implementing Tax-for-Profit" 1983, 475). But one tax official in his mid-fifties anticipated a more gradual transition: when asked how long the first step would last, he answered, "I may have retired when the current experiment is over" ("Finance Official Describes New Taxation System" 1983).

9. Officially, only losses caused by external, objective factors, not losses caused by poor management, were subsidized (Caizheng Bu Caishui Tizhi Gaige Zhu 1989, 145).

ence on Tax-for-Profit brought together 320 officials from central ministries and local governments to discuss and approve the plan, they had only a few minor quibbles.[10] First Zhao Ziyang and then the Standing Committee of the State Council met with the group to urge their acceptance of the plan ("Ministry of Finance Report" 1983, 469). According to some young reformist economists, "The first stage of the tax-for-profit reform proceeded very smoothly. The reason for its success was that it consolidated state revenue without touching the problem of distributing after-tax profits and the method of remitting and retaining after-tax profits remained the same as before" (Hua Sheng, Zhang Xuejun, Luo Xiaopeng 1988, no. 9:26).

One crucial compromise made by the MOF and the State Council in drafting the first-stage plan in early 1983 was to abandon their original intention to implement an adjustment tax set at a uniform rate (called a profit differential tax or *li cha shui*) on after-tax profits; instead, they allowed enterprises to continue to share profits with the state according to a variety of sharing mechanisms. The adjustment tax, an idea that had been around since the original tax-for-profit experiments, was viewed as a way to allow the state to extract a larger share of the earnings of the most profitable firms, earnings presumed to accrue from irrational prices and other objective factors, and thereby as a way to put enterprises at an equal starting line. For example, in the Wuhan experiments a fair rate of profit on sales was set at 12 percent, and an adjustment tax of 60 percent was levied on profits earned above that rate.[11] Critics of the Wuhan plan argued that it "protected the backward and restricted the advanced" (*baohu luohou, yizhi xianjin*) and failed to distinguish between objective and subjective sources of profitability; they

10. The conference adjusted the classification scheme for small retail commercial enterprises; deleted the fixed asset fee for small enterprises; restricted the fixed quota method for sharing the after-tax profits of large and medium-sized enterprises to mining enterprises only; reduced the tax rate for food and beverage service enterprises; reduced the tax rate for supply and marketing cooperatives; allowed regional variation in the tax rate for construction and installation enterprises; fixed the allowed uses of retained profits for basic metallurgical enterprises; allowed small enterprises to follow the example of larger enterprises in repaying loans from pre-tax profits; permitted special concessions in minority autonomous regions; and guaranteed county treasuries against any negative impact from the policy ("Ministry of Finance Report" 1983, 469–71).

11. Adjustment tax (*at*) equals sales income (*si*) multiplied by 60 percent of the figure obtained by deducting 12 percent from the profit rate (*pr*) of sales: $at = si \times .6(.88pr)$.

advocated a system tailored to individual enterprise differences instead (Mo Huilin and Zhu Congguang 1983, 45). In the Shanghai tax-for-profit experiment the adjustment tax rate was set for each individual enterprise (author's interviews). In the Liuzhou (Guangxi Province) experiment the base rate of profit on sales was set at 15 percent, and profits above that were taxed at a progressive rate[12] (author's interviews). When the Beijing tax-for-profit experiments were analyzed, the conclusion was that the crux of accelerating the implementation of tax-for-profit was establishing an adjustment tax that could be used to adjust income gaps and encourage the advanced enterprises ("A Discussion on the Question of Tax-for-Profit" 1983, 30).[13]

The industrial ministries and coastal provinces were alarmed at the thought of the MOF imposing a uniform adjustment tax on their most profitable enterprises and mustered their forces to strike the adjustment tax from the draft plan. In late 1982 and early 1983 research and financial simulations done by the "relevant departments" (which undoubtedly included industrial ministries and local governments as well as the MOF and the Reform Commission) on the basis of six thousand factories in Shanghai, Tianjin, and Jinan found that the profitability gaps among different sectors and among factories in the same sectors in different cities were just too wide to set fair uniform adjustment tax rates (Jin Renxiong and Yuan Zhenyu 1983, 81; Caizheng Bu Caishui Tizhi Gaige Zhu 1989, 144). In this first round of tax-for-profit discussions the official representatives of the big, profitable factories in coastal China blocked the adjustment tax. The final draft plan included an adjustment tax only as one of several options that enterprises could adopt for dividing after-tax profits.[14]

Once the regulations for the first stage of tax-for-profit had been adopted by the State Council, the conflict of interest between central financial officials and ministry and local industrial officials came into the open again. The minister of finance made menacing noises

12. Profits of 15–20 percent were taxed at a 60 percent rate; 20–30 percent at a 70 percent rate; and over 30 percent at an 80 percent rate.
13. According to the financial specialists, taxes had to be unified and standardized (*tongyi* and *yi dao qie*). The idea of giving each enterprise its own tax rate was antithetical to the principle of tax-for-profit and no different from profit retention (Jin Renxiong and Yuan Zhenyu 1983, 76).
14. The plan proposed one adjustment tax rate for base profits and a 60 percent lower rate for profits above that amount ("Ministry of Finance Report" 1983, 474).

about adjusting the profit-retention base percentage for sectors and firms that "had retained an unreasonably high percentage of profits. . . . They are not allowed to retain their vested interests" (Wang Bingqian 1983, K6). Suspicious enterprises and local governments were described as "lacking understanding of the importance of substituting taxes for profit delivery" and "worried that substituting taxes for profit delivery might affect and reduce enterprise income." Some local governments reacted by not following central regulations but "coming up with their own notions" and "going their own way" instead ("Prepare Well" 1983, K7). The general tone of national press articles during spring 1983 was tough, reflecting the MOF perspective that tax-for-profit should put pressure on enterprises and not just enliven them: "If there is not a certain degree of pressure and if the enterprises are allowed to get a share of profits too easily, we will not be able to urge our enterprises to make progress" ("Major Principle" 1983, K2). The message from Beijing was loud and clear: Zhao Ziyang and the State Council would not let anything stand in the way of enforcing tax-for-profit.

The pace of implementation was very rapid. Zhao Ziyang, with the backing of Deng Xiaoping, was determined to enforce this policy to deflate Hu Yaobang's contracting wind and prove his own leadership abilities. Zhao's sense of urgency was reinforced by central financial officials who were anxious to replenish the dwindling treasury. Even though the tax regulations were not promulgated until April 1983, tax collection work was scheduled to begin in June, and taxes were to be calculated retroactive to 1 January 1983 ("Ministry of Finance Regulations on Implementing Income Tax Collection" 1983, 916). A May 1983 MOF directive ordered that local governments and ministries begin collecting taxes on 1 June on the basis of estimates even if the negotiations over enterprise tax rates and profit-sharing ratios had not yet been concluded ("Finance Ministry Circular" 1983). The big push paid off: 98 percent of state profit-making enterprises (91,136 of 93,085) paid income taxes and remitted profits under tax-for-profit in 1983 (Caizheng Bu Caishui Tizhi Gaige Zhu 1989, 146). And although the policy did not work any miracles on the state treasury (1983 government revenues were 11 percent higher than 1982 revenues, but expenditures were 12 percent higher, producing a deficit 48 percent larger; *Statistical Yearbook* 1989, 657), enterprises implementing tax-for-profit earned 11.1 percent more profits and retained 28.2 percent more profits than they had the previous year (Tian Yinong et al. 1988, 89). The figures for industrial enterprises alone were 10.9 percent more profit earned and 25.8 percent more profit retained (Xu Yi 1984, 5).

The Decision to Accelerate the Second Stage of Tax-for-Profit

The ink on the MOF regulations for the first stage of tax-for-profit was hardly dry when Zhao Ziyang in April 1983 proposed accelerating the urban economic reforms; in August 1983 he requested that the MOF investigate the possibility of moving up the timetable for the second stage of tax-for-profit (Caizheng Bu Caishui Tizhi Gaige Zhu 1989, 147; P. Lee 1987, 207). During September and October 1983 the MOF and the State Commission on Economic System Reform formed a joint investigation group to travel around the country and investigate the feasibility of implementing the second stage. Following their investigations, the MOF did a financial simulation of more than ten possible tax systems on more than 40,000 state industrial enterprises, 12,000 state commercial enterprises, and 28,000 urban collective enterprises (Caizheng Bu Caishui Tizhi Gaige Zhu 1989, 147). Based on the MOF and Reform Commission report, Zhao Ziyang announced at the Second Session of the Sixth National People's Congress in May 1984 that the second stage would be implemented during the last quarter of 1984. A national work conference was called at the end of June 1984 to decide the specific contents of the second stage; and on 1 October 1984 the second stage of tax-for-profit was implemented.

What was the rush? Why did Zhao Ziyang launch the second stage of tax-for-profit sooner than planned without waiting for a comprehensive price readjustment? The decision to accelerate the transition to a full-fledged tax system was Zhao Ziyang's, backed by Deng Xiaoping and the CCP Politburo, which had to have approved Zhao's NPC speech (author's interviews). Both the economic and political environment persuaded Zhao to speed up the process.

The economic environment in late 1983 and early 1984 was very promising. A buyers' market, unprecedented in China, had been created by an ample supply of goods, which in turn was produced by a dramatic improvement in the performance of agriculture because of decollectivization and increases in purchase prices (Chen Yizi 1990, 72). This loose economic environment created the possibility of accelerating the pace of market reforms without provoking inflation or reducing living standards. The dramatic success of the agricultural reform stimulated the demand for industrial goods and convinced top party leaders in the Standing Committee of the Politburo, Chen Yun included, that the time was right to introduce a comprehensive package of industrial reforms (author's interviews; Caizheng Bu Caishui Tizhi Gaige Zhu 1989, 147).

In early 1984 the CCP and State Council began to prepare an agenda for the Third Plenum of the Twelfth Central Committee in October 1984, which was to launch a multifaceted urban economic reform aimed at creating an environment conducive to enterprise efficiency. In preparation for the plenum, plans for reforming planning, foreign trade, and commerce were announced in summer and fall 1984, following a May document called the "Ten Points" that greatly expanded the autonomy of enterprise managers ("State Council Decision on Measures to Expand the Autonomy of State-Run Industrial Enterprises" 1984). (There was even a group working on price adjustments, but no decisions were announced; see below.) The momentum of the reform drive quickened as policymakers rushed to take advantage of the propitious economic conditions.

The political environment was more complex. Throughout 1983 Chen Yun and the conservative elders exercised substantial behind-the-scenes influence on economic reform policy-making. They had signaled their strength in the theoretical debate on the priority of the plan over the market in 1981 and 1982. Their preference for tax-for-profit over profit contracting made tax-for-profit the best reform approach for building a coalition within the top reaches of the CCP. Zhao Ziyang's speech at the First Session of the Sixth National People's Congress in June 1983 was so much in harmony with Chen Yun's ideas that Chen could have written it himself. Its vision of a "new economic system with Chinese characteristics" combined the dramatic challenge of reform ("reform is a revolution") with a conservative commitment to perfect the socialist system but not overturn it. Zhao appealed to the conservative wing of the party by declaring that each and every reform had to fulfill the plan, preserve national economic balance, take into consideration the interests of state, enterprise, and individual, and guarantee the gradual increase in state financial revenue (Zhou Taihe et al. 1984, 205; Zhao Ziyang 1983).

In October 1983 Deng Xiaoping sought to appease the ascendant conservative political elites in the party by launching the Anti-Spiritual Pollution Campaign, an ideological campaign against the cultural degeneration caused by corrosive influences from abroad.

Emboldened by this evidence of their own power, party conservatives, particularly those in the CCP Propaganda Department, aimed
their ideological weapons not only at the pornography and corruption that entered China through the open door but also at the domestic economic reforms. They began to attack reformers both in
the countryside and in the city. Even though Deng Xiaoping himself
had instigated the campaign, he brought it to a hasty close in January 1984 to prevent it from subverting his cherished economic reforms. As one official said, "Deng Xiaoping stood strongly behind
the economic reforms. The critical factor was the success of the
agricultural reform. When the Spiritual Pollution Campaign started
to criticize the agricultural reform, the Central Committee and Deng
got upset" (author's interview).

The momentum of the reform drive accelerated in 1984 after
Deng Xiaoping slapped down the conservatives for overreaching
themselves in the Spiritual Pollution Campaign. After January 1984
the reforms no longer had to "lie low"; they could "go on the offensive" (author's interview). Even Chen Yun was forced on the defensive. His Third Plenum speech in October 1984 modified his
position on the primacy of planning by admitting that 1950s planning methods could not be imposed on a 1980s Chinese economy
that was larger and more complicated (Chen Yun 1984). But why
did the party leadership go on the reform offensive with the tax-
for-profit approach instead of profit contracting?

The widely heralded success of the rural reform, which used
contracts to divide responsibilities and earnings between the household and the collective, encouraged the advocates of industrial
profit contracting to revive their cause during 1983–84 (Chen Yizi
1990, 71). If contracting had worked so well in the countryside, why
not apply it to cities as well? However, although the MOF and the
conservative defenders of the interests of the central state could
support agricultural contracting because such a small share of state
revenues came from agriculture, they opposed contracting in industry, where state financial interests were more directly at stake.
The tax-for-profit approach to enterprise finance, which gave priority to central revenues, was much more congenial to them than was
the contracting model. Zhao Ziyang, in arguing against a mecha-
nistic application of rural contracting to the urban context, put the
issue squarely:

> Reforms in the cities are more complex than in the country-
> side. Therefore, we should draw from the rural reform
> experience only what is common to both and must not me-

chanically apply the specific forms of operation and management suited only to agriculture to urban industrial and commercial enterprises and other undertakings. *Since more than 80 percent of state revenue comes from urban industrial and commercial enterprises, the outcome of reforms in the cities has a vital bearing on the national economy as a whole.* (Zhao Ziyang 1983, 1)[15]

Zhao Ziyang tried to win high-level CCP support for himself and tax-for-profit by emphasizing the value of the tax approach to the central state. In the same speech he contrasted his own approach to reform with the approach of others (by insinuation, Hu Yaobang), which was "impetuous" and based on a erroneous view "that reform simply means decentralization of power and interests" (Zhao Ziyang 1983, 1). As CCP general secretary, Hu Yaobang could have prevailed over government premier Zhao Ziyang, but not with the other members of the Politburo and Standing Committee of the Politburo arrayed on Zhao's side.

Moreover, the fiasco of the Spiritual Pollution Campaign was not read by Chinese officials simply as the death knell of conservative elites within the CCP. The message communicated by Deng Xiaoping's actions—first starting the campaign and then ending it when it threatened the reforms—was that the elderly generation of leaders, many of whom had retired from their official posts, were still a formidable political force, but that Deng Xiaoping would not let them roll back reforms to restore the old command economy. A reform policy that was acceptable to the conservative elders, as was tax-for-profit, was more likely to win a coalition of support in the Politburo and Standing Committee of the Politburo than was one that made the conservative elders nervous. Making the acceleration of tax-for-profit the "breakthrough point" of the urban reform was a way for Zhao to win support for himself and the reform drive at the top reaches of party power.[16] By building up steam behind tax-for-profit at the end of 1983 and the beginning of 1984, Zhao Ziyang

15. Tian Jiyun also sold tax-for-profit with the revenue argument. He stated in September 1983, "The greatest advantage of this system is that it ensures, in law, the attainment of the principle of 'the state getting the largest share, the enterprises enjoying a big share, while the individuals get the remainder,' and also assures the steady growth of state revenue on the basis of production development" (Huang Changlu and Zhu Minzhi 1983, K12).

16. Before Zhao introduced his reform package to the Third Plenum, he tried it out in letter form to Deng Xiaopeng, Li Xiannian, Chen Yun, and Hu Yaobang to see if it was acceptable to the elders (Zhao Ziyang 1984).

was able to win most of the battles over the reform manifesto prepared at the party's Third Plenum, Twelfth Central Committee (October 1984). The document confirmed Zhao's position that the rural reform model, that is, contracting, would not be transferred mechanically to the urban setting ("Decision of the Central Committee" 1984, 24).[17]

The question remains, why did Zhao abandon his original intention to wait until prices were rationalized before carrying out the second stage of tax-for-profit? Why didn't Zhao make price rationalization the cornerstone of his 1984 big push to market reform? Conservative elites within the CCP were by no means unalterably opposed to price adjustments or even to price reforms that would allow some prices to float according to the market. The dual-price system, with low plan prices and higher above-quota market prices for most goods, made the planners' job of enforcing plan procurement very difficult; the best solution was to adjust plan prices upward (author's interviews). Moreover, the gap between agricultural procurement prices, which had been raised in 1979 as part of the rural reform, and the low purchase price of food in the cities translated into a heavy subsidy burden for the central treasury; the best solution was to allow at least some urban food prices to fluctuate with the market.[18] Therefore, the SPC and the MOF, along with their elderly patrons, were a natural lobby for price adjustments or reform. Like everyone, they worried about the possibility that price adjustments would stimulate inflation and spark social unrest, but they were generally sympathetic to the need to rationalize prices.

The obstacle to price reform was not high-level opposition but the irreconcilability of bureaucratic interests, especially in the context of divided leadership. Price adjustments, particularly of raw materials and fuels, would please the extractive industries and the inland provinces where extractive industries were concentrated but would antagonize the manufacturing industries and the coastal provinces where manufacturing industries were concentrated. When

17. Both tax-for-profit and profit contracting claimed roots in the rural responsibility system, but the partisans of contracting argued that the rural model could be adapted by factories, whereas the partisans of tax-for-profit argued that the forms of the model had to be modified to suit the different environment of urban industry (Wang Jui 1983, 30).
18. A year later, at the beginning of 1985, Chen Yun and Yao Yilin successfully proposed freeing urban purchase prices of secondary food products (vegetables, meat, fish, etc.) as a way of reducing the burden on the central budget (Chen Yizi 1990, 72).

Zhao Ziyang created a State Council task force to develop a strategy for rationalizing prices and began to tackle the price problem in earnest, he discovered that it was going to be the knottiest issue of reform. As one account explained, "Many comrades thought that the second stage of tax-for-profit would not be carried out until after price readjustment, and of course that would have been smoother, but the price problem is extremely complicated [*fuza*] and not easy to solve in a short time, so the tax-for-profit reform could not wait for price reform to be carried out" (Chu Tan and Zhang Feng 1983, 72).

After only a few months of preliminary work on price adjustments, Zhao realized that if he wanted to show dramatic progress, price reform was not the best route. In September 1983 Tian Jiyun told reporters that he had a new plan for the second stage of tax-for-profit: "Bypass the readjustment of the price system which is a 'stumbling block,' accelerate the pace of taxation reform, complete the transition of substituting taxes for delivery of profits from the first to the second step as quickly as possible, and use the perfected system of substituting taxes for delivery of profits to bring along the reform of the price system and other work" (Huang Changlu and Zhu Minzhi 1983, K12). Because Zhao and Tian were unable to push through the stone wall of the Chinese bureaucracy with price rationalization, they found an opening with tax reform instead.

Of course, this change in strategy involved completely reconceptualizing the connection between prices and taxes. Originally Zhao and his advisers thought that a standardized tax system could be introduced only on the basis of rational prices. Now they viewed taxes as a way to compensate for irrational prices and a host of other objective factors. Taxes could be used to mitigate (*huanhe*) the harm of irrational prices (author's interviews). In other words, tax reform became a politically feasible substitute for price reform. As one participant put it, "Tax-for-profit affects the interests of the producing departments just like price reform does, but unlike price reform it does not affect people's livelihood or the interests of the consuming departments because the prices remain unchanged" (author's interviews). Instead of creating a genuine market environment with rational prices, Zhao Ziyang took the path of creating a pseudo market environment through the administrative mechanism of taxes.[19]

19.   The Chinese effort to create a market environment by means of ad-

Building Bureaucratic Consensus on the Second
Stage of Tax-for-Profit

The impetus to accelerate the implementation of the second stage of tax-for-profit came from the top down, from Zhao Ziyang and his supporters at the top levels of the CCP. Within the government bureaucracy the MOF was the prime mover, whereas the enterprises, ministries, localities, and the SEC were in no hurry to move forward along the path of tax-for-profit. The interview and documentary sources describe officials from localities, ministries, and enterprises as "worried" that the second stage of tax-for-profit would "diminish their activism" by "reducing their profits" (Ji Naifu and Chen Naijin 1984, K13; "Let Enterprises Invigorate Themselves" 1984, K15; author's interviews). Many managers and officials clearly preferred profit contracting.[20] The pressure from above meant that the bureaucrats were going to have to get together to work out an acceptable tax package.[21] But because the bureaucrats were aware of Hu Yaobang and the profit-contracting alternative lurking in the wings and because they themselves felt no incentive to expedite the second stage, they fought hard to make sure their interests were preserved in the package.[22]

---

ministrative mechanisms without actually freeing economic activity from administrative control is a good example of the tendency of communist governments to approach reform by "playing market as children play war, railroad, or school" (Heilbroner 1990, 97).

20. The tax-for-profit team tried to convince enterprise managers that tax-for-profit was quite "compatible with the system of contracted responsibilities implemented by the enterprises." They meant that whereas the relationship between the state and the enterprises was set by the tax system, within the enterprise managers were free to use various types of contract responsibility systems to solve the relationship between enterprises and employees (Ji Naifu and Chen Naijin 1984, K13).

21. At the June–July 1984 national work conference responsible for working out the specific contents of the policy, Zhao Ziyang told the delegates in no uncertain terms that the second stage of tax-for-profit must go forward: "If we do not make a breakthrough in this matter we will be unable to carry out the ten-point regulations on extending the decision-making power of the enterprises; further reforms will also be out of the question" (Ji Naifu and Chen Naijin 1984, K13).

22. Another reason that the bargaining over the second stage of tax-for-profit was particularly intense was the principle, established by the State Council leadership to win bureaucratic support for the policy, that no enterprise's retained profits would be reduced below the 1983 level. Because 1983 was a very good year for most enterprises, this principle required that the policy guarantee a high base of profits for the enterprises even though 1984 was likely to be a less favorable year for business (author's interviews).

The proposed second stage of tax-for-profit was truly a comprehensive (*peitao*) reform with many reform objectives riding on it (Hua Sheng, Zhang Xuejun, Luo Xiaopeng 1988, no. 9:26). More than two hundred different categories of product taxes (combined with value-added taxes for fourteen products and turnover taxes for commercial enterprises) would be used to reduce the distorting effects of irrational prices and enable enterprises producing different products to compete under equal conditions.[23] Within sectors, comparability would be enhanced by a fixed asset tax to compensate for different legacies of past state investments in equipment and a natural resource tax on extractive industries to compensate for variation in natural endowments. These taxes were intended to offset the differences in enterprise profitability caused by factors beyond the control of managers and eliminate sources of unfairness in inter-enterprise competition. Once these taxes were levied, enterprises would pay a uniform income tax and a set of local taxes, keep the remaining profits, and be responsible for their own profits and losses. The distribution relationship between the state and enterprises would be fixed according to law, and enterprises would become true "economic entities owned by the state that can independently carry out operation and management, pay taxes according to law, and assume sole responsibility for their profits and losses" ("Major Breakthrough" 1984). After implementing tax-for-profit, the state could legitimately end its bailouts of losing firms and force them to stand on their own; managers would no longer be able to claim that their losses were due to uneven features of the economic environment.

Another radical feature of the second stage of the proposal was that it required all enterprises, regardless of whether they were run by localities or ministries, to pay their taxes directly to the center.[24] The fiscal system of "eating in separate kitchens" would be abolished and a new system of local taxes established to fund local governments. The tax reform would reconstitute the fiscal relationship between center and localities. At the same stroke it would dissolve the link between enterprises and the financial interests of ministries and territories and free enterprises from the bonds im-

23. "By rationally readjusting the rate of product tax, the differential incomes resulting from the higher prices of certain products exceeding their real value will be transferred to the state. This will ease the present contradiction resulting from unreasonable prices" (Jin Xin 1984, K11). In the past the industrial commercial tax rates were set by sector, with only approximately forty rates in all (author's interview).
24. Local officials would still collect central taxes.

posed by vertical and horizontal (*tiaotiao, kuaikuai*) administration (Chu Tan and Zhang Feng 1983, 1).

A value-added tax levied on fourteen manufacturing industries was intended to increase the incentives for enterprise specialization and discourage firms from excessive vertical integration (a phenomenon the Chinese label as "large but complete" [*da er quan*] and "small but complete" [*xiao er quan*]).[25]

The draft plan had real teeth, almost as sharp as those of a genuine market. If this original version of tax-for-profit had been implemented, enterprises for the first time would have faced the risk of failure and felt real pressure to improve efficiency. As one financial official said, the tax policy's "purpose is to create a situation in which the enterprises will become extinct if they do not make progress" (Song Yifeng 1984, K5).

Not surprisingly, many enterprise managers and industrial bureaucrats in China fought long and hard to defeat the toughest features of the plan and preserve their security. The battlefield was the National Work Conference on the Second Stage of Tax-for-Profit, which met from 22 June to 7 July 1984 to work out the policy details. After the formal opening, the participants, more than six hundred officials from the provinces and ministries, were greeted by an impromptu speech by Tian Jiyun, who told them that they had no choice but to go ahead with tax-for-profit.[26] Tian identified the two worries on the minds of the officials attending the work conference:

> Now, everyone has two worries: The first one is whether or not the interests of the enterprises would be affected; the second one is whether or not local revenues would be affected. Those who have these worries should feel at ease. What kind of reform would it be if our practice of replacing profit delivery with tax payments would dampen the enthusiasm of the enterprises? . . . As for the relationship between state and local revenues, the practice in the past three decades has proven that the highly centralized methods are useless. Now, we

25. The fourteen industries included farm machinery, automobiles, Western medicine, silk, machinery, consumer electric appliances, dyeing, rolled steel, sewing machines, ships, and bicycles (author's interviews).
26. "The orientation in replacing profit delivery with tax payments must be unswervingly upheld. It is necessary to resolutely follow this road and keep going. This practice has been approved by the Second Session of the Sixth NPC and reaffirmed by Premier Zhao Ziyang's government work report" ("Tian Jiyun Addresses Meeting" 1984).

need not worry too much about local revenues. ("Tian Jiyun Addresses Meeting" 1984)

Tian's assurances had little effect. The conference was a contentious affair.[27] The MOF was kept busy revising the contents of the policy, producing more than twenty drafts before a final version was accepted (author's interviews; Hua Sheng, Zhang Xuejun, Luo Xiaopeng 1988, no. 9:26). The first-stage tax-for-profit meeting had merely tinkered with minor points in the policy, but the second-stage meeting—confronted by a serious reform with real redistributive consequences—took the policy apart and put it together again in a completely different way to preserve egalitarian balance. Every controversy was resolved in such a way as to protect the weaker enterprises, sectors, and regions.

There was a clear regional dimension to the conference debates. China's loss-suffering enterprises are concentrated in a few sectors—coal, machinery, chemicals, foodstuffs, building materials, and textiles—and lie mainly in the inland provinces ("Over 6000 State Factories, Mines Lose Money" 1988). The rate of deficit enterprises is more than 100 percent higher in the middle and western regions of China than it is in the eastern regions (Xu Kehong 1988). As a rule, processing industries are more profitable than are extractive industries (because of irrational, administratively set prices), and most processing industries are located on the coast whereas most extractive industries are inland (Li Yunlin et al. 1989, 33). The hefty package of taxes in tax-for-profit threatened the precarious financial status of inland regions and was likely to widen the already sizable gap between coastal and inland regions. Even though more of the loss-making enterprises were run by central ministries than by local authorities ("Over 6000 State Factories, Mines Lose Money" 1988), the local authorities from inland provinces felt responsible for these enterprises and joined with the ministries in putting up strong resistance to the package at the conference (author's interviews).

The issue that drew the greatest fire was that of product tax rates. Product taxes took a big bite out of enterprise earnings and provided the largest share of tax revenue (Caizheng Bu Caishui Tizhi Gaige Zhu 1989, 149). The product tax rates were originally

27. Leaders of the State Council attended from time to time and were regularly briefed by Li Peng, who at the time was vice minister of finance (Ji Naifu and Chen Naijin 1984, K13).

set at a level appropriate for a firm of above-average profitability in order to put pressure on firms. Ministries and local governments protested on behalf of their weaker enterprises, and enterprise managers wrote letters of complaint (author's interviews). Simulations by the MOF (some of them done collaboratively with the technically sophisticated Finance Bureau in Shanghai) showed that if the product tax rates were set at the above-average level, more than 40 percent of enterprises would take a loss and would be unable to pay any other taxes (author's interviews; Hua Sheng, Zhang Xuejun, Luo Xiaopeng 1988, no. 9:26).[28] Places with good economic efficiency, such as Shanghai, Tianjin, and other coastal cities, would have no problems with above-average product tax rates, but places with poorer economic efficiency would not be able to tolerate them (author's interviews).

In the end the meeting agreed to reduce product tax rates to the level of firms of average or below-average profitability in order to take care of (*zhaogu*) backward firms and regions (author's interviews). Even with the rates lowered, some enterprises were unable to pay their product tax. The conference decided to allow them to have their tax forgiven or reduced temporarily (author's interviews; "Major Breakthrough" 1984).[29]

Product tax rates were adjusted (some were raised and some lowered) to build support for the compromise among a broad coalition of provincial officials. The most important reductions (amounting to 1.05 billion yuan, or 49.8 percent of the total reduction) were for tobacco, wine, and sugar factories, processing plants from which local governments drew much of their revenues. Naturally, the inland provinces, with their high concentration of low-profit extractive industries, had the most to lose from high product tax rates. Therefore, the next most important reductions (77 million yuan, or 36.5 percent of the total) were for fuel products including coal, liquefied natural gas, and crude oil (producing less than 5 million tons) that were produced mainly in the inland provinces. Product tax increases were focused on items produced from low-priced raw materials (such as products refined from oil, electric power, gas-

28. The MOF estimate of the number of enterprises that would take losses under the original plan (which included above-average product tax rates, the three equalization taxes, and local taxes) was reported by officials I interviewed as ranging from 25 to 50 percent.
29. The justification for leniency toward enterprises unable to pay their product taxes was that the irrational price system *still* had not been solved ("Major Breakthrough" 1984).

made fertilizer, and steel products) and on high-profit items (such as machinery, pharmaceuticals, perfume, and consumer durables). The net effect of these adjustments was that "the appearance of a big gap in profit rates was solved to a certain degree. . . . From the angle of different territories, because of the diversity in economic conditions, the change in losses was not completely balanced, but *the losses in most territories were reduced*" (Caizheng Bu Caishui Tizhi Gaige Zhu 1989, 153; my emphasis).

Even after the product tax rates were adjusted to blunt the impact of tax-for-profit on less profitable firms, there were loud objections to the new fixed asset and natural resource taxes designed to equalize the economic environment. During the conference much of the debate was framed in terms of the choice between either high product tax rates or the fixed assets tax because to levy both would constitute an impossible burden on weak enterprises. Young economists were particularly worried about abandoning the fixed assets tax. A group of them wrote to Zhao Ziyang five times pleading to reduce product tax rates in order to retain the fixed assets tax. (The fixed assets tax had been part of the tax-for-profit experiment in Shanghai and had worked extremely well. Shanghai officials asked to be allowed to retain the fixed assets tax [author's interviews].) Although the leaders paid some attention to the young economists and the Shanghai officials, "for all kinds of reasons it was impossible to change the huge administrative machine that was moving in its established track." The final decision, even after the product tax rates were reduced, was to give up the fixed assets tax to avoid too big a gap among strong and weak enterprises (Hua Sheng, Zhang Xuejun, and Luo Xiaopeng 1988, no.9:26).[30]

The main opposition to the fixed assets tax came from the coal industry, which had a huge accumulation of equipment but very low profits and which simply refused to go along with the tax unless it included variable rates. According to Coal Ministry officials and officials from Shanxi and other inland provinces with many coal mines, it would be unfair to tax the fixed assets of coal enterprises at the same rate as the fixed assets of petrochemical enter-

30. According to one official, the fixed assets tax was dropped before the June work conference because it had aroused so much opposition at earlier meetings. "The enterprises with a lot of fixed assets are usually those with poor economic results so they cannot handle the burden of fixed assets tax. If they had implemented the fixed assets tax at a unified rate, they would have had to reduce it or forgive it for many enterprises" (author's interview).

prises; both industries had a lot of fixed assets, but petrochemicals were much more profitable than coal. The MOF, already over-whelmed by the complexity of the new tax system, refused to agree, insisting that a fixed assets tax with variable tax rates would be too unwieldy (author's interviews).[31]

The other tax designed to create a level playing field, the natural resource tax, also met opposition at the work conference. The orig-inal intention of the natural resource tax was to compensate for production cost differences caused by different natural endow-ments of coal mines, ore mines, oil fields, and natural gas fields. The tax was opposed by all the affected ministries, with the most outspoken being the powerful Metallurgical Ministry (author's in-terviews). These ministries preferred to solve the problem internally by redistributing profits from low-cost, high-profit facilities to high-cost, low-profit ones. Because all the extractive industrial ministries were lined up against this tax, its scope was cut so far back as to be virtually eliminated.[32]

The ministries instead obtained a major side payment to win their acquiescence to the rest of the package. The coal, oil, metal-lurgy, and petrochemical ministries (along with the railroad and military ministries) were granted ministry contracts with the state.[33] In exchange for a certain amount of retained profit and state in-vestment, they supplied the plan with a certain amount of products

31. Some Chinese economists advocated combining the fixed assets tax with a differential land tax (*jicha shui*) designed to adjust for differences among localities in the availability of transport and communications (au-thor's interviews). The idea of differential land rent (*jicha dizu*) was origi-nally proposed by Marx and Ricardo as a way to extract from enterprises the differential income derived from their geographic location. In a socialist economy a factory in Shanghai may pay the same low rent for its land that a factory in Urumchi does despite the obvious disparities in the economic advantages offered by the two settings. The differential land tax would even out interprovincial differences so that the burden of fixed asset and other taxes would not fall too heavily on the less developed regions. As far as I can tell, this technically complicated proposal never got on the bar-gaining table.
32. The tax remained on the books but was not implemented except for a number of the best endowed and most profitable coal mines and oil and natural gas fields (Caizheng Bu Caishui Tizhi Gaige Zhu 1989, 151; author's interviews). The tax burden was negotiated as part of ministry contracts and redistributed by the ministries among their enterprises.
33. The Railroad Ministry's progressive remission contract for after-tax profit was actually approved by the State Council in May 1983 as part of the first stage of tax-for-profit (Zheng Derong et al. 1987, 262).

and then were free to sell their above-quota output on their own at higher prices.[34] Ministry contracts were favored by the SPC and Material Supply Bureau because they made it easier to enforce plan procurement in the context of a dual-track economy, but they obviously clashed with the reform principles of "separating enterprises from administration" (*zhengqi fenkai*) by tightening the hold of the ministries on the enterprises (author's interviews). Ministry contracts were a political tactic to buy the support of some powerful heavy industrial ministries for the tax-for-profit package and other reform initiatives.

Most of the two weeks during the conference were spent on bargaining over product tax rates and the two other taxes intended to equalize the economic environment, with the net result being a softening of the pressure on less profitable enterprises, sectors, and regions. The resolution of minor issues also reflected the need to appease provinces and ministries with weak enterprises. For example, the categories for the eight-grade progressive income tax on small enterprises were widened to reduce the burden on these enterprises.[35] And the right to repay bank loans out of pretax profits was extended from small state enterprises to large and medium-sized ones (Lu Baifu 1988).

Even after reducing product tax rates, eliminating the fixed assets tax, and cutting back the natural resources tax, enterprises and local governments were still opposed to implementing the proposed set of local taxes.[36] Both were dead-set against replacing the system of "eating in separate kitchens." If local taxes were set too high, many enterprises would be forced into the red; if they were set too low, the local governments would go broke.[37] After the conference

34. For details on the coal ministry contract, see Cao Jingquan 1986.
35. Under the original proposal an enterprise with a profit of 10,000 yuan would have paid an income tax of 32.06 percent; after the revisions made by the work conference, it paid at a rate of 24.2 percent (Caizheng Bu Caishui Tizhi Gaige Zhu 1989, 154). There was little discussion of the comparatively low tax rates for small state enterprises and private and collective enterprises. The tax-for-profit system subsidized small enterprises at the expense of large ones and created incentives for large firms to form joint ventures with small ones.
36. Four local taxes were proposed: facilities tax (*fangchan shui*), land-use tax (*tudi shiyong shui*), license tax, and city construction and maintenance tax (*chengshi jienshi weihu shui*; author's interviews).
37. Local governments were also apprehensive about the practical challenges of implementing taxes such as the land-use tax. Often bureau offi-

had argued over the national tax issues for two weeks, the State Council leaders were afraid that prolonged disagreement over how to divide taxes between center and locality and how to set local tax rates would impede the timely implementation of the second stage. They knew they did not have the capacity (*liliang*) to resolve the local tax issue expeditiously (author's interview); therefore, they preempted debate by agreeing to leave local taxes on the book but not implement them (Ji Naifu and Chen Naijin 1984, K13). The resolution of the financial relationship between center and locality would have to wait. For the meantime, "eating in separate kitchens" would continue, and provinces were guaranteed their 1983 revenues despite any perturbations caused by tax-for-profit.[38]

The outcome of the work conference was predictable: to ease the pressure on weaker enterprises, their tax burden was reduced by adjusting product tax rates, cutting back natural resources taxes, and dropping fixed asset and local taxes. These compromises were necessary to get ministry and local government officials to agree to the second-stage tax policy. The officials knew they could hang tough because the leadership was divided on the question of tax-for-profit versus profit contracting and because Zhao Ziyang was in a hurry to get tax-for-profit in place.

The price for reaching consensus was paid by the central treasury, which faced a large shortfall in revenue created by collecting fewer taxes. The MOF did not raise the problem of the revenue shortfall at the time of the work conference but soon afterward came to the State Council with new simulations revealing the problem. (According to one official, the MOF's behavior on this occasion was "sneaky"; author's interview.) The only way to fill the revenue gap created by the revised tax package, the MOF said, was an adjustment tax (*tiaojie shui*) to extract funds from the most profitable enterprises. If they did not levy an adjustment tax, there would be a "chunk of income" the state couldn't "grab" (author's interview).

The idea of an adjustment tax had been in the minds of MOF officials since the first stage of tax-for-profit. According to one MOF

cials and managers did not know how much land a unit actually occupied because its workshops were so dispersed (author's interviews). Managers of large heavy industrial plants and oil fields that occupied a lot of land were particularly opposed to the land-use tax.

38. For example, the center increased Shanxi's ratio of revenue retention to compensate the province for revenue losses caused by tax-for-profit (Lieberthal and Oksenberg 1988, 345).

bureaucrat, the focus of all the many MOF drafts on the second stage of tax-for-profit was whether or not to use some form of adjustment tax to equalize the situation of the enterprises and claim more revenues for the center. The earliest MOF drafts for the second stage had included an adjustment tax, but the draft the State Council approved for submission to the work conference did not (author's interviews). At first the MOF wanted to adopt an adjustment tax called "profit differential tax" (*li cha shui*), which used a uniform formula to tax away all profits earned over an average level of profitability. From the standpoint of the MOF the profit differential tax was a simpler, easier way to even out enterprise profit disparities attributed mostly to external factors, far better than a set of several complicated taxes on fixed assets and natural resources (Yan Yi 1984, 40). But the enterprises strongly opposed such a tax because it punished enterprises that made money because of good management (author's interviews).

The 1984 simulation presented by the MOF to the State Council was based on a draft that included the fixed asset and natural resources taxes and local taxes but no adjustment tax.[39] The MOF used the simulation to confirm the work conference's conclusions that this package of taxes left too many enterprises in the red. MOF officials talked about enterprise losses, but what they really cared about was revenue (author's interview). They advocated following the conference's decisions to reduce product tax rates and eliminate many of the other taxes and proposed equalizing profits and replacing the revenue that would have been provided by these taxes by means of an adjustment tax instead. After all, the MOF had always preferred an adjustment tax because it was easier than setting rates for all the new taxes (author's interviews). The MOF also argued that because the tax-for-profit package had been modified to reduce product tax rates, restrict the natural resources tax, and eliminate the fixed assets tax, profit differentials caused by objective factors would continue to be a problem unless the government used an adjustment tax.

In the end the State Council reversed itself and on 18 September 1984 adopted a final tax-for-profit plan that included an adjustment tax on after-tax profits to be levied on approximately ten thousand

39. The MOF used the Shanghai Finance Bureau's sophisticated computer equipment to do the simulation arguing for an adjustment tax (author's interview). Ironically, Shanghai was the city most fiercely opposed to the adjustment tax.

of the most profitable large and medium-sized enterprises, most of which were located in coastal cities, especially Shanghai and Tianjin (Xu Yi 1984).[40] (Of the 10 billion yuan in revenues collected from the adjustment tax in 1984, 1.8–2 billion came from Shanghai factories alone; author's interviews.)[41] Tax rates were to be determined individually for each enterprise (*yi hu yi lu*) because the situation of enterprises was too varied to use a uniform formula. The rate would be set to preserve the 1983 level of retained profits for enterprises and remain constant for seven years to encourage the enterprises to make progress. The profits earned over the previous year's level were to be taxed at a rate 70 percent lower than the base rate (Caizheng Bu Caishui Tizhi Gaige Zhu 1989, 148).

It was widely acknowledged that the adjustment tax was not a genuine tax because it was not standardized (author's interviews). Rather, it was bargained out between finance departments and industrial departments and then again between industrial departments and enterprises, much as profit-sharing contracts had been.[42] The adjustment tax and the flexibility built into the regulations for product and income taxes (i.e., income tax could be reduced for a limited time to allow enterprises to reach their 1983 profit-retention level and product tax could be reduced to maintain "rational levels of profit retention") perpetuated the particularistic bargaining practices established under profit-retention contracts.[43] Managers appreciated

40. When the State Council (represented by Minister of Finance Wang Bingqian) asked the Standing Committee of the National People's Congress to empower them to pass the final tax-for-profit draft (including the adjustment tax), the committee allowed them to approve it only as a temporary policy to be revised later in light of experience (Caizheng Bu Caishui Tizhi Gaige Zhu 1989, 148). This stance on the part of the legislative leaders may have reflected some reservations about the adjustment tax or other features of the policy package.
41. According to one MOF official, the final tax-for-profit package would net the center 20–30 billion yuan less per year than the earlier package, which included more types of taxes and higher product tax rates, would have netted. They expected to collect 10–12 billion from the adjustment tax, still leaving a shortfall (author's interview).
42. The ministry-level Chinese National Petrochemical Corporation was very unhappy about the high adjustment tax rate (90 percent of its base after-tax profits and 9 percent of its incremental profits) that was set in its negotiations with the MOF. SINOPEC complained to the State Council, which settled the issue (*xietiao*) by guaranteeing SINOPEC that they could renegotiate their adjustment tax if the raw materials they used (i.e., unprocessed oil) increased in price (author's interview).
43. As one critic said, "The previous wrangling over base figures and ratios that occurred during the time when all profits were retained and all

the chance to bargain tax rates with financial and industrial officials, and the officials were glad to trade favors for political support.

No economist or economic official in China, not even those from the MOF, defended the economic logic of the adjustment tax. It was accepted only because "there was no other way to solve the problem" (author's interviews). The problem, they explained, was not just state revenue but also the large gap between advanced and backward areas of the country (author's interviews). The original tax package would have widened the gap between coastal and inland China. Once extraneous sources of unearned profits were taxed away, profit levels would have reflected the huge differences in internal efficiency between coastal and inland enterprises, and substantial numbers of factories in the interior would have been forced out of business. Inland officials exercised their veto at the national work conference and other meetings to prevent this eventuality. The only way to obtain consensus on any tax reform was to turn a redistributive policy into one that preserved everyone's original vested interests.

The saga of tax-for-profit reveals that when economic reforms are processed through the traditional communist decision-making system, the contradiction between balance and efficiency is resolved in favor of balance, especially if the leadership is divided on the reforms. The practical requirements of obtaining consensus in a bureaucratic policy-making system evolve into the normative principle of "balancism." As an ideology, "balancism" shapes the thinking of even those groups who are penalized by it. For example, in an account of the tax-for-profit story, the manager of a large, profitable automobile plant in a coastal city explained the rationale for the adjustment tax: "The adjustment tax was to protect the backward. Of course, from the larger perspective it was to preserve peace and unity, because historically China's development has not been balanced. The inland areas have needed construction and development" (author's interview).

The tax-for-profit policy that emerged from the Chinese bureaucratic bargaining process bore little resemblance to the original vision of Zhao Ziyang, Tian Jiyun, and their economist advisers. The attempt to use tax policy to simulate the level playing field of the

losses accountable [under profit contracting] has now turned into wrangling over base figures and 'rational levels of profit retention' [under tax-for-profit]" (Wang Qingling 1985, 20).

market failed. Product tax rates were adjusted (mostly down) so that they failed to even out the effects of irrational prices. Because taxes on fixed assets and natural resources were not implemented or were cut back drastically, disparities in these objective factors continued to distort enterprise profit levels. Because the unfair features of the economic environment persisted, it was impossible to require enterprises to take responsibility for their profits and losses. Large and medium-sized firms were no more financially independent under tax-for-profit than they had been under profit contracting. The subordination relations between local governments and local enterprises were slightly attenuated by the second stage of tax-for-profit, which required all enterprises to pay national taxes (which were split with localities) instead of paying taxes according to the level that managed them. But local governments, without the originally planned set of separate local taxes to support them, continued to depend on revenue-sharing contracts with the center under the "eating in separate kitchens" arrangement. The relations between center and locality were not put on a new foundation. Finally, the tax-for-profit package failed to establish uniform, standardized legal rules for enterprise finance. Thanks to the addition of the adjustment tax, which was negotiated on an individual basis, particularism still pervaded the financial structure. There was plenty of room for bargaining between finance officials and industrial officials. Managers and industrial bureau officials continued to have an incentive to focus their energies on bargaining good deals instead of raising production efficiency.

The final tax-for-profit package satisfied the MOF because it was relatively simple to implement and strengthened legal guarantees of state revenues.[44] The outcome was a victory for the inland provinces and heavy (especially extractive) industries, which used their political clout to retain the protections and subsidies they had come to enjoy under the command economy. The more efficient and prof-

---

44. One high-level MOF official smugly noted that the final tax package closely resembled the ministry's original plan. The final package included eleven taxes, including the four local taxes that were not implemented. The taxes that were implemented were the product tax, value-added tax, business tax (on commercial and service units), salt tax (which had existed in China for more than two thousand years), the natural resources tax (levies on a very small set of enterprises), income tax, and adjustment tax (author's interviews). The state also collected six other taxes covering construction; bonuses; slaughter; agriculture, forestry, and fisheries; tariffs; and fuel consumption (author's interviews).

itable economies of China's coastal cities were the big losers; the tax system kept them harnessed to a state bent on egalitarian balance instead of freeing them to exploit their potential. The unhappy representatives of Shanghai, Tianjin, and other coastal areas complained that the adjustment tax discriminated against the best enterprises, or as the Chinese put it, "beat the fastest oxen." But they were unable to block the adjustment tax or veto the package because Zhao Ziyang, supported by Deng Xiaoping and party conservatives, was pushing hard from the top down.

The following chapter continues the story of enterprise finance. The consensus achieved in 1984 under conditions of divided leadership, with one set of leaders pushing hard from the top down, was not a genuine policy equilibrium. After the second stage of tax-for-profit was implemented in 1984, the big enterprises began almost immediately to agitate for a financial system less disadvantageous to their interests. Even under the perverse incentives of an egalitarian tax system, their economic dynamism in an era of partial marketization widened their lead over inland industry and translated into political pressure to reverse the 1984 decision. In the face of actual shifts in relative economic positions and the divisions between Zhao and Hu Yaobang on enterprise finance reforms, how long could the traditional communist political system continue to produce policies that punished the advanced to take care of the backward?

13   The Power of Particularism

Abortive Price Reform and the
Revival of Profit Contracting, 1985–88

Chinese advocates of the contracting approach to economic reform labeled their approach "socialist economic system reform with Chinese characteristics," tainting rival approaches with the implication that they were overly influenced by foreign, bourgeois ideas. Strategic use of economic rhetoric aside, particularistic contracting was a persistent and distinctive feature of Chinese economic reform. Time after time reform policies emerged from Chinese political institutions in the form of particularistic contracting. Sometimes other types of reform policies were proposed, policies that used uniform formulas and rules to create a sound environment for market competition, policies such as tax-for-profit or reform of irrational administratively set prices. But such standardization policies either emerged from the bureaucratic bargaining machine transformed into particularistic policies, as in the case of tax-for-profit, or sank without a trace and never emerged at all, as in the case of price reform.

Why did reform policies always come forth from Chinese political institutions in the form of particularistic contracts that shared power and resources between center and locality, government and enterprises, on an ad hoc basis? The answer lies in the political incentives and choice rules structured by Chinese political institutions.

The career incentives of Chinese politicians at every level of the system from center down to localities led them to favor contracting over universalism. The opportunity to allocate special deals to individual subordinates translated into political resources. An ambitious Beijing politician could build a base of political supporters at the provincial and municipal level by rewarding them with special reform experiments (see chapter 10), generous revenue-sharing contracts (see chapter 9), and the authority to build their own political machines by bargaining out profit-sharing contracts with local enterprise managers. CCP General Secretary Hu Yaobang, until his purge in January 1987, led the drive for enterprise profit contracting, thereby expanding and consolidating the nationwide network of supporters he had built as former head of the Communist Youth League. Meanwhile, Premier Zhao Ziyang, who as a former provincial official had to prove himself to the Beijing establishment and who, according to his advisers, genuinely believed in the necessity for standardization reforms, pushed for approaches such as tax-for-profit and price reform. But as soon as Hu Yaobang was eliminated from the succession and the contest was reframed between Zhao the reformist and Li Peng the conservative, Zhao immediately switched positions to advocate contracting and abandon standardization.

The incentives of bureaucrats and delegation by consensus also tilted the outcome toward contracting. From the standpoint of bureaucrats anxious to preserve the vested interests of their agencies, contracting appeared much less threatening than did fundamental changes in the tax and price systems. Because contracting gave every organization the opportunity to retain its privileges through bargaining, it was easier for contracting to win a consensus of bureaucratic support than for inherently redistributive policies such as tax or price reform to do so. Most foreign economists, and many Chinese ones, would assert that contracting was a less effective mechanism for improving industrial efficiency than was reforming irrational prices or forcing enterprises to pay uniform taxes and take responsibility for their own profits and losses. The costs of continuing inefficiency, however, were diffused among all economic actors, whereas the benefits of contracting were concentrated on specific enterprises and bureaucracies and potentially available to all. In contrast, the costs of moving to a strict tax system or rational prices would be concentrated on certain sectors and regions, whereas the benefits of increased efficiency would be widely diffused. In the institutional context of delegation by consensus, a system that grants veto power to a broad set of bureaucratic interests, it is no surprise that contracting was preferred to tax or price reform.

Some Chinese economists in favor of contracting frankly acknowledged its practical political advantages over tax or price reform. Yu Guangyuan (1987) put a theoretical gloss on political pragmatism when he wrote that the simplicity and clarity of con-

tracting suited China's cultural level during the early stage of socialism:[1] cadres and employees of low cultural level could easily
figure out the effects of the contracting system on the interests of
factories, workshops, and employees, whereas the effects of other
types of reforms were harder to calculate. Li Yining, an economist
who supported contracting as a means of eventually transforming
the ownership system, identified a difference in what he called the
"psychological effect" of reform policies: price reform makes people
think about what they're going to lose, whereas contracting and
ownership reform make people think about what they're going to
gain ("Thoughts on Which One to Do First" 1986). In other words,
from the perspective of Chinese employees, managers, and industrial officials, tax and price reform looked like much pain and little
gain, whereas contracting looked like much gain and little pain.

This chapter tells the story of Chinese industrial reform policy-
making during 1986–87. The main plot of the story is the triumph
of enterprise profit contracting over tax-for-profit and price reform.
Contracting lost a battle to tax-for-profit in 1983 (see chapter 11),
but it won the war in 1987. The moral of the story is that economic
logic and political logic are not the same thing and that in economic
policy-making, political logic prevails. Economic policy outcomes in
all political systems are shaped by the individual incentives and
choice rules in each distinctive set of political institutions. In the
Chinese case the incentives of politicians and the consensus choice
rules tilted outcomes toward contracting.

Enterprise Finance after Second-Stage Tax-for-Profit

Why was it possible for enterprise profit contracting to replace tax-
for-profit less than three years after the tax scheme had been implemented? The tax scheme was an easy target for the broadly popular
contracting approach. As described in the previous chapter, many
elements of the tax plan were never put into effect because they
drew too much opposition. The final package clearly failed to

---

1. Zhao Ziyang's much-touted theoretical contribution to Marxism articulated at the Thirteenth Party Congress in November 1987 was the idea
that China was in the early stage of socialism and that the unequal wages,
commodity (market) economy, and diverse ownership forms associated
with the reform drive were entirely appropriate to this early stage of socialism. Of course, the problem with this formulation was the implication
that historical progress would impel China away from the market and toward the plan, a path that would reverse the overall direction of reform
policies.

achieve its objective of leveling profit disparities caused by irrational prices, previous investments, or natural resources. Given continuing inequities in the economic environment, enterprises could not be required to take full responsibility for their profits and losses; enterprises could justify perpetuating the practice of repaying bank loans out of pretax earnings; and local governments had a rationale for continuing to interfere in enterprise management. Those favoring the contracting method argued that because tax-for-profit had not solved the problems it was intended to solve, the only solution was to carry out contracting instead (Song Yifeng 1985).

Second, the last-minute addition of the ad hoc adjustment tax on the most profitable enterprises perverted the tax scheme with particularism. Enterprise managers bargained out their adjustment tax rates with their bureaucratic superiors, who in turn bargained out an aggregate rate with financial officials. Managers and industrial bureaucrats often were able to plead unfair hardship from factors beyond their control and obtain rate reductions or exemptions from other taxes as well. Officials were permitted, even encouraged, to use "flexible methods" in tax work; as a result, there were no clear, uniform rules about taxes (Zhang Shaojie and Zhao Yujiang 1987). In practice, the new tax system proved to be just as subjective and particularistic as profit contracting.[2] Contracting advocates could justifiably claim that contracting was even more "fixed" (*guding*) than tax-for-profit (Zhou Guanwu 1986, 13).

To compound the problems, local officials actively colluded with local firms in outright tax evasion, looking the other way when managers hid enterprise profits through various ingenious tricks. Officials were also willing to reassign medium-sized firms to the category of small firm to lower their tax rates ("Second Stage Tax-for-Profit" 1984). The press described local governments as "acting in the interests of the local economy by breaking rules to reduce the tax burden on enterprises" ("Tax-Dodging Enterprises Face State Clampdown" 1984). Officials estimated that 70 percent of enterprises practiced some form of tax evasion (author's interviews). Given the fiscal rules, local governments had an incentive to cooperate in tax evasion to keep funds at home rather than sharing them with the center.

2.   Christine Wong (1990) argues that the hope of a standardized, legal tax system was effectively killed in 1984 when policymakers promised managers that the second stage of tax-for-profit would guarantee their 1983 level of retained profits.

There was even some question about how widely tax-for-profit actually was implemented. It was reported in 1987 that although fewer than one hundred firms had received formal national approval to retain the contracting method, in fact, Jilin Province had stuck to enterprise profit contracting continuously since 1983, and Guangdong, Heilongjiang, Hebei, Hubei, Shanxi, and Beijing had been using profit contracting before it became national policy ("Four Thousand Large and Medium-Sized Enterprises" 1987; Lu Dong 1988, 24). With Hu Yaobang, the SEC, and the Institute of Industrial Economics continuing to praise the advantages of profit contracting over tax-for-profit, it is not surprising that some localities simply failed to implement the national tax policy.

Finally, economic performance did not confirm the wisdom of tax-for-profit. During late 1984 and the first half of 1985 the Chinese economy experienced severe overheating. Industry grew too fast, capital investment expanded drastically, wages skyrocketed, prices rose, and fuel and power were in short supply (Wu Jinglian, Li Jiange, and Ding Ningning 1985; Wu Jinglian 1985; Wu Jinglian 1985a; Wu Jinglian, Li Jiange, Ding Ningning, and Zhang Junkuo 1986).[3] Central planning and finance officials were disappointed to find that the new tax system proved unable to enhance macroeconomic control of enterprise behavior. Moreover, with production costs rising and enterprise efficiency improving slowly, the central treasury's burden of subsidizing enterprise losses grew bigger and bigger. According to one procontracting source, enterprise profits declined for twenty-two consecutive months from the time tax-for-profit was adopted over profit contracting at the end of 1983; he claimed that the adverse trend was reversed only after 1987, when contracting was finally extended on a national basis (Yang Peixin 1990, 42).

All of these features of the situation made tax-for-profit vulnerable to criticism. Nevertheless, like many other economically ineffective Chinese policies, it might have remained in place for years. What finally did in tax-for-profit was the growing political pressure, particularly from large and medium-sized state industrial enter-

3. During 1985 there was a fierce debate within the ranks of reformist economists over macroeconomic policy, with the more cautious reformers, led by Wu Jinglian, arguing the risks of economic overheating and the need for better central macroeconomic control, and the radical reformers, led by the young economists at the State Council Economic Reform Institute, arguing on the basis of a version of Keynesianism that high growth was a positive force for reform.

prises, to retract it. The final tax package, which included the controversial, last-minute adjustment tax, was not a policy equilibrium. The managers and bureaucrats of large state factories complained vehemently that the adjustment tax was unfair discrimination against the most dynamic enterprises, and once these influential industrial forces started making noise, it became difficult to sustain tax-for-profit.

The Fast Oxen Stampede: Large Enterprises Lobby Against Tax-for-Profit

No sooner had the regulations for the second stage of tax-for-profit been promulgated than the managers of China's largest state factories began to challenge them. In August 1984 the Institute of Industrial Economics organized a meeting of twenty-five large state enterprises that already had profit contracts and wanted to expand the use of them (author's interviews).

As of 1985, 5,837 enterprises were categorized as large and medium-sized state enterprises, the majority of them in heavy industrial sectors producing energy, raw and semifinished materials, and equipment. Although these enterprises constituted only 2 percent of the total number of enterprises, they contributed 47.1 percent of total national industrial output value, 65.7 percent of total fixed assets, and 65.9 percent of profits and taxes delivered to the state (Luo Yuanming 1985; "Strive to Create the Conditions" 1985, K15). The national plan and treasury depended heavily on these enterprises.[4]

The managers of large and medium-sized industrial enterprises wielded formidable political clout. The managers of giant firms such as Anshan Iron and Steel Company and Daqing Oilfield held official cadre ranks as high as some province and ministry heads and were on the center's nomenklatura list. These titans of industry were usually prominent national figures who gave speeches, wrote articles, and were frequently invited to participate in policy work

4. In 1988 the category of large and medium-sized enterprises was expanded to approximately ten thousand enterprises, which accounted for 70 percent of total fixed assets and 62.8 percent of total profits and taxes handed to the state (Yang Peixin 1989, 40; "State Enterprises Report Profits" 1989). Another 1989 source claims that the 9,900 large and medium-sized enterprises provided about 80 percent of the country's financial income (Wang Yuling 1989, 43). The same source states that the output value of the 450 largest industrial enterprises occupying the top 50 positions in 9 major sectors amounted to 20.24 percent of the total national industrial output value.

conferences. Most of the largest factories were administered direct-ly by ministries, and their managers played an active political role within the ministerial industrial systems.[5]

The State Economic Commission was an influential political ally of the large state enterprises. During the reform decade the SEC acted as political entrepreneur on behalf of reforms that would give enterprise managers more authority and more resources. Most of the 1985–87 conferences at which the managers of large firms com-plained about restrictions on their autonomy and funds were orga-nized by the SEC. Provincial-level economic commissions also actively pressed the claims of large enterprises (An Qihong 1985, K10). The power of the large enterprises was greatly amplified by the bureaucratic initiatives of the SEC.

During the second half of the 1980s the managers of large enter-prises began for the first time to organize their own independent lobbying campaigns to supplement the bureaucratic efforts of the industrial ministries and the SEC. Individual managers from prom-inent Beijing firms—among them Zhou Guanwu, the manager of the Capital Iron and Steel Corporation, and Xu Xiaochun, the man-ager of the Beijing Printing and Dyeing Mill—used their proximity to national power to good advantage. They invited reformist leaders such as Hu Yaobang and Zhao Ziyang to visit their plants so they could publicize their pitch on behalf of large state enterprises. Local groups of managers started to write letters to local newspapers calling on higher-level departments to change policies or to imple-ment existing policies. In 1985 managers from thirty-one large fac-tories in Taiyuan wrote to *Shanxi ribao* complaining that many of the 1984 reforms had never been implemented and that provincial officials continued to tie their hands; the managers won more de-preciation funds and a lower adjustment tax ("Many Provincial Units Begin Responding" 1985, R1). Lobbying efforts at the pro-vincial level were so effective that some provincial governments drew up special regulations to enliven large enterprises as early as January and February 1985 ("Zhejiang to Attempt Reform" 1985; "Liaoning Issues Regulations" 1985).

5. The interests of the large firms were articulated more by the ministries (*tiao*) than by the localities (*kuai*). In fact, spokespersons for the large en-terprises often griped that local officials showed favoritism toward the smaller local enterprises instead of supporting the big national ones; as they put it, all officials should support the "national team" as well as their "local teams" (Wang Jinjia 1989, 37). If given the opportunity, managers of small local factories might have made the opposite complaint, that ministry officials neglected them while favoring the large enterprises.

The collective action problems of large enterprise managers were reduced by the emergence during the era of reform of new governmental or quasi-governmental organizations such as the Enterprise Management Association, which was founded by the SEC.[6] These organizations created local and national networks of large enterprise managers.

The ability of large enterprise managers to organize collective action was also enhanced by their concentration in a few coastal urban areas. In Shanghai alone 98.5 percent of state industrial enterprises were required to pay adjustment tax. Forty percent of Jiangsu state factories paid adjustment tax. The proportion was lower but still sizable in Beijing and Tianjin (author's interviews). Not surprisingly, Shanghai was the headquarters of the lobbying campaign against the adjustment tax, and the Shanghai proreform newspaper, *World Economic Herald* (*Shijie jingji daobao*), organized forums and other collective activities that brought the managers of large enterprises together.

By 1986 the managers of large enterprises were organizing regional and national associations of their own. The Golden Triangle Entrepreneurs Club, based in Shanghai, brought together the managers of thirty-one large enterprises, including Baoshan Iron and Steel Corporation, at its first national meeting and issued a manifesto that was published in the *People's Daily* ("Reflections and Demands" 1986). The manifesto asserted in sharp language that the respect, authority, and rewards given to enterprise managers were not commensurate with the economic and political risks they faced. They argued that contracting systems were the best way to give the managers their due and to invigorate large enterprises and that the managers needed an independent association of entrepreneurs to give them a political voice in policy-making. Golden Triangle held a second annual national meeting in 1988, with fifty-one enterprises represented, and issued another manifesto for enterprise invigoration ("Nine-Point Proposal on Invigoration" 1988).

All the letters, articles, speeches, and meetings articulating the demands of large enterprise managers for more powers and funds had an impact on government policy. As one official said in late 1984, "The State Council listens because it is now paying attention to large enterprises" (author's interview).

6. A 1989 forum of managers of large and medium-sized enterprises in Liaoning was organized by the provincial Structural Reform Committee, the Association of Entrepreneurs, and the Enterprise Management Association ("Enterprise Directors Forum" 1989, 62).

Before the introduction of the Chinese reforms, foreign experts on market reforms in socialist systems believed that factory managers generally opposed such reforms (Nove 1983, 177). The lobbying efforts of the managers of large enterprises on behalf of economic reforms showed China to be an exception to this pattern. True, Chinese managers of large firms were at first leery of market reforms that threatened to shake them out of their comfortable dependence on the state. But the wrenching experience of the 1980–81 readjustment (see chapter 10) gave them a new appreciation of the opportunities offered by the market, and their envy of the benefits of reform enjoyed by smaller enterprises and nonstate enterprises motivated them to demand that these benefits be extended to their own enterprises (author's interviews). When employees of large firms saw their counterparts in small local firms rapidly raising their living standards under the new reform rules, they started to demand the same freedoms for themselves. The management attitude of large state factory managers was transformed; they paid more attention to the market because they knew they could sell at a higher price and make more money there (author's interview). Large enterprise managers changed from lazy conservatives coddled by the state to active reformers challenging the state. This transformation is illustrated by one 1985 article that put the relationship between the backbone enterprises and the state in these terms:

> Under our socialist system, the interests of enterprises and the state are basically identical, but they could be contradictory under certain circumstances. One rather conspicuous contradiction at present can be observed in the distribution of profits that our enterprises have earned: Who should retain more, the state or the enterprises? ("Large State Enterprises Need Such Administrators" 1985, K21)

Of course, the kinds of reforms preferred by the managers of large state firms were those that gave them more freedoms and more funds, but not more risk. During 1985–86 they focused their complaints on two problems: the continuing administrative restrictions on their managerial autonomy, and the adjustment tax, which left them inadequate funds for self-development.

The managers of large firms chafed under the controls of the centrally planned economy, which still dominated their operations despite five years of reforms. Most of their output still was procured at low prices by the plan, whereas smaller local firms were making money hand over fist producing for the market. Although the monopoly of the central Ministry of Foreign Economic Relations and Trade officially had been ended, the ministry still prohibited all but a few enterprises from direct contact with the international market and impeded the attempts of industrial ministries to become trading companies representing their own enterprises (author's interviews).[7] Administrative decentralization had increased local administrative interference in enterprise management and unauthorized financial extractions from enterprises. New local corporations had stolen the managerial autonomy and funds that were supposed to be delegated to enterprises.[8] Reforms established in 1984 to grant powers to enterprises—for instance, the Ten Points—were on the books but were not being implemented because of the power struggle (*zhengchuan*) between corporations and enterprises. The advocates of enterprise interests demanded that power be turned over to the enterprises without corporations skimming any off the top (Yuan Baohua 1985). Managerial actions were hamstrung by too many "mothers-in-law" (*popo*) who poked their noses into everything and demanded payoffs to approve anything (author's interviews).

The large enterprise managers' main complaint was financial. They argued that the adjustment tax left them with insufficient funds to carry out the technological renovation of their outmoded equipment. Moreover, the tax-for-profit system was rigged against them: rural village and township enterprises gave the state only 30 percent of their profits; urban collective enterprises gave 50 percent; but large state enterprises were required to pay 80–90 percent

7.   These complaints about tight administrative controls over the activities of large enterprises were still being made in 1989; see Yang Peixin 1989, 40.
8.   Factory managers' complaints about the tyranny of corporations were especially widespread in Shanghai, where the corporations had been founded in 1956 and where their power was entrenched. Managers described how prior to tax-for-profit they contracted with the corporation for a certain amount of bonus funds in exchange for remitting a certain amount of profit; sometimes the corporation simply broke the contract, withholding bonus funds and diverting them to subsidize other, less profitable firms. Managers hoped tax-for-profit would give them a direct relationship to the state and eliminate the arbitrary interventions of the corporation. In fact, corporations continued to negotiate tax rates, especially adjustment tax rates, with the finance bureau and then disaggregate them in egalitarian fashion among their subordinate firms (author's interviews; also see Dong Huanliang 1984, 2).

("Strive to Create the Conditions" 1985, K14). After paying taxes and additional exactions (*tanpai*) imposed by local and central governments, enterprises had very little real retained profit (Liu Tonglin, Li Lian, Lu Fengling, and Wang Lun 1987). Large Chinese firms had to pay 50–55 percent of net income for product tax, value-added tax, business tax, urban construction and maintenance fees, additional educational fees, and so on. In addition, enterprises were required to pay 55 percent of remaining profits as income tax and 5 to 25 percent as adjustment tax. They also had to take 15 percent of their retained profits to give the central energy and communication funds. Finally, they had to buy state treasury bonds and shares of key construction projects. The government claimed that enterprises retained 40 percent of their profits, but actually they were left with only 10 percent (Gao Shangquan 1987, 134). Some of the largest firms, such as the Yanshan Chemical Plant and Jinshan Chemical Plant, had to pay out 95 percent of their earnings. A 1985 survey of eleven well-run large enterprises in Tianjin found that although officially the enterprises kept 11.3 percent of their profits, they actually kept only 8.36 percent, with only 3.68 percent for development; another 1986 survey of water and electric power enterprises throughout the country found that they retained only 6.14 percent of their profits, with only 3.2 percent for development (Yang Peixin 1987, 13). One commentator noted, "Due to the fact that enterprises had to pay high taxes, that they had to supply goods at low prices in accordance with mandatory planning, and that they had to remit their foreign exchange income to the state, they had no money even for maintaining simple reproduction, let alone technical transformation" (Yang Peixin 1989a, 15). Another account remarked that Soviet and Eastern European firms were allowed to retain more profits than Chinese ones (Gao Shangquan 1987, 134), and yet another pointed out that Western capitalist countries were trying to reduce their tax rates to allow enterprises to keep about 50 percent for reinvestment (Yang Peixin 1987, 13).

Advocates of profit contracting argued that the tax-for-profit policy was to blame for draining the blood from China's most dynamic industries: "The policy of substituting tax for profits in two stages continually increased the tax burden on state-run enterprises and dampened their production capability for self-expansion" (Yang Peixin 1989a, 15; see also Zhou Guanwu 1986, 13). The Chinese talked about this problem with animal metaphors that reflected the society's rural character. The adjustment tax was criticized for "beating the fastest oxen" (*bianda kuai niu*), or punishing the enterprises that made the greatest contribution. The overall tax burden was blamed for the situation of "monkey in the tree, tiger in the cage, and lion being tied": small rural industries were free and prosperous, military industries faced restrictions, and large and medium-sized industries were bound up (Yang Peixin 1989, 40).

The campaign to liberate and invigorate large enterprises and to give them more funds for upgrading their equipment was spearheaded by the SEC beginning in November 1984, when the commission announced a new priority on the technical modernization of outmoded factory equipment at a national conference on technical advancement. Ninety billion yuan would be spent on technical renovation projects between 1985 and 1987 ("Accelerate the Technical Progress" 1984). The diversion of these investment funds from new construction to technical renovation was a bureaucratic victory for the SEC, which allocated renovation funds, over the SPC, which allocated construction funds. The pressing need for technical renovation of equipment became the rationale for demanding that heavy industrial enterprises be allowed to keep more of their own funds.

A few months later, in February 1985, the SEC made the invigoration of large and medium-sized enterprises the theme of a national economic work conference. This theme harkened back to the major CCP statement on economic reform from the Third Session of the Twelfth Central Committee in October 1984, which had said, "Socialism with Chinese characteristics should, first and foremost, be able to instill vitality to enterprises. . . . [T]he key to restructuring the national economy, with the focus on the urban economy, is invigoration of enterprises, particularly the large and medium-sized enterprises owned by the whole people" ("Decision of the Central Committee" 1984). The February work conference put forward the objective of invigorating all large and medium-sized enterprises in three years' time and came up with ten measures designed to promote this objective (Luo Yuanming 1985).[9] The conference promised large enterprises greater powers for direct foreign trade, a reduction of adjustment tax for the best-run enterprises, an introduction of internal management responsibility systems, a system linking wages to profits, greater freedom to obtain materials and sell products on the market, and closure of corporations that imposed bur-

9. Another source lists eleven points from the February conference because it includes one point on technical renovation and technology import ("Eleven Policy Measures" 1985).

dens on enterprises ("Eleven Policy Measures" 1985; "Enterprises' Greater Autonomy" 1985). By September 1985 the State Council had translated the sentiment for invigorating large enterprises into a set of fourteen regulations ("State Council Approves the State Economic Commission and Economic System Reform Commission Circular" 1985).

During 1985 the lobbying efforts of large enterprises won a gradual reduction in adjustment tax rates for some enterprises that made big contributions and were left with comparatively small retained profit. They also succeeded in getting the State Council to reduce their depreciation rates and to shift all depreciation funds to enterprises—a measure clearly aimed at facilitating technical renovation (Tian Yinong et al. 1988, 93; author's interviews). But they still were stuck with an onerous tax system, and they had made no apparent progress at instituting their preferred financial scheme, profit contracting. The reason was Zhao Ziyang's continued preference for standardization approaches to reform over particularistic contracting.

Zhao Ziyang's Tough Response

Premier Zhao Ziyang supported the general principle of invigorating large and medium-sized enterprises but resisted the pressure to give away more funds and more powers to the enterprises. Beginning in late 1984, he visited large enterprises such as the Beijing Printing and Dyeing Plant to let them know that they should rely on their own potential instead of waiting for the state to hand down more power and cut their taxes. You already have been given a lot of power and funds, he said, and you have equipment and talent that is superior to that of smaller enterprises. There is no reason that you should not be able to compete with smaller enterprises. Do not always look upward to the state to give you benefits; look inward and improve your management to exploit your own potential (author's interviews). He toured large enterprises, such as the Shangyang Electric Cable Plant, that had improved their performance by internal reforms to praise them and publicize their methods (Li Xinyan 1985). The slogan associated with Zhao Ziyang's approach to invigorating large enterprise was "Do not direct your eyes upward, look inward instead" (*Yao yu yenjing xiang shang, zuan wei xiang nei*; see, for example, Yuan Baohua 1985; Xu Jingan 1985). Zhao was fighting the tendency of managers to invest more energy in seeking rents from their bureaucratic patrons than in improving firm efficiency.

Zhao Ziyang's report to the Third Session of the Sixth National People's Congress in March 1985 offered expressions of sympathy for the plight of large enterprises but little tangible aid. Zhao said that until then, "The cities had supported the rural reform and the large enterprises had supported the reform of the small enterprises. . . . Now the time had come to place the invigoration of large and medium-sized enterprises on the agenda." But except for gradually reducing adjustment tax rates (which had been the original intention back in 1984, when the second stage of tax-for-profit was set), he offered no additional help. His report emphasized that large enterprises should use different kinds of internal management responsibility systems to exploit their potential (Zhao Ziyang 1985a, 697). In spring and summer 1985 articles echoing Zhao's position envisioned a third stage of tax-for-profit in which the adjustment tax was reduced and the tax package perfected ("Third Stage Reform of Tax-for-Profit" 1985).

This tough talk from Zhao Ziyang clearly identified him with the conservative wing of the party, who worried about economic overheating and central budget deficits, and not with the reformers and industrial interests pressing to put more resources in the hands of managers. In 1985–86 both sides, central finance officials as well as industrial managers and bureaucrats, perceived a clear contradiction between controlling excessive growth and central budgetary deficits and enlivening large enterprises. Zhao Ziyang clearly placed the concerns of the central state over industrial interests.

Large enterprise managers were being squeezed by raw material price rises resulting from the two-track system; after they paid fixed tax rates and an adjustment tax whose rate was set for seven years, they felt poorer than ever. From their point of view, they were being unfairly punished by the tax system while the smaller enterprises were flourishing thanks to the tax system. And now their premier was telling them that their problems were their own to solve. No wonder industrial interests publicly asserted themselves: "To invigorate large and medium-sized enterprises owned by the State, efforts should be made not only within these enterprises but also from outside" ("*Economic Daily* on Invigoration" 1984).

From the standpoint of central financial and planning officials and of the conservative elders within the party, the state could not afford to disperse more funds to the enterprises. They also were afraid that greater financial autonomy for enterprises would make them less amenable to direction from Beijing. As one official said, "If the enterprises get too much money, will they listen to the state? Will they leave the plan [*likai guojia jihua*]?" (author's interview). Central planners believed that investment decisions made by the enterprises themselves would be less rational and more wasteful than investment decisions made by the center (author's interviews). One critic of the argument that enlivening enterprises required them to retain more profits pointed out that the logic of the argument was similar to the Laffer curve and supply-side economics promoted during the Reagan administration in the United States. Although tax reductions had clearly stimulated American enterprises, the increased income from growth had not compensated for the losses suffered through reduced taxes, so that the budget deficit and accumulated debt had still grown (Dai Yuanchen and He Suoheng 1987).

Zhao Ziyang's position on this policy issue was strategic.[10] During 1985 the conservative elders within the party were showing their strength. The reformist leaders were vulnerable because their 1984 initiatives had caused the economy to overheat in late 1984 and 1985 and added to widespread official corruption. Student protests in September 1985 against official corruption and Japanese business penetration alarmed party officials, particularly the conservatives. Chen Yun reportedly wrote a letter in September 1985, later circulated as a CCP study document, that accused both Hu Yaobang and Zhao Ziyang of allowing their children to trade on their official connections to profit from foreign business activities (Lo Ping 1986). The Central Committee and State Council issued a joint circular aimed at eliminating corruption and abuses of power among officials ("Circular Urges Correction" 1985; "Curbing Abuses" 1985). The student protests worked against the reformists and for the conservatives by raising the specter of social chaos (*luan*) caused by reforms (Chang Chuan 1985).

Deng Xiaoping tried to protect the reformist leaders and consolidate the future of the economic reform drive by replacing elderly

---

10. Zhao may have sincerely believed that a cautious approach to economic reform emphasizing tax and price reform and retaining central controls over enterprises was economically more rational than were reform approaches such as contracting that concentrated on improving enterprise incentives, but he was willing to switch his position almost overnight after Hu Yaobang was purged.

conservatives with younger proreform officials in the leadership organs of the CCP.[11] In September 1985 he called a national party congress two years ahead of time by designating it a national party "conference" instead of a party congress (such an extraordinary conference had been called only once before, by Mao Zedong in 1949). The conference retired 64 of the 210 Central Committee members and 10 of the 25 Politburo members, all of whom were in their seventies or eighties. At the conference (and subsequently at the November 1987 Thirteenth Party Congress) Deng succeeded in filling the Central Committee with officials committed to economic reform. Paradoxically, the message communicated by the conference was that the elderly conservatives continued to have tremendous power within the party. The old veterans managed to retain their seats in the Standing Committee of the Politburo and continued to dominate that top body.[12] Chen Yun, the veteran most influential in the economic policy arena, gave a hard-line speech stressing the conservative themes of grain farming, planning, opposition to corruption, and ideological work. Sharing the podium with Chen Yun, Deng Xiaoping made a conference speech that sounded very defensive ("Chen Yun's Speech at the CCP National Conference" 1985; "Deng Xiaoping's Speech" 1985). Feeling intense heat from the conservatives, Zhao Ziyang made a speech that defended the value of reform but took a cautious, centralizing approach to reform, leaving Hu Yaobang, who continued to be associated with contracting, politically isolated (Zhao Ziyang 1985). (During 1985 even Hu Yaobang took a more cautious line on reform: he remained silent about profit contracting and emphasized changes of the management team within enterprises as the key to running enterprises well [Yuan Baohua 1985].)

The September 1985 State Council regulations for invigorating large enterprises reflected Zhao's emphasis on improving internal management, not granting new powers or funds. The document reminded the managers of large enterprises that they already had benefited from the ten points on expanding enterprises' decision-making power ("State Council Decision on Measures" 1984), the

11.   In June 1985 Deng Xiaoping showed that he too was feeling the heat from the conservative elders when he made statements about the Special Economic Zones being experiments, not permanent institutions. Such statements signaled that he was hedging his commitment to a reform institution that he previously had supported unambiguously.
12.   Except for the resignation of Ye Jianying, the membership of the Standing Committee remained unchanged.

planning system reforms ("State Council Approves the State Planning Commission Circular" 1984), and the ten points on enterprise technical renovation ("Accelerate the Technical Progress and Technical Renovation of Existing Enterprises" 1984) promulgated in 1984. The way to enliven large enterprises was simply to implement these established policies, exercise the powers the enterprises had already been delegated, and carry out internal reforms to exploit their favorable conditions ("State Council Approves the SEC and Economic System Reform Commission Circular" 1985; Luo Yuanming 1985).[13]

The internal reforms urged on large enterprises laid the groundwork for the later return to enterprise profit contracting. The managerial responsibility system was based on a nested set of contract relationships in which subunits such as workshops and individual managerial personnel contracted to remit a certain amount of profit in return for a certain level of wages and other rewards. The factory manager signed a contract with the department that appointed him specifying his tenure, responsibilities, powers, rewards, and punishments ("State Council Approves the SEC and Economic System Reform Commission Circular" 1985; Chen Junsheng 1985). The contractual form of the relationship between different levels of the administrative hierarchy within firms, which of course was inspired by the successful agricultural responsibility system, was established in 1985. It was only a small step from the managerial responsibility system to the enterprise profit-contracting system when, in 1987, the fall of Hu Yaobang changed the political context.[14]

The Abortive Price Reform of 1986

During 1985 and 1986 the split in the ranks of reformist leaders and economists became more open and acrimonious (Xiao Jie 1986). A fierce debate about the rate of growth and macroeconomic control raged during 1985 simultaneously with the debate over the tax system and the invigoration of large enterprises. Hu Yaobang and some reformist economists (often labeled the "radical" reform

13. In his September 1985 Party Conference speech, the only external assistance Zhao promised large enterprises was the gradual reduction in adjustment tax rates and getting the corporations off their backs (Zhao 1985).
14. The managerial responsibility system and profit contracting were in effect the same thing for subordinate factories or branch factories that contracted with the main factory or corporation above them; see Dong Huanliang 1987.

group) adopted a kind of Chinese Keynesianism that defended rapid growth as necessary for structural reform. According to them, any excessive growth was due not to the dispersion of too much power and funds to the enterprises but to the absence of a mechanism like private ownership or contracting to give the enterprise a sense of financial responsibility. As they put it, "Investment expansion is government behavior, not enterprise behavior" (Yang Peixin 1987a). Some of the economists from the radical wing of the reformist movement came to believe that the only way to combine authority and responsibility in enterprises was to give them real property rights and eventually change their ownership (Hua Sheng, He Jiacheng et al. 1986a; Tong Zongkun 1986). Dong Furen, head of the Institute of Economics of the Chinese Academy of Social Sciences Institute of Economics, was a leader in the movement to reform enterprise property rights; Dong recruited a group of bright young economists (including Hua Sheng; see below) who were interested in using contracting as a transition to property rights reform (author's interviews). Li Yining, a Beijing University economics professor who advocated ownership reform, spent much time advising Hu Yaobang and his close ally in the Politburo, Hu Qili (author's interviews). The young economists in the State Council Research Institute on Economic System Reform (*Tigaisuo*) advocated contracting as a way to separate ownership from management—in other words, to give enterprises authority and responsibility while maintaining state ownership—but they backed away from full ownership reform, which they believed was politically infeasible (author's interviews).

Meanwhile, Zhao Ziyang, positioning himself as the cautious reformer, argued for tough contractionary policies to counteract the overheating of late 1984 and the first half of 1985. Zhao and his economist advisers, Liu Guoguang, Xue Muqiao, and Wu Jinglian, were alarmed by the massive issuance of credit at the end of 1984 and the inflation created by it (Zhao Ziyang 1985a).[15] Zhao's advisers argued that China needed a "comprehensive" (*peitao*) reform to establish a sound economic environment in which supply and demand were balanced and price signals were rational and that central controls over enterprise investments were a short-term necessity to

15. Wu Jinglian's interpretation of this debate and his own point of view are summarized in Wu Jinglian, Li Jiange, Ding Ningning, and Zhang Junkuo 1986 and in other essays collected in his *Explorations in Questions on Economic Reform* (Wu Jinglian 1987).

assure the long-term future of market reforms.[16] Zhao emphasized the prudence of his own approach to reform, making the implicit contrast with Hu Yaobang's rashness. He articulated this position on controlled growth in his March 1985 speech to the Third Session of the Sixth National People's Congress (Zhao Ziyang 1985a), in his speech to the September 1985 Party Conference (Zhao Ziyang 1985), and in his speech to the national planning conference in mid-January 1986 ("Zhao Outlines Tasks for 1986 Reform" 1986). Given the political and economic context—the strength of the conservative elders within the CCP and serious shortages, inflation, and deficits—Zhao Ziyang's point of view prevailed. By the September 1985 Party Conference Zhao had won the debate over macroeconomic policy (author's interviews).

The political and economic problem facing Zhao Ziyang in 1985 and 1986 was how to sustain the momentum of reform without counteracting contractionary policies. Zhao had to show progress on market reforms to demonstrate that he was a reformist—perhaps a cautious reformist, but a reformist nonetheless. If he wanted to build a coalition of support for the reform drive and for his own career, he could not afford to sound like a clone of Chen Yun. His speeches defended the reform drive: it was wrong to blame economic reforms for all the current economic and social problems, he argued (Zhao Ziyang 1985, 25). But his speeches also stressed the importance of moving ahead on reforms in a gradual, cautious manner ("feeling one's way across the river from stone to stone," *mozhe shitou guohe*) and warned against the "fallacy of rash advance," which everyone knew referred to the position of Hu Yaobang and the radical reformers ("Zhao Comments" 1985; "Reform Is Advancing" 1985).[17] Zhao groped for a reform agenda that would make economic sense and fit his political incentives.

16. Wu Jinglian's argument that market reform requires a loose economic environment—a buyer's market with supply slightly bigger than demand— is in part a political one: "To make the economic structural reform a success, it is imperative to let most people benefit from the reform. Nevertheless, as the economic results of the reform are only apparent after a period of time, during the process of reform we should have abundant materials and funds as reserve, to reduce the conflicts during the process of resolving economic interests" (Wu Jinglian 1987a, 8).
17. Among the newspaper articles published in 1985 stressing the importance of prudence in pursuing reforms, one attributed the failure of the late Ching dynasty one-hundred-day reforms to their rashness and lack of realism (Kong Xiangji 1985).

If the contractionary policies worked, perhaps this was the moment for price reform. The Third Plenum of the Twelfth Central Committee document in 1984 had made a commitment to price reform as "the key to the reform of the entire economic structure." Price reform was widely recognized among Chinese and foreign economists as a prerequisite for successful transition to market socialism. The existing administratively set prices were like "funny mirrors" (*haha jin*) that distorted reality and sent economic decision-makers perverse signals. Zhao's economic adviser, Wu Jinglian, believed that "the price mechanism is the pivot of the entire structure of market economy" (Wu Jinglian 1987a, 7). Wu insisted that the only way to have price reform without massive inflation was to combine it with strict monetary control.

Zhao Ziyang had always taken a cautious stance toward price reform. Early in the reform drive the premier had been persuaded by his advisers and by Eastern European and other foreign economists that successful market reform required price rationalization (author's interviews). He established a State Council Price Office in 1981 and directed it to calculate theoretical prices in 1982 (author's interviews). But fearing opposition from party conservatives if prices spiraled out of control and from the industrial ministries whose costs would go up with rising input prices, he was reluctant to tackle a large-scale price reform head-on. His willingness to expend political capital on price reform was questionable from the beginning, and his decision to create a two-track system by allowing enterprises to sell above-quota output at market prices was a pragmatic strategy designed to avoid bureaucratic conflict (author's interviews).

The two key choices in price reform are, first, whether to free prices and allow them to float according to the market or merely to adjust them administratively, and, second, whether to change prices in one giant step or in a series of small steps. Freeing prices in one fell swoop was never considered a politically feasible option in China. The debate concentrated on how to carry out price adjustments—all at once or gradually. "Gradually" was generally defined as over a period of five years or longer (author's interviews).

During 1984 a group of young economists tried to convince Zhao Ziyang to raise prices of raw materials and fuel (e.g., coal, timber, pig iron) in one giant step (Lou Jiwei and Zhou Xiaochuan 1984). They argued that the enterprises could afford the increase in costs and that forcing them to reduce waste and increase efficiency would be beneficial. Zhao Ziyang asked his senior aides and advisers to meet with the youngsters ("young-old dialogue," *qinglao duihua*) to consider the proposal. The Price Bureau, the MOF, and the SPC all did their own simulations of the effects of giant-step price adjustments, and they all reached the same conclusion: giant-step adjustments could spin the economy out of control, and therefore gradual adjustments were less risky.[18] The only voices raised in favor of one-shot drastic price rises were those of economists at various institutes and think tanks. Not surprisingly, Zhao and the officials were not persuaded that the economic and political risks of giant-step industrial price adjustments were justified (author's interviews).

As price rises for industrial inputs were discussed in bureaucratic meetings during 1984, the manufacturing industrial ministries insisted that the price increases be slow and gradual and that their enterprises be allowed to compensate for the cost increases by raising the prices of their own products (author's interviews). The main consuming industries that would be affected by increases in the prices of coal, timber, and pig iron were electric power, steel, railroads, and machine building, with steel, railroads, and electric power being the primary users of coal (author's interviews).

These preliminary discussions within the government bureaucracy of industrial price reform generated information about the attitudes of various ministries that gave early warning to Zhao Ziyang and other party leaders about how divisive the price issue was. In 1984 Zhao backed away from price reform and implemented the second stage of tax-for-profit without it, sticking with two-track prices instead. Zhao's 1985 plans for industrial price reform were very modest: a rise in the price of short-distance rail transport, price differentials permitted for goods of different quality and in different localities, and a continued reliance on the indirect two-track ap-

18. Key conservative central bureaucracies such as the SPC and Material Supply Bureau, although leery of drastic price reform measures, were basically sympathetic to the idea of price reform because the price differentials created by the two-track system had made it difficult for them to procure products for the plan. One solution proposed to the problem of enforcing plan procurement in the context of the two-track system was to move to a three-tier price system like that used in agriculture (one price for plan quota, a higher price for above-quota sales to the state, and another price for market sales). However, such a system was never introduced because it would have cost the state treasury too much (author's interviews).

proach for prices of raw materials and fuels (plan prices would remain unchanged, but producers would continue to be permitted to sell above-quota output on the market at floating prices; Zhao Ziyang 1985a, 700).[19]

How, then, can we explain the top CCP leadership's bold move in early 1985 to free urban prices of secondary agricultural produce (fruits and vegetables, meat and fish)? Of course, the liberalization of food prices was desirable from the standpoint of party leaders because it benefited farmers and reduced the government's financial burden of agricultural price subsidies.[20] But wasn't such a move politically dangerous? In other countries, food price rises always provoke more mass protest than do price rises of other products. If the CCP leadership was almost paranoid about the threat of social unrest caused by inflation, why would they risk raising the prices of food consumed by urban citizens when they were reluctant to raise the prices of products consumed only by factories?[21] The best explanation is that the main obstacle to price reform in China was delegation by consensus in bureaucratic policy-making and not the leaders' fear of social unrest. Raising the prices of industrial materials redistributed benefits away from manufacturing industries to extractive industries; the manufacturing industries would veto any such price increase unless they were compensated so that they were no worse off than before. By contrast, raising the prices of vegetables and meat threatened no central bureaucratic interests, only the interests of ordinary consumers who were not represented in the policy-making process. (From the viewpoint of local officials, however, rises in vegetable and meat prices were politically more dan-

19. The March 1985 national work conference on economic reform experiments reflected the same caution and concluded that when carrying out wage and price reform, the government could not lower its guard against loss of macroeconomic control ("State Council Office Issues a Circular" 1985, 677).

20. An earlier experiment with liberalizing prices of urban subsidiary food products in Guangdong had been very successful. The prices of vegetables and fish first rose but then dropped as production increased (author's interviews).

21. Six days after the Third Plenum of the Twelfth CCP Central Committee in 1984, which had issued a major communiqué declaring an intention to tackle the reform of irrational prices, there was a wave of urban consumer "panic buying." Coincidentally, many national government employees in Beijing had been given their annual clothing subsidy (of approximately twelve yuan) a few days after the plenum and rushed to the stores to acquire low-priced goods. Even this scare did not deter the CCP leadership from the urban food price liberalization in early 1985.

gerous than rises in the prices of industrial inputs. In most cities the 1985 liberalization of food prices was short-lived because local officials soon slapped on price controls to prevent consumer discontent.)

In 1986 Zhao Ziyang decided to work toward curbing inflation and getting control over the economy that he might lay the groundwork for major reform initiatives in 1987. Even without any major reforms of industrial prices, the price reform of urban nonstaple foodstuffs added to the excessive issuance of bank credit at the end of 1984 and resulted in serious inflation in 1985, when the urban consumer price index went up 11.9 percent (Naughton 1990). Zhao tried to reassure the bureaucracy and society by announcing at the January 1986 national planning conference that there would be no major reform initiatives and no new price reforms that year; instead, 1986 would be devoted to "consolidating, digesting, supplementing and improving on last year's reforms . . . and making preparations for larger steps in reforms over the next two years" ("Zhao Outlines Tasks for '86 Reform" 1986, 6). Vice Premier Tian Jiyun told the January meeting of party cadres in central government organs that the bureaucrats could relax: the State Council had decided that the main task of the 1986 price reform would be "to let all concerned digest and perfect measures that have already been put into effect so as to keep the general commodity price level basically stable" (Tian Jiyun 1986, K15).[22]

Despite Zhao Ziyang's record of avoiding conflict on redistributive issues such as price reform, his advisers believed that they had a mandate from him to work out a plan for comprehensive reform

22. In this speech Tian Jiyun told the government bureaucrats that he and Zhao would not "coerce" them to accept reforms but would instead let them "act at their own pace": "The overall reform of the economic structure is, in a sense, a readjustment of power and interests, in which a large amount of contradictions exist. Among them are the contradictions between the central authorities and the localities; between the state, the collective, and the individual; between one department and another; between one locality and another; between departments and localities; and so on and so forth. . . . Only by perfectly handling the various kinds of contradictions in the course of reform can the enthusiasm of all spheres for carrying out the reform be aroused and protected, and can the consolidation and development of a political situation in which there are stability and unity be promoted at the same time" (Tian Jiyun 1986, K21). In other words, Tian and Zhao promised not to override the bureaucratic policy-making process that required all reform policies to be approved by consensus.

centered on massive price adjustments during 1986 (unless otherwise noted, the following account is based on the author's interviews). At a January meeting of Zhao and his advisers to decide
reform strategies for the next five-year plan, four alternatives were
proposed (Wu Jinglian 1987b, 280–81): (1) privatization beginning
with small enterprises, which would be leased and eventually sold;
(2) a type of contracting for large enterprises, called the "asset management responsibility system" (*zichan jingying zerenzhi*), under
which managers would be evaluated according to how much they
had increased the value of enterprise assets during their tenure;[23]
(3) price reform beginning with housing prices; (4) comprehensive
reform beginning with price reform of raw material and transportation prices. Zhao Ziyang reviewed the proposals (he had received
written proposals ahead of time) and decided that the asset management responsibility system was not practical because it would
be impossible to determine the economic value of assets. He urged
that the two price reform proposals be combined to formulate a
comprehensive strategy centered on price rationalization. Beginning in February 1986 a group of Zhao's economic advisers formed
a planning group (*fangan ban*) to devise concrete measures for comprehensive reform of prices, taxes, and finance (banking reform
was added in May 1986). The planning group, formally established
in April 1986, was under Tian Jiyun and led by An Zhiwen, a cautious veteran who was the number two leader (under Zhao Ziyang)
of the Commission on Economic System Reform. During March and
April Zhao Ziyang came out in favor of comprehensive reform
based on price reform at meetings of the Finance and Economics
Small Group and Standing Committee of the State Council.

The planning group worked hard to come up with a set of specific price adjustments for raw materials, fuels, and transportation.
They referred to three sets of prices: two-track prices calculated
beginning in 1981 with the help of the Czech economists recommended by Ota Sik; world market prices; and Chinese free-market
prices. The group's tax proposal recommended greater reliance on
value-added taxes and restoration of the fixed asset and natural
resources taxes originally included in tax-for-profit. The financial
system proposal essentially was to assign different taxes to different

23. For a detailed explanation, see "The Draft Plan for Trial Implementation of the Assets Management Responsibility System" 1987; Hua Sheng,
He Jiacheng et al. 1986.

administrative levels and establish a new national tax collection agency. The banking proposal was for an independent banking system.

While Zhao's economic advisers worked out reform proposals in the planning group, pressure against this comprehensive approach to reform began to build from within the bureaucracy and to be expressed at national work conferences. At a national conference on urban reform organized by the Commission on Economic Structural Reform and the SEC in March 1986, many provincial and municipal officials complained loudly about the tight macropolicy. As Zhao's adviser Xue Muqiao described the scene, "The various localities cried production backslide and asked for more loans" (Xue Muqiao 1988, 19). There was a full-scale debate about the relative merits of the two-track price system and price reform and about the costs and benefits of fiscal decentralization. Local cadres pressed for more funds and power, and some of Zhao Ziyang's advisers criticized the trend toward localism by citing the negative example of Yugoslavia.

Despite his public commitment to tight macropolicy and comprehensive economic reform based on price reform, Zhao Ziyang caved in to the pressure from local officials. After the March work conference he (with the approval of the State Council) ordered the bank head Chen Muhua to turn the faucet and reopen the flow of credit for circulating capital (Yang Peixin 1989a, 14). Although this action was defended as "flexibility in the midst of contraction" (*jinzhong youhuo*), it was in fact a turnabout in monetary policy. The loosening of credit caused a rapid increase in the money supply and stimulated industrial growth.

Zhao Ziyang felt he could not deny the local officials this infusion of credit. After all, stringent contractionary policies had made the situation of local enterprises and governments desperate. And Zhao was well aware that local leaders were the largest bloc in the Central Committee, which held the formal authority to select leaders. Still, during spring 1986 Zhao appeared to hold the line against the pressure from big enterprises, localities, and the radical reformist economists in the Economic Reform Research Institute to replace his price reform strategy with some form of enterprise profit contracting. His planning group believed he still was genuinely committed to price reform.

According to two informants, in May 1986 the advocates of enterprise profit contracting pulled a fast one on Zhao Ziyang. When

Zhao traveled to Hubei to investigate the site of the proposed Three Gorges Dam, his aide, Bao Tong, suggested that he take along the young economist Hua Sheng, who favored enterprise contracting approaches to property rights reform. On the train Hua Sheng tried to persuade Zhao of the merits of the assets management responsibility system. To make it more practical, Hua introduced an idea he had gotten from another economist, namely a bidding system (*tou biao*) to solve the problem of evaluating assets: individuals would submit bids to serve as manager of a particular firm and take on the responsibilities and rewards specified in the managerial contract. Zhao was still not convinced. After the group returned from Hubei, Hua Sheng and his associates contacted reporters and launched a publicity blitz claiming that Zhao had approved the asset responsibility system. People in the planning group believed that actually Zhao did not change his mind and abandon price reform for contracting until the very end of 1986. But the impact of the May 1986 publicity was that more than one hundred experiments in assets management contracting were established in localities throughout the country.

In the summer of 1986 Deng Xiaoping began to talk about political reforms. Although his own notions of political reform were modest, Deng's initiative encouraged intellectuals to discuss radical democratic reform possibilities at public forums and in the press. The political motivation for Deng's actions during the summer of 1986 remains mysterious; his actions signaled a tilting toward reformists and away from party conservatives. The outraged conservatives leaned on Deng and got him to announce the indefinite postponement of political reforms at the Sixth Plenum of the CCP Central Committee in September 1986. The public debate on political reform sparked by Deng was widely believed to have encouraged large student prodemocracy protests in December 1986.

Deng's political reform initiative emitted confusing signals to his subordinates who had been delegated responsibility for economic policy-making. Did Deng's actions mean a tilting toward reform at the top party levels? What was the meaning of Deng's backing down on political reform in September? Party politicians and government bureaucrats must read the policy preferences of top party leaders and the power balance among them so they can shape their own proposals accordingly. During the second half of 1986 the information about CCP leadership politics was ambiguous. Hu Yaobang, already cast in the role of the rash reformer, barreled ahead in response to Deng's words about political reform, eagerly committing himself to political reform and urging his associates to speculate about China's democratic future almost without restraint. By contrast, Zhao Ziyang seemed uncertain how to behave. With characteristic caution, he did not come out in favor of radical political reforms, and he equivocated on price reform.

Given that Zhao Ziyang was feeling political pressure both from CCP conservatives and from reformist procontracting forces and that he had a record of avoiding political conflict on price reform, the planning group's draft proposals were unrealistic. Their plan called for giant-step price adjustments (*yibu daowei*, "reaching the correct level in one step") of a large number of producer goods (*duojia liandong*, "many prices revised at once"). The State Council Commission on Economic System Reform, which had long practice at anticipating the policy preferences of their political superiors, reshuffled the membership of the planning group to moderate its recommendations in June 1986.

In July 1986 the planning group's proposals were presented to a national work conference. The idea of a giant-step price adjustment of many industrial materials and fuels drew a great deal of fire. Some participants, such as the Capital Iron and Steel manager Zhou Guangwu, argued for profit contracting over price reform. Except for the producers of raw materials and the representatives of provinces where these materials were produced, almost no one was enthusiastic about price reform. The Shanghai officials were a notable exception.[24]

Most participants took for granted the necessity of compensating sectors and regions whose costs would be raised by input price adjustments. The only way to obtain bureaucratic consensus on price reform was to blunt its redistributive effects so that no one was made worse off than they were in their present situation. To avoid inflation of consumer prices, compensation would be provided not by allowing the industries that would be the hardest hit by the big increases to raise their own prices but by cutting their product tax rates. The tax breaks would protect the vested inter-

24. Shanghai officials may have calculated that given the comparatively good efficiency of Shanghai firms and high quality of Shanghai products, price reform would work for them in the long term. And because the burden of the adjustment tax fell particularly hard on them, they were eager to get rid of tax-for-profit.

ests of the consuming industries and maintain their original relative positions.[25]

Tax breaks for price reform would cost the central treasury. The increase in the prices of raw materials such as coal would reduce the center's burden of subsidizing coal mines and other extractive enterprises operating at a loss. But this financial gain would be more than offset by the reduction of profits of manufacturing enterprises, not to mention any cut in revenues from slashing product taxes. Some economists advocating price reform believed that "the central government should spend money for reform if it has to" (author's interviews).[26] But how much would it cost, and where was the money to come from?

The MOF expressed a commitment to the principle of price reform but announced regretfully that it simply could not afford it.[27] MOF officials calculated that between 1979 and 1986 various price adjustments already had cost the central treasury 300 billion yuan; more than 200 billion yuan had gone to subsidies for agricultural price increases (Tian Yinong et al. 1988, 98). At the 1986 work conference the MOF estimated that the large-scale adjustment of industrial input prices would cost them more than 20 billion yuan; facing a sizable budget deficit, they did not have the money for it. Arguing for the feasibility of the proposal, the planning group estimated the cost to be only 10 billion yuan. There was no resolution

25. One advocate of this pragmatic approach to winning a consensus on price reform disagreed with the young economists who insisted that enterprises absorb increased costs by raising their efficiency. He argued that efficiency had to do with competition within the same industry whereas price reform would have its greatest impact on the relative burdens and profitability of different industries (author's interview).
26. Some less pragmatic pro-price-reform economists insisted that enterprises should be pressured to absorb all the cost increases by improving efficiency. Other, more pragmatic ones proposed cutting product taxes, but only for those industries that could not tolerate the cost increases (e.g., they would not cut taxes for electrical consumer appliance manufacturers that don't use much raw material and have very high profits) and only to a lower-middle rate that protected the majority of enterprises in an industry. According to one pragmatist, if product taxes were not reduced, "the industries will make noise and ruin the reform" (author's interviews).
27. "For a long time we have recognized that price reform was beneficial to improving enterprise efficiency and raising financial revenue, but changing the comparative prices of various products naturally will have the effect of changing financial income and expenditures. Therefore, whether in China or any other socialist country, price reform cannot be separated from state financial support" (Tian Yinong et al. 1988, 97).

of the conflicting estimates, although the final outcome suggests either that government bureaucrats and party leaders found the MOF estimate more credible or that they accepted the larger estimate because they were averse to risk. The conference, while failing to reach a consensus on the proposed reform package, did not decisively kill it either.

After the contentious work conference the price reform proposal moved to the top leadership of the State Council.[28] The government leaders, headed by Zhao Ziyang, scrapped the large-scale price adjustment package and replaced it with a reform of steel prices only. This decision effectively gutted the comprehensive reform because the reforms of taxes and the financial system depended on adjusting the prices of all industrial materials, not just steel.

Obtaining bureaucratic consensus on a radically redistributive policy such as price reform was impossible in the absence of a strong, unified leadership commitment to the policy. During the 1986 deliberations about price reform Hu Yaobang and his profit-contracting alternative still lurked in the background. At the time, rumors of Hu's weakening political position were rife in Beijing. Party conservatives were obviously unhappy about the freewheeling discussions of democratic reforms encouraged by Hu. Deng Xiaoping himself had initiated these discussions, yet there were rumors that he was losing confidence in Hu. The officials I interviewed believed that when Hu Yaobang's position slipped in the summer of 1986, Zhao Ziyang's ambitions to succeed Deng Xiaoping as preeminent leader intensified; until then, although Zhao and Hu, as the two leading second-rung leaders, were competitors, Zhao's ambitions were limited by the reality that Hu as party general secretary was the presumptive heir, and Zhao had focused primarily on building a bureaucratic coalition of support for the reform drive. With his eyes now more focused on the succession contest and his rival slipping from favor, Zhao faced new dangers and opportunities. Imposing an unpopular policy on central government officials, many of whom also served in the selectorate, was now too risky for Zhao.

The planning group went back to calculate a detailed list of several thousand prices of steel products. In August 1986 the steel price adjustments were approved by a leadership meeting at Bei-

28. The proposal moved either to the Standing Committee of the State Council or to the Finance and Economics Small Group; the officials I interviewed were not sure which body made the decision.

daihe, the seaside resort where the Beijing leaders spend their summers. When the leaders returned to Beijing, Zhao Ziyang's will failed. In the end he carried out no price reform at all, not even one limited to steel.

According to Hua Sheng, a young economist who advocated contracting, "The 1986 project to take joint actions in the field of prices, taxes, and finance miscarried owing to the failure to balance the interests of different groups" (Hua Sheng, Zhang Xuejun, Luo Xiaopeng 1988, no. 9:30). The comprehensive reform package, designed to create a fair environment for enterprise competition, sank like tax-for-profit into what Hua Sheng called the "Bermuda Triangle" of prices, taxes, and finance (Hua Sheng, Zhang Xuejun, Luo Xiaopeng 1988, no. 9:27). The failure of Zhao Ziyang's 1986 comprehensive reform initiative demonstrated once again the inability of Chinese authoritarian bureaucratic institutions to make policies that redistribute benefits among sectors and regions. A redistributive policy stands a chance only if the government has the financial wherewithal to buy off those who stand to lose by the policy or if the party leadership is united and strongly committed to the policy. By backing away from price reform, even one limited in scope, Zhao Ziyang retained central bureaucratic support for the reform drive; but he lost the chance to dramatically improve enterprise efficiency by rationalizing prices.

The Fall of Hu Yaobang, Zhao Ziyang's About-face, and the Victory of Profit Contracting

By the end of 1986 Zhao Ziyang apparently had decided that comprehensive reform was political suicide. He began spending more time with his procontracting aides and advisers such as Bao Tong and Chen Yizi (head of the State Council Research Institute on Economic System Reform) and, through them, with radical economists such as Li Yining, who advocated ownership reform. Li Yining said to Zhao that the current failure of economic reform was due to the failure of price reform, but that the success of price reform could not lead to the success of economic reform (Zhang Weiguo 1988; author's interviews). The argument was based on both political pragmatism and economic theory: policies such as price reform could never win a consensus of support; only policies that did not challenge the vested interests of any group stood a chance. Even if prices were rationalized, enterprises would be unable to respond to them unless they had real autonomy. Anyway, two-track pricing, which already existed, gave market signals to enterprises (Wu and Reynolds 1987, 11).

After the disillusioning experience of price reform Zhao Ziyang was receptive to Li Yining's ideas and turned his attention from the economic environment to enterprise enlivening. The State Council issued a December 1986 directive, "Some Decisions on Deepening Enterprise Reform and Strengthening Enterprise Invigoration," which emphasized the separation of ownership from management as the key to enterprise reform and suggested three methods of separating ownership from management: leasing all small enter- prises and the medium-sized enterprises that were running at a loss or earning small profits; implementing various forms of contracted management responsibility in large and medium-sized enterprises; and experimenting with shareholding in some suitable large and medium-sized enterprises (Liu Tonglin et al. 1987, 219). That same month Zhao ordered a number of large cities (including Shanghai, Beijing, Wuhan, Shenyang, and Chongqing) to experiment with shareholding in some enterprises (author's interviews).[29] Zhao ap- peared to have concluded that universalistic approaches to reform were a lost cause; they did not receive strong support even from the MOF or conservative party leaders such as Chen Yun. Zhao was hitting his head against the stone wall of the Chinese bureaucracy, and he was doing neither the reform drive nor his own political career any good.

In early January 1987 the party octogenarians told Deng Xiaoping that CCP Secretary Hu Yaobang had gone too far and had to be fired. Hu's encouragement of open debate about democratic reform and the massive student prodemocracy demonstrations in Decem- ber 1986 stimulated by this debate threatened party rule and social stability. Although Hu's specific economic policy positions were not a publicly stated reason for his dismissal, his impulsive actions in both the political and economic realm were cited as reasons by the Politburo. Hu's ouster threw the plans for leadership succession and the reform drive into disarray. Deng tried to preserve the future of reforms by appointing Zhao Ziyang as CCP general secretary,

29. This experiment drew a lot of opposition for threatening to disperse the financial power of the central state. Some of the radical reformists in the Research Institute on Economic System Reform, a delegation of whom had learned about the institutional complexity of capital markets during a recent visit to the United States, advised against the shareholding experi- ment because Chinese conditions were not yet ripe (author's interviews).

but the elderly hard-liners insisted that Vice Premier Li Peng be moved up to be premier at the same time.[30]

. With Hu out of the picture the succession contest was set differently, with Zhao the market reformer versus Li the central planner.[31] In economic policy Zhao went all-out to play the reformer, building a constituency among the two groups who had benefited from reforms—provincial and municipal officials, especially from coastal regions, and the industrial officials linked to large enterprises. As a provincial politician lacking a national network of clients, Zhao was anxious to inherit Hu Yaobang's extensive network by making common cause with them. Zhao's strategy for transferring the allegiance of Hu's clients to himself was to adopt Hu Yaobang's position in favor of enterprise contracting and to exploit the extensive patronage opportunities offered by enterprise contracting.[32]

Zhao's shift toward what in China had become defined as a more radical reformist position (enterprise contracting) from what had become defined as a more conservative reformist position (comprehensive reform) would not have been predicted by a spatial model of Chinese elite political competition. With Hu positioned as the radical reformer, Zhao previously had been forced to play both sides of the fence in the selectorate, trying to appear as a committed reformer to the local officials and industrial officials and as a cautious protector of central state interests to the conservative elders and MOF and SPC officials. But with Hu gone and Li Peng now the opposition, Zhao automatically became the reformer; Hu's pro-reform constituency had no choice but to stick with Zhao, and Zhao could use the threat of capitulating to Li Peng's supporters to keep the proreform elements in line more easily than he could before. In a spatial model Zhao Ziyang would have had no incentive to change his stance from comprehensive reform to profit contracting.

30. As CCP general secretary, Zhao was principal and Premier Li Peng the agent, but Zhao himself was the agent of Deng Xiaoping and the elders who continued to exercise authority at the top of the party.
31. Under the hegemony of the reform ideology, it was politically impossible for conservative types such as Chen Yun or Li Peng to advocate a return to the pre–Cultural Revolution centrally planned economy, but they clearly favored a version of reform that preserved central economic control.
32. Zhao never formally abandoned the policy aimed at price reform. The current priority on enterprise contracting was justified as a way to deal with the immediate problems of an overheated economy, to reduce the scale of construction and control inflation, and thereby to create the favorable conditions for carrying out price reform several years later (Xue Muqiao 1988, 19).

Why, then, did Zhao Ziyang shift his position on enterprise reform? Why didn't the spatial logic hold? Several explanations for Zhao's about-face toward profit contracting suggest themselves. One is that victory in leadership competition in China may depend more on clientalist politics than on bureaucratic constituency politics (see chapter 4). Particularistic policies that enable contenders to nourish their network of clients with patronage trump more standardized policies that please some bureaucratic groups but not others. Zhao saw a good opportunity to take over Hu's clientalist network by pushing the particularistic approach of enterprise contracting.[33]

Another explanation was that Zhao had learned from the debacle of price reform and the unraveling of the tax-for-profit compromise that redistributive formulas could not achieve genuine, lasting consensus in the Chinese political system unless party leaders were in strong agreement on them. In the context of leadership competition the leader who promotes such policy formulas does no political good for himself. Anticipating competition and disagreement between Li Peng and himself, Zhao Ziyang abandoned the quixotic hope of comprehensive reform for the more realistic course of contracting, which offered Zhao a better way to make a dramatic "breakthrough" in reform (Ai Feng and Dai Yuqing 1988, 35). In contrast to standardization reforms that made almost everyone unhappy, enterprise contracting made almost everyone happy.

Zhao Ziyang made the invigoration of large and medium-sized enterprises the centerpiece of his National People's Congress speech in March 1987 and announced in that speech his support of the contracted management responsibility system (*chengbao jingying zirenzhi*) as the best method to achieve this invigoration (Zhao Ziyang 1987c). In May 1987 Zhao Ziyang visited Liaoning, where his enthusiasm for contracting was fueled by provincial officials who touted the dramatic success of their contracting experiments (author's interviews). Throughout 1987 Zhao continued to advocate contracting (Zhao Ziyang 1987a; 1987b); it was a point of emphasis in his November 1987 Thirteenth Party Congress speech (1987). By 1988 contracting had become Zhao's own personal policy, so much so that the official world of Beijing had a saying, "There are two things that, like the tiger's rear, one does not dare touch, Deng

33. Andrew Nathan (1973) argues that given the personal nature of patron-client ties, factions cannot be inherited.

Xiaoping's 'mao' (cat) and Zhao Ziyang's 'bao' (contract system)" (Hood 1988, 25).[34]

Many of the radical reformist economists previously associated with Hu Yaobang favored contracting only as a way station to ownership reform.[35] But Zhao Ziyang recognized that the hard-liners at the top of the party who had shown their strength by ousting Hu Yaobang would never go along with dismantling state ownership; he told his advisers that ownership reform was dead (author's interviews). Instead, Zhao advocated contracting as a broadly acceptable method to combine state ownership with a commodity economy.[36] The government would delegate managerial power to enterprise managers while retaining state ownership (Zhao Ziyang 1987b). Still, some radical economists continued to view contracting as a transitional method; over the years, as the enterprise's own capital investments came to constitute a larger and larger share of the enterprise's assets, the enterprise would in effect come to own itself (Xiao Zhuoji 1987, 10).[37]

The managers and industrial bureaucrats linked to large and medium-sized enterprises welcomed contracting because it voided tax-for-profit, with its hated adjustment tax, and allowed enterprises to keep more profits. The lobbying effort against tax-for-profit by the managers of large enterprises, the industrial ministries, and the SEC had succeeded, and all of them were sure that the shift to contracting would result in more money remaining in the hands of managers. There were several different types of enterprise contracts, some of which committed the enterprise to pay the state a fixed amount or percentage of their earnings and one, called progressive profit contracting (*dizeng lilun baogan*), that committed the enterprise to pay an increasing percentage to the state each year.

34. Deng Xiaoping's "cat" refers to Deng's famous statement of pragmatism over ideology: "It doesn't matter whether a cat is black or white so long as it catches mice."
35. As one radical reformist economist said, "We pushed contracting because we couldn't find any better method to resolve the ownership problem . . . and it was a step on the way to a joint-stock system" (author's interview).
36. Although Zhao Ziyang adopted Hu's procontracting position, he was anxious to avoid alienating the elders and therefore took a much more orthodox line on political-ideological issues than Hu Yaobang had done (for example, see Zhao 1987e).
37. As David Granick (1990) notes, property rights in China are determined by who paid for the capital investments.

Even with the latter system, which was used by the model enterprise Capital Iron and Steel, managers were confident in their ability to prosper. They could use their political clout to negotiate favorable baselines and percentages with financial officials. Once they were given a real profit incentive and the authority to make their own investment decisions, they were bound to grow and earn more money than they did when their hands were tied by the state.[38]

Managers also favored contracting because it would enhance their independence from corporation and bureau officials who interfered in enterprise operations and appropriated enterprise funds. The contracting method included a formal delegation of personnel and other managerial authority to the enterprise manager. Once the enterprise's obligations to the state were fixed in a notarized contract, the enterprises would have a legal basis for resisting additional bureaucratic demands (Liu Tonglin et al. 1987).

In addition, managers viewed contracting as the "best way to solve discrepancies among enterprises in their history and environment during the process of transition" (Qiu Siyi 1987)—in other words, as the solution to the problem of the "gap between suffering and happiness." Instead of using the standardization approach of tax-for-profit to create a level playing field, they preferred the flexibility of enterprise contracting (Liu Tonglin et al. 1987).[39] Under a

---

38.   "The results of investments made by enterprises themselves are better than those made in a concentrated and unified way by the state" (Yang Peixin 1989a, 15).

39.   As one contracting advocate explained, "Some comrades held that the contract system is not a standardized reform. . . . The targets of contracts and the responsibility, power, and interest of the enterprises are not measured by the same yardstick. They are decided by each enterprise according to its own subjective and objective conditions and using different yardsticks. The state will take more from enterprises whose profit is large, take less from enterprises whose profit is small, and subsidize some loss-suffering enterprises. . . . The practice over the past few years indicates that due to the irrational price system, poor market environment, and the lack of scientific macroeconomic management, enterprises lack a rational operational mechanism. If we conduct standardized reform under these conditions, we will cause large gaps between suffering and happiness in different trades and different enterprises that are formed in an organic way. This appears to be equality, but in essence is inequality. Therefore we must find some transitional forms under which enterprises not only have clear responsibility, power, and interest, but can also maintain a flexible regulatory mechanism in handling the relationships of interest between the state, collectives, and individuals. The contract system is a form of business man-

particularistic bargaining system the managers trusted in their ability to negotiate with higher-level officials to protect their firm's competitive position.

Theoretically, the contracted management responsibility system was supposed to establish once and for all the enterprise's full responsibility for its losses as well as profits, a prospect that hardly would have been welcomed by managers if they had believed in it. In principle, the contract was to remain fixed for three to five years regardless of changes—for instance, price hikes—in the economic environment. A portion of retained profits would be reserved as a "risk preparedness fund" (*fengxian zhunbei jin*) to enable the firm to meet its financial obligations in the face of economic uncertainty (Ren Kelei et al. 1987). Such an arrangement obviously would have put enterprises under greater financial risk; some versions of contracting would even have created personal liability for managers.[40] Why, then, were industrial managers so enthusiastic about contracting? Because they never believed that a contracting system with real teeth would ever be implemented; they predicted that they would be able to renegotiate their contracts to compensate for any external factors that reduced their revenues (Liu Tonglin et al. 1987), and they were right. Under the contracting system, enterprises contracted only for profits and not for losses. They faced no more risk than they had under any previous rules, and the version of contracting assigning personal liability to managers never got off the ground.

The industrial bureaucracies also preferred contracting to tax-for-profit. Under tax-for-profit the taxes of centrally administered enterprises were paid to the MOF. But under contracting, enterprise profits and taxes were pooled, and the profits and taxes of enterprises run by ministries were channeled through the ministries to the state, just as they had been under the original command economy. This arrangement enabled ministries to carry out redistribution among their enterprises and to skim some development funds off the top before paying the MOF. Contracting reinforced the financial control of ministries and bureaus over their subordinate enterprises and was congruent with the ministerial contract deals that some ministries had obtained. This authority to negotiate with en-

---

agement that has been developed to meet this kind of special need" (Zuo Mu 1987, K21).

40. In one Shenyang experiment, factory managers were required to list their family property and one-third of their annual income as collateral ("Shenyang Plant Directors" 1986).

terprises over their contract terms gave individual industrial officials the power to construct networks of clients among enterprise
managers.

Local officials favored enterprise contracting for the same reasons. Under tax-for-profit, taxes from all enterprises, regardless of
which level "owned" them, had been paid to the central treasury,
with the locals receiving a share of the total. Contracting restored
the financial linkage between local governments and their enterprises; local governments retained all the remitted profits of the
enterprises they "owned" (Ding Xuedong 1987; Qiu Siyi 1987).

The flexibility of enterprise contracting created even greater political opportunities for local officials than for ministerial officials.
Under tax-for-profit, enterprise tax rates (except for the adjustment
tax) were fixed, and local governments simply served as tax collectors for the central government, taking a set share of the tax revenues. But under profit contracting, the provincial and municipal
governments had the power to allocate financial obligations to the
enterprises they managed through industrial bureaus. This system
gave local officials the opportunity to promote their own careers by
building political machines based in the industrial bureaucracy.

Enterprise contracting was truly a policy with something for
everyone. Not only was it attractive to the key groups in the reform
coalition, namely, local politicians and industrial managers and bureaucrats, but it also offered some advantages to normally conservative central bureaucrats in the SPC and MOF.

The appeal of enterprise contracting to Beijing officials worried
about macroeconomic control was obvious. In the first quarter of
1987 enterprise economic performance was poor. The longtime advocates of profit contracting in the SEC made the case for the
method primarily as a mechanism to regulate enterprise behavior.
Under profit contracting, the SEC officials argued, it would be possible to achieve the objectives of the current campaign for "Double
Increase and Double Savings"—that is, to raise production and
practice economy, raise revenues and reduce expenditures ("The
Momentum in the Development of 'Dual Increase and Dual Reduction' Is Good" 1987). An official from the Jilin Provincial Planning
Commission, on the basis of his province's experience with the
method since 1983, made the case that contracting enhanced strict
control over enterprise capital construction. By specifying in each
enterprise's contract what percentage of its retained profits it could
spend for various purposes, including reinvestment for capital con-

struction, the government strengthened its hand over enterprise expansion (Qiu Siyi 1987). Planners also realized that they could introduce procurement quotas, energy conservation targets, and other stipulations into contracts to make it easier to enforce the plan.[41]

Enterprise contracting resembled central planning in that it was an ad hoc negotiated exchange arrangement between different levels of industrial administration; and like central planning, enterprise contracting enabled the state to control enterprise behavior. From the perspective of central planners, enterprise contracting was a good way to achieve a combination of "macroeconomic control" and "microeconomic flexibility" (Ai Feng and Dai Yuqing 1988, 36; Zhou Shulian 1988, 8).

The MOF continued to defend tax-for-profit against the contracting trend during 1987 (author's interviews), but it was no match for the combined forces of industrial and local interests. Vice Premier Tian Jiyun, who had spearheaded the tax-for-profit effort for Zhao Ziyang and who continued to defend the policy against the contracting onslaught, was demoted from his position as executive vice premier. Formally speaking, tax-for-profit was never abrogated. An enterprise's tax obligation was calculated according to the tax rules and then combined with a profit-sharing deal so that the enterprise handed over a lump sum to the government. But because both the center and the enterprise were guaranteed the level of revenues they had received the previous year (1986), the tax rules lost their force.[42] The MOF complained that under contracting, "the actual tax rate . . . is determined by negotiations between the competent department and the enterprises" (Xu Jian 1989, 29). The MOF tried to protect the integrity of the tax system by arguing that at the very least, taxes ought to be collected independently of profits instead

41. Soon after contracting was implemented, the State Statistical Bureau reported that industrial enterprises were doing a better job than previously in fulfilling their plan procurement quotas of steel, coal, timber, cement, and other key materials (Guo Zhongshi 1988). But just months later the SPC complained that enterprise procurement quotas for these materials were not being fulfilled by enterprises ("Enterprises Fail to Fulfill Contract Obligations" 1988).

42. Moreover, enterprises continued to be allowed to repay bank loans before paying taxes, thereby creating a perverse incentive to expand credit and stimulate enterprise expansion. One proposal, never implemented, was to force enterprises to repay loans from after-tax earnings by compensating them with a reduction in their total tax rates to 35 or 40 percent (Lu Baifu 1988).

of being pooled with profits as they were under the contracting system (Ding Xuedong 1987).[43]

MOF opposition was muted when in the last three quarters of 1987, after contracting was implemented, the profits and taxes handed over to the state treasury increased by 7.4 percent over the same period of the preceding year.[44] Although they preferred on principle a legalized tax system to a particularistic contracting system, they had to accept the fact that contracting was the only politically feasible way to resolve the contradiction between enterprise enlivening and state revenue (Yang Peixin 1987). The central treasury simply could not afford any of the other alternatives, such as maintaining the tax system but cutting the tax rates or implementing comprehensive price reform.[45] Enterprise contracting might not be a perfect system, but at least it guaranteed that the center would receive no less revenue than it had previously received.[46] And the progressive profit-contracting system, which was implemented on a widespread basis in 1987, gave the center a fixed claim on the growth in enterprise profits as well.[47]

The enterprise contracting system was approved and implemented smoothly and rapidly, in marked contrast to the bureaucratic obstacles that had impeded the previous tax and price reform initiatives.

43. Under such an arrangement the enterprise would pay taxes according to set rates, and then at the end of the year the tax department would refund to the enterprise the proper amount based on its contract (Fang Xiaoqiu 1987, 13). The State Council regulations on contracting included this arrangement ("Provisional Regulations" 1988).

44. One MOF spokesman, looking back on 1987, acknowledged that contracting "at the beginning played a positive role in preventing a drastic drop in financial revenue" (Xu Jian 1989, 29).

45. One MOF official said that the ideal tax system would require the unification of tax categories and reduction of tax rates, abolition of all tax exemptions and preferences, and requirement that loans be repaid from after-tax funds. But because the central budget deficit prevented the MOF from increasing enterprise after-tax retained profits, the ministry was unable to impose any improvements in the tax system on the enterprises. In this situation the only thing they could do was go with contracting and flexible methods for the time (Ding Xuedong 1987).

46. "The contracting system does not require the state to reduce taxes or profits. It takes the tax or profit handed to the state in the previous year or three years before as the base, and the promised amount increases year after year; it is a guarantee, not a reduction of financial income" (Yang Peixin 1989, 40).

47. According to one official, the adoption of progressive profit contracting was designed to win the support of the MOF for the contracting approach (author's interview). But one MOF official in a 1987 article opposed the popularization of the progressive profit-contracting method (Ding Xuedong 1987).

The industrial ministries and localities were for it, and it did not cost the MOF anything. After Zhao Ziyang announced his support for contracting approaches to invigorating large enterprises in his National People's Congress speech of March 1987, many large and medium-sized enterprises began to "experiment" with the method. Zhao asked the State Council Commission on Economic System Reform (administered by the prominent contracting advocate An Ziwen) and the SEC (headed by another contracting enthusiast, Lu Dong) to convene several conferences to discuss the method (author's interviews). In March, Zhao urged that an SEC report advocating the contracting method be widely disseminated and discussed; according to one report, the central authorities (presumably the State Council) "having fully weighed the advantages and disadvantages" of contracting, decided to introduce it throughout the country (Ai Feng and Dai Yuqing 1988, 35). This decision, announced at the April conference of provincial governors, was greeted enthusiastically ("Advantages of the Contracted Management Responsibility System" 1987; Ai Feng and Dai Yuqing 1988). Later that month the SEC drew up the specific measures to implement the contracting method, including five different contracting methods (Ai Feng and Dai Yuqing 1988; author's interviews).[48] In July, Lu Dong promoted contracting as the focus of the "Double Increase and Double Savings" campaign at a national meeting to exchange experiences in carrying out the campaign ("Four Thousand Large and Medium-Sized Enterprises" 1987); the next day the *People's Daily* reported that the leadership of the State Council confirmed Lu Dong's views ("Enterprise Contracting Method" 1987). At the end of June 1987 an SEC survey of twenty-eight provincial-level units found that 4,046 of the total of 7,814 large and medium-sized industrial enterprises (51.8 percent) had already implemented some type of enterprise contracting system (Lu Zhihui 1987, 277; "Four Thousand Large and Medium-Sized Enterprises" 1987). By the end of the year 76 percent of large and medium-sized industrial enterprises and 75 percent of all state-owned industrial enterprises were using contracting, and Zhao Ziyang was commending the SEC for its work in popularizing the method ("Enterprise Contracted Management Wins a Great Breakthrough in 1987" 1988).[49]

48. The State Council approved the "Provisional Regulations Governing the Contracted Managerial Responsibility System Among Publicly Owned Industrial Enterprises" (1988) drawn up by the SEC in February 1988.
49. Only 8 percent of state enterprises were using progressive profit contracting ("Reform of State-Run Enterprises" 1987).

At first the contracting method was described as a "transitional form" to cope with the present situation ("Beneficial Both to the Enterprise and the State" 1987, K14; Zuo Mu 1987, 21), but by the end of 1987 the *People's Daily* was reassuring managers that it was a "long-term policy" and not just an "expedient measure" ("Perfecting the Contracted Management Responsibility System" 1987, 22). And during 1988 the contracting "wind" blew even harder, with schools, beauty parlors, military units, and, indeed, every kind of work unit rushing to get more power and money by signing their own contracts.

The only minor controversy that arose during the formulation of contracting policies was over the idea to evaluate managers by how much they had increased the value of enterprise assets (the assets management responsibility system), a concept originally proposed by Hua Sheng and other radical reformist economists. When the SEC came up with its list of approved types of enterprise contract methods, it did not include the assets management responsibility system because it was too cumbersome (Ren Kelei et al. 1987; author's interviews; "Provisional Regulations" 1988). Moreover, the SEC wanted to avoid provoking concerns about eroding state ownership by raising the issue of the dispensation of the assets purchased with retained enterprise profits (author's interviews). In May some of Zhao Ziyang's advisers who favored comprehensive price reform over contracting criticized the one-on-one bargaining feature of contracting as arbitrary. The terms of the contract depended more on the bargaining ability and personal connections of the manager than on any economic factors.

Zhao Ziyang responded by retrieving the bidding idea from Hua Sheng's plan while leaving out the other parts of the plan dealing with enterprise assets.[50] Managerial positions would be advertised and open to competitive bidding by individuals who desired to serve. The hiring of managers and the setting of contract targets would be accomplished simultaneously. Competitive bidding would eliminate the subjectivity of contracting and make it a fair, impartial system.[51]

50. Hua Sheng and his colleagues nevertheless continued to advocate the assets management responsibility system; for example, see He Jiacheng and Bian Yongzhuang 1987 (4). But the method was not popular and few enterprises adopted it (Lin Ling 1988).
51. In theory, bids were supposed to be received and evaluated by a Bid Assessment Committee including specialists from the same industry (social specialists) and workers' representatives as well as officials from the responsible bureau (Lu Dong 1988). According to one view, the workers' representatives should constitute at least one-third of the committee (Mi-

From May 1987 on, the official policy on contracting articulated by Zhao Ziyang, the SEC, and everyone else was to make competitive bidding an integral part of the contract method ("Zhao Ziyang Converses" 1987; "Enterprise Contracting Method" 1987; "Key Point of Contracting" 1988). However, as Zhao himself acknowledged, most of the time competitive bidding was omitted when the contracting method was implemented or what was called competitive bidding was not genuinely competitive ("Key Point of Contracting" 1988). The regulations requiring competitive bidding were rarely enforced ("Provisional Regulations" 1988). One important reason for this lackadaisical enforcement was the reluctance of the CCP Organization Department to see its power to appoint cadres diluted.[52]

Although Zhao Ziyang's public advocacy of the contracting method was unambiguous, he privately told some of his advisers that he wished he could find a way to combine the economic advantages of price reform with the political advantages of contracting. Zhao recognized the importance of price reform but told his advisers that no statesman could carry it out unless he operated under martial law. Therefore, he said, "We must figure out a way to avoid price reform but still have a market economy" (author's interviews). During the summer of 1987 a few economists suggested calculating "decision-making prices," shadow prices "that could be used to evaluate enterprise performance and reduce the subjective element in contracting." Zhao liked the idea and asked the SPC to calculate the prices; however, the idea was technically complicated and was never implemented (author's interviews).

Why Another Attempt at Price Reform in 1988 Never Stood a Chance

The contracted management responsibility system was a policy equilibrium in the Chinese political system. It could defeat any

---

croeconomic Research Office 1988). Bidding was intended to "safeguard the steady increase in state financial revenue" (Zuo Mu 1987, K24). The competition among managerial aspirants and the participation of specialists from outside the responsible bureau in evaluating contracts were mechanisms to protect state interests by weakening the monopoly power of the enterprise in the bargaining process.

52. The CCP Organization and Personnel departments issued a circular stating that although selecting managers through a bidding scheme was good for small and medium-sized enterprises, large enterprises should introduce it only gradually as an experiment, and very large enterprises should not use it at all ("Organization Department and Personnel Department" 1988, 37).

standardization policy such as tax reform or price reform. The particularism of the contracting approach offered short-term political opportunities for building support networks to Chinese politicians from top to bottom of the political system. Contracting was favored by industrial and local interests and was acceptable to central planning and finance officials. It was easy to obtain bureaucratic consensus on contracting because it was nonredistributive, allowing sectors, localities, and enterprises to hang onto their original relative positions. Both reformists and conservatives, both Zhao Ziyang and Li Peng, recognized its political advantages. When Zhao Ziyang began advocating enterprise contracting in 1987, Li Peng did not publicly disagree. In fact, at a February 1988 national conference on the system both Zhao Ziyang and Li Peng spoke in favor of the policy ("Li Peng Pushes Contract System at Forum" 1988).

The economic logic of contracting was not nearly as compelling as its political logic. By allowing enterprises to get more power and profits and avoid risk, contracting did not pressure managers to improve industrial efficiency. By giving managers an incentive to increase profits by expanding capacity, rewarding workers, and raising prices, contracting contributed to overheating and inflation. But despite its disappointing economic results, the system was unshakable. Too many bureaucratic actors had developed a vested interest in the perpetuation of this version of partial reform.

From 1987 on, economic criticisms of enterprise contracting were heard from all quarters. Press articles on contracting invariably concluded with a list of the method's shortcomings that needed to be resolved. Yet almost no one except some economists and some people in the MOF suggested that the method be scrapped. The imperfections of contracting identified in the press included:

Particularism. The contents and form of management contracts varied from enterprise to enterprise, industry to industry, and locality to locality. The contracting regulations allowed wide latitude in the contents of the contract and the way base quotas and sharing rates were calculated ("Provisional Regulations" 1988). Every enterprise operated according to different rules. According to one survey of twenty cities, more than thirty different forms of contracts were being used (Xu Yaozhong 1988, 41). The contracting method was too arbitrary to discriminate between well and poorly run enterprises. A manager could more easily increase a firm's retained profits by bargaining down the base figure or remittance rate than by cutting costs or increasing sales.

No genuine competitive bidding. Supervising bureaus either did not use bidding at all or used it in a phony, unfair way, "inviting tenders in name but designating certain applicants in reality." When they hired managers, bureau officials relied too much on personal relationships and feelings and discriminated against applicants from outside their own unit ("Contract Dispensor" 1988).

Contracts as "unequal treaties." Contracts between different levels in the administrative hierarchy were not contracts between equals but were imposed unilaterally on lower levels by higher levels (Wu Fumin and Yu Xi 1988). The contract became a pretext for administrative interference in enterprise management and strengthened, not weakened, subordinate relationships.

Too many targets. Enterprise profit contracts were gradually replaced by comprehensive contracts including many different economic targets (Xu Yaozhong 1988; Microeconomic Research Office 1988). The regulations left open the variety of targets to be included in contracts ("Provisional Regulations" 1988). Government planners and industrial officials enforced control over enterprise behavior by loading the contract with such items as plan targets, cost reduction targets, and specifications of the use of retained profits. Contracting came more and more to resemble mandatory planning.

Contract changes caused by external fluctuations. Any changes in the Chinese economy, such as price rises or devaluation of the renminbi, affected contracts by raising production costs. Increasing inflation in 1987 and 1988 put contracts under strain, and many managers demanded the renegotiation of their contracts ("Rising Prices" 1988).[53] Although contracts were supposed to remain stable for at least three years ("Provisional Regulations" 1988), many of them were renegotiated every year.

Lack of risk. Although the original vision of management contracts was to force managers to confront the risk of going out of business, this tough version of contracting was never implemented.[54] When they were facing financial difficulties, managers

---

53. Commitment to the halfway house of contracting made people highly resistant to price reform. As one procontracting economist said, "The implementation of the contract system needs a stable external environment rather than drastic changes. However, price reform will certainly cause some changes in such a stable external environment. This is a contradiction" (Li Jun 1988, 40). See also Ren Kelei et al. 1987.

54. One of the rare instances when the tough version of contracting was seriously discussed was at a July 1988 national meeting on the contract method ("Zhao Ziyang at Contract Responsibility Symposium" 1988). This meeting occurred during the period when Zhao Ziyang was under intense

simply renegotiated their contracts. The idea of making the manager personally accountable never got far because the personal assets of individual managers were insignificant compared with the assets of state-run enterprises (Qiu Yuan 1987). Because the current version of contracting did not change state ownership of factory assets, even those purchased with retained profits, the responsibility for potential bankruptcy still fell on the state, which had every reason to avoid it. Profit incentives without risk led managers to make poor decisions.

Short-term perspective. One consequence of not allowing enterprises to own the assets they purchased was that managers spent retained profits on worker bonuses and nonproductive construction—items of short-term value—instead of investing to improve productive capability.[55] Some officials compared Chinese factory managers to trade union heads in foreign countries; the goal of both is to put as much money as possible into workers' pockets (author's interviews).

Incentive to raise prices. Under contracting, enterprises could increase their retained profits if they increased their total profits by raising the prices of their products. These managerial incentives contributed to worsening inflation during 1987 and 1988.

Conflicts between managers and workers. The most widely used form of contracting involved signing contracts with individual managers. Under this arrangement firm employees had no responsibility and cared mainly about their own present income. Some managers sensed employee resentment of the managerial bonuses written into contracts and therefore declined them. The wages of employees and managers were governed by egalitarianism. The employees, not comprehending the risks managers faced, discouraged managers from receiving what they were entitled to ("Jilin's Gao Di on Income of Contractors" 1987). Economists such as Jiang Yiwei proposed solving this problem by letting the employees contract for an enterprise and then hire a manager themselves. Zhao Ziyang expressed sympathy for this idea (Jiang Yiwei 1988), but it was never carried out on a widespread basis.

Despite these serious problems, the contracting system remained firmly entrenched. Some reformist economists continued to argue

---

pressure from Li Peng and CCP conservatives for the spiraling inflation sparked by the 1988 price reform initiative.

55.   The lack of property rights also deterred individual farmers from investing in their land under the rural contracting system. But at least farmers were allowed to own their own equipment and draft animals.

that only a joint-stock system and a genuine transformation of ownership would give enterprises rational economic incentives and genuine autonomy ("Shareholding System May Become 'Key' to Reform" 1988; Li Yining 1989). Others continued to assert that there was no way to create a market environment without tackling the fundamental issue of price reform (Xue Muqiao 1988). But neither alternative strategy of reform made much headway against the widely popular contracting.

In spring 1988 this policy equilibrium was tested by another round of discussions about price reform. Chinese officials I interviewed had different views about who was responsible for initiating these discussions. According to some officials, Deng Xiaoping was responsible and caught everyone, including Zhao Ziyang, by surprise.[56] Deng declared for price reform in a talk with Korean leader O Chin-u on 18 May (Chai Shikuan 1988). This unexpected and inexplicable intervention in the reform process threw everyone for a loop; Zhao Ziyang did not even express his support for Deng's suggestion until five days later ("Zhao Ziyang Meets American Guests" 1988). The Politburo held a meeting 30 May–1 June to confirm Deng Xiaoping's declared policy of moving ahead quickly on price reform ("CCP Politburo Meeting" 1988).[57] On 3 June, Deng and Zhao both spoke in favor of price reform at an international conference. Deng said that price reform, although risky, was critical: "It is better to bear short-term sufferings than the long-term ones" ("Deng Discusses Price Reform" 1988). Zhao added, "Price reform may be the most difficult problem encountered by all socialist countries in the course of reform. We are prepared to try it and take some risks" ("Zhao Ziyang on Price Reform" 1988).

Other officials believe that Zhao Ziyang and Deng Xiaoping had consulted and agreed to revive the price reform effort before Deng Xiaoping spoke out.[58] Deng's meeting with O Chin-u took place the

56. According to one Beijing observer, Li Tieying, then head of the Economic Reform Commission, was the person who convinced Deng to push price reform (author's interviews).
57. According to one report, some officials who were not Politburo members attended the meeting as observers, but the meeting was not labeled an enlarged Politburo meeting. The meeting was described as a "mobilization meeting," not a meeting to deliberate (Liu Jui-shao 1988).
58. According to one account, Zhao's decision to press again for price reform resulted from several reports he had commissioned from the Research Institute on Economic System Reform, one on the East European reform experiences (which found that the absence of thorough price reform

day after Zhao Ziyang had presented his views on eight current issues to an enlarged meeting of the Politburo Standing Committee (Liu Jui-shao 1988). Joseph Fewsmith interprets this sequence of events to mean that Deng was coordinating with his general secretary (Fewsmith 1989). But Zhao's remarks at the meeting were never reported by the PRC press.

The case for blaming Deng Xiaoping for the sudden return to the price reform agenda is mainly that even Zhao Ziyang's advisers who previously had supported price reform thought it would be crazy to try it in the context of the 1988 economic environment, which could hardly have been less favorable. Because the contractionary policies of 1985–86 and 1987 had been feeble, the economy was growing too fast. The gap between plan and market prices was widening. People were already unhappy about high rates of inflation. The press reported declining living standards, workers' strikes, and a sense of crisis in society. Having abandoned price reform in the more favorable economic environment of a year before, why should Zhao Ziyang return to it now? Because I am unable to answer this question, I find the story of Deng Xiaoping's responsibility for the 1988 initiative more plausible than the story attributing the initiative to Zhao Ziyang.

When the population heard Deng Xiaoping, whom they recognized as the preeminent leader with supreme authority over all policy decisions, declare himself for price reform, they believed that price rises were imminent. They rushed to protect themselves against price rises by converting their money into goods, a rational economic response inaccurately labeled "panic buying." Naturally, prices shot up even higher as a result of consumers' actions. Not surprisingly, when top government and party leaders met at their annual summer session in Beidaihe, they backed away from price changes. Although everyone expressed a commitment to the notion of price reform, no one except a few economists and the bureaucratic supporters of extractive industries really wanted to carry it out at that time.[59] In the current economic context it was obvious

---

prevented their full marketization) and another on China's growing budgetary burden of price subsidies. A third report, based on the visit to Latin America by the institute's leader, Chen Yizi, proposed that inflation, even at the high Latin American rates, could be managed if proper measures were taken (You Ji 1991).

59. For the Coal Ministry's position in support of price reform, see Ge Fu 1989.

that price rises would further destabilize an already fragile social situation. At a meeting of 26–30 September 1988 the Central Committee approved a decision shelving price reform for at least two years.

The abortive price reform initiative of 1988 jeopardized the future of the reform drive. Li Peng blamed the fiasco on Zhao Ziyang in an effort to discredit Zhao's stewardship of the economy.[60] The July 1988 Beidaihe meeting reduced Zhao's authority over economic policy and handed it over to the conservative leaders Li Peng and Yao Yilin instead. The elders were pressuring Deng to fire Zhao long before the spring 1989 protests in Tiananmen Square.

If Deng Xiaoping was actually responsible for the ill-timed price reform imitative, Zhao's downfall would follow a pattern that also fits Hu Yaobang's fall in 1986–87. Deng Xiaoping had a habit of making erratic interventions to accelerate reform at times when conservative leaders were already flexing their muscles. The first intervention was in 1987, when Deng Xiaoping pushed political reform; that initiative backfired against Hu Yaobang, who was deposed in January 1987. The second intervention was in 1988, when Deng Xiaoping pushed price reform; that initiative backfired against Zhao Ziyang, who was deposed in May 1989. Like his predecessor, Mao Zedong, Deng Xiaoping knocked off his successors one after another. But Deng's machinations were channeled through the reform policy process and did serious mischief to the reform drive as well as to the succession.

The misfiring of price reform in 1988 also diluted public support for the economic reform and for the CCP that was leading it. Frustrated and disturbed by the confusing on-again, off-again signals about price reform, the public was beginning to doubt the competence of all the reformist party leaders, Deng as well as Zhao. They also were discontent because their living standards, battered by inflation, were not keeping up with their raised expectations. China was suffering the onus of inflation without having received the bonus of genuine price rationalization.

After the price reform disaster Li Peng and his elderly backstage supporters at the top of the party took charge of economic policy and carried out contractionary policies. But despite their commit-

60. Li Peng had distanced himself from the policy accelerating price reform on 24 May 1988, when he told American guests, "It will take a long time to rationalize the price structure, and we need to play carefully whenever a step is taken" ("Li Peng Discusses Reform" 1988).

ments to central planning and macroeconomic control the CCP conservatives did not dismantle either enterprise contracting or provincial fiscal contracting. The vested interests in the contracting versions of partial reform were too strong. Recognizing that they would face a tough succession contest after Deng Xiaoping's death, Li Peng and his allies did not dare go against the provincial and municipal officials, managers of large factories, and industrial bureaucrats who supported contracting. Nor did they attempt to replace contracting with more effective standardized rules such as tax laws; they realized that in the Chinese political system, as the 1986–87 history of price reform and contracting showed, particularistic sharing arrangements would always win out over redistributive standardization formulas.[61]

Even when the conservatives' hold on the CCP strengthened after 1989, party policies on reform did not negate enterprise or fiscal contracting. With Hu Yaobang and Zhao Ziyang out of the picture and the power of the conservatives demonstrated to all in the Tiananmen crackdown, we might have expected the CCP to roll back reforms and return to central planning or at least to recentralize financial control over funds dispersed by enterprise and fiscal contracting. The party's unified will to control inflation by enforcing tough contractionary policies was effectively brought to bear on the overheated economy in 1990–91. Elderly conservatives such as Chen Yun and Yao Yilin did advocate the unpopular notions of fiscal recentralization and a real tax system. But Li Peng and other middle-aged leaders refused to jeopardize their careers by abandoning enterprise and fiscal contracting for either the old command

61. One 1989 account described how contracting was better at "handling interest relations" than were standardized methods: "The base figures specified in contracts represent vested interests. Since the contract system protects vested interests, it is therefore acceptable to all relevant parties. . . . In the past, we tried to solve the problem of the highly uneven distribution of benefits among enterprises by applying standardized methods. For example, all enterprises were required to pay income taxes according to the same rates, and the results were far from uniform: Some enterprises still had a great deal of profits left after paying taxes, others had little, and some money-losing enterprises could barely survive. . . . The contract system features the application of nonstandardized methods as a means for solving the problem of the uneven distribution of benefits among enterprises. . . . A balance of interests is achieved among enterprises and the problem of the uneven distribution of work and benefits is roughly solved" (Song Tingming 1989, 33).

system or a comprehensive tax or price reform.[62] On the contrary, Li Peng took up the cause of the hard-pressed large and medium-sized state industries and demanded a better deal for them in the framework of particularistic contracting ("Li Peng Stresses Economic Efficiency" 1991; Li Peng 1991).[63]

62. During 1990–91 there was plenty of talk about replacing both enterprise and fiscal contracting with a tax system dividing central and local taxes, but there was no progress in implementing such a system. As for prices, comprehensive price reform was abandoned as politically impractical and replaced instead with "small-step microadjustments" in the prices of coal, railway transport, cement, crude oil, refined oil, pig iron, and steel and with a major increase in the urban prices of grains and edible oils. These price adjustments were aimed primarily at reducing the budgetary burden of price subsidies.

63. At Li Peng's urging, the State Council in 1991 announced eleven preferential policies for large and medium-sized enterprises that would be applied directly by the center to "particular projects and enterprises" on a particularistic basis (Li Peng 1991, 35). Such an approach enabled Li Peng and other central officials to monopolize the patronage opportunities of the policies.

4

CONCLUSION

14 The Political Lessons of Economic Reform in China

The reform experiences of the Soviet Union and China stand in vivid contrast. In the Soviet Union, Mikhail Gorbachev introduced democratic political reforms to create the political framework for economic reform. Because the central communist party-state was strong, institutionalized, and wedded to the command economy, Gorbachev expanded the political arena to enfranchise citizens more likely to support market reforms. To get around the obstruction of conservative Communist Party opponents of reform, he shifted authority from party to government institutions. The consequences of Gorbachev's bold strategy were political chaos and economic failure. Communist Party rule collapsed, ethnic conflicts erupted, the Soviet Union disintegrated, the command economy came to a standstill, and market reforms went nowhere.

In China, Deng Xiaoping took the more cautious approach of introducing economic reforms without political reforms. Every reform policy had to be channeled through existing communist authoritarian bureaucratic institutions. Yet the Chinese version of communism proved to be surprisingly flexible. The central bureaucracy had been weakened by the Cultural Revolution, and previous waves of decentralization allowed provincial officials to become a political counterweight to the conservative center. Over the period 1979–89 bureaucratic support for the reform drive broadened and the momentum of reform was sustained despite periodic retrenchments. By the end of the decade the Chinese people were still suffering the social control of the communist regime, but their living standards were dramatically improved. Real per capita GNP grew 7.2 percent annually from 1978 to 1990 (McMillan and Naughton 1991, 3).

The conservative leaders of the CCP, beleaguered by their own society and isolated internationally after the Tiananmen crackdown and the fall of communism in the Soviet Union and Eastern Europe, have exploited the contrast between the Soviet and Chinese reform outcomes to argue for the superiority of socialism and communist party rule. The Soviet people face starvation while in China the food and goods in the shops "are a feast for the eyes" ("Two Different Outcomes of Reform" 1990, 3). Compare and draw your own conclusions, say the Chinese leaders.

Our own political values impel us to decry the continuation of oppressive Communist Party rule in China. Those of us who frequently visit China and have Chinese friends know very well the terrible personal price paid when people are forced to mouth slogans they no longer believe or to criticize a friend for a deviant political view they themselves share.

It is undeniable that the Chinese formula of economic reform without political reform has been more successful in economic terms than has the Soviet approach of political reform before economic reform, but the Soviet Union probably did not have the option of taking the Chinese way. Soviet communist institutions were more centralized and less flexible; the Soviet central bureaucracy, if left intact, would have blocked any market reform initiatives. Still, the lesson of the Chinese case is that in some varieties of communism, it is possible to move from a command economy to market competition without changing the political rules of the game. Communist rule in and of itself is not an insuperable obstacle to economic transformation.

The political challenge of economic reform in China was nevertheless formidable. Authoritarian communist regimes may look like strong states, but they rarely have the capacity to impose painful policies over the heads of bureaucrats. The Chinese leaders had to delegate reform decision-making to a bureaucracy that included groups who would lose from the reforms as well as those who would potentially gain from them. The political institutions created by the CCP leaders in the 1950s were designed to enhance the political influence in the policy-making process of groups favored by the command economy, particularly heavy industry. The political challenge of economic reform was to build a constituency for reform from among the groups who would potentially benefit from it, namely, provincial officials, light industry, and agriculture, and to reorient the preferences of the groups with vested interests in the command economy. This task required artful strategy on the part of the political entrepreneurs at the top of the CCP. An important element in that strategy was to introduce reforms not in a comprehensive package, but gradually, and to transform the economy not by abolishing the plan, but by allowing markets and nonstate firms to grow out of the plan.

A strategy that built a bureaucratic constituency for the reform drive was not necessarily one that vastly improved economic efficiency. Chinese-style economic reform, according to one Chinese economist, meant "transferring power to lower levels and allowing lower levels to gain more profits" (author's interview). Fiscal and industrial reforms designed to turn provincial and enterprise officials into a proreform counterweight to the conservative center produced a hybrid economic system that stimulated rapid growth and raised living standards but made only modest headway in improving industrial efficiency. The Chinese reforms generated extensive growth under reform conditions, not intensive growth.

Although the Chinese strategy effectively moved the country from central planning to partial marketization, at the end of the decade reform policy-making had stalled halfway down the road. Many party and government officials had acquired vested interests in economic reform. Yet the version of reform they were committed to was a patchwork of particularistic bargains for sharing funds between center and province and between province and enterprise that generated political rents for politicians at all levels but barely improved the economic efficiency of state-owned industrial firms.[1] Given their vested interests in partial reform, provincial and industrial officials blocked efforts to improve economic outcomes by moving toward comprehensive reform. Party leaders who won political points for particularistic giveaways were loath to retract them or alienate their bureaucratic supporters by imposing universalistic policies on them.

Despite the political impasse on comprehensive reforms, the dynamism of the nonstate sector kept the reform drive alive. The decision to create a two-track economy during a protracted period of transition may have been economically less optimal than a comprehensive package of reforms, but as a second-best approach it had positive economic consequences. Even when officials were deadlocked on new reforms for state industry, the actual behavior of state firms was moving them further and further away from the

1. "Contracting prevents further reform because it fixes all the institutions in a complex network of rents" (Wu Jinglian 1988, 3).

plan, drawn away by the dynamic growth of nonstate industry and the expansion of market sales.

Chinese Political Institutions and Reform Outcomes

The Chinese decision to attempt economic reform without political reform meant that reform policies were hammered out in existing authoritarian bureaucratic communist institutions. As a result, reform policies reflected the political logic of these institutions more than any economic logic. Chinese policymakers and economists lacked a technical road map to guide them in the transition from command economy to market economy (C. Lin 1989). But the path they took was not random; it was laid out for them by the incentives and rules of the game of Chinese political institutions.

THE PATH OF CHINESE ECONOMIC REFORMS

Reforms were enacted in a gradual, piecemeal fashion, not according to a comprehensive plan. Instead of tackling the planned economy head-on, decisionmakers pursued marketization sideways by creating a two-track system in which plan and market and state and nonstate firms coexisted during an extended period of transition. Fiscal decentralization to local governments, agricultural decollectivization, expansion of private and collective businesses, and foreign investment special zones were introduced at an early stage of the reform drive and progressed with little opposition. Redistributive reform policies, such as the replacement of profit remission with taxes, were approved only after compromises that left no one worse off than before. Policies that took the form of particularistic contracts between the government and subordinate units, such as fiscal contracting to provinces and profit contracting to enterprises, always won out over policies taking the form of universal rules—for instance, price reform and tax reform.

CHINESE POLITICAL INSTITUTIONS

Chinese economic reform policies were shaped by the institutional setting in which the policies were made. Five key dimensions of Chinese political institutions affected economic reform policies:

Authority relations among institutions. The CCP has formal political authority over the government, and party leaders delegate to the government the formulation and implementation of economic policies. The authority of the party results in reform policies that reflect the preferences of the party and changes in the top leadership of the party. The initiative to launch the reform drive came from the reformist party leaders. When the conservatives increased their dominance in the party beginning in 1987, and even more after 1989, the reforms of state-owned industry were put on hold.

Leadership incentives. CCP leaders are chosen by an elite "selectorate" composed of the Central Committee, the revolutionary elders, and top military leaders (fewer than five hundred "selectors" in all). The largest blocs within the selectorate are provincial party and government officials, central party and government officials, and PLA officers. On the one hand, public officials within the selectorate are beholden to the top party leaders who appointed them to their posts; on the other hand, the party leaders are beholden to the officials who have the power to replace them, creating a relationship between leaders and officials of *reciprocal accountability*. Communist politicians compete for party leadership by promoting policies that enable them to claim credit and win support from members of the selectorate as bureaucratic groups and as individual clients. In the case of economic reforms, party politicians in Beijing and, indeed, at every level of the system had a political incentive to generate political support for themselves by pushing policies that took the form of particularistic contracting even though such policies were less conducive to efficiency than uniform rules would have been. The fact that industrial reforms were introduced as "experiments" granting special treatment and that fiscal contracts and enterprise profit contracts always prevailed over more universalistic approaches reflects the compelling political logic of particularistic contracting in the context of Chinese leadership incentives.

Bargaining arena. Chinese economic policies are formulated and implemented by a government bureaucracy that is organized hierarchically. Leverage over policy depends on the formal rank of an organization. Central government ministries organized by function and sector and provincial governments have equivalent rank. Bureaucratic organizations afford virtual (i.e., nonelectoral) representation to social interests. Party authorities expect bureaucrats to advocate the preferences of their organizations. The bureaucracy is the sole arena in which conflicts of group interests can be resolved. All economic reform proposals were channeled through the government bureaucracy. Decisions were made slowly, and debate over reform policy issues was highly contentious, with organizations previously favored by the command economy (e.g., heavy industrial ministries and inland provinces) opposing any changes that would leave them worse off.

Groups enfranchised in the policy process. Economic sectors are represented by ministries. The organization of the Chinese central government bureaucracy gives industry more clout than agriculture, and within industry, gives heavy industry more clout than light industry. Given this pattern of political enfranchisement, economic reform policies had to protect the interests of heavy industry. The political clout of heavy industry explains the ministerial contract system for particular heavy industrial ministries, compromises in the tax-for-profit policy, the turn away from tax-for-profit to profit contracting, and the failure to carry out price reform. Agricultural reform moved ahead because agriculture's voice in the central bureaucracy was weak and because price increases for manufactured farm inputs and price subsidies for urban consumers guaranteed that agricultural reform in no way threatened the interests of industry. After a decade of reform the shares of central government investment remained essentially unchanged, with heavy industry still favored and agriculture's share even further reduced.

Provinces have no permanent formal representation in the bureaucratic arena. However, reform policies were made in policy work conferences to enhance the influence of provinces. In the work conference setting, provinces obtained policies that benefited them, including fiscal decentralization and a compromise version of tax-for-profit.

Decision rules. At each level of the Chinese bureaucratic hierarchy, agency representatives make decisions by a consensus rule. If they agree, the decision is automatically ratified by the next level; if not, the issue is kicked up to the next level or is dropped. Government ministries or provinces that have strong objections to policy proposals can veto them or force them to be modified. Hierarchical control gives bureaucrats an incentive to reach agreement through compromise, but under a divided political leadership this incentive is weakened. Because all economic reform policies had to work their way through the Chinese bureaucratic bargaining machine during a period of leadership competition, marketization was gradual, indirect, and partial. Under the consensus rule and given the divisions in the CCP leadership, redistributive reform policies such as price reform could not win approval; other policies, such as tax-for-profit, were approved only by devising compromises to protect the interests of all bureaucratic organizations and were then reversed. Compromises and side payments had to be found to protect groups with vested interests in the command economy, particularly heavy industry. The most drastic redistributive reforms had to be postponed indefinitely because they threatened these vested interests. Party leaders, conservatives and reformists alike, trying to create constituencies among subordinate bureaucrats designed reforms to allocate favors to these bureaucrats on a selective basis.

Unanswered Questions about Communist Institutions and Policy-Making

I have begun to describe the distinctive features of communist political institutions and analyze the ways these institutions shape the policy-making process. The attempt to make explicit the lines of authority, the political incentives of leaders and officials, and the rules of collective decision-making in Chinese communist institutions has helped make sense of the story of China's economic reforms during 1979–89. Yet we are still a long way from a genuine model of communist political institutions and policy-making. In studying the Chinese reform, I often found myself unable to explain changes in policies by the institutional context and fell back on ad hoc explanations instead. Following are a few questions about communist institutions we will have to answer to develop an appropriate model of them.[2] (I hope that readers will add to this list of questions.) Most of the questions deal with the leadership incentives that derive from leadership selection; leadership selection is the most opaque process in communist politics, particularly in China, where the institutionalization of this process lags behind the Soviet Union and Eastern Europe.

1. What is the choice rule by which the formal and informal bodies in the selectorate select leaders?

2. In a selectorate that is not limited to the officials in the Central Committee but includes elders (and a preeminent leader)

2. As communist regimes disappear one by one, the value of developing an institutional model of communist policy-making may appear questionable. I would argue that the effort is not merely an exercise in historical or formal political analysis. The building of postcommunist institutions and patterns of postcommunist policy-making will undoubtedly reflect the lessons participants "learned" from the functioning of communist institutions. In the case of China, of course, a functioning communist political system still exists.

with informal influence but no formal posts, in what circumstances do political aspirants concentrate their appeals on Central Committee groups and in what circumstances on the elders?

3. Is the authority of the elders and the preeminent leader based solely on their unique status as members of the founder generation, or is it a permanent feature of Chinese communist institutions?

4. What is the authority relationship between the military and the communist party? Does the military have veto power in leadership selection or policy-making? If not veto power, does the military have an influence disproportionate to its membership in the selectorate? Is the political influence of the military derived from the critical importance of internal security in authoritarian states or from other, possibly historical, factors?

5. On what basis do members of the selectorate choose party leaders? How do members weigh the following dimensions of candidates: the value of their policy stances to different bureaucratic groups (group interests); their record in delivering patronage to particular individuals (clientalism); and their ability and character (qualifications)?

6. What are the political incentives of local communist party leaders and government officials? What is their relationship with subordinate officials? Are they linked by reciprocal accountability? How are local leaders chosen? Why do local leaders press for policies that give them control over patronage?

7. What is and is not distinctive about the preference of communist politicians for policies that allow them to distribute patronage to subordinates? Politicians in all political systems (e.g., the United States, Japan) prefer private goods policies that allow them to claim credit with their constituents to public goods policies with benefits that are diffuse and nonexcludable and therefore of less political value to politicians. The only obvious exception to this universal preference appears in parliamentary governments with electoral systems that produce strong parties (for instance, the United Kingdom); in such governments party labels have more electoral value to politicians than patronage does. How does a communist regime in which politicians distribute patronage to subordinate officials differ from a democratic regime in which politicians distribute patronage to citizens?

Evaluating China's Gradual Approach to
Economic Reform

The decision of China's leaders to retain existing political institutions and introduce a market through a communist bureaucracy prolonged the period of transition. It is easy to find fault with the Chinese strategy of gradualism, especially if one focuses on the continuing low efficiency of state-owned industry. During the first decade of reform, to make the economic reform a political success, it was necessary to let most people benefit from reform (Wu Jinglian 1987a). Building consensus required compromising or postponing the tough but economically necessary redistributive measures such as price and tax reform while moving full-steam ahead to extend particularistic financial contracts to local governments and enterprises. Chinese economists who advocate comprehensive (*peitao*) reform criticized this sequencing of policies; although politically practicable, it did less to improve the efficiency of industrial enterprises than comprehensive reform would have done (Wu Jinglian and Zhou Xiaochuan 1988). Moreover, the perpetuation of the dualtrack economy created strong incentives for officials to make corrupt profits from arbitrage between plan and market. Recognizing how far away from a full-fledged market economy China remained after more than a decade of reform, Western economists urged the countries of Eastern Europe and the Soviet Union to eschew gradualism and adopt a comprehensive "big-bang" reform instead.

A closer look at the Chinese reform experience suggests that gradual transition from plan to market as a second-best approach has more positive economic consequences than Western economists have appreciated.[3] One positive consequence of Chinese gradualism was the reorientation of the preferences of officials, managers, and even workers in state-owned industry. During the decade of transition, people in state-owned industry learned that market competition offered them rewards as well as risks. As a result, they no longer opposed market reform and even demanded more market freedoms for themselves. How did this learning occur?[4] It was a

3. Two efforts to build theories of gradual economic reform on the basis of the Chinese experience are Jefferson and Rawski 1991 and McMillan and Naughton 1991.
4. The Chinese talk about economic learning as the *renshi* (understanding) issue.

response to the competitive pressure of nonstate firms on state firms. Between 1979 and 1989 the state's monopoly on industry was destroyed as private and collective firms were allowed, and even encouraged by concessionary financial treatment, to compete with state firms.

This book focuses on the political conflicts sparked by the introduction of reforms in state-owned industry through a communist bureaucracy. At the time I began researching the book in 1984, state-owned industry was the center ring of the Chinese economic reform. Officials spent more time and energy debating policies designed to improve the performance of state industry than on agriculture, nonstate businesses, and foreign trade combined. The central Chinese state was financially dependent on the profits of state industry.

By the time I was completing the book in 1991, the reform action had shifted away from state industry toward the nonstate sector. While Chinese government officials had been busy chasing one another's tails, fighting over the relative gains and losses to different industrial sectors, regions, and levels of government implied in each reform policy targeted at state industries, private, collective, and foreign joint venture businesses had expanded dramatically. Policies regarding nonstate businesses had presented no immediate challenge to bureaucratic vested interests and were approved easily.

The dynamism of Chinese privately and collectively owned businesses, located mostly in rural areas, was astounding. The output of nonstate industrial firms grew at an annual rate of 17.6 percent between 1978 and 1990, compared to a growth rate in state industry of 7.6 percent. As a result, state-owned firms accounted for only 55 percent of industrial output in 1990, down from 78 percent in 1978 (McMillan and Naughton 1991, 4). When commercial, agricultural, and foreign trade businesses are included, less than 40 percent of China's national income originated in the state sector by 1989. As Nicholas Lardy observed (1991, 6), "By that standard the role of the state in economic matters in China has shrunk to a level approaching that of both Italy and France, where state-owned firms produce a third of national output." Nonstate industrial firms, although they did not meet the standard of the purely competitive firms of economic models, were profit-seekers operating in an environment more market-oriented than that of the state firms (Lardy 1991; McMillan and Naughton 1991).

State firms were given the incentive and the wherewithal to respond to the competition of nonstate firms by reforms that permitted them to sell their above-quota output on the market and to retain a share of their profits. This modest change in the incentives facing state firms might have had only marginal effects on the behavior of these firms were it not for two changes in the economic environment: the reduction in the scale and scope of the central plan and competition from nonstate firms. Episodes of economic retrenchment when the central government drastically cut plan output quotas (particularly 1981–82) taught state industrial officials and managers that they could not rely on the plan to survive. But when they turned to the market, they found that the nonstate firms held the competitive edge. Unlike state firms, private and collective firms were unencumbered by burdens imposed by government— plan quotas, low plan prices, labor quotas, mandated welfare expenditures, adjustment taxes, or profit contracts.[5] Government bureaus and party committees still hired the managers of state-owned firms and told them what to do, whereas private, collective, and joint venture firms were largely on their own.

At the start of the reform drive, industrial ministry officials and the managers of large state-owned factories believed that the security of the plan was preferable to the risks of market competition. But by the end of the decade their views had changed. Having watched the nonstate sector prosper even during periods of economic retrenchment when state industry suffered, they concluded they could do better escaping from the plan than by clinging to it.

The nonstate sector became a magnet, drawing state industry away from the plan and toward the market. Under the two-track system the higher prices in the market leached the best products, labor, and managers out of the plan (Liu Guoguang and Zhao Renwei 1985). Especially after painful retrenchment periods, such as those in 1981–82 and 1990–91, the managers of large state factories and their Beijing spokespersons demanded "full decision-making rights" comparable to those of nonstate factories (Lu Dong 1991).[6]

5. By contrast, the plan offered cheap material supplies.
6. Lu Dong, former head of the SEC and closely identified with large state enterprises, contrasted the situation of nonstate and state firms: "[Nonstate enterprises] are guided by the market and profit and are independent in making policy decisions concerning their operations, development strategy, marketing, and internal distribution as well as their employment system

To escape the plan, state enterprise managers also began to diversify ownership forms within their enterprises, leasing or otherwise spinning off parts of their operations to collective owners. In 1991 the SPC condoned the trend toward "one factory, two systems" (*yi chang liang zhi*) because it was the only way for large state enterprises to survive (author's interviews). Some managers also resorted to illegal ruses to escape the plan; one such ruse involved becoming a foreign joint venture by setting up a dummy corporation in Hong Kong (author's interviews).

The establishment of different ownership forms within state enterprises and the flourishing of private and collective businesses in Chinese cities also changed the thinking of Chinese state workers. They became increasingly willing to trade off the security of the "iron rice bowl" offered by state firms for the higher wages and opportunities for advancement offered by nonstate firms.

The disequilibrium created by the dynamism of the nonstate sector and the pressure from state industry to escape the plan meant not only that the Chinese system would never return to the pre-reform command economy but also that it would inexorably move away from state ownership. The trend is not one of privatization (McMillan and Naughton 1991). Although the growth of private businesses may raise the hackles of the ideological specialists within the CCP, it is much less economically significant than is the expansion of collective and joint venture enterprises. Nationally, only about 2 percent of national income is produced by private firms, although the figure is higher in major cities, especially in Southern China.[7] Collective ownership, even in the form of joint stock com-

---

and establishment of departments. When making such decisions, they are free from external interference. However, every link of the production and management of state-owned enterprises is restricted by many factors. Basically speaking, they are still dependent on the administrative departments. They are still perplexed by the distorted price system, egalitarian distribution system, excessive examination and appraising, and unnecessary organizations. Whether the enterprises have full decision-making rights in operation and management is the key problem to be solved in transforming their operational mechanism" (Lu Dong 1991, 59).

7. The state regulation of private markets in Chinese cities has gone a long way to build public confidence in private commercial businesses and prevent criminal organizations from putting the squeeze on these businesses. As a result, private commerce has expanded. The former Soviet Union presents a contrasting picture of scant private businesses, public suspicion of private businesspeople, and mafia disruption of private markets.

panies, is more ideologically palatable because it can be disguised as social ownership (He Wei 1990). But it raises the specter of loss of state control over economic life and the fundamental ideological question, Is this still socialism?[8]

Can China undergo a transformation away from state ownership of industry within the context of existing communist political institutions? Some Chinese reformist economists have come to believe that the only way to break out of the imbroglio of price, wage, capital investment, and tax reforms is to change the ownership of state industry.[9] The experience of some Eastern European countries suggests that ideological resistance to ownership reform under socialism may not be insuperable (Bartlett 1990; Staniszkis 1984). The political advantages of deflecting the blame for price rises, unemployment, and other painful consequences of marketization away from the party and government onto factory managers help political leaders overcome any queasiness they might have about private property. The prospect of eliminating central budget deficits with the windfall earned by selling off state factories also makes this radical reform particularly attractive to central financial officials. As one Chinese commentator said in 1990, "At present, price reform and the reform of state-run enterprises are 'under a long siege,' and are entering a 'state of impasse.' Under these conditions, we should change our ideas and first carry out some reforms which 'require less money' and involve less vested economic interests. As far as I can see, at present we can take adjustment of the ownership system as a new starting point for deepening system reform" (Fan Gang 1990, 27).

In ideological terms, ownership reform seems a more radical approach to reform than restructuring prices, wages, capital invest-

---

8. Ideological diehards within the CCP put it this way: "If socialist countries cannot uphold the four cardinal principles and cannot persist in the struggle with bourgeois liberalization in the course of deepening the reform of the economic structure, and cannot win victory in the struggle, socialist countries will be faced with the danger that economic privatization will be realized. . . . Therefore, the struggle over the direction in which the reform of the economic structure should be deepened is a fundamental aspect of socialist countries opposing the 'peaceful evolution' policy promoted by the two international counterrevolutionary forces" (Wang Haibo 1990, 6).

9. Dong Furen was the most avant-garde in advocating privatization (see Dong Furen 1979). By 1990 even Liu Guoguang, formerly an advocate of comprehensive reform, was supporting ownership reform (Liu Guoguang 1990a).

ment, and taxes, yet it may nevertheless be more politically feasible in the context of communist political institutions. If national political institutions continue to be unable to implement painful, redistributive universalistic reforms of state enterprises, Beijing leaders may opt instead simply to divest themselves of responsibility for the enterprises.

Institutional Prerequisites for Communist Transformations from Planning to Markets

China's economic reform experience must be judged an overall economic success. The reforms transformed China from a command economy to one in which the market and non-state-owned businesses dominate economic life. Despite the slow improvement of the efficiency of state-owned industrial firms, the economy as a whole has grown rapidly and living standards have risen considerably.

What are the institutional lessons of the Chinese reform experience? The fact that the Chinese reforms succeeded without changing China's political institutions challenges much of the standard wisdom about the rigidity of communist systems. The success of China's approach of economic reform without political reform—especially when contrasted with the failures of Soviet and Eastern European communist regimes to accomplish economic reform without political reform and the disastrous consequences of Gorbachev's experiment in political reform before economic reform—raises fundamental questions about what it takes politically to implement economic reforms.

Another way of putting this question is, What are the institutional prerequisites for the dynamic transformation of an economic system? All societies need the capacity to innovate in response to changes in their environment; in other words, they need the capacity to reform. Some features of institutions may be conducive to political stability but may impede political actors from revising the economic rules of the game to confront new economic, technological, or military challenges. Other institutional features may enhance both stability and the capacity to reform.

The success of the Chinese experience and the failure of the Soviet experience suggest two features of political institutions that are necessary for economic reform. The first is *flexibility*. The key to flexibility is the presence of choice-making institutions with internal rules and an enfranchisement formula that encourages (or can be modified to encourage) innovation. Institutions vary as to how con-

ducive to innovation are their internal rules (agenda setting, decision gates, choice rules). For example, legislatures that make
decisions by majority rule tend to be better able to innovate than
are bureaucracies that make decisions by consensus. Winning a
simple majority for change is easier than winning a consensus for
change. This is an advantage that Western democracies have over
China.

As for enfranchisement, the key issue is whether decision-
making institutions' formula of representation (how decisionmakers
are chosen and which social interests they represent) gives political
weight to groups who will benefit from reforms. When founding
elites establish governing institutions, they structure them to promote a particular economic development strategy by enhancing the
power of the groups identified with this development strategy.

Changing a development strategy requires institutions whose
formula of representation permits the social groups who will benefit from the economic changes to raise their voices in decision-
making. Thus, if the rule for enfranchisement does not automatically incorporate new social forces, the mechanisms for changing
the internal rules and representation formula of decision-making
institutions are critically important for the capacity of a political
system to reform.

Democratic systems that give all citizens the right to elect representatives are the most adaptable. Changes in the size or economic importance of social groups can be immediately translated into
policy changes through elections. Democratic legislatures can be
redistricted to amplify or diminish the representation of various
groups. Yet a universal franchise, by its very definition, empowers
everyone, including the masses of citizens who will feel the pinch
of the price rises and unemployment that are the inevitable costs of
economic restructuring. Unless painful but crucial measures such
as tax reform, price reform, and enterprise bankruptcy are introduced at a very early stage when popular economic expectations
remain low, gaining approval for them can be even harder under
democratic rules than it is under authoritarian ones.

Authoritarian leaders may adapt the franchise by reconfiguring
their government and party institutions to favor particular policy
outcomes. Some communist leaders, Janos Kadar in Hungary for
one, promoted market reforms by the institutional strategy of merging specialized industrial ministries into one comprehensive Ministry of Industry. Chinese party leaders regularly revise the CCP

constitution to shift the authority over the Secretariat back and forth between the Politburo and Central Committee to make an end run around Politburo members who are resistant to policy change.[10] Because neither the size nor the membership of communist authoritative institutions is set by law, communist leaders can readjust them to empower groups who favor reforms.

Not all communist systems are equally flexible in this respect, however; the more institutionalized the communist regime, the less flexible it is. It was more difficult for Gorbachev, bound by party rules and norms of collective rule, to alter the membership of the Soviet Party Central Committee than it was for Deng Xiaoping, who strengthened the proreform forces in the Chinese Party Central Committee by increasing the number of local officials. The greater institutionalization of Soviet party institutions limited the flexibility of the Soviet regime and convinced Gorbachev that he would be unable to build political support for economic reform without shifting authority from the party to elected government institutions. Deng Xiaoping took advantage of the looser and more personalistic character of the Chinese regime to pack party institutions with proreform forces. Deng was not a personal dictator unconstrained by party collective norms, however (Teiwes 1979, 1984, 1991); not until the Thirteenth Party Congress in 1987 was he able to shift the conservative elders out of the Politburo and the Politburo Standing Committee.

A second institutional desideratum for achieving economic reform is *authority*. Reforming an economic system cannot be done without inflicting some pain on the groups who are favored and protected by the status quo. A political system that cannot exert authority over its agents will find economic transformation an impossible task.

The Chinese approach to the authority problem was to retain the CCP's nomenklatura power to appoint government officials. Deng

10. Reorganizations of the government bureaucracy occur frequently in China, but none during the past decade was designed to shift the balance of power toward proreform groups. A special State Council group was formed to sketch a plan for streamlining the bureaucracy by merging and eliminating ministries to foster marketization, but the plan was never announced or carried out (author's interviews). The lack of institutional redesign during the Chinese economic reform era suggests that the problem of reciprocal accountability and competition for power among communist elites may constrain the efforts of communist leaders to restructure institutions.

Xiaoping used this power to replace thousands of officials who had loyally served the command economy for decades with younger, better-educated officials more supportive of economic reforms. The party's power to promote and demote officials gave subordinate officials a career incentive to go along with reform compromises even when they did not benefit their own agencies. The party's control over personnel appointments also facilitated the implementation of reforms among factory managers and workers.[11]

The retention of authoritarian institutions does not mean that leaders can impose a set of reforms on a recalcitrant bureaucracy. Only if an authoritarian leader is a ruler of royal birth, a charismatic dictator, or a tyrant relying on terror is his authority sufficiently independent to free him of accountability to subordinates. Even with a high degree of insulation from political pressures, leaders cannot run the country without delegating authority. Once a leader relies on agents for information and for policy implementation, his policies must take the interests of agents into account. And because communist politicians are also politically dependent on officials in a relationship of reciprocal accountability, they must design a reform package that wins the support of bureaucratic constituents. In the less institutionalized Chinese version of reciprocal accountability, the dominance of the top-down authority of party leaders in this relationship prevents leaders' political dependence on subordinates from deterring innovation.

The Chinese case suggests that authority without immobilism can be achieved when the combination of power over appointments with responsiveness to bureaucratic agents is joined to a flexible formula of enfranchisement. This combination cannot obtain bureaucratic agreement on a policies that severely hurt important agencies—for instance, price reform—but it can make progress on many other less painfully redistributive reform measures.

In the more rule-bound version of communism in the Soviet Union, Gorbachev voluntarily renounced the Communist Party's authority to establish a democratic political authority for economic reforms. Gorbachev believed that putting political power on a firmer legal foundation and sharing responsibility with nonparty elements were the only solutions to the political challenge of market

---

11. Despite the growth of employment opportunities in collective and individual enterprises, two-thirds of industrial workers still work in state enterprises (*Statistical Yearbook* 1989, 256), where they are under the thumb of managers and CCP secretaries (Walder 1986).

reforms.[12] The new, democratically elected legislatures in the former Soviet states, however, were reluctant to accept the responsibility that comes with authority. Their individual political incentives discouraged them from identifying themselves with redistributive reforms. When politicians are elected by citizens and no longer chosen by subordinate officials, their political incentives and policy preferences shift. Instead of handing out benefits to lower-level bureaucrats, they become populists, handing out benefits more broadly to mass constituents. Although the threat of redistributing resources among bureaucratic organizations no longer dooms reform initiatives, the threat to guarantees of mass welfare does. Populist immobilism is even more stubborn than bureaucratic immobilism.

No one has yet discovered a sure political formula for moving an economic system from command to market. Democratization is not a panacea for the economic problems of centrally planned economies, a fact graphically illustrated by the downward economic spiral in the Soviet Union under Gorbachev and the post-Soviet states under Boris Yeltsin. Once communist leaders give up their authority to legislatures who are reluctant to use it, populist immobilism can result.[13] In a communist regime with a flexible enfranchisement formula, retaining the far-reaching authority of the communist party over the government and society, while distasteful in moral terms, may be the best short-term political strategy of economic reform.

Eventually, communist institutions are unlikely to survive the marketization of a socialist economy. Communist parties will be unable to satisfy the new social demands stimulated by economic transformation, particularly the demand from collective and private businesses for genuine property rights, without fundamental constitutional reform. In the Soviet Union and Eastern Europe communism was toppled from the top down by elite political entrepreneurs hoping to remove the political obstacles to economic reform. When communism ends in China, it may be undone by a real revolution unleashed by the success of economic reform.

12. The Polish communist leaders made a similar calculation. The Polish communists were viewed by Poles as agents of the Soviet Communist Party. Their domestic political authority was too weak to enable them to take sole political responsibility for economic reforms.
13. In order to muster the authority for embarking on serious market reforms, Yeltsin has had to violate the spirit if not the letter of the new constitution by postponing elections and making himself both president and premier of the Russian Republic. It may not be communism, but it is still authoritarianism.

Bibliography

"Accelerate the Technical Progress and Technical Renovation of Existing Enterprises." 1984. *Renmin ribao* (People's daily), 15 Nov., 1.

"Accelerating the Development of Light Industry and Textiles Is Necessary for Economic Readjustment." 1981. Editorial. *Renmin ribao*, 23 Jan., 1.

"Achievements in Restructuring Industry Noted." 1982. Beijing Domestic Service, 22 Jan.; *Foreign Broadcast Information Service, Daily Report: China (FBIS)*, 29 Jan., K5.

"The Advantages of the Contracted Management Responsibility System Truly Outweigh the Disadvantages." 1987. *Shijie jingji daobao* (World economic herald), 4 May, 2.

Ai Feng and Dai Yuqing. 1988. "In the Commodity Economy Perspective, Commenting on the Economic Situation in 1987 and the Role of the Law of Value." *Renmin ribao*, 15 Feb.; *FBIS*, 29 Feb., 34–37.

Ames, Barry. 1987. *Political Survival: Politicians and Public Policy in Latin America*. Berkeley and Los Angeles: University of California Press.

An Qihong. 1985. "Some Comments Deriving from the Turning About of a Big Ship." *Hongqi* (Red flag), no. 20 (16 Oct.); *FBIS*, 15 Nov., K8–11.

Bachman, David. 1991. *Bureaucracy, Economy, and Leadership in China: The Institutional Origins of the Great Leap Forward*. Cambridge: Cambridge University Press.

Bahry, Donna. 1987. *Outside Moscow: Power, Politics, and Budgetary Policy in the Soviet Republics*. New York: Columbia University Press.

Barnett, A. Doak. 1985. *The Making of Foreign Policy in China: Structure and Process*. Boulder: Westview.

———. 1967. *Cadres, Bureaucracy, and Political Power in Communist China*. New York: Columbia University Press.

Bartlett, David L. 1990. "Reforming Money and Property in a Socialist System: The Political Economy of Transition in Hungary." Ph.D. diss. University of California, San Diego.

Bates, Robert H. 1983. *Essays on the Political Economy of Rural Africa*. Berkeley and Los Angeles: University of California Press.

———. 1981. *Markets and States in Tropical Africa*. Berkeley and Los Angeles: University of California Press.

Bates, Robert H., and Paul Collier. 1991. "The Politics of Economic Reform in Zambia." Unpublished manuscript.

351

Bates, Robert H., and Da-hsiang Donald Lien. 1985. "A Note on Taxation, Development, and Representative Government." *Politics and Society* 14, no. 1:53–70.

"Beijing CCP Adopts Reorganization Measures." 1988. *Xinhua* (New China), 29 June; *FBIS*, 11 July, 63.

"Beijing Speeds Up Reform of Industrial Economic Setup." 1983. *Jingji ribao* (Economics daily), 4 Jan.; *FBIS*, 20 Jan., K9–10.

"Beneficial Both to the Enterprise and the State." 1987. *Renmin ribao*, 15 May; *FBIS*, 21 May, K12–15.

Bergson, Abram. 1978. *Productivity and the Social System: The USSR and the West*. Cambridge: Harvard University Press.

Bo Yibo. 1991. "Investigations, Exploration Conducted Before and After the Compilation of 'On the Ten Great Relationships.'" *Qiushi* (Seek truth), no. 12 (16 June); *FBIS*, 5 Aug., 26–39.

"Bo Yibo on Machine Building Industry's Advance." 1982. *Xinhua*, 14 Feb.; *FBIS*, 17 Feb., K11–12.

"Breaking with Departmental Bias, on the Importance of Strengthening Sectoral Management During Industrial Reform." 1984. *Renmin ribao*, 17 July, 1.

Breslauer, George W. Forthcoming. "Politics, Ideology, and Learning in Soviet Economic Reforms since Stalin." In Peter Hauslohner and David Cameron, eds., *Political Control of the Soviet Economy*. Cambridge: Cambridge University Press.

———. 1982. *Khrushchev and Brezhnev as Leaders: Building Authority in Soviet Politics*. London: George Allen and Unwin.

Brown, Alan A., and Egon Neuberger. 1968. "Basic Features of a Centrally Planned Economy." In Brown and Neuberger, eds., *International Trade and Central Planning*, 405–16. Berkeley and Los Angeles: University of California Press.

Brus, Wlodzimierz. 1973. *The Economics and Politics of Socialism*. London: Routledge and Kegan Paul.

Brzezinski, Zbigniew, and Samuel P. Huntington. 1964. *Political Power: USA/USSR*. New York: Viking.

Bunce, Valerie. 1981. *Do New Leaders Make a Difference? Executive Succession and Public Policy under Capitalism and Socialism*. Princeton: Princeton University Press.

Burns, John P. Forthcoming. "The Politics of Personnel Policy in China: The 1990 CCP Central *Nomenklatura*." *China Quarterly*.

———. 1988. "Reform of Contemporary China's Civil Service System: Proposals of the Thirteenth Party Congress." Paper presented to the Annual Meeting of the Association for Asian Studies, Mar.

———. 1987. "China's Nomenklatura System." *Problems of Communism* 36, no. 5 (Sept.–Oct.): 36–51.

Byrd, William, and Gene Tidrick. 1987. "Factor Allocation and Enterprise Incentives." In Gene Tidrick and Chen Jiyuan, eds., *China's Industrial Reform*, 60–102. New York: Oxford University Press.

Caizheng Bu Caishui Tizhi Gaige Zhu. 1989. *Caishui gaige shinian* (A decade of financial and tax reform). Beijing: China Finance and Economics Publishers.

————. 1988. "Deepen the Reform of the Budget Management System to Promote Economic Development." *Jingji guanli* (Economic management), no. 10:35–37, 39.

Cao Jingquan. 1986. "Some Questions in Continuously Perfecting and Implementing Comprehensive Contracting." *Meitan jingji yanjiu* (Coal economics research), no. 4:10–12.

"CCP Circular on Hubei Rail Transport Holdup." 1983. *Xinhua*, 5 June; *FBIS*, 9 June, K18–21.

"CCP Politburo Meeting Stresses Economic Reform." 1988. *Xinhua*, 1 June; *FBIS*, 1 June, 22.

Chai Shikuan. 1988. "DPRK Defense Minister Meets with Deng Xiaoping." *Xinhua*, 19 May; *FBIS*, 19 May, 8–9.

Chang Chuan. 1985. "Letter from Beijing." *Cheng ming* (Contention) (Hong Kong), 1 Dec.; *FBIS*, 13 Dec., W1–3.

Chang, Parris H. 1990. *Power and Policy in China*. 3d ed. Dubuque, Iowa: Kendall, Hunt.

————. 1970. "Research Notes on the Changing Loci of Decision in the CCP." *China Quarterly*, no. 44 (Oct.–Dec.): 169–94.

Chao Hao-sheng. 1989. "Yao Yilin on the Economic Situation in China." *Ta kung pao* (Hong Kong), 23 Dec.; *FBIS*, 26 Dec., 24–26.

Chen Chieh-hung. 1991. "Chen Yun Opposes the Practice of 'One Dominating View' at the Decisionmaking Level, While Li Xiannian Speaks on the Responsibility for the 1989 'Turmoil.'" *Ching Pao* (Capital daily) (Hong Kong), 10 Jan.; *FBIS*, 17 Jan., 15–17.

Chen Jianping. 1991. "The Central Authorities Decide to Support the Building of Special Science and Technology Zones." *Wen wei po* (Hong Kong), 22 Mar.; *FBIS*, 12 Apr., 42–43.

Chen Junsheng. 1987. "Increase the Work Efficiency of Public Organs." *Renmin ribao*, 19 Mar.; *FBIS*, 1 Apr., K33–39.

————. 1985. "The Key Lies in Arousing the Enthusiasm of the Managers and Producers, Investigation Report on Enhancing the Internal Vitality of Big and Medium-Sized Enterprises." *Renmin ribao*, 18 Nov.; *FBIS*, 4 Dec., K24–29.

Chen Wei-chun. 1991. "Army Generals Request Big Increase of Military Expenditure; Jiang Zemin and Li Peng Endorse the Demand." *Kuang chiao ching* (Broad angle mirror) (Hong Kong), 16 Feb.; *FBIS*, 15 Feb., 21–23.

Chen Yizi. 1990. *Zhongguo: Shinian gaige yu ba jiu min yun* (China: A decade of reform and the 1989 democracy movement). Taipei: Lien jing pinglun.

Chen Yongzhong and Li Xiaoping. 1984. "On Progressive Profit Contracting." *Jingji tizhi gaige* (Economic system reform), Mar., 28–32.

Chen Yun. 1984. "Speech at the Third Plenum of the Twelfth Central Committee." In Chinese Communist Party Central Documents Research Office, ed., *Shier da yi lai* (After the Twelfth Party Congress), 588–91. Beijing: People's Publishing House, 1985.

———. 1982. "Strengthen the Planned Economy." In *San zhong quanhui yi lai zhongyang wenxian xuanbian* (Collection of important documents after the Third Plenum of the Eleventh Central Committee), 1132–34. Beijing: People's Publishing House.

———. 1981. "Some Viewpoints on Economic Work." In *San zhong quanhui yi lai zhongyang wenxian xuanbian* (Collection of important documents after the Third Plenum of the Eleventh Central Committee), 1057–60. Beijing: People's Publishing House, 1982.

———. 1980. "The Economic Situation and the Lessons of Experience." In *San zhong quanhui yi lai zhongyang wenxian xuanbian* (Collection of important documents after the Third Plenum of the Eleventh Central Committee), 601–2. Beijing: People's Publishing House, 1982.

Chen Yun and Zhang Guimin. 1990. "Minister Calls for an End to Local Protectionism." *Xinhua*, 10 Apr.; *FBIS*, 20 Apr., 43.

"Chen Yun's Speech at the CCP National Conference." 1985. *Beijing Review*, 30 Sept., 18–20.

Cheng, Terry. 1991. "Sources Speculate on Eighth Plenum Outcome." *Hong Kong Standard*, 21 Nov.; *FBIS*, 21 Nov., 24–25.

Cheung Po-ling. 1990. "Regions Reported to Get Concessions in Next Plan." *Hong Kong Standard*, 24 Nov.; *FBIS*, 26 Nov., 28–29.

Ch'ien Tuan-sheng. 1961. *The Government and Politics of China*. Cambridge: Harvard University Press.

Chinese Communist Party Central Documents Research Office, ed. 1986. *Shier da yi lai* (After the Twelfth Party Congress). Beijing: People's Publishing House.

"Chinese Communist Party Document Number One on Rural Economic Policies." 1983. *Xinhua*, 10 Apr.; *FBIS*, 13 Apr., K1–13.

Chu Tan and Zhang Feng. 1983. "Several Questions on Current Aspects of Economic System Reform That We Must Emphatically Study." *Jingjixue dongtai* (Trends in economics), no. 12:1–5.

"Circular Urges Correction of 'Unhealthy Practices.'" 1985. *Xinhua*, 9 Dec.; *FBIS*, 10 Dec., K1–3.

Clarke, Christopher M. 1981. "China's Energy Plan for the 80's." *China Business Review* 8, no. 3 (May–June): 48–51.

Colton, Timothy J. 1986. *The Dilemma of Reform in the Soviet Union*. New York: Council on Foreign Relations.

Comisso, Ellen. 1986. "Introduction: State Structures, Political Processes, and Collective Choice in CMEA States." In Ellen Comisso and Laura D'Andrea Tyson, eds., *Power, Purpose, and Collective Choice: Economic Strategy in Socialist States*, 19–62. Ithaca: Cornell University Press.

"Communiqué of the Third Plenary Session of the Eleventh Central Committee of the Communist Party of China." 1978. *Beijing Review*, no. 52 (22 Dec.): 6–16.

"A Contract Dispensor Should Also Be Able to Provide a High-Mark Answer." 1988. *Renmin ribao*, 3 June; *FBIS*, 16 June, 45–46.

Crane, George T. 1990. *The Political Economy of China's Special Economic Zones*. Armonk, N.Y.: M. E. Sharpe.

"Curbing Abuses." 1985. *China Daily*, 16 Dec., 4.

Cyert, Richard M., and James G. March. 1963. *A Behavioral Theory of the Firm*. Englewood Cliffs, N.J.: Prentice Hall.

Dahl, Robert A. 1956. *A Preface to Democratic Theory*. Chicago: University of Chicago Press.

Dai Yuanchen and He Suoheng. 1987. "Macroeconomic Policy Options Faced in Times of Financial Difficulties." *Jingji yanjiu* (Economic research), 20 June, 26–32.

Dai Yuanchen et al. 1989. "Short-Term Measures for Freeing Reform from Its Current Difficulties." *Jingji yanjiu*, 20 July, 3–12.

Dai Yuqing. 1985. "The Two Sides of Decision-Making Power." *Renmin ribao*, 1 Apr.; *FBIS*, 3 Apr., K12–13.

Daniels, Robert V. 1989. "Political Processes and Generational Change." In Archie Brown, ed., *Political Leadership in the Soviet Union*, 96–126. Bloomington: Indiana University Press.

———. 1971. "Soviet Politics since Khrushchev." In John W. Strong, ed., *The Soviet Union under Brezhnev and Kosygin*, 16–25. New York: Van Nostrand–Reinhold.

"Decision of the Central Committee of the Communist Party of China on Reform of the Economic Structure." 1984. Adopted by the Twelfth Central Committee of the Communist Party of China at Its Third Plenary Session, 20 Oct. 1984. Beijing: Foreign Languages Press.

"Decisions on Some Questions Concerning the Acceleration of Agricultural Development." 1979. *Xinhua*, 5 Oct.; cited in Harold C. Hinton, ed., *The People's Republic of China, 1979–1984: A Documentary Survey* 2:513–23. Wilmington: Scholarly Resources, 1986.

"Deng Discusses Price Reform, Policy on Hong Kong." 1988. *Xinhua*, 3 June; *FBIS*, 3 June, 17.

"Deng to Give Up CCP Job." 1982. *Agence France-Press* (Hong Kong), 23 Aug.; *FBIS*, 24 Aug., K8–9.

Deng Xiaoping. 1984. *Selected Works of Deng Xiaoping (1975–1982)*. Beijing: Foreign Languages Press.

———. 1980. "On the Reform of the System of Party and State Leadership." In Deng, *Selected Works of Deng Xiaoping*, 302–25.

"Deng Xiaoping's Important Speech Delivered at the Central Work Conference on December 25, 1980." 1981. *Ming pao* (Hong Kong), 1 May; *FBIS*, 1 May, W2.

"Deng Xiaoping's Speech at the CCP National Conference." 1985. *Beijing Review*, 30 Sept., 15–18.

Deng Yingtao and Xu Xiaobo. 1987. "The Effect of Extrabudgetary Funds on Capital Construction and Countermeasures." *Jingji ribao*, 24 Feb.; *FBIS*, 11 Mar., 16.

Dernberger, Robert F. 1986. "Economic Policy and Performance." In U.S. Congress, Joint Economic Committee, *China's Economy Looks Toward the Year 2000*. Washington D.C.: Government Printing Office.

———. 1981. "P.R.C. Industrial Policies: Goals and Results." Unpublished paper.

"Different Types of Contracted Managerial Responsibility Systems Used by Enterprises." 1987. *Shijieh jingji daobao*, 25 May, 7.

Ding Xuedong. 1987. "Combine Substituting Tax-for-Profit and the Contracted Management Responsibility System." *Shijie jingji daobao*, 18 May, 15.

"A Discussion on the Question of Tax-for-Profit by Some Enterprise Leaders in Beijing City." 1983. *Jingji guanli*, Mar., 28–30.

Dittmer, Lowell. 1990. "Patterns of Elite Strife and Succession in Chinese Politics." *China Quarterly*, no. 123 (Sept.): 405–30.

————. 1989. "The Tiananmen Massacre." *Problems of Communism* 38, no. 5 (Sept.–Oct.): 2–15.

————. 1984. "Ideology and Organization in Post-Mao China." *Asian Survey* 24, no. 3 (Mar.): 349–69.

"Do a Still Better Job in the Reform of Expanding Enterprises' Decision Making Powers." 1981. *Xinhua*, 5 Mar.; *FBIS*, 11 Mar., L25.

"Do Not Put Up New Blockades in the Course of Reform." 1984. *Xinhua*, 18 July; *FBIS*, 23 July, K9–10.

"Documents Urge Enterprise Consolidation." 1983. *Xinhua*, 30 June; *FBIS*, 1 July, K8.

Dong Furen. 1982. "Further Develop the Study of China's Economic Development Strategy." *Jingjixue wenzhai* (Economics digest), no. 4:5–7.

————. 1979. "On Questions Regarding the Forms of Socialist Ownership in China." *Jingji yanjiu*, no. 1.

Dong Huanliang. 1987. "Changzhou Dongfeng Printing and Dyeing Factory Practices the System of Linking Remunerations with Profits." *Renmin ribao*, 22 Apr.; *FBIS*, 29 Apr., K31–33.

————. 1984. "Corporations Cannot Fight for Power with Enterprises." *Renmin ribao*, 16 Nov., 2.

Dong Yuguo. 1991. "Looking Towards Modernization by the Mid-21st Century: An Interview with Yuan Mu." *Beijing Review*, no. 13 (1–7 Apr.): 12–22.

Donnithorne, Audrey. 1981. *Centre-Provincial Economic Relations in China*. Contemporary China Papers, no. 16. Canberra: Australian National University.

————. 1972. *The Budget and the Plan in China*. Contemporary China Papers, no. 3. Canberra: Australian National University.

————. 1967. *China's Economic System*. New York: Praeger.

"The Draft Plan for Trial Implementation of the Assets Management Responsibility System." 1987. *Jingjixue dongtai*, no. 1.

"Draft Revision of Some Articles of the Constitution of the Chinese Communist Party." 1987. *Renmin ribao*, 2 Nov.

Dunmore, Timothy. 1980. *The Stalinist Command Economy, The Soviet State Apparatus and Economic Policy, 1945–53*. London: Macmillan.

"Eating from Individual Plates Urged." 1984. *China Daily*, 26 Dec., 3.

"*Economic Daily* on Invigoration of Big Enterprises." 1984. *China Daily*, 7 Nov., 3.

Ehrlich, Eva, and Gyorgy Szilagyi. 1980. "International Comparison of the Hungarian Infrastructure, 1960–1974." *Acta Oeconomica*, no. 24:57–80.

"Eleven Policy Measures to Invigorate Large and Medium-Sized Enterprises." 1985. Speech by Lu Dong at National Economic Work Conference. In Shen Chong and Xiang Xiyang, eds., *Shinian lai: lilun, zhengce, shijian, ziliao xuanbian* (The decade: theory, policy, and practice, a collection of documents) 3:262–63. Beijing: Seek Truth Publishing House.

"Enterprise Contracted Management Wins a Great Breakthrough in 1987." 1988. *Renmin ribao*, 28 Jan.; rpt. in Shen Chong and Xiang Xiyang, eds., *Shinian lai: lilun, zhengce, shijian, ziliao xuanbian* (The decade: theory, policy, and practice, a collection of documents) 3:283–85. Beijing: Seek Truth Publishing House.

"Enterprise Contracting Method Suits China's National Conditions." 1987. *Renmin ribao*, 20 July, 1.

"Enterprise Directors Forum Held 9 September." 1989. *Liaoning ribao* (Liaoning daily), 12 Sept.; *FBIS*, 16 Oct., 62.

"Enterprises Fail to Fulfill Contract Obligations." 1988. Beijing Domestic Service, 8 May; *FBIS*, 1 June, 35.

"Enterprises' Greater Autonomy." 1985. *Xinhua*, 6 Feb.; *FBIS*, 7 Feb., K10.

Esherick, Joseph W., and Elizabeth J. Perry. 1983. "Leadership Succession in the People's Republic of China: 'Crisis' or Opportunity?" *Studies in Comparative Communism* 16, no. 3:171–77.

"Establish a System of Planned Management More Suitable to Our Country's Situation" (Special commentator). 1982. *Renmin ribao*, 21 Sept., 4–5.

Fan Gang. 1990. "Appropriately Readjust the Ownership Structure." *Jingji cankao* (Economic reference), 4 Dec.; *FBIS*, 21 Dec., 26–28.

Fang Weizhong. 1982. "A Basic Principal from Which We Cannot Waver." *Hongqi*, no. 9 (Sept.): 13–19.

———. 1979. "Some Tentative Ideas on Carrying Out the Reform of the Economic Management Structure." *Renmin ribao*, 21 Sept., 3.

Fang Weizhong et al. 1984. *Zhonghua renmin gongheguo jingji dashiji* (Chronicle of economic events in the PRC). Beijing: Chinese Social Science Publishers.

Fang Xiaoqiu. 1987. "A Probe into the Question of Accelerating Financial Reform." *Renmin ribao*, 14 Dec.; *FBIS*, 24 Dec., 12–15.

Feng Zonghao. 1984. "A Mathematical Evaluation of the 'Contracting Method' and the 'Sharing Method.'" *Jingji guanli*, no. 3 (Mar.): 25–26.

Fewsmith, Joseph. 1989. "China's Price Reform: Intellectual Approaches and Policy Conflict." Paper presented at the annual meeting of the Association for Asian Studies, Mar.

Field, Robert Michael. 1986. "China: The Changing Structure of Industry." In U.S. Congress, Joint Economic Committee, *China's Economy Looks Toward the Year 2000*, 505–47. Washington, D.C.: Government Printing Office.

"Fifty-two Cities Carry Out Economic Reform." 1984. *Renmin ribao*, 20 Oct., 3.

"Finance Ministry Circular on Tax Collection." 1983. *Xinhua*, 26 May; *FBIS*, 27 May, K5.

"Finance Official Describes New Taxation System." 1983. *Xinhua*, 16 Mar.; *FBIS*, 17 Mar., K15.

"Finance Official Interviewed on New Tax Plan." 1983. *Xinhua*, 27 Apr.; *FBIS*, 3 May, K7–13.

"Forum Discusses Deng's Speech." 1987. *Xinhua*, 5 July; *FBIS*, 6 July, K5–8.

"Four Thousand Large and Medium-Sized Enterprises Carry Out Contracted Management: Double Increase and Double Savings Obtains Clear Economic Benefit." 1987. *Renmin ribao*, 18 July, 1.

Friedrich, Carl. 1963. *Man and His Government*. New York: McGraw-Hill.

Fujimoto, Akira. 1980. "The Reform of China's Financial Administration System." *China Newsletter* (Japan External Trade Research Organization), Mar., 2–9.

"Fully Understand the Long-Term Character and Difficulty of the Reform." 1987. *Hongqi*, Mar.; *FBIS*, 16 Mar., K13–15.

Gao Jie. 1982. "The Vitality of Industrial Economy as Seen from Several Figures." *Ban yue tan* (Fortnightly talks), 25 July; *FBIS*, 13 Aug., K7–9.

Gao Shangquan. 1987. *Jiunianlai de zhongguo jingji tizhi gaige* (China's economic system reform during the past nine years). Beijing: Renmin Chubanshe.

Ge Fu. 1989. "Comprehensive Arrangements Are Necessary for Coal Price Reform." *Jingji guanli*, no. 8:16–20.

Goldstein, Avery. 1991. *From Bandwagon to Balance-of-Power Politics: Structural Constraints and Politics in China, 1949–78*. Stanford: Stanford University Press.

Goodman, David S. G. 1984. "Provincial Party First Secretaries in National Politics: A Categoric or a Political Group?" In Goodman, ed., *Groups and Politics in the People's Republic of China*, 68–82. Cardiff: University College Cardiff Press.

Gorbachev, M. S. 1987. "Restructuring Is a Vital Affair of the People." Speech at the Eighteenth Congress of USSR Trade Unions. *Pravda*, 26 Feb.; *Current Digest of the Soviet Press* 39, no. 8:7–8, 13–14.

Granick, David. 1990. *Chinese State Enterprises: A Regional Property Rights Analysis*. Chicago: University of Chicago Press.

———. 1987. "The Industrial Environment in China and the CMEA Countries." In Gene Tidrick and Chen Jiyuan, eds., *China's Industrial Reforms*, 103–31. New York: Oxford University Press.

Gu Mu. 1985. "Opening Up to the World: A Strategic Decision to Make China Strong and Prosperous." *Kaifang* (Opening), no. 9 (8 Sept.); *FBIS*, 10 Oct., K2.

Guan Shaofeng. 1988. "The Relationships Between Local Party Committees, People's Congresses, and Governments—A Perspective." *Liaowang* (Outlook) *Overseas Edition*, 2 July; *FBIS*, 28 July, 16–19.

Guo Daimo and Yang Zhaoming. 1979. "Different Viewpoints in a Discussion on the Reform of the Economic Management Structure." *Renmin ribao*, 21 Sept., 3.

Guo Zhongshi. 1988. "Supply of State-Monopoly Goods Is Improved." *China Daily*, 23 Mar., 1.

Guojia Caizheng Gailun Bianxie Zhu. 1984. *Guojia caizheng gailun* (Introduction to national finance). Beijing: Finance and Economics Publishers.

Gustafson, Thane. 1981. *Reform in Soviet Politics: Lessons of Recent Policies on Land and Water*. Cambridge: Cambridge University Press.

Halpern, Nina P. 1989. "Economic Reform and Democratization in Communist Systems." *Studies in Comparative Communism* 22, nos. 2–3 (Summer–Autumn): 139–52.

Hammond, Thomas H., and Gary J. Miller. 1985. "A Social Choice Perspective on Expertise and Authority in Bureaucracy." *American Journal of Political Science* 29, no. 1 (Feb.): 1–28.

Hamrin, Carol Lee. 1990. *China and the Challenge of the Future: Changing Political Patterns*. Boulder: Westview.

———. 1984. "Competing 'Policy Packages' in Post-Mao China." *Asian Survey* 29, no. 1 (Jan.): 487–518.

Han Guochun. 1982. "A Brief Introduction to the System of 'Apportioning Revenues and Expenses Between the Central and Local Authorities, While Holding the Latter Responsible for Their Own Profit and Loss in Financial Management.'" *Caizheng* (Finance), no. 7 (5 July); *Joint Publications Research Service*, no. 82018 (19 Oct.): 16–19.

Hao Zhen, Zuo Linshu, and Wang Zhiliang. 1983. "The State Must Get the Biggest Part, and the Enterprise Must Have Prospects." *Jingji guanli*, no. 5:24–25.

Harding, Harry. 1981. *Organizing China: The Problem of Bureaucracy, 1949–1976*. Stanford: Stanford University Press.

Hayek, F. A. 1935. *Collectivist Economic Planning*. London: Routledge.

He Jiacheng and Bian Yongzhuang. 1987. "Assets Proposal Offered as a Solution." *China Daily*, 10 Sept., 4.

He Shaoming. 1990. "Intensification of Contradictions among the Party, Government, and Army." *Cheng ming* (Hong Kong), 1 Jan.; *FBIS*, 2 Jan., 23–25.

He Wei. 1990. "Some Rough Conceptions of Reform in State-Owned Enterprises." *Gongren ribao* (Workers' daily), 23 Nov.; *FBIS*, 27 Dec., 43–44.

He Zhuoxin. 1983. "To Emulate the Shoudu Iron and Steel Company, Efforts Must Be Exerted to Improve the Way of Doing Basic Tasks." *Xinhua*, 28 Dec. 1982; *FBIS*, 3 Jan. 1983.

Heilbroner, Robert. 1990. "After Communism." *New Yorker*, 10 Sept., 91–100.

"Henan Governor Cheng Weigao Sternly Criticized 'Internal Battles.'" 1988. *Renmin ribao*, 22 Mar.; *FBIS*, 23 Mar., 16–17.

Henderson, Gail E., and Myron Cohen. 1984. *The Chinese Hospital: A Socialist Work Unit*. New Haven: Yale University Press.

Hirschman, Albert O. 1963. *Journeys Toward Progress*. New York: Twentieth Century Fund.

———. 1958. *The Strategy of Economic Development*. New Haven: Yale University Press.

Hirszowicz, Maria. 1980. *The Bureaucratic Leviathan: A Study in the Sociology of Communism*. Oxford: Martin Robinson.

Ho, Samuel, and Ralph W. Huenemann. 1984. *China's Open Door Policy: The Quest for Foreign Technology and Capital*. Vancouver: University of British Columbia Press.

Ho Po-shih. 1991. "Inside Story of the Seventh Plenum." *Tangtai* (Contemporary) (Hong Kong), 5 Jan.; *FBIS*, 8 Jan., 28–30.

Hood, Marlowe. 1988. "Beijing's Contract System Keeps the Competitive Spirit Flowing." *South China Sunday Morning Post* (Hong Kong), 27 Mar.; *FBIS*, 28 Mar., 25–26.

Hough, Jerry F. 1991. "Understanding Gorbachev: The Importance of Politics." *Soviet Economy* 7 (Apr.–June): 89–109.

———. 1980. *Soviet Leadership in Transition*. Washington, D.C.: Brookings Institution.

———. 1977. *The Soviet Union and Social Science Theory*. Cambridge: Harvard University Press.

———. 1969. *The Soviet Prefects: The Local Party Organs in Industrial Decision-Making*. Cambridge: Harvard University Press.

Hough, Jerry F., and Merle Fainsod. 1979. *How the Soviet Union Is Governed*. Cambridge: Harvard University Press.

"How Shoudu Boosts Profits." 1982. *China Daily*, 11 Oct., 2.

"How Shoudu Steelworks Has Become a National Success." 1982. *China Daily*, 9 Oct., 2.

Hsiao, Katherine Huang. 1987. *The Government Budget and Fiscal Policy in Mainland China*. Taipei: Chung-Hua Institution for Economic Research.

Hu Guohua. 1988. "Party-State Separation Has Strengthened, Not Weakened, Party Leadership." *Liaowang*, 8 Feb.; *Joint Publications Research Service*, 19 May, 59.

Hu Qiaomu. 1978. "Observe Economic Laws." *Renmin ribao*, 6 Oct.; *FBIS*, 11 Oct., E1–22.

Hu Yaobang. 1982. "Report to the Twelfth CCP National Congress." In *The Twelfth National Congress of the CCP*, 9–85. Beijing: Foreign Languages Press.

"Hu Yaobang Resigns as General Secretary." 1987. *Xinhua*, 16 Jan.; *FBIS*, 16 Jan., K1–2.

Hua Sheng, He Jiacheng, et al. 1986. "The Bridge Integrating Public Ownership with the Commodity Economy." *Jingjixue dongtai*, no. 1.

———. 1986a. "On the Restructuring of Microeconomic Foundations." *Jingji yanjiu*, no. 3.

Hua Sheng, Zhang Xuejun, Luo Xiaopeng. 1988. "Ten Years of Chinese Reform: Review, Reflection, and Prospects." *Jingji yanjiu*, no. 9 (Sept.): 13–37; no. 11 (Nov.); no. 12 (Dec.).

Hua Xing. 1983. "The Components Will Be Stimulated When the Whole Is Handled Well." *Xinhua*, 17 Apr.; *FBIS*, 21 Apr., K10–11.

Huan Gudan. 1979. "A Look at the CCP Central Committee's Working Conference." *Cheng ming* (Hong Kong), no. 20 (1 June); *FBIS*, 8 June, U1–6.

Huang Changlu and Zhu Minzhi. 1983. "An Interview with Tian Jiyun." *Liaowang*, 29 Sept.; *FBIS*, 26 Oct., K10–14.

Huang Yasheng. 1988. "'Web' of Interests and Patterns of Behavior of Chinese Local Economic Bureaucracies and Enterprises During Reforms." Unpublished paper.

"*Hunan ribao* on Enterprise Responsibility Systems." 1981. *Hunan ribao*, 21 Aug.; *FBIS*, 24 Aug., P1–2.

"Immediately Stop Additional Levies of Local Energy and Transportation Construction Funds." 1984. *Renmin ribao*, 24 Nov., 2.

"The Important Matter of Substituting Tax for Profits Delivered to the State Must Be Grasped Firmly and Well." 1983. *Chengdu Sichuan Provincial Service*, 29 June; *FBIS*, 6 July, Q1–2.

"Industrial Management: Planning of Structural Changes." 1979. *China News Analysis*, no. 1165 (12 Oct.): 1–7.

"Industrial Production, Transport Conference Opens." 1981. *Xinhua*, 15 Apr.; *FBIS*, 16 Apr., K1–3.

"It Is Necessary for All to Cling to the Goal of Reform." 1986. *Xinhua*, 2 Nov.; *FBIS*, 3 Nov., K11–12.

Janos, Andrew. 1976. "Systemic Models and the Theory of Change in the Comparative Study of Communist Politics." In Janos, ed., *Authoritarian Politics in Communist Europe*, 1–31. Berkeley: Institute of International Studies.

Jao, Y. K., and C. K. Leung, eds. 1986. *China's Special Economic Zones*. Hong Kong: Oxford University Press.

Jefferson, Gary H., and Thomas G. Rawski. 1991. "A Theory of Economic Reform." University of Pittsburgh, Department of Economics, Working Paper no. 273, 26 Sept.

Jefferson, Gary H., Thomas G. Rawski, and Yu Xinzheng. Forthcoming. "Growth, Efficiency, and Convergence in China's State and Collective Industry." *Economic Development and Cultural Change*.

Ji Chongwei and Wang Zhenji. 1978. "On the Question of Increasing Enterprise Profits and Speeding Up the Accumulation of Funds." *Jingji yanjiu*, no. 4 (20 Apr.): 8–16.

Ji Naifu and Chen Naijin. 1984. "Meeting on Second Stage Tax Reform Held in Beijing." *Xinhua*, 7 July; *FBIS*, 9 July, K12–13.

Jiang Yiwei. 1988. "On Managerial Authority in Socialist Enterprises." *Gongren ribao*, 18 Mar.; *FBIS*, 31 Mar., 40–42.

———. 1983. "Some Questions about the Industrial Economic Responsibility System." *Jingji guanli*, no. 10 (Oct.): 22–27.

———. 1981. "The Theory of Enterprise Independence." *China Social Sciences*, no. 1.

Jilin Provincial Service. 1983. "Jilin's Governor Criticizes Malpractices." *Jilin Provincial Service*, 21 Feb.; *FBIS*, 24 Feb., S4–5.

"Jilin's Gao Di on Income of Contractors." 1987. *Dongbei jingji bao* (Northeast economic journal) (Shenyang), 13 Oct.; *FBIS*, 23 Oct., 38–39.

Jin Renxiong and Yuan Zhenyu. 1983. *Yi shui dai li jianlun* (A simple discussion of substituting tax for profit). Beijing: Chinese Finance and Economics Publishers.

Jin Xin. 1984. "Discussing the Second Step in the Reform of Substituting Taxes for Delivery of Profits." *Renmin ribao*, 22 June; *FBIS*, 27 June, K10–13.

———. 1983. "Appropriately Increase the Ratio of State Revenue to the National Income." *Renmin ribao*, 15 July; *FBIS*, 21 July, K10–12.

Jing Ping. 1983. "Everyone Must Support Key Construction." *Hongqi*, no. 8 (16 Apr.): 16–18.

Joffe, Ellis. 1987. *The Chinese Army after Mao*. London: Weidenfeld and Nicolson.

"Joint Report of the State Economic Commission, State Council Economic Reform Office, State Planning Commission, Ministry of Finance, Ministry of Commerce, Ministry of Foreign Trade, State Material Supply Bureau, State Labor Bureau, State Price Bureau, and the People's Bank of China on 'Thoroughly Carry Out the State Council's Regulations on Expanding Enterprise Autonomy and Firmly Improve Concrete Methods for Carrying Out the Work on Enterprise Autonomy.'" 1981. *The Communiqué of the State Council*, no. 14 (5 Sept.): 439–51.

Jones, Ellen. 1984. "Committee Decision Making in the Soviet Union." *World Politics* 36 (Jan.): 165–88.

"The Key Point of Contracting Is to Introduce the Competitive Mechanism." 1988. *Renmin ribao*, 13 Feb.; cited in Shen Chong and Xiang Xiyang, eds., *Shinian lai: lilun, zhengce, shijian, ziliao xuanbian* (The decade: theory, policy, and practice, a collection of documents) 3:285–86. Beijing: Seek Truth Publishing House.

Kiewiet, D. Roderick, and Mathew D. McCubbins. 1991. *The Logic of Delegation: Congressional Parties and the Appropriations Process*. Chicago: University of Chicago Press.

Kobayashi, Shigeru. 1981. "The 'Reality of Readjustment' in China." *Metalworking Engineering and Marketing* (Japan), Nov., 22–31.

Kokubun Ryosei. 1986. "The Politics of Foreign Economic Policy-Making in China: The Case of Plant Cancellations with Japan." *China Quarterly*, no. 105 (Mar.): 19–44.

Kong Xiangji. 1985. "A Reexamination of the Causes of the Failure of the One-Hundred Day Reform." *Renmin ribao*, 21 Oct.; *FBIS*, 5 Nov., K1–4.

Krueger, Anne. 1974. "The Political Economy of the Rent-Seeking Society." *American Economic Review* 64:291–302.

Kuan Chen, Gary Jefferson, Thomas Rawski, Wang Hongchang, and Zheng Yuxin. 1988. "Productivity Change in Chinese Industry, 1953–85." *Journal of Comparative Economics* 12:570–91.

Kuan, Daniel. 1990. "Regional Cadres Said Demanding More Powers." *South China Morning Post*, 13 Nov.; *FBIS*, 13 Nov., 27–28.

Kuhn, Philip. 1970. *Rebellion and Its Enemies in Late Imperial China: Militarization and Social Structure, 1798–1864*. Cambridge: Harvard University Press.

Kuo Chien. 1991. "PLA General Political Department Issues New Brainwashing Document: The CCP Is Tightening Control over the Army." *Tangtai* (Hong Kong), 15 May; *FBIS*, 21 May, 52–55.

Kyodo. 1987. "PRC Sources Note Hu Yaobang 'Ran Recklessly.'" *Kyodo* (Tokyo), 17 Jan.; *FBIS*, 20 Jan., K5–7.

Lam, Willy Wo-lap. 1991. "Party Elders Resist Abolishing Advisory Commission." *South China Morning Post* (Hong Kong), 12 June; *FBIS*, 17 June, 26–27.

———. 1989. "Further on CCP Central Work Conference." *South China Morning Post* (Hong Kong), 3 Nov.; *FBIS*, 3 Nov., 13.

Lampton, David M. 1987. "Chinese Politics: The Bargaining Treadmill." *Issues and Studies* 23, no. 3 (Mar.): 11–41.

———. 1987a. "Water: Challenge to a Fragmented Political System." In Lampton, ed., *Policy Implementation in Post-Mao China*, 157–89. Berkeley and Los Angeles: University of California Press.

Lardy, Nicholas R. 1991. "Redefining U.S.-China Economic Relations." The National Bureau of Asian and Soviet Research, *NBR Analysis Series Paper* no. 5.

———. 1983. *Agriculture in China's Modern Economic Development*. Cambridge: Cambridge University Press.

———. 1979. *Economic Growth and Distribution in China*. Cambridge: Cambridge University Press.

Lardy, Nicholas R., and Kenneth G. Lieberthal, eds. 1983. *Chen Yun's Strategy for China's Development: A Non-Maoist Alternative*. Armonk, N.Y.: M. E. Sharpe.

"Large State Enterprises Need Such Administrators." 1985. *Xinhua*, 28 Jan.; *FBIS*, 29 Jan., K21–22.

Lawler, Edward E., III. 1976. "Control Systems in Organizations." In Marvin Dunnette, ed., *Handbook of Industrial and Organizational Psychology*, 1247–92. Chicago: Rand McNally.

"Leading Party Groups to Be Dissolved." 1988. *Xinhua*, 31 July; *FBIS*, 1 Aug., 29.

Lee, Hong Yung. 1991. *From Revolutionary Cadres to Party Technocrats in Socialist China*. Berkeley and Los Angeles: University of California Press.

Lee, Peter N. S. 1987. *Industrial Management and Economic Reform in China, 1949–1984*. Hong Kong: Oxford University Press.

———. 1986. "Enterprise Autonomy in Post-Mao China: A Case Study of Policy-making, 1978–83." *China Quarterly*, no. 105 (Mar.): 45–71.

"Let Enterprises Invigorate Themselves." 1984. Beijing Domestic Service, 7 July; *FBIS*, 9 July, K14–15.

Li Anding. 1983. "Enterprises Try Self-Management in Foreign Trade." *Xinhua*, 12 May; *FBIS*, 17 May, K14–15.

Li Haibo. 1983. "Shoudu Steel: A Success Story." *Beijing Review*, 11 Apr., 19–25.

Li Huifen. 1984. "Some Methods and Experiences from Our Carrying Out the Progressively Increasing Profit Remittance Contracting System." *Jingji guanli*, no. 4:19–22, 25.

Li Jianli. 1982. "Will Concentrating Funds for Capital Construction Investment Affect the Improvement in the People's Living Standard?" *Beijing ribao*, 1 Nov., 3.

Li Jun. 1988. "The Contract System and Price Reform." *Liaowang Overseas Edition*, 11 July; *FBIS*, 20 July, 38–41.

Li Kaixin. 1983. "Concentrate Materials to Ensure Keypoint Construction." *Hongqi*, no.17:16–19.

Li Ling. 1983. "Large Scale Production and Small Enterprises." *Renmin ribao*, 2 Sept.; *FBIS*, 14 Sept., K10–15.

Li Peng. 1991. "Further Deepen Reform, Invigorate Large and Medium-Sized Enterprises." *Xinhua*, 23 May; *FBIS*, 24 May, 31–37.

————. 1991a. "Report on the Outline of the Ten-Year Program and the Eighth Five-Year Plan for National Economic and Social Development." Speech delivered at the Fourth Session of the Seventh National People's Congress. Beijing Domestic Service, 25 Mar.; *FBIS*, 27 Mar., 9–34.

————. 1990. "Make Great Efforts to Adjust the Economic Structure and Improve Enterprises' Economic Results." Speech to the National Planning Meeting. *Xinhua*, 31 Dec. 1990; *FBIS*, 2 Jan. 1991, 18–29.

————. 1989. "Maintain Orientation, Firm Up Confidence, Advance with Steady Steps." *Zhongguo jingji tizhi gaige* (Chinese economic system reform), no. 2 (23 Feb.); *FBIS*, 8 Mar., 21–24.

————. 1988. "Li Peng Addresses Party Work Meeting." *Xinhua*, 22 Mar.; *FBIS*, 23 Mar., 15–16.

"Li Peng Chairs State Council Executive Meeting." 1988. *Xinhua*, 12 July; *FBIS*, 13 July, 19.

"Li Peng Discusses Reform of Price Increases." 1988. *Renmin ribao*, 25 May; *FBIS*, 31 May, 26.

"Li Peng, Others Hold Final News Briefing." 1991. Beijing Central Television, 9 Apr.; *FBIS*, 10 Apr., 18–20.

"Li Peng Pushes Contract System at Forum." 1988. *Xinhua*, 12 Feb.; *FBIS*, 16 Feb., 16–17.

"Li Peng Stresses Economic Efficiency." 1991. *Xinhua*, 12 Feb.; *FBIS*, 13 Feb., 36–39.

Li Rui. 1985. "Do Not Blindly Seek a Higher Rate of Development." *Guangming ribao*, 7 May; *FBIS*, 15 May, K11.

Li Shangzhi and He Ping. 1991. "Newsletter: Lighthouse That Illuminates a Ten-Year Voyage: On the Conception of the Outline of the Ten Year Program and the Eighth Five-Year Plan for National Economic and Social Development." *Xinhua*, 6 Apr.; *FBIS*, 10 Apr., 27–30.

Li Ximing. 1989. "Li Ximing Speaks at Beijing Plenum." *Beijing ribao*, 12 Oct.; *FBIS*, 11 Dec., 46–47.

Li Xinyan. 1985. "Zhao Ziyang Praises Shenyang Plant's Reform." *Xinhua*, 4 Mar.; *FBIS*, 5 Mar., K9–10.

Li Yining. 1989. "We Are Faced with Inflation Related to the Economic System." *Shijie jingji daobao*, 6 Mar., 2.

Li Yunlin, Guo Lian, and Zhu Jun. 1989. "An Experiment in Commenting on China's Regional Inflation." *Guangming ribao*, 7 Jan.; *FBIS*, 19 Jan., 33–35.

Liao Shixiang and Huang Moya. 1988. "Several Thoughts on the Separation of Party and Government." *Guangming ribao* (Bright daily), 1 Aug.; *FBIS*, 15 Aug., 24–26.

"Liaoning Issues Regulations on Large Enterprises." 1985. Liaoning Provincial Service, 11 Feb.; *FBIS*, 14 Feb., S1–2.

Liaoning jingji tongji nianjian (Liaoning yearbook of economic statistics), *1987*. 1987. Beijing: Zhongguo Tongji Chubanshe.

Lieberthal, Kenneth G., and Bruce J. Dickson. 1989. *A Research Guide to Central Party and Government Meetings in China, 1949–1989*. Armonk, N.Y.: M. E. Sharpe.

Lieberthal, Kenneth G., and Michel Oksenberg. 1988. *Policy Making in China: Leaders, Structures, and Processes*. Princeton: Princeton University Press.

Lin, Cyril Zhiren. 1989. "Open-Ended Economic Reform in China." In David Stark and Victor Nee, eds., *Remaking the Economic Institutions of Socialism*, 95–136. Stanford: Stanford University Press.

Lin, Justin. 1988. "The Household Responsibility System in China's Agricultural Reform: A Theoretical and Empirical Study." *Economic Development and Cultural Change* 36, no. 3 (Apr.): S199–224.

Lin Ling. 1988. "Some Questions on Deepening Enterprise Reforms." *Guangming ribao*, 13 Feb.; *FBIS*, 25 Mar., 59–63.

———. 1983. "Several Questions Regarding the Relationship Between the State and the Enterprise." *Jingji guanli*, no. 10 (Oct.): 34–36.

Lin Ruo. 1988. "A Successful Attempt to Reform the Financial System." *Renmin ribao*, 21 Mar.; *FBIS*, 6 Apr., 55–57.

Lindblom, Charles E. 1977. *Politics and Markets*. New York: Basic.

Link, Perry. 1986. "Intellectuals and Cultural Policy after Mao." In A. Doak Barnett and Ralph N. Clough, eds., *Modernizing China, Post-Mao Reforms and Development*, 81–102. Boulder: Westview.

Liu Guoguang. 1990. "Problems Regarding the Economic Mechanism Must be Resolved While Improving the Economic Environment and Rectifying the Economic Order." *Ching chi tao pao* (Economic herald) (Hong Kong), 22 Jan.; *FBIS*, 5 Feb., 22–23.

———. 1990a. "A Study of the Reform of China's State Owned Economy." *Zhongguo jingji tizhi gaige*, 23 Nov.; *FBIS*, 27 Dec., 44–48.

———. 1989. "China's Economic Readjustment and the Fate of Reform." *Jingji ribao*, 28 Feb., 3.

Liu Guoguang and Zhao Renwei. 1985. "The Question of Dual Structure in the Course of Pattern Transformation." *Guangming ribao*, 2 Nov.; *FBIS*, 13 Nov., K18–20.

Liu Hong. 1988. "The Party Leadership Is Political Leadership." *Ban yue tan*, no. 1 (10 Jan.); *FBIS*, 8 Feb., 14–16.

Liu Jui-shao. 1988. "Enlarged Meeting of CCP Political Bureau Decides on Tough Action on Prices and Other Problems." *Wen wei po* (Hong Kong), 31 May; *FBIS*, 31 May, 19.

Liu Lixin and Tian Chunsheng. 1983. "Conscientiously Control the Scale of Investments in Fixed Assets." *Renmin ribao*, 21 Feb.; *FBIS*, 24 Feb., K15–18.

Liu Rongcang. 1987. "Increasing the Results in Funds Utilization Is an Important Link in Increasing Production and Economizing." *Renmin ribao*, 17 Apr., 5.

Liu Tonglin, Li Lian, Lu Fengling, and Wang Lun. 1987. "The Contracted Responsibility System: Special Points and Problems That Must Be Solved." *Shijie jingji daobao*, 27 Apr., 14.

Liu Tonglin et al. 1987. "Several Questions on Carrying Out the Contracted Responsibility System." *Renmin ribao*, 18 May 18; rpt. in Shen Chong and Xiang Xiyang, eds., *Shinian lai: lilun, zhengce, shijian, ziliao xuanbian* (The decade: theory, policy, and practice, a collection of documents) 3:218–20. Beijing: Seek Truth Publishing House, 1988.

Liu Yiqun et al. 1989. "An Analysis of the Causes of Increase and Decrease in Savings Deposits." *Jingji guanli*, no. 6:57–59, 62.

Lo Ping. 1991. "Notes on a Northern Journey." *Cheng ming* (Hong Kong), 1 June; *FBIS*, 4 June, 28–30.

———. 1989. "Notes on a Northern Journey." *Cheng ming* (Hong Kong), 1 Dec., 6–8.

———. 1988. "Notes on a Northern Journey." *Cheng ming* (Hong Kong), 1 Apr.; *FBIS*, 1 Apr., 42–46.

———. 1987. "Notes on a Northern Journey." *Cheng ming* (Hong Kong), 1 Feb.; *FBIS*, 29 Jan., K1–8.

———. 1987a. "Notes on a Northern Journey." *Cheng ming* (Hong Kong), 1 Mar.; *FBIS*, 3 Mar., K1–3.

———. 1987b. "Notes on a Northern Journey." *Cheng ming* (Hong Kong), 1 July; *FBIS*, 2 July, K5–11.

———. 1986. "Notes on a Northern Journey." *Cheng ming* (Hong Kong), 1 Jan.; *FBIS*, 6 Jan., W3–8.

———. 1985. "Notes on a Northern Journey." *Cheng ming* (Hong Kong), 1 May; *FBIS*, 3 May, W1–4.

———. 1985a. "Notes on a Northern Journey." *Cheng ming* (Hong Kong), 1 June; *FBIS*, 6 June, W2–11.

———. 1981. "Reorganization of the Nucleus of the Chinese Communist Party—The Truth of Hua Guofeng's Resignation and the New Troika." *Cheng ming* (Hong Kong), 1 Feb.; *FBIS*, 2 Feb., U1–6.

Lo So. 1989. "Why Has Deng Xiaoping Retired at This Time?" *Ching pao* (Hong Kong), 10 Dec.; *FBIS*, 13 Dec., 10–14.

Lou Jiwei and Zhou Xiaochuan. 1984. "On the Direction of the Reform of Our Country's Price System and Other Related Models and Measures." *Jingji yanjiu*, no. 10 (20 Oct.): 13–20.

Lu Baifu. 1988. "Theory and Policy on Reform of Enterprise Loan Repayment." *Renmin ribao*, 11 Mar., 5.

Lu Dong. 1991. "Transforming the Operational Mechanism Is the Key to Invigorating Large and Medium-Sized State Enterprises." *Renmin ribao*, 6 May; *FBIS*, 22 May, 58–63.

———. 1988. "Perfectly Link Up the Parts to Deepen and Develop the Contract Managerial Responsibility System, Speech at the National Forum on the Contract Managerial Responsibility System for Enterprises." *Renmin ribao*, 14 Feb.; *FBIS*, 4 Mar., 24–27.

Lu Feng. 1991. "Vigorously Promote the Work of the Cadre Reshuffles." *Renmin ribao*, 19 Jan.; *FBIS*, 25 Jan., 33–34.

Lu Xiansheng. 1982. "Mandatory Planning Is the Most Important Form of the Planned Economy." *Guangming ribao*, 17 Oct., 3.

Lu Zhihui. 1987. "Summary of the Situation of Implementing the Contracted Responsibility System in the Nation's Regions." *Ti gai xinxi* (System reform news), no. 19; rpt. in Shen Chong and Xiang Xiyang, eds., *Shinian lai: lilun, zhengce, shijian, ziliao xuanbian* (The decade: theory, policy, and practice, a collection of documents) 3:277–82. Beijing: Seek Truth Publishing House, 1988.

Luo Liewen and Ruan Jiangning. 1989. "The Establishment of Scientific and Democratic Procedures for Making Policy Decisions Must Not Be Delayed Any Longer, Famous Economist Jiang Yiwei Points Out the Defects of Current Policy-Making Procedures." *Shijie jingji daobao*, 17 Apr., 1–2.

Luo Yuanming. 1985. "Enterprises Should Rely on Their Own Efforts for Invigoration." *Shijie jingji daobao*, 22 July, 2.

Lyons, Thomas P. 1990. "Planning and Interprovincial Co-ordination in Maoist China." *China Quarterly*, no. 121 (Mar.): 36–60.

———. 1987. *Economic Integration and Planning in Maoist China*. New York: Columbia University Press.

Ma Daying. 1982. "On Unified Financial Authority and Concentrated Finance Resources." *Caijing wenti yanjiu* (Research on finance and economic problems), no. 1 (Jan.): 6–12.

Ma Hong. 1987. "Ma Hong, General Director of State Council Economic and Social Development Research Center, Answers Reporter's Questions." *Guangming ribao*, 29 Oct.; *FBIS*, 13 Nov., 37–38.

———. 1982. "A New Road for Developing China's Socialist Economy." *Ta kung pao* (Hong Kong), 11 Dec. 1981; *FBIS*, 21 Jan. 1982, W3–6.

———. 1982a. "Strengthen the Planned Economy, Improve Planning Work." *China Finance and Trade Journal*, 20 June.

Ma Hong and Sun Shangqing, eds. 1981. *Zhongguo jingji jiegou wenti yanjiu* (Research on problems of China's economic structure). Beijing: Zhongguo Shehui Kexue Chubanshe.

McCubbins, Mathew, and Thomas Schwartz. 1984. "Congressional Oversight Overlooked: Police Patrols vs. Fire Alarms." *American Journal of Political Science* 28 (Feb.): 165–79.

MacFarquhar, Roderick. 1988. "Passing the Baton in Beijing." *New York Review of Books*, 18 Feb., 21–22.

———. 1983. *The Origins of the Cultural Revolution*. Vol. 2, *The Great Leap Forward, 1958–1960*. New York: Columbia University Press.

———. 1974. *The Origins of the Cultural Revolution*. Vol. 1, *Contradictions among the People, 1956–57*. New York: Columbia University Press.

McMillan, John, and Barry Naughton. 1991. "How to Reform a Planned Economy: Lessons from China." Unpublished paper, 14 Nov.

McMillan, John, John Whalley, and Zhu Lijing. 1989. "The Impact of China's Economic Reforms on Agricultural Productivity Growth." *Journal of Political Economy* 97, no. 4:781–807.

The Macroeconomic Management Project Group of the Institute of Economics, Chinese Academy of Social Sciences. 1987. "Uphold the Direction of an Appropriate Degree of Decentralization, Remodel the State Management Structure." *Jingji yanjiu*, June, 16–25.

"Main Points of Comrade Yang Shangkun's Speech at Emergency Enlarged Meeting of the Central Military Commission, May 24, 1989." 1989. *Ming pao* (Hong Kong), 29 May; *FBIS*, 30 May, 17–20.

"A Major Breakthrough, the Aim and Significance of Carrying Out the Second-Stage Reform in Tax-for-Profit." 1984. *Renmin ribao*, 8 July, 1.

"A Major Principle, the State Takes the Biggest Slice." 1983. *Renmin ribao*, 17 Apr.; *FBIS*, 19 Apr., K1–3.

Manion, Melanie. 1991. "Policy Implementation in the People's Republic of China: Authoritative Decisions Versus Individual Interests." *Journal of Asian Studies* 50, no. 2 (May): 253–79.

Mann, Jim. 1989. *Beijing Jeep: The Short Unhappy Romance of American Business in China*. New York: Simon and Schuster.

Mann, Susan. 1987. *Local Merchants and the Chinese Bureaucracy, 1750–1950*. Stanford: Stanford University Press.

"Many Provincial Units Begin Responding to the Call of the Thirty-one Factory Directors." 1985. *Shanxi ribao* (Shanxi daily), 16 June; *FBIS*, 2 July, R1–2.

Maruyama, Nobuo. 1981. "Regional Development Policy: Part II." *China Newsletter* (Japan External Trade Research Organization), no. 33 (July– Aug.): 16–22.

"Metallurgical Conference's New System Approved." 1985. *Xinhua*, 10 Feb.; *FBIS*, 12 Feb., K16–17.

Microeconomic Research Office of the Chinese Economic Structural Reform Institute. 1988. "Development of the Contract System and Deepening Enterprise Reform." *Renmin ribao*, 25 Jan., 26 Jan.; *FBIS*, 4 Feb., 15–17, 10 Feb., 29–31.

"Minister of Finance Addresses Financial Meeting." 1988. *Xinhua*, 24 July; *FBIS*, 25 July, 42–43.

Ministry of Finance. 1983. "Ministry of Finance Temporary Regulations on Financial Management Questions in Carrying Out Replacing Profit with Tax in State Industrial and Transportation Enterprises." In *Guoying chiyeh ligaishui wenjian huibian* (Collection of documents on replacing profit with tax in state enterprises), 15–16. Beijing: Chinese Financial Economics Publishing House.

"Ministry of Finance Regulations for Implementing Tax-for-Profit in State Enterprises." 1983. *State Council Bulletin*, no. 11 (30 June): 475–78.

"The Ministry of Finance Regulations on Implementing Income Tax Collection in State Enterprises." 1983. Rpt. in *Jingji tizhi gaige wenjian huibian 1977–83* (Collection of documents on the State Economic System reform), 916–18. Beijing: Beijing Finance and Economics Publishers, 1984.

"Ministry of Finance Report on the National Tax-for-Profit Work Conference." 1983. *State Council Bulletin*, no. 11 (30 June): 468–74.

Mo Huilin and Zhu Congguang. 1983. "We Should Do Research on the Tax-for-Profit Method to Improve It." *Jingji guanli*, Feb., 44–45.

"The Momentum in the Development of 'Dual Increase and Dual Reduction' Is Good." 1987. *Renmin ribao*, 1 Apr.

Mu Fu. 1985. "Confrontation Between Two Factions at the September Conference of Party Delegates." *Cheng ming* (Hong Kong), 1 Oct.; *FBIS*, 3 Oct., W1–7.

Nathan, Andrew J. 1973. "A Factionalism Model for CCP Politics." *China Quarterly*, no. 53 (Jan.–Mar.): 34–66.

"National Meeting of Enterprises Using Progressive Profit Contracting Called in Beijing." 1984. *Jingji tizhi gaige*, Jan., 63.

Naughton, Barry. Forthcoming. *Growing out of the Plan: Chinese Economic Reform, 1978–90*. Cambridge: Cambridge University Press.

———. 1990. "Inflation: Patterns, Causes, and Cures." In U.S. Congress, Joint Economic Committee, *China's Economic Dilemmas in the 1990's* 1:135–59. Washington, D.C.: Government Printing Office.

———. 1990a. "Macroeconomic Obstacles to Reform in China: The Role of Fiscal and Monetary Policy." Unpublished paper.

———. 1989. "Monetary Implications of Balanced Economic Growth and the Current Macroeconomic Disturbances in China: Policy and Institutional Factors." In Dieter Cassel and Gunter Heiduk, eds., *China's Contemporary Economic Reforms as a Development Strategy*, 109–44. Baden-Baden: Nomos.

———. 1989a. "The Pattern and Legacy of Economic Growth in the Mao Era." In Joyce Kallgren, Kenneth Lieberthal, Roderick MacFarquhar, and Frederick Wakeman, eds., *Perspectives on Modern China: Four Anniversaries*, 226–54. Armonk, N.Y.: M. E. Sharpe.

———. 1988. "The Chinese Industrial Enterprise: Structure and Capabilities." Background paper prepared for the World Bank, Aug.

———. 1988a. "The Third Front: Defense Industrialization in the Chinese Interior." *China Quarterly*, no. 115 (Sept.): 351–86.

———. 1987. "The Decline of Central Control over Investment in Post-Mao China." In David M. Lampton, ed., *Policy Implementation in Post-Mao China*, 51–80. Berkeley and Los Angeles: University of California Press.

———. 1986. "Finance and Planning Reforms in Industry." In U.S. Congress, Joint Economic Committee, *China's Economy Looks Toward the Year 2000* 1:604–29. Washington, D.C.: Government Printing Office.

———. 1985. "False Starts and Second Wind: Financial Reforms in China's Industrial System." In Elizabeth J. Perry and Christine Wong, eds., *The Political Economy of Reform in Post-Mao China*, 223–52. Cambridge: Harvard University Press.

Nee, Victor. 1989. "A Theory of Market Transition: From Redistribution to Markets in State Socialism." *American Sociological Review* 54:663–81.

Nee, Victor, and Su Sijin. 1990. "Institutional Change and Economic Growth in China: The View from the Villages." *Journal of Asian Studies* 49, no. 1 (Feb.): 3–25.

"New Management System to Categorize Cadres." 1987. *Xinhua*, 18 Nov.; *FBIS*, 18 Nov., 17–18.

"Nine-Point Proposal on Invigoration by Leading Officials from Fifty-one Major Enterprises." 1988. *Guangming ribao*, 11 Feb.; *FBIS*, 9 Mar., 33–36.

"Nineteen Eighty-Five Document Number One on Rural Economic Reform." 1985. *Xinhua*, 24 Mar.; *FBIS*, 25 Mar., K1–11.

Nolan, Peter, and Dong Fureng, eds. 1989. *Market Forces in China, Competition and Small Business: The Wenzhou Debate*. London: Zed.

Nove, Alec. 1983. *The Economics of Feasible Socialism*. London: Allen and Unwin.

———. 1980. *The Soviet Economic System*. London: Allen and Unwin.

"NPC Presidium Holds Fourth Meeting April 5." 1988. *Xinhua*, 5 Apr.; *FBIS*, 5 Apr., 11–12.

"Official Discusses Party Role in Enterprises." 1989. *Xinhua*, 24 Dec.; *FBIS*, 29 Dec., 4–6.

Oi, Jean C. 1990. "The Fate of the Collective After the Commune." In Deborah Davis and Ezra Vogel, eds., *Chinese Society on the Eve of Tiananmen: The Impact of Reform*, 15–36. Cambridge: Harvard University Press.

————. 1989. *State and Peasant in Contemporary China: The Political Economy of Village Government*. Berkeley and Los Angeles: University of California Press.

————. 1988. "The Chinese Village Incorporated." In Bruce L. Reynolds, ed., *Chinese Economic Policy*, 67–88. New York: Paragon House.

Oksenberg, Michel. 1987. "China's Thirteenth Party Congress." *Problems of Communism* 36, no. 6 (Nov.–Dec.): 15–16.

————. 1982. "Economic Policy-Making in China: Summer 1981." *China Quarterly*, no. 90:165–94.

————. 1971. "Policy Making under Mao, 1949–68: An Overview." In John M. H. Lindbeck, ed., *China: Management of a Revolutionary Society*. Seattle: University of Washington Press.

Oksenberg, Michel, and Bruce J. Dickson. 1991. "The Origins, Processes, and Outcomes of Great Political Reform." In Dankwart A. Rustow and Kenneth Paul Erickson, eds., *Comparative Political Dynamics: Global Research Perspectives*, 235–61. New York: Harper and Row.

Oksenberg, Michel, and James Tong. 1990. "The Evolution of Central-Provincial Fiscal Relations in China, 1971–1984: The Formal System." Unpublished paper.

————. 1987. "The Evolution of Central-Provincial Fiscal Relations in China, 1950–1983: The Formal System." Unpublished paper.

————. 1984. "The Fiscal Reform in China and Its Effects on Interprovincial Variations in Social Services, 1979–1983." Unpublished paper.

"On 'Wrangles.'" 1986. *Liaowang*, 22 Sept.; *FBIS*, 23 Sept., K17–18.

"An Opinion on Eight Enterprises Experimenting with Tax-for-Profit in Guangdong Province." 1983. *Jingji guanli*, May, 26–28, 33.

"Organization Department and Personnel Department of the CCP Central Committee Issue Joint Circular on Introduction of Competitive Mechanism to Enterprises to Reform the Personnel System." 1988. *Renmin ribao*, 31 May; *FBIS*, 8 June, 37–38.

"Over 6000 State Factories, Mines Lose Money." 1988. *Xinhua*, 31 Aug.; *FBIS*, 1 Sept., 32.

Paltiel, Jeremy T. 1989. "China: Mexicanization or Market Reform?" In James A. Caporaso, ed., *The Elusive State: International and Comparative Perspectives*, 255–78. Newbury Park, Calif.: Sage.

————. 1985. "The Interaction of Party Rectification and Economic Reform in the CCP, 1984." Unpublished paper.

Parish, William L., ed. 1985. *Chinese Rural Development: The Great Transformation*. Armonk, N.Y.: M. E. Sharpe.

Pearson, Margaret. 1991. *Joint Ventures in the People's Republic of China: The Control of Foreign Direct Investment under Socialism*. Princeton: Princeton University Press.

"Perfecting the Contracted Management Responsibility System in the Course of Practice." 1987. *Renmin ribao*, 12 Dec.; *FBIS*, 21 Dec., 22–24.

Perry, Elizabeth J., and Christine Wong. 1985. "The Political Economy of Reform in Post-Mao China: Causes, Content, and Consequences." In Perry and Wong, eds., *The Political Economy of Reform in Post-Mao China*, 1–27. Cambridge: Harvard University Press.

Pratt, John W., and Richard Zeckhauser, eds. 1985. *Principals and Agents: The Structure of Business*. Boston: Harvard Business School Press.

"Prepare Well for Across-the-Board Substitution of Taxes for the Profit-Delivery System." 1983. *Renmin ribao*, 28 Apr.; *FBIS*, 29 Apr., K6–8.

"Progress Made in Industrial Reorganization." 1982. *Xinhua*, 3 Jan.; *FBIS*, 6 Jan., K13–14.

"The Proposals of the CCP Central Committee Said to Have Been Revised Twice." 1991. *Ming pao* (Hong Kong), 29 Jan.; *FBIS*, 30 Jan., 16–17.

"Provisional Regulations Governing the Contracted Managerial Responsibility System among Publicly Owned Industrial Enterprises." 1988. *Xinhua*, 2 Mar.; *FBIS*, 7 Mar., 56–60.

Pryor, Frederick L. 1985. "Growth and Fluctuations of Production in OECD and East European Countries." *World Politics* 37, no. 2:204–37.

Pye, Lucian W. 1981. *The Dynamics of Chinese Politics*. Cambridge: Oelgeschlager, Gunn, and Hain.

Qi Xiangwu and Hou Yunchun. 1982. "Why Is It Necessary to Oppose Regional Economic Blockades?" *Hongqi*, no. 9 (1 May).

Qiu Siyi. 1987. "Enlightenment from Contracted Responsibility's Improvement of Macro Management." *Shijie jingji daobao*, 17 Aug., 7.

Qiu Yuan. 1987. "Contracted Management Bears a Distinct Transitional Character." *Guangming ribao*, 19 Sept.; *FBIS*, 28 Sept., 16–17.

"Reducing the Scale of Capital Construction Is an Important Supporting Measure for Reform." 1988. *Renmin ribao*, 2 Sept.; *FBIS*, 9 Sept., 64–65.

"The Reflections and Demands of Thirty-one Entrepreneurs." 1986. *Renmin ribao*, 15 Dec.; rpt. in Shen Chong and Xiang Xiyang, eds., *Shinian lai: lilun, zhengce, shijian, ziliao xuanbian* (The decade: theory, policy, and practice, a collection of documents) 3:214–17. Beijing: Seek Truth Publishing House, 1988.

"Reform Is Advancing in the Course of Exploration." 1985. *Renmin ribao*, 26 Apr.; *FBIS*, 29 Apr., K7–8.

"The Reform of State-Run Enterprises Deepens Continuously." 1987. *Renmin ribao*, 9 Aug., 3.

"Reforms Must Be Carried Out Step by Step." 1985. *Gongren ribao*, 13 Mar.; *FBIS*, 25 Mar., K26–27.

"Rejuvenation Called 'Key Reason' for Hu's Downfall." 1987. *Hong Kong Standard*, 6 Feb.; *FBIS*, 9 Feb., K2–3.

Ren Kelei et al. 1987. "Several Questions on Carrying Out the Contracted Management Responsibility System." *Shijie jingji daobao*, 27 Apr., 13.

Ren Tao. 1982. "In the Final Analysis What Is the Effect of Industrial Management Reforms on National Financial Revenue?" *Jingji guanli*, Nov., 31–34.

"Ren Zhongyi's Talk on the Relationship Between Replacement of Profit with Tax and the Contract System." 1983. *Yangcheng wanbao* (Guangzhou), 17 May; *FBIS*, 19 May, P1–2.

"Report of the Opinions of the State Economic Commission on the Situation and Future of the Task of Experiments in Expanding Enterprise Autonomy." 1980. *Communiqué of the State Council*, no. 14 (20 Nov.).

"Resolutely Stop Acts of Wrangling Detrimental to the Overall Interests." 1983. *Renmin ribao*, 21 Jan.; *FBIS*, 24 Jan., K5–6.

"Resolve Must Be Great, Work Must Be Meticulous, Realistically Grasp This Year's Economic Work." 1987. *Renmin ribao*, 15 Apr.; *FBIS*, 20 Apr., K22.

Reynolds, Bruce. 1982. "Reform in Chinese Industrial Management: An Empirical Report." In U.S. Congress, Joint Economic Committee, *China under the Four Modernizations* 1:119–37. Washington: Government Printing Office.

———, ed. 1987. *Reform in China, Challenges and Choices*. Armonk, N.Y.: M. E. Sharpe.

Richman, Barry M. 1969. *Industrial Society in Communist China*. New York: Random.

Rigby, T. H. 1980. "A Conceptual Approach to Authority, Power, and Policy in the Soviet Union." In T. H. Rigby, Archie Brown, and Peter Reddaway, eds., *Authority, Power, and Policy in the USSR*, 9–31. London: Macmillan.

———. 1964. "Crypto-Politics." *Survey*, no. 50 (Jan.): 183–94.

Riggs, Fred W. 1964. *Administration in Developing Countries: The Theory of Prismatic Society*. Boston: Houghton Mifflin.

"Rising Prices Strain Managerial Contract System." 1988. *Xinhua*, 19 July; *FBIS*, 20 July, 37–38.

Roeder, Philip G. Forthcoming. *Red Sunset: Origins of the Soviet Constitutional Revolution*. Princeton: Princeton University Press.

———. 1990. "Reforming the Constitution of Stalinism: Gorbachev's Institutional Problem." Paper delivered at the Annual Meeting of the American Political Science Association, 30 Aug.–2 Sept.

———. 1985. "Do New Soviet Leaders Really Make a Difference? Rethinking the 'Succession Connection.'" *American Political Science Review* 79:958–76.

Rozelle, Scott D. Forthcoming. *Policy Implementation in the Provinces: Successes and Failures of China's Local Policies and Regional Development Strategies*.

Rui Jun. 1988. "Economists on How to Deal with Inflation in China." *Liaowang Overseas Edition*, 24 Oct.; *FBIS*, 31 Oct., 44–45.

Rush, Myron. 1968. *Political Succession in the USSR*. 2d ed. New York: Columbia University Press.

Safire, William. 1990. "Games Asians Play." *New York Times*, 20 Sept., A20.

Schurmann, Franz. 1968. *Ideology and Organization in Communist China*. 2d ed. Berkeley and Los Angeles: University of California Press.

————. 1967. "Politics and Economics in Russia and China." In Donald W. Treadgold, ed., *Soviet and Chinese Communism*, 297–326. Seattle: University of Washington Press.

Schwartz, Thomas. 1988. "The Meaning of Instability." Paper presented to the Department of Political Science, University of California, San Diego, June.

————. 1987. "Votes, Strategies, and Institutions: An Introduction to the Theory of Collective Choice." In Mathew D. McCubbins and Terry Sullivan, eds., *Congress, Structure and Policy*, 318–45. Cambridge: Cambridge University Press.

"The Second Stage Tax-for-Profit Must Strictly Carry Out State Regulation." 1984. *Renmin ribao*, 5 Dec.

"*Selected Works of Deng Xiaoping* Reveals Background to Gao-Rao Case." 1983. *Wen wei po* (Hong Kong), 30 June; *FBIS*, 1 July, W1.

"Shaanxi Prefecture on Unauthorized Aid Requests." 1985. *Xinhua*, 19 Mar.; *FBIS*, 26 Mar., T2–3.

Shambaugh, David L. 1989. "The Fourth and Fifth Plenary Sessions of the Thirteenth CCP Central Committee." *China Quarterly*, no. 120 (Dec.): 852–62.

"Shareholding System May Become 'Key' to Reform." 1988. *Xinhua*, 11 Apr.; *FBIS*, 15 Apr., 39–40.

Shen Chong and Xiang Xiyang, eds. 1988. *Shinian lai: lilun, zhengce, shijian, ziliao xuanbian* (The decade: theory, policy, and practice, a collection of documents). Vol. 3. Beijing: Seek Truth Publishing House.

Shen Liren. 1986. "Transformation of Economic Development Strategy." *Jingji guanli*, no. 9 (5 Sept.).

"Shenyang Plant Directors Hired under New System." 1986. *Xinhua*, 4 Sept.; *FBIS*, 5 Sept., S1.

Shepsle, Kenneth A. 1979. "Institutional Arrangements and Equilibrium in Multidimensional Voting Models." *American Journal of Political Science* 23 (Feb.): 27–59.

Shirk, Susan L. 1989. "The Political Economy of Chinese Industrial Reform." In Victor Nee and David Stark, eds., *Remaking the Economic Institutions of Socialism: China and Eastern Europe*, 328–62. Stanford: Stanford University Press.

————. 1988. "The Acquisition of Foreign Technology in China: The Bargaining Game." Paper presented to the Seventeenth Pacific Trade and Development Conference, Bali, Indonesia, July.

————. 1981. "Recent Chinese Labor Policies and the Transformation of Industrial Organization in China." *China Quarterly*, no. 88 (Dec.): 575–93.

Solinger, Dorothy J. 1988. "Disinvestment and the Politics of Pleading." Paper presented at the Annual Meeting of the Association for Asian Studies, Mar.

————. 1983. *Chinese Business under Socialism*. Berkeley and Los Angeles: University of California Press.

————. 1982. "The Fifth National People's Congress and the Process of Policymaking: Reform, Readjustment, and the Opposition." *Asian Survey* 22, no. 12 (Dec.): 1238–75.

Song Tingming. 1989. "Public Ownership, Profit Mechanisms, Contract Responsibility System." *Renmin ribao*, 27 Feb.; *FBIS*, 7 Mar., 30–33.

————. 1985. "A Key to Solving the Problem of Investment Expansion." *Jingji ribao*, 24 Aug., 1–2.

Song Yifeng. 1985. "Improve Enterprise Management to Suit the Situation of Reform." *Renmin ribao*, 19 Aug.; *FBIS*, 30 Aug., K11–14.

————. 1984. "Tax System Reform and Improving Enterprises' Quality." *Renmin ribao*, 6 Feb.; *FBIS*, 16 Feb., K3–5.

"Specifics on Shanxi Tax Payment System." 1983. *Shanxi ribao*, 22 Apr.; *FBIS*, 19 May, R5–6.

Staniszkis, Jadwiga. 1984. *Poland's Self-Limiting Revolution*. Princeton: Princeton University Press.

"State Council Approves the Ministry of Finance Circular on the Report on Strengthening Tax Bureau Organs in Provinces and Autonomous Regions." 1982. Rpt. in *Jingji tizhi gaige wenjian huibian 1977–83* (Collection of documents on the State Economic System reform), 897. Beijing: Beijing Finance and Economics Publishers, 1984.

"State Council Approves the State Economic Commission and Economic System Reform Commission Circular on Carrying Out Measures on Several Problems of Strengthening the Invigoration of Large and Medium-Sized State-Run Industrial Enterprises." 1985. Rpt. in Chinese Communist Party Central Documents Research Office, *Shier da yi lai* (After the Twelfth Party Congress), 770–78. Beijing: People's Publishing House, 1985.

"State Council Approves the State Economic Commission and Ministry of Finance Directive on the Method for Implementing Profit Retention in State Industrial Enterprises." 1980. *Communiqué of the State Council*, no. 23 (22 Jan.).

"State Council Approves the State Planning Commission Circular on Several Measures to Improve the Planning System." 1984. Rpt. in Chinese Communist Party Central Documents Research Office, *Shier da yi lai* (After the Twelfth Party Congress), 545–57. Beijing: People's Publishing House, 1985.

"State Council Circular on Economic Restructuring." 1991. *Xinhua*, 10 Feb.; *FBIS*, 11 Feb., 44–46.

"State Council Decision on Measures to Expand the Autonomy of State-Run Industrial Enterprises." 1984. *Renmin ribao*, 12 May; rpt. in Shen Chong and Xiang Xiyang, eds., *Shinian lai: lilun, zhengce, shijian, ziliao xuanbian* (The decade: theory, policy, and practice, a collection of documents) 3:260–62. Beijing: Seek Truth Publishing House, 1988.

"State Council Decision to Improve the Method of Local Financial Contracts." 1988. *Caizheng*, no. 10:1.

"State Council Discusses Gansu, Ningxia Development." 1983. *Xinhua*, 18 Jan.; *FBIS*, 27 Jan., T1–2.

"State Council Issues Notice on Profit Delivery." 1984. *Xinhua*, 18 July; *FBIS*, 20 July, K4–5.

"State Council Issues Regulations for Implementing the Contracted Managerial Responsibility System in State-Owned Industrial Enterprises." 1988. Rpt. in Shen Chong and Xiang Xiyang, eds., *Shinian lai: lilun, zhengce, shijian, ziliao xuanbian* (The decade: theory, policy, and practice, a collection of documents) 3:286. Beijing: Seek Truth Publishing House, 1988.

"State Council Notice on Carrying Out the Financial Management System of 'Apportioning Revenues and Expenditures While Contracting Responsibility According to Levels.'" 1981. In *Zhongguo jingji nianjian* (Chinese economic yearbook), II-130. Beijing: Beijing Jingji Guanli Caizhishe.

"State Council Notice on Carrying Out the Financial Management System of 'Linking Revenues and Expenditures, Sharing Total Revenues, Contracting the Percentages, and Fixed for Three Years.'" 1979. Rpt. in *Jingji tizhi gaige wenjian huibian 1977–83* (Collection of documents on the State Economic System reform), 803–4. Beijing: Beijing Finance and Economics Publishers, 1984.

"State Council Notice on Improving the Financial Management System of 'Apportioning Revenues and Expenditures While Contracting Responsibility According to Levels.'" 1982. Rpt. in *Jingji tizhi gaige wenjian huibian 1977–83* (Collection of documents on the State Economic System reform), 841. Beijing: Beijing Finance and Economics Publishers, 1984.

"State Council Office Issues a Circular on the Summary of the National Work Conference on Economic System Reform Experiments." 1985. Rpt. in Chinese Communist Party Central Documents Research Office, *Shier da yi lai* (After the Twelfth Party Congress), 675–84. Beijing: People's Publishing House, 1986.

"State Council on Ensuring Financial Balance." 1981. *Xinhua*, 3 Feb.; *FBIS*, 5 Feb., L6.

"State Council on Marketing Industrial Products." 1982. *Xinhua*, 20 Apr.; *FBIS*, 21 Apr., K9–11.

"State Economic Commission May Be Restored." 1989. *Wen wei po* (Hong Kong), 19 Sept.; *FBIS*, 19 Sept., 31–32.

"State Enterprises Report Profits." 1989. *Xinhua*, 12 Sept.; *FBIS*, 5 Oct., 44.

State Statistical Bureau. 1990. "Statistical Report on the 1989 National Economic and Social Development." *Renmin ribao*, 22 Feb., 3.

———. 1989. "Initial Results Scored in Improvement of the Economic Environment and Rectification of the Economic Order, Grim Situation Remains." *Renmin ribao*, 21 Oct.; *FBIS*, 27 Oct., 20–25.

Statistical Yearbook. 1991. Beijing: Chinese Statistical Publishers.

———. 1990. Beijing: Chinese Statistical Publishers.

———. 1989. Beijing: Chinese Statistical Publishers.

———. 1987. Beijing: Chinese Statistical Publishers.

———. 1985. Beijing: Chinese Statistical Publishers.

———. 1984. Beijing: Chinese Statistical Publishers.

———. 1983. Beijing: Chinese Statistical Publishers.

———. 1981. Beijing: Economic Management Periodical Publishers.

"Strive to Create the Conditions for Invigorating Large- and Medium-Sized Enterprises." 1985. *Xinhua*, 6 Sept.; *FBIS*, 10 Sept., K14–15.

Su Wenming et al. 1982. *Economic Readjustment and Reform*. Beijing: Beijing Review.

"Summary of the National Meeting of Progressive Profit Contracting Enterprises." 1984. *Jingjixue dongtai*, Apr., 1–3.

Sun Ru. 1978. "Socialist Accumulation and Enterprise Profit." *Jingji yanjiu*, no. 4 (20 Apr.): 17–20.

Sun Yun. 1982. "How to Improve Control of Extra-Budgetary Funds." *Caimao jingji*, no. 7 (15 July).

Tang Tian. 1987. "The Readjustment of the Cadre Distribution Structure Is Imperative." *Liaowang*, no. 36 (7 Sept.); *FBIS*, 18 Sept., 18–19.

"Tax-Dodging Enterprises Face State Clampdown." 1984. *China Daily*, 6 Dec., 1.

"Tax-for-Profit Is the Direction of Reform." 1983. *Renmin ribao*, 2 Mar., 1.

Teiwes, Frederick C. 1991. "Introduction to the Second Edition of *Politics and Purges in China*." Unpublished manuscript.

———. 1984. *Leadership, Legitimacy, and Conflict in China*. Armonk, N.Y.: M. E. Sharpe.

———. 1979. *Politics and Purges in China: Rectification and the Decline of Party Norms,1950–1965*. White Plains, N.Y.: M. E. Sharpe.

———. 1966. "The Purge of Provincial Leaders, 1957–1958." *China Quarterly*, no. 27 (July–Sept.): 14–32.

"The Temporary Provisions for Carrying Out a Financial Management System of Apportioning Revenues and Expenditures Between the Central and Local Authorities, While Holding the Latter Responsible for Their Own Profit and Loss." 1980. *Caizheng*, no. 12 (Dec.); *Joint Publications Research Service*, no. 77592 (16 Mar. 1981): 35–39.

"The Third Stage Reform of Tax-for-Profit." 1985. *Jingji zhoubao* (Economics weekly), 5 May.

"Thoughts on Which One to Do First, Price Reform or Ownership Reform." 1986. *Shijie jingji daobao*, 8 Nov.

Tian Jia, Zhu Limin, and Cao Siyuan. 1987. "Further Perfect Reform of Separately Listing Cities in the State Plan." *Shijie jingji daobao*, 26 Oct., 10.

Tian Jiyun. 1986. "Speech at a Conference of Central Organs" (6 Jan.). *Xinhua*, 11 Jan.; *FBIS*, 13 Jan., K5–21.

———. 1983. "A Suggestion on Accelerating the Implementation of 'Tax-for-Profit.'" *Jingji guanli*, no. 1 (Jan.): 9–10, 13.

———. 1983a. "We Can't Use the Rural Contracting Method to Solve the Distribution Relationship Between the State and Enterprises." *Jingji ribao*, 3 May, 1.

"Tian Jiyun Addresses Meeting." 1984. *Xinhua*, 22 June; *FBIS*, 25 June, K16.

Tian Yinong, Xiang Huaicheng, and Zhu Fulin. 1988. *Lun zhongguo caizheng tizhi gaige yu hongguan tiaokong* (On China's financial system reform and macroregulatory control). Beijing: China Finance and Economics Publishers.

Tidrick, Gene, and Chen Jiyuan, eds. 1987. *China's Industrial Reform.* New York: Oxford University Press.

Tong, James. 1989. "Fiscal Reform, Elite Turnover, and Central-Provincial Relations in Post-Mao China." *Australian Journal of Chinese Affairs*, no. 22 (July): 1–28.

Tong Zongkun. 1986. "Reflections on Choosing Targets of Reform of the Ownership System." *Jingjixue dongtai*, no. 1.

Tsou Tang. 1983. "Back from the Brink of Revolutionary-'Feudal' Totalitarianism." In David Mozingo and Victor Nee, eds., *State and Society in Contemporary China*, 53–88. Ithaca: Cornell University Press.

Tullock, Gordon. 1987. *Autocracy.* Dordrecht: Kluwer Academic Publishers.

"Two Different Outcomes of Reform." 1990. *Wen wei po* (Hong Kong), 13 Dec.; *FBIS*, 21 Dec., 3–4.

Tyson, Laura D'Andrea. 1983. "Investment Allocation: A Comparison of the Reform Experiences of Hungary and Yugoslavia." *Journal of Comparative Economics* 7:288–303.

"U.N. Calls East Slide at Depression Point." 1991. *New York Times*, 3 Dec., C6.

Unger, Jonathan. 1987. "The Struggle to Dictate China's Administration: The Conflict of Branches vs. Areas vs. Reform." *Australian Journal of Chinese Affairs*, no. 18 (July): 15–45.

"Visitors of Hunan Origin Attend Economy Forum." 1984. *Changsha Hunan Province Service*, 5 July; *FBIS*, 9 July, P3–4.

Vogel, Ezra F. 1989. *One Step Ahead in China, Guangdong under Reform.* Cambridge: Harvard University Press.

Walder, Andrew G. 1987. "Wage Reform and the Web of Factory Interests." *China Quarterly*, no. 109 (Mar): 22–41.

————. 1986. *Communist Neo-Traditionalism, Work and Authority in Chinese Industry.* Berkeley and Los Angeles: University of California Press.

————. 1986a. "The Informal Dimension of Enterprise Financial Reforms." In U.S. Congress, Joint Economic Committee, *China's Economy Looks Toward the Year 2000*, 630–45. Washington D.C.: Government Printing Office.

Waldron, Arthur. 1990. "Warlordism Versus Federalism: The Revival of a Debate." *China Quarterly*, no. 121 (Mar.): 116–28.

"Wan Li Chairs Second Presidium Meeting." 1989. *Xinhua*, 30 Mar.; *FBIS*, 30 Mar., 12.

Wang Bingqian. 1990. "Report on the Implementation of the State Budget for 1989 and on the Draft Budget for 1990." *Xinhua*, 7 Apr.; *FBIS*, 12 Apr., 16–24.

————. 1987. "Report on the Implementation of the State Budget for 1986 and on the Draft State Budget for 1987." *Xinhua*, 13 Apr.; *FBIS*, 15 Apr., K11–21.

————. 1983. "Finance Minister Interviewed on New Tax Plan." Beijing Domestic Television, 27 Apr.; *FBIS*, 3 May, K4–13.

Wang Depei. 1991. "An Analysis of Trends in Enlivening Large, Medium-Sized Enterprises." *Jingji guanli*, 5 June; *FBIS*, 7 Aug., 36–40.

Wang Haibo. 1990. "The Direction in Which to Deepen the Reform of the Economic Structure." *Jingji guanli*, no. 2:6–10.

Wang Hui. 1989. *Zhongguo de guanchang bing* (China's disease of bureaucracy). Tianjin: China Women's Publishing House.

Wang, James C. F. 1989. *Contemporary Chinese Politics: An Introduction*. Englewood Cliffs, N.J.: Prentice Hall.

Wang Jijiang and Zhou Baohua. 1983. "Lessons Learned from Fushan Steel Plant." *Renmin ribao*, 10 Oct.; *FBIS*, 19 Oct., S1–5.

Wang Jinjia. 1989. "On the Local Right to Make Decisions and the 'Vassal Economy.'" *Jingji ribao*, 11 Nov.; *FBIS*, 30 Nov., 36–38.

Wang Jui. 1983. "On the Economic Responsibility System." *Jingji yanjiu*, Oct., 28–31.

Wang Mengkui. 1990. "Improve the Pattern of National Income Distribution." *Jingji ribao*, 26 Oct., 3.

Wang Min. 1985. "Be Clearheaded, Advance Steadily." *Liaowang*, 29 Apr.; *FBIS*, 9 May, K7.

Wang Qingling. 1985. "My Views on Perfecting the System of Replacing Profit Remission with Taxes." *Jingji guanli*, no. 10:19–21.

Wang Renzhi and Gui Shiyong. 1982. "On Mandatory Planning." *Chinese Social Science*, Nov., 47–58.

Wang Yuling. 1989. "Invigorating Large Enterprises Is the Key to Stabilizing the Economy: An Interview with Song Tingming." *Jingji ribao*, 19 Oct.; *FBIS*, 9 Nov., 43–44.

Wang Zhaodong and Shi Xichuan. 1983. "The Second Springtime in the History of Planning." *Jingji ribao*, 10 Jan.; *FBIS*, 24 Jan., K13–17.

Ward, Benjamin. 1980. "The Chinese Approach to Economic Development." In Robert F. Dernberger, ed., *China's Development Experience in Comparative Perspective*, 91–119. Cambridge: Harvard University Press.

———. 1967. *The Socialist Economy: A Study of Organizational Alternatives*. New York: Random.

Wei Lichun. 1985. "On Controlling the Scale of Investment in Fixed Assets." *Hongqi*, no. 17:35–38.

Weingast, Barry R., and Mark J. Moran. 1983. "Bureaucratic Discretion or Congressional Control? Regulatory Policymaking by the Federal Trade Commission." *Journal of Political Economy* 91, no. 5:765–800.

"What Is Unnecessary Should Be Given Up So That What Is Necessary Can Be Achieved." 1988. *Renmin ribao*, 4 Dec.; *FBIS*, 15 Dec., 34–37.

"The Whole Party and the People of the Whole Country Must Attend to the Overall Interests of the Nation." 1983. *Renmin ribao*, 19 May; *FBIS*, 23 May, K7–9.

Wong, Christine P. W. 1990. "Central-Local Relations in an Era of Fiscal Decline: The Paradox of Fiscal Decentralization in Post-Mao China." Unpublished paper.

———. 1987. "Between Plan and Market: The Role of the Local Sector in Post-Mao China." *Journal of Comparative Economics* 11, no. 3:385–98.

———. 1986. "The Economics of Shortage and Problems of Reform in Chinese Industry." *Journal of Comparative Economics* 10, no. 4:363–87.

————. 1986a. "Ownership and Control in Chinese Industry: The Maoist Legacy and Prospects for the 1980's." In U.S. Congress, Joint Economic Committee, *China's Economy Looks Toward the Year 2000* 1:571–603. Washington D.C.: Government Printing Office.

————. 1985. "Material Allocation and Decentralization: Impact of the Local Sector on Industrial Reform." In Elizabeth J. Perry and Christine Wong, eds., *The Political Economy of Reform in Post-Mao China*, 253–78. Cambridge: Harvard University Press.

Woodall, Jean. 1982. *The Socialist Corporation and Technocratic Power: The Polish United Workers' Party, Industrial Organization and Workforce Control, 1958–80.* Cambridge: Cambridge University Press.

Wu Fumin and Yu Xi. 1988. "Why Is It Difficult to Introduce Competitive Mechanisms into Managerial Contracts?" *Xinhua*, 5 Jan.; *FBIS*, 15 Jan., 28–29.

Wu Jinglian. 1990. "The Strategic Options of Reform and the Evolution of Economic Theories: An Analysis of China's Example." Unpublished paper.

————. 1988. "The Rent-Seeking Theory and Some Negative Phenomena in the Chinese Economy." *Jingji ribao*, 30 Sept., 3.

————. 1987. *Jingji gaige wenti tansuo* (Explorations in questions on economic reform). Beijing: Zhanwan Publishers.

————. 1987a. "Some Views on the Choice of a Strategy for Reform." *Jingji yanjiu*, no. 2 (20 Feb.): 3–14.

————. 1987b. "Taking Improvement of Macroeconomic Control as the Goal to Carry Out Three Basic Links in Comprehensive Reform." In Wu Jinglian, ed., *Explorations in Questions on Economic Reform*, 279–82. Beijing: Zhanwan Publishers.

————. 1985. "Another Discussion of Preserving a Positive Economic Environment for Economic Reform." *Jingji yanjiu*, no. 5 (20 May): 3–12.

————. 1985a. "The Question of the Direction of Development and Macroeconomic Control During the Early Stages of Economic Reform." *Renmin ribao*, 11 Feb., 5.

Wu Jinglian, Li Jiange, and Ding Ningning. 1985. "Control Growth Rate of the National Economy Within an Appropriate Range." *Renmin ribao*, 17 May.

Wu Jinglian, Li Jiange, Ding Ningning, and Zhang Junkuo. 1986. "Correctly Handle the Relationships among Economic Construction, System Reform, and Improving People's Livelihood." *Jingji fazhan yu tizhi gaige* (Economic development and system reform), June, 15–32.

Wu Jinglian and Bruce Reynolds. 1987. "Choosing a Strategy for China's Economic Reform." Paper presented at the annual meeting of the American Economic Association, Dec.

Wu Jinglian and Zhao Renwei. 1987. "The Dual Pricing System in China's Industry." *Journal of Comparative Economics* 11:309–18.

Wu Jinglian and Zhou Xiaochuan. 1988. *Zhongguo jingji gaige de zhengti sheji* (The integrated design of China's economic reform). Beijing: Zhanwan Publishers.

Wu Minyi. 1990. "Some Thoughts on the Activities of Local Governments." *Jingji yanjiu*, no. 7 (20 July): 56–60.

Xiang Yuanpei and Du Linfeng. 1980. "Questions on Enterprise Profit Retention." *Jingji guanli*, no. 4:20–23.

Xiao Jiabao. 1989. "Forsake the Theory of Quick Success and Discard the Theory of Pessimism." *Jingji cankao*, 27 Feb.; *FBIS*, 15 Mar.; 42–44.

Xiao Jie. 1986. "Diverse Views on the Focus of Economic Reform in the Seventh Five Year Plan Period." *Shijie jingji daobao*, 6 Jan., 3.

Xiao Min and Shao Fei. 1961. "A Preliminary Study of the Problem of the Profit of Socialist Enterprise." *Guangming ribao*, 11 Dec. 1961; *Survey of the China Mainland Press*, no. 2661 (Jan. 1962): 7–15.

Xiao Zhuoji. 1987. "The Contracting System Hinges on Affirming the Enterprise Ownership System." *Shijie jingji daobao*, 5 Oct., 10.

"*Xinhua* Policy Terminology Series on NPC." 1991. *Xinhua*, 26 Mar.; *FBIS*, 27 Mar., 53.

Xu Jian. 1989. "An Attempt to Discuss Monetary and Financial Policies During the Austerity Period." *Jingji ribao*, 12 May; *FBIS*, 8 June, 26–30.

Xu Jingan. 1985. "Looking Inward, Streamlining Administration, and Decentralizing Power." *Renmin ribao*, 19 Apr.; *FBIS*, 25 Apr., K10–12.

Xu Kehong. 1988. "Measures Proposed to Reduce Enterprise Deficits." *Xinhua*, 30 Aug.; *FBIS*, 1 Sept., 32.

Xu Yaozhong. 1988. "New Trend in Enterprise Contracting." *Liaowang*, 8 Feb.; *FBIS*, 29 Feb., 40–42.

Xu Yi. 1984. "On the Second Stage Reform of Tax-for-Profit." *Renmin ribao*, 10 Sept., 5.

———. 1983. "Correctly Handle the Relationship Between Planning and Freedom in Economic Management System." *Jingji kexue* (Economic science), no. 5 (20 Oct.): 8–13.

———. 1982. "Several Questions on the Current Economy." *Caizheng yanjiu* (Financial research), no. 5:1–11.

Xue Muqiao. 1988. "Seriously Sum Up the Experiences of Ten Years of Reform." *Guangming ribao*, 17 Dec.; *FBIS*, 5 Jan., 18–23.

———. 1983. "China's Current Economic Situation, Analysis and Prospects." *Renmin ribao*, 3 June; *FBIS*, 13 June, K34–41.

———. 1982. "The Planned Economy Is Primary, Market Regulation Is Secondary." *Hongqi*, no. 8:30–33.

———. 1982a. *Wo guo guomin jingji di tiaozheng he gaige* (The readjustment and reform of China's national economy). Beijing: Renmin Chubanshe.

———. 1981. "Adjust the National Economy and Promote Comprehensive Balance." *Jingji yanjiu*, no. 2 (20 Feb.): 27.

Yan Jiaqi. 1988. "'Separation of Party and Government Work' in China as Viewed from a Comparative Angle." *Wen wei po* (Hong Kong), 23 Mar.; *FBIS*, 14 Apr., 42–45.

Yan Yi. 1984. "A Suggestion to Use Product Tax and Product Differential Tax to Adjust Profit Levels of Enterprises." *Jingji tizhi gaige*, Jan., 38–41.

Yang Baibing. 1991. "Party's Absolute Leadership, Soul and Foundation of Our Army Building." *Renmin ribao*, 24 June; *FBIS*, 26 June, 34–38.

Yang Peixin. 1990. "Reform in Urban Areas Remains Centered on the Contract System." *Renmin ribao*, 3 July; *FBIS*, 16 July, 41–42.

———. 1989. "Bring into Full Play the Role of Large and Medium-Sized Enterprises as the Mainstay." *Renmin ribao*, 20 Nov.; *FBIS*, 5 Dec., 40–42.

———. 1989a. "Reviewing Reform over the Past Ten Years, We Come to the Conclusion: Only by Persisting in Reform Can We Check Inflation." *Shijie jingji daobao*, 27 Mar., 14–15.

———. 1987. "Invigorate Enterprises and Adjust the Tax Burden." *Shijie jingji daobao*, 7 July, 13.

———. 1987a. "Reverse the Current Macroeconomic Situation from Its Roots." *Shijie jingji daobao*, 6 July, 3.

Yang Qixian. 1983. "On the Principle of Whether Management or the State Should Get the Largest Share in Enterprise Contracts." *Jingji guanli*, no. 5:22–23.

Yang Ruiming. 1985. "Pointing the Way to Reforming the Education System, Report on the Formulation of the 'Decision of the CCP Central Committee on Reform of the Education System.'" *Liaowang*, 10 June; *FBIS*, 26 June, K11–17.

Yao Yilin. 1981. "Report on the Readjustment of the 1981 National Economic Plan and State Revenue and Expenditure." *Beijing Review*, no. 11:14–27.

"Yao Yilin Attends Forum on Enterprise Management." 1981. *Xinhua*, 2 Feb.; *FBIS*, 3 Feb., L1.

Yeung, Chris. 1991. "Guangdong Officials on Payments to the Center." *South China Morning Post*, 27 Mar., 10.

Ying Guang. 1983 "On the Socialist Unified Market." *Renmin ribao*, 28 Feb.

You Ji. 1991. "Zhao Ziyang and the Politics of Inflation." *Australian Journal of Chinese Affairs*, no. 25 (Jan.): 69–91.

Yu Guangyuan. 1987. "Some of My Opinions on the Contracting System." *Shijie jingji daobao*, 5 Oct., 10.

Yu Zuyao. 1983. "Maintain the Good Momentum of the Steady Growth of Light Industrial Production." *Guangming ribao*, 24 Apr.; *FBIS*, 4 May, K8.

Yuan Baohua. 1985. "The Task of Enterprise Rectification in 1985." *Jingji ribao*, 3 Jan., 2.

———. 1979. "China's State Economic Commission." *China Business Review*, July–Aug., 16–17.

"Yuan Baohua Speaks on Enterprise Consolidation." 1983. *Xinhua*, 28 May; *FBIS*, 31 May, K11.

Zaslavskaya, Tatyana. 1984. "The Novosibirsk Report." *Survey* 28, no. 1 (Spring): 88–108.

Zelin, Madeleine. 1984. *The Magistrate's Tael: Rationalizing Fiscal Reform in Eighteenth Century China*. Berkeley and Los Angeles: University of California Press.

Zeng Jianhui. 1985. "A New Milestone, Notes on the Plenary Sessions of the CCP Central Committee and the National Conference of Delegates." *Liaowang*, 7 Oct.; *FBIS*, 30 Oct., K4–10.

Zhang Chaowen. 1989. "Chinese Premiers and the Datong-Qinhuangdao Railway." *Liaowang Overseas Edition*, no. 4 (23 Jan.); *FBIS*, 31 Jan., 24–27.

Zhang Jianming. 1982. "The Question of Centralization or Decentralization of Power Inside Integrated Enterprises." *Caiwu yu kuaiji* (Financial affairs and accounting), no. 9 (20 Sept.); *Joint Publications Research Service*, no. 82348 (Economics 288; 30 Nov.): 44–51.

Zhang Jingfu. 1982. "Speech to the Meeting Founding the State Economic Commission." *Zhongguo caimao bao* (China finance and trade journal), 27 May, 1.

Zhang Shaojie and Zhao Yujiang. 1987. "The Separation of Profit and Tax." *Shijie jingji daobao*, 11 May, 5.

Zhang Weiguo. 1988. "Professor Li Yining Introduces the 1988–95 National Program for Reform of the Economic System Proposed by Beijing University." *Shijie jingji daobao*, 23 May, 12.

Zhang Zhenbin. 1988. "My Opinion on Several Questions Regarding Financial Reform." *Renmin ribao*, 18 Mar.; *FBIS*, 5 Apr., 25–26.

Zhang Zhuoyuan. 1981. "Build a Rational Economic Structure to Promote Socialist Modernization." In Ma Hong and Sun Shangqing, eds., *Research on Problems of China's Economic Structure*. Beijing: Zhongguo Shehui Kexue Chubanshe.

Zhao Chunxin. 1981. "On How the Structure of Distribution Can Function in Regulation of the Economic Structure." In Chinese Finance Society, ed., *Lun caizheng fenpei yu jingji di guanxi* (On the relations between financial distribution and the economy). Beijing: Chinese Finance and Economics Publishing House.

"Zhao Comments." 1985. *Xinhua*, 1 Jan.; *FBIS*, 2 Jan., K9–10.

"Zhao Outlines Tasks for '86 Reform." 1986. *Beijing Review*, no. 5 (3 Feb.): 6–7.

Zhao Renwei. 1990. "Two Contrasting Phenomena in China's Income Distribution." *Cambridge Journal of Economics* 14:345–49.

Zhao Ziyang. 1987. "Advance along the Road of Socialism with Chinese Characteristics." Work Report to Thirteenth National CCP Congress. *Xinhua*, 25 Oct.; *FBIS*, 26 Oct., 10–34.

———. 1987a. "Different Forms of the Contracted Management Responsibility System Are Imperative." *Renmin ribao*, 26 Apr.; rpt. in Shen Chong and Xiang Xiyang, eds., *Shinian lai: lilun, zhengce, shijian, ziliao xuanbian* (The decade: theory, policy, and practice, a collection of documents) 3:276–77. Beijing: Seek Truth Publishing House, 1988.

———. 1987b. "Genuinely Implement the Giving of Managerial Power to the Enterprises." *Renmin ribao*, 19 Dec.; rpt. in Shen Chong and Xiang Xiyang, eds., *Shinian lai: lilun, zhengce, shijian, ziliao xuanbian* (The decade: theory, policy, and practice, a collection of documents) 3:282–83. Beijing: Seek Truth Publishing House, 1988.

———. 1987c. "Report on the Work of the Government." Presented to the Fifth Session of the Sixth National People's Congress. Beijing Domestic Service, 25 Mar.; *FBIS*, 26 Mar., K1–25.

————. 1987d. "On the Separation of Party and Government." Speech to the Preparatory Meeting for the Seventh Plenary Session of the Twelfth Central Committee, 14 Oct. *Xinhua*, 26 Nov.; *FBIS*, 27 Nov.; 13–16.

————. 1987e. "Speech at the Spring Festival Gathering." *Xinhua*, 29 Jan.; *FBIS*, 30 Jan., K4–8.

————. 1985. "Explaining the Formulation of the Proposed Seventh Five Year Plan." Speech to the National Party Conference, 18 Sept. *Renmin ribao*, 26 Sept.; *Xinhua yuebao* (New China monthly), Sept., 24–27.

————. 1985a. "The Present Economic Situation and Economic System Reform." Report on the Work of the Government presented to the Third Session of the Sixth National People's Congress. Rpt. in CCP Central Documents Research Office, *Shier da yi lai* (After the Twelfth Party Congress), 685–710. Beijing: People's Publishers, 1986.

————. 1984. "Opinions on Three Issues in Economic Structural Reform." Rpt. in CCP Central Documents Research Office, *Shier da yi lai* (After the Twelfth Party Congress), 533–38. Beijing: People's Publishers, 1986.

————. 1983. "Report on the Work of the Government." Presented to the First Session of the Sixth National People's Congress. *Renmin ribao*, 24 June, 1.

————. 1982. "Report on the Sixth Five Year Plan." Presented to the Fifth Session of the Fifth National People's Congress. *Beijing Review*, no. 51 (20 Dec.): 10–35.

————. 1982a. "Some Questions on Current Economic Work." Speech delivered at the National Work Conference on Industrial and Transportation Work, 4 Mar. *Hongqi* (Red flag), no. 7:2–10.

————. 1980. "Investigate Problems, Set Economic Reform on the Right Lines." *Renmin ribao*, 21 Apr., 1–2.

"Zhao Ziyang at Contract Responsibility Symposium." 1988. Beijing Domestic Service, 16 July; *FBIS*, 25 July, 37–38.

"Zhao Ziyang Converses with Guests from Poland." 1987. *Renmin ribao*, 22 Aug.

"Zhao Ziyang Meets American Guests." 1988. *Renmin ribao*, 25 May; *FBIS*, 31 May, 25–26.

"Zhao Ziyang on Price Reform, Detente, Pollution." 1988. *Xinhua*, 2 June; *FBIS*, 3 June, 17–18.

"Zhao Ziyang Talks on Responsibility Systems." 1982. *Ming pao* (Hong Kong), 14 Jan.; *FBIS*, 22 Jan., W5.

"Zhejiang to Attempt Reform in Major Enterprises." 1985. Zhejiang Provincial Service, 16 Jan.; *FBIS*, 22 Jan., O3.

Zheng Derong et al. 1987. *Zhongguo jingji tizhi gaige jishi* (A record of China's economic system reform). Beijing: Spring and Autumn Publishers.

Zhou Guanwu. 1986. "Reform Is to Move Forward in Liberating Productive Power." *Jingji guanli*, no. 4:12–17.

————. 1984. "Lessons from the Five-Year Experience of Economic Reform at Capital Iron and Steel." *Jingji guanli*, no. 3:19–24.

Zhou Shulian. 1988. "The Enterprise Contracted Management Responsibility System Is Full of Vitality." *Jingji guanli*, no. 5 (20 May): 4–8.

Zhou Taihe. 1982. "The Development and Perfecting of the Industrial Economic Responsibility System." *Hongqi*, no. 23; rpt. in *Xinhua yuebao*, no. 1 (1983): 114–17.

Zhou Taihe et al. 1984. *Dangdai Zhongguo de Jingji Tizhi Gaige* (China's current economic system reform). Beijing: Chinese Academy of Social Sciences Publishers.

Zhou Yi. 1987. "The Question of Party Leadership During Political Structure Reform." *Lilun yuekan* (Theoretical monthly), no. 7 (25 July); *FBIS*, 1 Sept., 18–23.

Zhu Mingchun. 1990. "Increasing the Economic Results of Industry Is an Important Task in the Next Phase of Rectification and Consolidation." *Jingji guanli*, no. 10 (5 Oct.): 10–12, 38.

———. 1990a. "Local Barriers Should Be Handled in a Comprehensive Manner." *Guangming ribao*, 3 Nov.; *FBIS*, 12 Dec., 40–42.

Zuo Chuntai. 1982. "Certain Experiences in Restructuring China's Financial Management System." *Guangming ribao*, 23 Aug.; *Joint Publications Research Service*, no. 81938 (Economics 271; 6 Oct.): 16–23.

Zuo Mu. 1987. "On the Contracted Management Responsibility System." *Renmin ribao*, 15 June; *FBIS*, 24 June, K21–25.

Zweig, David, Kathy Hartford, James Feinerman, and Deng Jianxu. 1987. "Law, Contracts, and Economic Modernization: Lessons from the Recent Chinese Rural Reforms." *Stanford Journal of International Law* 23, no. 2:319–64.

Index

ment, 210; reorganization of, 111; role and structure of, 93, 96n.6, 96–97, 97nn.7,9; *xietiao* function of, 121, 122

State enterprises: adjustment tax for, 137–38, 258, 258n.14; agencies controlling, 29–30, 30–31n.10; bank loans repaid by, 217, 217n.25; bureaucrats' stake in, 101–2; under "central cities" reform, 179; competing with nonstate sector, 16, 42–44, 131, 343–44, 343–44n.6; consolidation of, 213–14; economic performance of, 144–45, 144–45n.20; extensive growth of, 17–18; government's financial ties with, 187n.53, 187–88, 249–50, 267, 267n.24; hiring practices of, 45–46; inefficiency of, 17n.11, 17–18, 28–29, 31, 32n.13, 32–33, 33n.15; interviews with, 19; large and medium-sized, 285n.4, 285–86; modified profit-retention for, 204–5; named experimental firms, 201, 201n.7, 202–3, 226–27; opposing local taxes, 273n.36, 273–74, 273–74n.37; profit contracting for, 217–18, 226, 228–29, 232, 236, 241–42, 319, 319n.49; protected by balancism, 131–32; provincial interference in, 187–88; recentralization for, 165, 165n.23, 198n.2, 198–99; regional characteristics of, 269, 270–71, 277; revenues provided by, 152, 152n.4, 161, 161n.17; SEC's support of, 98, 98n.10, 286, 291–92; suspicious of tax-for-profit, 253, 259, 266, 266nn.20,22, 268; tax evasion by, 283; tax-for-profit consequences for, 248–50, 253–56, 259–60, 267nn.23,24, 267–73, 289–91, 293; technological reno-

vation of, 235, 235n.13. *See also* Large enterprises

State managers: advocating market freedom, 43–44; collective lobbying by, 286, 287, 287n.6, 313; colluding with local government, 230n.8, 230–31; controlled by party committees, 61; favoring profit contracting, 312–15; hiring responsibility of, 46; lacking personal accountability, 323–24, 323–24n.54; poor quality of, 32–33; reacting to readjustment, 211n.16, 211–13, 212nn.17,18, 218; selection of, 320–21, 320–21n.51, 321n.52; in transitional economy, 130. *See also* State enterprises

State Planning Commission (SPC): departmental contracts with, 139; favoring readjustment, 210–11; price adjustment simulations by, 300, 300n.18; profit-retention stance of, 219, 238, 239; reorganization of, 111; representing sectoral views, 99, 99n.13; role and ideology of, 93, 93n.2, 95; SEC conflict with, 98

State Production Commission (*guojia shengchan weiyuanhui*), 97n.9

State revenues. *See* Central revenues

State Science and Technology Commission, 93, 231

"State self-interest" (*guojia benwei lun*), 232. *See also* Profit contracting

Student demonstrations, 4, 76, 76n.12

"Subordination relations" (*lishu guanxi*), 155

"Substituting tax for profits" (*li gai shui*). *See* Tax-for-profit

Supply-side economics, 294

Taiwan, 97n.8

Compositor: Recorder Typesetting
Text: 10/13 Palatino
Display: Palatino
Printer: Thomson-Shore, Inc.
Binder: Thomson-Shore, Inc.